BUSINESS JOURNALISM

Its Function and Future

BUSINESS JOURNALISM

Its Function and Future

BY

JULIEN ELFENBEIN

Editorial Director, Haire Publishing Company

HARPER & BROTHERS PUBLISHERS

NEW YORK AND LONDON

BUSINESS JOURNALISM: Its Function and Future

This book is complete and unabridged
in contents, and is manufactured in strict
conformity with Government regulations
for saving paper.

To

ANDREW J. HAIRE

CONTENTS

LIST OF CHARTS

FOREWORD

By Stanley A. Knisely

Executive Vice-President of
The Associated Business Papers, Inc.

Here, at last, is a work on business journalism that builds a monument worthy of its famous history and points a future in keeping with the magnitude and importance of so vital an influence in helping the world make an ever-better living.

No stodgy, orthodox, dry-as-dust textbook confined to a weary recital of mere mechanics or techniques—and doomed to gather dust, unopened, on musty library shelves.

How many business executives have ever leaned back in their swivel chairs for as much as a minute and asked themselves:

"Where would my business—my personal fortunes—be today had it not been for the business press?" and—

"What would happen to my business—my personal fortunes— if the business press closed its doors tonight and threw away the keys?"

Business historians may well attribute the phenomenal growth of industry and commerce in this country to the fact that we have had a business press of outstanding virility—at least one, and frequently two or more papers, devoted to each and every important phase of agriculture, mining, manufacture, transportation, and marketing. There are the professional business papers for the doctor, lawyer, and architect; merchandising papers for dealers and jobbers in every line; institutional papers in the hotel, school, hospital, and restaurant fields; specialized papers in the fields of sales, advertising and marketing; and industrial papers covering every important branch of manufacturing activity.

True, the colonists found here unlimited wealth in natural resources, but other countries had similar wealth. Our pioneers found a vast, undeveloped area awaiting only the ingenuity and toil of man to transform it into gold; but the same is true of Russia, China, and other parts of the world. Our American Indians did not develop these resources. The American Indian slaved to lay up venison and maize for the winter while his squaw worked all summer to weave one blanket.

Why is it, then, starting only a few hundred years ago—after many nations of the world had been at it for centuries—that we caught up with the leaders and passed them in so relatively short a time? Why is the United States the wealthiest nation? Why does it surpass all others in the fields of manufacture, transportation, and communications? In short, what has American business possessed that was not generally available to business throughout the world?

Broadly, we possessed these things: a sound democratic form of government, an economic system of competitive enterprise, and the largest, most active, unbiased independent and authoritative business press in the world. Many thousands of foreign businessmen and technicians subscribe regularly to American business papers. Japan, Germany, and Italy were heavy subscribers but were cut off following Pearl Harbor to prevent technical "know-how" from reaching enemy hands. Japan's special envoy Saburo Kurusu tried vainly to subscribe for American aviation papers even after he was incarcerated in Greenbrier, West Va., in the early days of World War II.

In this country, hardly a machine or a material or a process but owes much of its rapid development and speedy acceptance to the fact that the business press picked it up out of its crib, nursed it along in its creeping stages, and spread the news of its birth and growth.

And today, what do we find? A new low-alloy high-tensile steel is developed by the metallurgists who are constantly studying their businesspapers; and before you can turn around, thousands of mechanical and design engineers, thousands of top business executives, and thousands upon thousands of other important key men in all lines of industry know all about it, how it is made, how you can form it into myriad shapes, and how it saves millions of dollars in the transportation industry alone.

So it is with every development—plastics, magnesium, electronics, a helicopter, a new hair-do. No matter what it is, or in what line of activity, the business executive, master mechanic, airplane designer, or buyer in a lingerie store in Los Angeles, Amarillo, Spokane, or Duluth, knows all about it—all the details, figuratively speaking, almost overnight. How? Through the highly specialized business press, the information railway that transports know-how from where it is to where it is needed.

Does this mean anything to industry and trade?

Suppose the business press did close its doors tonight and throw away the keys. What other channel of public information and education now functioning could take over this highly technical service?

When we check them over—the colleges, newspapers, general magazines, radio, movies—we quickly discern their inability to man adequately the lines of business communication. What would result? The rate of progress in industry and trade would falter alarmingly. The standard of living would level off and start to decline. If we believe that true wealth in our nation depends upon ever-increasing production and ever-wider distribution at ever-lower costs and prices, we can readily understand what national retrogression would ensue if the business communication lines were cut.

Mr. Elfenbein's thesis that high-level employment will depend on more efficient distribution of the world's goods and services, under the guidance and inspiration of the specialized business press, is developed with an understanding that comes from eighteen years of practical experience as a working business journalist in the fields of distribution. He left the law school of the University of Texas twenty-seven years ago to join the U.S. Army Intelligence Service during World War I. In the quarter-century interregnum between wars he was newspaper reporter, commercial artist, advertising agency copywriter and account executive, trade association official, and businesspaper editor. When we entered World War II, Donald Nelson appointed him a member of the Business Paper Editors Advisory Council of the War Production Board. He is a former chairman of the New York Business Paper Editors. He is a member of the executive committee of the National Conference of Business Paper Editors and chairman of its postwar committee on distribution. He has lectured on business journalism at a number of universities and on business practice in many national forums.

Remember, the business press begins where the schools and colleges and textbooks leave off. The businesspaper is a new textbook, and a new, self-conducted examination every month. Who can say how much of our progress is due to a more universal burning of the midnight oil and the fact that the business press has helped mightily to provide us with the oil to burn and the information on how to burn it?

PREFACE

The ultimate strongholds of freedom are the minds of free men.
—JUSTICE ROBERT H. JACKSON

Work on this book was begun before our country entered World War II. It was designed to serve as a textbook in schools of journalism, marketing, and business administration. With the entrance of our country into the war, many of our schools and colleges were rapidly converted into military and naval training academies, where the curricula had neither room nor use for courses in journalism. Few schools, to begin with, could boast of courses in *business* journalism or even occasional lectures on the subject.

After Pearl Harbor, businesspaper editors and their staffs became engrossed in the task of helping industry convert from a peacetime to a wartime basis. Being a working journalist myself, I had to exercise some ambidexterity to complete this book and, at the same time, satisfy the exacting wartime demands of the businesspaper publishing organization of which I am a member.

Such an undertaking as this book, however, could not be ignored. To some people a book on business journalism at the time seemed remote from the pressing problems of a world at war or an immediate postwar world.

This book describes a war of which the physical struggles of human history, such as World Wars I and II, are only symptoms. The war with which journalists are concerned is not a struggle for millponds the cartographers once labeled "oceans" or for islands once designated "continents."

"*This war,*" as Archibald MacLeish so correctly identifies it, "*is a war for men's minds and for the kingdom which men have in their minds established—things which no oceans and no distance and no fleets of battleships could ever make secure.*

"The wars for men's minds are not won with dead shells—with

xvii

the banalities of unexploding words. They are won by a labor of *clarification* and *definition* and *illumination* which requires for its accomplishment all the machinery of the intellect [italics mine]."[1]

This book is such a labor. Candidly, it was written partly because the writer himself had a personal need for self-administered adult education, and a desire which William James best expresses: "*a desire to attain a conception of the frame of things which shall on the whole be more rational than that somewhat chaotic view which everyone by nature carries about with him under his hat.*"

The first textbook on business journalism was written by a publisher in 1923.[2] Prior to that, a series of lectures given at New York University were published, in 1915, with an introduction by Albert Frederick Wilson of the Department of Journalism.[3] In 1921 another series was published.[4] Since then only five treatises dealing with specific phases of business journalism have appeared in print: a manual on editing by an editor,[5] a book on advertising and selling by the space buyer of an advertising agency,[6] a manual on businesspaper writing by two businesspaper correspondents,[7] and a collection of essays by leading editors, managers, and publishers, compiled by a business writer.[8] In contrast, literally thousands of books have been published on all phases of newspaper journalism.

For many valuable suggestions and criticism of chapters in this book I am indebted, first of all, to my friend, Stanley Knisely, executive vice-president of the Associated Business Papers, Inc.

---

[1] *Books in This World at War*, by Archibald MacLeish, Assistant Secretary of State, former Librarian of Congress, former assistant director, Office of War Information, New York *Times Book Review*, December 6, 1942.

[2] *Industrial Publishing*, by Horace M. Swetland. New York Business Publishers Association, 1923.

[3] *Industrial Journalism*, published by *Advertising & Selling*. New York, 1915.

[4] *Lectures on Business Journalism*, New York Business Publishers Association, Inc., in collaboration with the Business Training Corporation, 1921.

[5] *The Business Paper Editor at Work*, Douglas G. Woolf, McGraw-Hill Book Co., 1936.

[6] *Advertising and Selling Through Business Publications*, Mabel Potter Hanford. Harper & Brothers, 1938.

[7] *Business Paper Writing—A Career*, Pauline & Wilfrid Redmond. Pitman Publishing Co., 1939.

[8] *Careers on Business Papers*, Benn Hall. Duell, Sloan & Pearce, 1940.

My thanks, also, to the following: Dr. Ordway Tead, editor of social and economic books, Harper & Brothers; James Blackburn, Jr., vice-president and director of circulation, of the McGraw-Hill Publishing Co.; Carl Gazley, executive director of the Audit Bureau of Circulations; Frank Avery, executive director of Controlled Circulation Audit; R. O. Eastman; A. R. Hahn, managing editor of *Sales Management*; Sidney D. Kirkpatrick, editor of *Chemical and Metallurgical Engineering*; L. S. Morrow, editor of *Factory Management and Maintenance*; Harwood Merrill, editor of *Modern Industry*; Dr. Leo Lion, formerly businesspaper chief of the House of Ullstein in Germany; J. K. Lasser, C.P.A., auditor and consultant to the Associated Business Papers, Inc.; Harry H. Van Aken, libel authority; and to George Nichols, editor of *Printers' Ink*, for permission to quote liberally from the fiftieth anniversary issue. My gratitude for helpful suggestions on Chapters III and VI must be expressed to Judge Thurman Arnold and Stuart Chase.

For historical research I am indebted to Alfred S. Moore of Belfast, Robin Walker of Dysart, Scotland, and Holbrook Jackson, editorial director, National Trade Press, Ltd., of London.

Thanks must be expressed also to authorities in many fields from whose works I have taken quotations and inspiration. I am in deep debt particularly to H. G. Wells's *Outline of History* and *The Outline of Man's Work and Wealth*; to Miriam Beard's *History of the Business Man*; to Lewis Mumford's *Technics of Civilization*; to Will Durant's *Story of Philosophy*; and to Dean Frank Luther Mott's *History of American Magazines*, for valuable reference.

I am particularly indebted to these men: Harold S. Smith, director of the budget; Morris A. Copeland, director of research, and Vladimir S. Kolesnikoff, chairman of the Technical Committee on Industrial Classification, of the Executive Office of the President, Bureau of the U.S. Budget, Division of Statistical Standards; C. J. Judkins, chief of Trade Association Unit, of the U.S. Department of Commerce; Carroll L. Wilson, director of the Bureau of Foreign and Domestic Commerce; J. C. Capt, Bureau of the Census; Thomas J. Fitzgerald, chief statistician for manufacturers; Vergil D. Reed, who introduced the S.I.C. to the International Congress on Distribution in Copenhagen, 1939; and to all their associates, for the existence of two monumental reference works, *Standard Industrial Classification Manual* (2 vols.) and the *Directory of Trade and Professional Associations.*

Thanks are due also to a number of businesspaper editors, publishers and business journalists here and abroad, trade association officials, librarians, government officials, college professors, advertising agency executives, and others who have eagerly cooperated in supplying information.

Finally, an expression of deep gratitude to my secretary, Marie Puglis, a young woman with a remarkable fund of patience, who is an expert at decoding hastily penciled author's alterations.

J.E.

New York City
February 1, 1945

BOOK ONE

CHAPTER I

THE BUSINESSPAPER FIELD
DEFINED

This muddled multitudinousness . . . this immense tangled affair, is our affair.
H. G. WELLS in *Outline of Man's Work and Wealth*

BASIC FUNCTIONS OF THE BUSINESSPAPER

THE time is overdue for a clearer understanding and appreciation of the business press: of the important part it plays in human affairs, and the vital role which is cast for an *integrated* business journalism in the emergent world economy.

To give understanding to the modern role of the businesspaper is not easy. Alongside a clear definition of business journalism must go a better definition of business itself. Indeed, it is an understanding of the functions of business that gives clarity to the functions of the business press.

The businesspaper is both a quasi-public agency of communication and a private profit enterprise. As a privately owned and operated business for profit it is run much like other private businesses. As a communication utility, the businesspaper performs nine basic functions:

1. *Adult education function:* providing encyclopedic materials or know-how for specialized instruction and information of men and women in industry, to improve technics and processes; a current textbook function.

2. *News function:* gathering, organizing and factually presenting authoritative business intelligence which management needs in order to make decisions.

3. *Editorial function:* crusading to elevate the status of industry

3

by advocacy of higher standards of conduct and performance; pioneering newborn industries; safeguarding the competitive character of private profit enterprise.

4. *Integrating function:* editorial guidance by judicious backgrounding; interpreting and explaining news events and trends; clarifying the reader's understanding; the editor seeks to give business a true perspective by impartially presenting all sides of an issue and revealing the relationship of that issue to other issues and to the totality of business; he then points out what course seems to offer the most good for the greatest number. The editor uses as a yardstick the largest area affected by the issue: if the area is global, he will consider, first, the world economy, second, the national economy, third, all industry, and last, that particular segment of industry his businesspaper serves.

5. *Forum function:* providing a meeting place in print for the discussion of business problems and processes, the constructive criticism of business practices and policies; also a place where the position of the businesspaper itself may be challenged and refuted by the readers.

6. *Advertising function:* providing a carrier for selling and educational messages addressed to specific markets or segments of industry, concerning goods and services; educating advertisers and potential advertisers on the importance of (a) business as a whole, (b) the specialized press as a whole, (c) the particular industry covered, and (d) the particular businesspaper and the justification for its existence; exercising vigilance in the maintenance and enforcement of high publishing and advertising standards.

7. *Research function:* surveying, analyzing, and distributing information about readers and markets, about production and distribution processes, to readers, to advertisers and advertising agencies, to private and public research organizations, to governmental and miscellaneous bureaus; the publication of trade directories, market studies, readership surveys, etc.

8. *Public relations function:* keeping the activities, interests, and objectives of the field covered, constantly before the eyes of industry as a whole, the government, labor, and the public; a program of education carried out through formal education,

lectures and speeches, consultation, press publicity releases, and through other media of which radio and the films are integral elements.

9. *Public Utility function:* the responsibility to provide continuous service at fair rates in return for the franchise from the public guaranteeing freedom to the press to print the truth without fear or prejudice.

These nine functions have no clean lines of demarcation. Advertising, for example, is often news to businesspaper readers. On the other hand, a news story about a product may result in the sale of that product more quickly than by an advertisement. All these categories overlap. Later we shall discuss these nine functions in detail, in terms of those who are responsible for their performance on the businesspaper.

Our first task is to explain the relationship of the business press to business, and the relationship of both to society.

WHY THERE IS CONFUSION ABOUT BUSINESSPAPERS

The mental confusion about businesspapers that now exists among businessmen and advertisers, among advertising agents and even publishers, among labor leaders, among our own and foreign government officials and diplomats, among educators, students, and even among the readers of the businesspapers themselves, is due in part to a misunderstanding of terminology.

Everyone knows what a newspaper is. But consider how variously today the businesspaper is labeled: trade journals, trade papers, resale papers, technical papers, industrial publications, commercial magazines, merchandising papers, administration and managerial papers, class papers, service periodicals, financial publications, professional magazines, reviews, gazettes, and businesspapers.

The business press is often bracketed in people's minds with manufacturers' circulars, house organs, trade association bulletins, and institutional publications. It is even placed in the same category with catalogues, directories, almanacs, newsletters, data books, and souvenir booklets.

The most popular term is "trade journal." For the etymologically curious, a "journal" originally meant a daily, being a relative of the word *diurnal*.[1] Today it is a term appearing in the masthead of some of our leading so-called "professional" publications which are issued usually monthly or quarterly instead of daily; for example, the medical "journals." Some prefer the term "magazine." Once a "magazine" was an "upstart collection of dullness and folly."[2]

There are not many businesspapers called gazettes, fortunately. Gazette was derived from *gazetta* (a small Venetian coin which bought a newspaper), while others say it came from *gazza* (a chattering magpie). "Review" was originally applied only to a collection of articles reviewing books. Scores of businesspapers are still called reviews today. Even the almost universal term "businesspaper" is partly a misnomer. A "paper" was the common term originally applied to any pamphlet or collection of unbound pamphlets, without stitching, stapling, or cover.

Confusion of terminology is not confined to the American business press. A similar misuse of words exists in the British and European business press. Especially confusing (to us) are the names of British publishing firms. For example, in the United States a reference to the "national trade press" would be taken to mean all those publishers whose businesspapers enjoy national coverage. In Britain, however, the "National Trade Press, Limited" is the corporate name of a single publisher of a group of business publications. In the United States, "industrial newspapers" would be commonly taken to refer to businesspapers, with a newspaper style of format, publishing the news of industry. In Britain, "Industrial Newspapers, Limited" happens to be a private concern publishing a number of businesspapers in many fields, some with magazine format.

Another English publisher calls his private corporation "Business Publishers, Limited." This title, if used in the United States, would suggest a trade association with a general membership of

---

[1] *History of American Magazines*, by Frank Luther Mott, Vol. I. D. Appleton & Co., New York, 1930 (Pulitzer Prize Winner).
[2] *The Dunciad*, Pope, Book I, 1743.

businesspaper publishers. In our country most publishers use their own names as the firm names.

Where confusion does not exist concerning the business press there is usually a vacuum. Many authors of books on journalism or marketing ignore the subject of business journalism outright. Grant Milnor Hyde, director and professor, School of Journalism, University of Wisconsin, in the foreword to *An Outline Survey of Journalism* describes that book as "comprising a survey of the entire field of journalism."[3] Twelve leading professors of journalism helped write it. There are four short paragraphs on "Industrial Publishing, An Adjunct to Business News Coverage." (*sic*)

A search of the latest edition of the Encyclopædia Britannica,[4] for example, fails to reveal a single reference to the business press under such headings as Trade, Business, Publishing, Journalism. For the editors of the Encyclopædia Britannica, business journalism is nonexistent, despite the fact that there were businesspapers flourishing in the late seventeenth century. One of them, *Lloyd's List*, perseveres to this day as one of Britain's outstanding business publications.

Moreover, under the general subject of Communication, the Encyclopædia Britannica makes no reference whatever to Printing, Publishing, or Journalism. Reference is made to Railways, Signaling, Wireless, Telegraph, Telephone, Broadcasting, Heliograph, Television, Semaphore, Morse Code, and the Fathometer. Elsewhere, under the J's, there does appear an essay on Journalism which recognizes the existence of *one medium*, the daily newspaper.

Encyclopaedia Americana in its latest edition[5] contains an article on Journalism, with a subdivision devoted to "class" publications in which "trade papers" and "college humor" magazines are bracketed. The author of the subdivision on "class" publications, Charles H. Cochrane, is listed as "a member of the editorial staff of *Newspaperdom*." The businesspaper known as *Newspaperdom* went out of existence in 1925, when it was merged with *Editor & Publisher*.

[3] *An Outline Survey of Journalism*, George Fox Mott, Editor. Barnes & Noble, New York, 1940.
[4] 14th Edition (1936).
[5] 1941 Edition.

The current *Americana* article on Journalism is, therefore, two decades old, at least.

People who buy advertising space in businesspapers for themselves or their clients, and who analyze this particular medium, are not particularly clear in their own minds about the specialized press. For some years the advertising agency Batten, Barton, Durstine & Osborne was the largest single purchaser of businesspaper advertising space for its clientele. In his book on advertising, Mr. Ben Duffy, vice-president in charge of that agency's marketing and plans, classifies the business press as follows:[6]

1. *Industrial* (concerned with production).
2. *Trade* (concerned with merchandising).
3. *Professional* (concerned with professions).

But Mrs. Mabel Potter Hanford, formerly businesspaper space buyer for this same agency, in her book on advertising, sets up a different classification:[7]

1. *General Business Magazines or Newspapers* ("treating broadly of general business news")

2. *Industrial Periodicals* "concerned with manufacturing industries and industries servicing industries such as mining, railroad, chemical engineering, etc."

3. *Trade or Commercial Periodicals* ("In general usage the trade paper is accepted as representing those addressed to a dealer or retailer and the distributor or jobber outlet").

4. *Service and Professional Periodicals* ("These are sometimes called 'class' magazines").

5. *Catalogues and Data-books* (These she describes as "collections of catalogues of various and allied industries furnished in one book for the convenience of a selected audience." Mrs. Hanford includes directories with data-books as "volumes of handy information").

Mrs. Hanford also divides her industrial group into two parts: *Vertical* and *Horizontal*.

[6] *Advertising Media & Markets*, by Ben Duffy. Prentice-Hall, Inc., New York, 1939.
[7] *Advertising and Selling through Business Publications*, by Mabel Potter Hanford. Harper & Brothers, New York, 1938.

Vertical is defined by Mrs. Hanford as "those addressed to a specific industry." *Horizontal* are "those which reach out into a variety of industries or manufacturing fields."

Dr. Hugh E. Agnew, professor emeritus of the Department of Marketing, New York University,[8] breaks down business publications into what he believes are "four fairly distinct types."

1. *"Administration or managerial"*
2. *"Technical and professional"*
3. *"Resale or trade"*
4. *"Industrial or commercial"*

To each of these experts, the same words mean different things. Dr. Agnew, under his fourth classification, has this to say:

Industrial or Commercial Publications

Although the term "industry" is usually connected with manufacturing processes, it is also extended to cover such activities as mining, the extraction of ores, and the like. The latter are sometimes called extractive industries. For the purpose of present classification, it is expedient to include transportation under this heading. This may be regarded as permissible, *inasmuch as mining is really a form of transportation.* So also with some of the other extractive industries. Also, in common parlance, it is not unusual to hear the phrase "railway industry" and, less often, "shipping industry." The difference seems to be primarily in the amount of service that is included in the charge made to the buyer. In selling coal or ores, this element is practically eliminated; so with many other raw materials. *In a sense, however, raw materials represent a large element of service.* Coal in its natural state in the mine, or iron ore similarly located, is of very limited value. The principal item of cost in each is that of transportation taking them from the place they are found to the place where they are consumed, obviously a service. These various processes of moving materials to a place where they serve a better purpose, or changing their form better to meet the demands of consumers, are on the borderlines of industry, and it is in this broad sense that the authors define industrial publications.[9] [Italics are the author's.]

[8] *Advertising Media*, Agnew & Dygert. McGraw-Hill, New York, 1938.
[9] Paul Mazur (*New Roads to Prosperity*, Viking Press, New York, 1931), goes Dr. Agnew one better and defines steel and production goods not as "basic" industries but as "service" industries.

The Blue Book[10] of the Associated Business Papers, the leading association of businesspaper publishers, recognizes only *three* major classifications of businesspapers:

1. *"Industrial and Technical Press"*
2. *"Merchandising or Trade Press"*
3. *"Professional and Institutional Press"*

Group 1 above is described by the A.B.P. Blue Book as "serving the interests of readers engaged in industry or in technical pursuits having to do with production."

Shying away from all these bewildering definitions and confused attempts to classify businesspapers, the publishing directories fall back on the alphabet method: "A" for Architects' publications; "B" for Butchers' and Bankers' publications; "C" for Candlestick Makers' publications; and let it go at that. One might as well try to understand New York City by reading its telephone directory.[11]

Why can we not agree on some simple classification of business so as to classify the press that serves business along equally simple lines? Why can we not agree that "trade" and "business" and "commerce" and "industry" mean the same thing? Is the physician less *industrious* than the miner? Do not butcher and banker *trade* what they have for what they need? Does not the maker of real locomotives have to *merchandise* his product as well as the maker of toy locomotives?

Trade, Industry, and Business Are the Same

Let us start with the simple, age-old word "trade," for once upon a time most businesspapers unashamedly answered to the name of trade papers. Trade comes from the Latin *trado*, meaning to hand over, which, it would seem, is the chief function of the human race. You trade something you have for something you need. If you are lucky you get an even break. The big idea, unfortunately, has always been to get better than an even break. In the dawn of the human race, Alexander Levene points out in a

[10] Last edition published in 1938 by the Associated Business Papers, Inc., New York.

[11] See *N. W. Ayer Newspaper Directory* (classification of Business Papers) and *Standard Rate and Data Service* (Business Paper Edition).

monograph on monopoly, trade did not exist. Every individual produced everything he consumed, until someone, more lazy than the rest, or perhaps with greater imagination, decided not to go hunting when his meat supply ran low. "Being adept at making stone axes," speculates Mr. Levene, "he exchanged a surplus ax with a neighbor for a supply of meat . . . barter became a human activity."[12]

But primitive barter gave way long ago to more complex forms of "trade." Someone invented money. In essence, however, people go right on trading, exchanging what they have for what they need—struggling for a living—and *every* businesspaper is concerned with *their ways of making a living*.

Ways change. Words change. Concepts change. To the authors of the Constitution of the United States, "industry" was *art* and "traffic" had a vulgar meaning. Stuart Chase writes:

Fifteen decades of cultural change lie between us and the words of the Constitution. What we now call "industry" the founding Fathers called "art." A "machine" was a symbol for a piece of workmanship composed with art to produce motion. It was also the "part which the deities, angels or demons perform in solving some knotty difficulty." A "manufacturer" symbolized a man who made things with his hands. The concept included, of course, the farmer. "Credit" was the symbol for trust reposed in the debtor. The vast machinery of modern credit transactions was unknown. A "banker" was a tradesman who dealt in money, not long removed from the goldsmithbanker. "Business" was beginning to be spelled with an *i*, but still meant busy-ness in most contexts. "Industry" symbolized the commendable behavior of ant and bee. "Traffick" had a vulgar connotation, as in "the slave traffick" or "traffick with hussies." "Trade" was more respectable. Large merchants as well as petty shopkeepers were "in trade." But "commerce" was held a stately word, symbol for all goods that moved.[13]

"Conclusions true in one generation are invalid in the next," says Dr. Richard T. Ely. "Terms and definitions appropriate to

[12] *Does Trade Need Anti-Trust Laws?* by Levene & Feldman. Long & Smith, New York, 1931.
[13] *The Tyranny of Words*, by Stuart Chase. Harcourt, Brace & Co., New York, 1938.

one stage of industry are misleading in a succeeding stage . . . even those laws or uniformities which science prizes as the finest products of its research are but statements of probabilities."[14]

In discussing the word "income" in the case of *Towne* v. *Eisner*, Mr. Justice Holmes laid down a principle worth remembering about words:

"It is not necessarily true that *income* means the same thing in the Constitution and the Act.[15] *A word is not a crystal, transparent and unchanged; it is the skin of a living thought and may vary greatly in color and content according to the circumstances and the time in which it is used.*"[16] (Italics are the author's.)

Consider the word "business" in our attempt to define a modern businesspaper:

A well-known spokesman for the business press, Colonel Chevalier, has declared: "Business, after all, is simply the process of producing and exchanging all of those things people want and are able to pay for. That is sometimes forgotten today when we hear business discussed in the most rarefied circles of our society."[17]

"Business," declares Professor Norman Scott Brien Gras of Harvard, "is the administration of labor and natural resources in partnership with capital, in a process which leads to a sale of goods or service, with other activities in a subordinate position . . . Business is administration that looks toward exchange. Private business expects a profit for its service. Public business would pretend to offer a service without profit."[18]

The well-known business authority, Harry Scherman, does not think the business process can be stated so simply as either Colonel Chevalier or Professor Gras states it. Nor does Mr. Scherman think of business as something bounded by Canada, Mexico, and two oceans as many Americans do. He writes: "If ever there was a shorthand word in common use, completely obliterating to ap-

[14] *Outlines of Economics*, by Richard T. Ely. Macmillan Co., New York, 1916.
[15] Income Tax Act.
[16] See also Alexander Levene, on the changing meaning of "Restraint of Trade." *Does Trade Need Anti-Trust Laws?* Long & Smith, New York, 1931.
[17] Colonel Willard T. Chevalier, vice-president, McGraw-Hill Publishing Co., before the Audit Bureau of Circulations, at a Chicago meeting in 1937.
[18] *Business & Capitalism*, by N. S. B. Gras. F. S. Crofts, New York, 1939.

prehension the actualities of daily existence, it is the word 'business.' "

Mr. Scherman, like Mr. Chase, points out that the original meaning of the word "business" was the state of being busy. "If it now meant only that," he says, "it would be a little curious to ask a man, *How is your busyness progressing? We* might as sensibly inquire, *How is your laziness getting along?"*

The word business refers not to the state of being busy, but to the activities men are busy performing. The business press is concerned with those activities separately and collectively. Mankind is busy carrying on exchanges of labor for money, money for goods, money for money. *The modern word "business" concerns the activities of two billion human beings.* More than that, it concerns an immense volume of deferred or incompleted exchanges by all the people on this planet, which affect the business of every person, no matter where he lives.

The true condition of a manufacturer's business is not judged by how much he is manufacturing, but by the number of orders on hand which he is now engaged in filling, or the orders he has just completed and is delivering; exchanges of his goods for someone else's money. A manufacturer's plant might be going full blast but business would be bad if he were not getting any orders. Similarly, the volume of crops a farmer grows does not make his business good or bad. *It is the volume of crops he can exchange for money, and for how much money, at a given time and place.*

The amount of business any concern does is measured by its sales, which is to say, by its exchanges. The same is true of wholesale distributors and retailers. The sum total of the exchanges of all individual enterprise is a picture of a nation and the even larger total of national exchanges tells the story of the chief human activities of two billion inhabitants of our world.

Mr. Scherman concludes: *"The wealth of all human society varies with and is determined by the volume of these exchanges, goods for money, services for money or money for money, all of which is encompassed in the single word 'business.' "*[19]

[19] *The Promises Men Live By*, by Harry Scherman. Random House, New York, 1938.

The business press provides the *carriers* of responsible information upon which businessmen make *decisions* that set in motion the business process.

When you hear someone say he is going to "state the case for business," you would imagine "business" was a watertight compartment in the scheme of things. On the contrary, business *is* the scheme of things. Leaders of industry sometimes find it necessary to remind their own associates of this important fact. Recently, Enders M. Voorhees, chairman of the finance committee of U. S. Steel Corporation, told a group of controllers:

> We who are in business are not litigants in a great cause, with the general public as our adversaries. *Business is not a thing apart. It is simply the same general public engaged in its own service of supply;* and business can no more live in a position adverse to those it supplies than the heart can take a position adverse to the lungs.[20] [Italics ours.]

If Mr. Voorhees' observations are sound, more people—especially students—need to understand the functions of business and business journalism. The businesspaper, in brief, is concerned with the fortunes of all human society, the exchange of all goods and services by mankind. Like business itself, the businesspaper must cut across political and national boundary lines to function properly as a social institution.

Horizontal and Vertical Businesspapers

The terms "horizontal" and "vertical," as used to describe types of businesspapers, are what Thurman Arnold calls "polar words." They have no meaning by themselves. Businesspaper editors disagree with each other, as to whether their *own* papers are "vertical" or "horizontal." The specialized job of a businesspaper may be said to be *vertical* and the over-all job *horizontal*. At best such terms provide only mental exercise. "Up" has no meaning apart from the term "down," as Arnold points out in a diverting chapter

[20] Address before the Controllers' Institute of America, Waldorf-Astoria Hotel, New York, Sept. 21, 1943.

on "Definitions and Polar Words," in one of his books.[21] Realization of this fact is the principle of *relativity* associated with Dr. Einstein's researches in physics. For centuries the terminology of traditional physics and of astronomy were full of polar words like "up in the sky" and "the sun does down." For thousands of years science was up against these false mental pictures, bound by these polar words, says Arnold. "Matter was little lumps, of which the atom was the smallest. Time was a sequence. Space was a frame. These word images were taken from the general images of the day. They could not be used to describe a world in which time was a dimension and matter a form of energy." By the same token "efficiency" is a polar word. Also "justice." "Justice," says Judge Arnold, "is such a nice word, we refuse to apply it to people who are struggling for things we do not like."

ENTIRE BUSINESS PRESS IS A "TECHNICAL PRESS"

Likewise, the term "technical" can give a false mental picture. Publishers of businesspapers covering the transformative and extractive industries often refer to their publications as "technical" papers. In this way they exclude, by implication at least, other businesspapers in fields which are held to be less technical, meaning that the technics are perhaps easier for more people to understand. Experience shows that the term "technical" may lead to a false classification. The use of logarithms does not make one business editor's columns more *technical* than another's. The editor of *Chemical and Metallurgical Engineering* might be just as mystified upon hearing a discussion of cumulative mark-on between the editors of *Chain Store Age* and *Department Store Economist* as the latter two editors might be on reading an article in *Chem. & Met.* on the formula for Buna-S (synthetic rubber).

The Greeks had a word for it: *Technikos*, meaning art. Latin, *technicus*. From *techne*, art, and *logos*, discourse, you get *technology* (Webster, 1942): "appertaining to art, science, profes-

[21] *Folklore of Capitalism*, by Thurman Arnold. Yale University Press, 1937; a sequel to *Symbols of Government* by the same author. Judge Arnold is a member of the U.S. Court of Appeals, Washington, D.C.

sion, handicraft, business or the like." That definition seems to cover the entire field of businesspaper publishing. All businesspapers are written by experts for experts. There are technics in every type of business activity and the subject matter is, therefore, technical. There are as many "kinds" of businesspapers as there are "kinds" of human effort in the struggle for existence. Each trade has its technics, or arts. Together they make up the technics of civilization. Every worth-while businesspaper is the current textbook of a technician somewhere, who wants to improve his art, or know-how.

"Technology" means the application of knowledge to a problem. It means getting a job done with a minimum of mistakes and a maximum of results.

In this one respect all kinds of businesspapers are alike: they are all concerned with the *know-how* of making a better living, with the technics of all branches of industry, with the methods of increasing efficiency (excuse the polar word) in every phase of human activity, with better ways of conducting profitable, legitimate business enterprise. All businesspapers are "technical" papers; all businesspapers are "industrial" papers; all businesspapers are "trade" papers. So from here on, we shall call them all *businesspapers*. Incidentally, there is no more reason to hyphenate the word *businesspaper* than the word newspaper.

The Businesspaper Compared with Other Media

Consider these essential differences in comparing the businesspaper with other carriers of information:

The Newspaper: spot news, politics, crime, divorces, society, woman's page, theater, comics, sports, crossword puzzles.

The General Magazine: fiction and nonfiction for popular information or entertainment, amusement, relaxation.

The News Weekly: digests of general news events, war, politics, crime, general economics with or without popular interpretation.

The Women's Magazines: fiction, fashions, home economics, household and garden equipment, decoration, humor, theater, movies.

case where papers are printed daily or weekly. Most publishers, however, use independently owned printing and engraving establishments.

The investment of the businesspaper publishing industry in its own machines and equipment is estimated at $100 million. The annual peacetime revenues are put at somewhere between $80 and $90 million, exclusive of farm journals, which have an annual revenue of about $20 million additional. Paid subscriptions of less than 150 leading businesspapers total $4 million a year.

In 1942, the 489 leading advertising agencies of the United States placed 212,332 pages of paid advertising in American businesspapers. *Wall Street Journal*, a well-known businesspaper, in its issue of August 19, 1943, described businesspapers as the "little giants" of publishing. *Iron Age*, for example, with a circulation of 17,000 copies a month, carried 6,640 pages of paid advertising in a year, as compared with 2,923 pages in *Time* and 2,372 pages in the *Saturday Evening Post*, the same year, despite the fact that these latter two general magazines have a total circulation of over 4 million readers.

Paper curtailment froze circulations of many businesspapers at January, 1943, levels during World War II. In April, 1943, one businesspaper publisher, typical of many, reported more than 8,000 unfilled subscriptions. Army, navy, air force, and government officials were priority subscribers during the war, depending heavily upon the latest technical information of the business press for the successful prosecution of the war effort both at home and on the fighting fronts.

Mechanical efficiency is an end product of businesspaper publishing. Describing the shuttle action of the British and German armies in the North African campaign in World War II, General L. J. Campbell, chief of ordnance, told businesspaper editors:

"It wasn't a question of who had the best soldiers, but purely one of who had the best and most *equipment*. Each drive, back and forth, across that desert [Libya] was a gigantic surge of mechanical energy."[23]

---

[23] Before the confidential National Conference of Business Paper Editors, Washington, 1943.

Men who *study* businesspapers made possible this mechanical efficiency for which American industry is famous; they made it possible for American industry to convert quickly into a war machine and supply vast quantities of matériel to the United Nations. Were it not for a half century of businesspaper publishing, the situation in World War II might have been tragic.

The average tonnage of a businesspaper is 47 tons annually, based on a survey, in March, 1943, of all businesspapers listed in *Standard Rate and Data Service*.[24] This would bring the estimated total tonnage of the business press (1,777 publications) to 84,000 tons a year. Tonnage is a poor way to judge the business press. The estimated tonnage of government printing alone, for 1943 (war year), was put at 782,000 tons. One issue of a ration book during World War II (No. 2 Point Rationing book in April, 1943) consumed more paper than 23 of the largest businesspapers would use in a year.

Jesse H. Neal, when he was secretary of the Associated Business Papers, Inc., several years ago, described the business press to a convention of the Associated Advertising Clubs of the World as *"information railways that connect mine and mill and factory in a solidly established system of main lines and branches."*[25]

The communication lines of the specialized business press, in point of fact, perform a more important economic function than the country's transportation systems. Railway, highway, seaway, skyway, and pipeway transport is largely dependent upon *decisions* by management. Decisions depend on specialized information.

Until there is a *meeting of minds* on both ends of the business

[24] A survey of the 1,777 businesspapers listed in *Standard Rate and Data* in March, 1943, elicited replies from 744 businesspapers. On this basis the 47-ton average was arrived at, W. J. Rooke, president of the Associated Business Papers, Inc., told a publishers' conference in the Waldorf-Astoria, New York, in March, 1943.

[25] "To the casual observer, the Industrial Press is about as exciting as the rows of wires that stretch along every road and railway . . . The simile is very apt. Both exist solely for the interchange of ideas. Both are typically American in the extent to which they have been developed and applied to the whole economy"—From a newspaper advertisement by the McGraw-Hill 'Network of Industrial Communication.' "

communication line, there is no sale, no contract, and no flow of goods.

"With the war," declared the editors of the businesspaper *Fortune* recently, "we have learned the importance of weighing the impact of individual decisions on each other and especially on the total work load of a burdened economy. Likewise we have learned how important is the behavior of total output for individual decision."[26]

We doubt if any responsible business executive ever makes a decision before he secures the latest specialized information provided by his own favorite businesspaper.

[26] "The Job Before Us," *Fortune*, January, 1944.

CHAPTER II

THE BACKGROUND OF INDUSTRY SERVED

Business is the way men make their living and because there are many men, with many talents and skills, the ways of making a living can be counted by the thousands. They are bound up with every activity of life. The complex sum of these activities we call the business world . . . this multitude of activities, so inter-related and cross-bound that every human unit in our society is inescapably allied to other human units seems at first glance to be an impenetrable maze.

MELVIN ANSHEN, *Introduction to Business*

THERE is no legitimate activity of life that is not guided and served by one or more businesspapers in the United States. Since there are more than two thousand active businesspapers published in North America, this chapter will serve to indicate further the tremendous scope of the business press as the information railway for this complex, modern social organization by which we all live, work, and accumulate wealth.

Two points in Professor Anshen's observation above deserve our special attention. Because every human unit in our society is allied to every other human unit, it is necessary for the student of business and the student of business journalism to see these units in relation to each other. Then, what seems at first a tangled and muddled affair becomes an orderly, integrated process, easy to understand.

How to Classify Businesspapers

There are many ways to classify businesspapers, depending upon your objective. They can be classified:

1. *By segments of industry*: businesspapers serve all segments of industry and, in this book, agriculture, labor, the professions and service trades, manufacture, commerce, transportation and communications, all are included in the term "industry."

2. *By commodity group*: producers' goods or services, and consumers' goods or services.

3. *By circulation*: character, quality, and type of reader, which will identify him with some kind of industry; but this bracket generally is used to indicate whether the reader pays for the paper or gets it free, and what kind of audit determines those facts.

4. *By geography*: international, national, regional, sectional, or local.

5. *By format*: magazine size (large and standard); newspaper size (large and tabloid); pocket size.

6. *By frequency*: daily, weekly, biweekly, semimonthly, monthly, bimonthly, quarterly, semiannually, and annually.

Monthly businesspapers are still the most popular. In 1937, *Standard Rate and Data Service* listed 1,509 businesspapers in their April Business Paper Section. These were grouped under 160 separate classifications. Frequency of publication was as follows:

Annually or semiannually	95
Quarterly or three times a year	32
Bimonthly or eight times a year	38
Monthly	1,062
Semimonthly	45
Biweekly	30
Weekly	189
Daily	18

Of the total, 447 were organs of trade or professional associations.

In July, 1944, *Standard Rate & Data Service* listed 1619 U. S. businesspapers. Of these, 298 were members of the Audit Bureau of Circulation (paid subscriptions), 159 were members of the Controlled Circulation Audit (free but independently audited), 553 were paid circulation with publishers' sworn statements, 235 were distributed free with publishers' sworn statements, and 374 refused to furnish any circulation information.

Businesspapers are sometimes classified as "producers' goods" (or capital goods) and "consumers' goods" papers, because the goods and services which industry produces are often divided into these two major commodity groups.[1]

---

[1] Method used by U.S. Department of Commerce.

Commodity groups are further broken down this way:

PRODUCERS' GOODS

    (a) Equipment, such as factory machinery and locomotives.
    (b) Construction (private).
    (c) Construction (government).

CONSUMERS' GOODS

    (a) Services, such as housing and medical care.
    (b) Perishable Goods, such as food and gasoline.
    (c) Semidurable Goods, such as clothing and tires.
    (d) Durable Goods, such as refrigerators and automobiles.

Producers' goods are used to fabricate consumers' goods. A machine tool, for example, is producers' goods. Consumers' goods are things people consume or destroy in use, sometimes quickly and sometimes slowly, but ultimately. A machine tool will wear out too, or be discarded for a better one. But the tool is not consumed in the sense that a refrigerator, which a machine tool helped to produce, is consumed. Coal is a raw material used to manufacture electricity or chinaware, but it is also "consumers' goods." The use of these terms, *producers' goods* and *consumers' goods*, to classify businesspapers is unsatisfactory. The first classification, *by segments of industry*, will best help students to understand the functions of business journalism.

But sensibly to classify the business press by segments of industry it is first necessary logically to classify industry into the separate segments which the business press serves. Such a logical classification of industry becomes at one and the same time a logical classification of the *specialized* business press.

THE FOUR MAJOR BRACKETS OF INDUSTRY

The most sensible classification of industry we are able to find is the *Standard Industrial Classification* (S.I.C.),[2] which arranges all

[2] *Standard Industrial Classification Manual*, describing 1,530 industries, was prepared by the Bureau of the Budget, Executive Office of the President of the United States, and is used by the Departments of Commerce and Labor, Federal Reserve System and Federal Trade Commission.

PLAN FOR THE CLASSIFICATION OF INDUSTRY*

I EXTRACTIVE

Agriculture (General, Dairy, Grain, Cotton, Fruit, Livestock and Truck Farms)	Forestry (Timber tracts, Logging camps, Nurseries, etc.)	Fisheries Fish Farms and Hatcheries and Fishery Services	Mining (Metal & Coal Mines, Oil and Gas Wells, Quarries, etc.)

II TRANSFORMATIVE

Food	Furniture	Leather	Electrical Machinery
Tobacco	Paper	Stone, Clay, Glass	Machinery and Tools
Textiles	Chemicals	Iron & Steel	Automobiles
Apparel	Petroleum	Ordnance	Transportation Equipment
Lumber	Rubber	Nonferrous Metals	Miscellaneous

III CONTRIBUTIVE

Management	Finance, Insurance & Real Estate	Medical & Health Services	Advertising, Merchandising
Heat, Light, Power		Legal Services	Selling & Promotion
Water & Sanitary Services	Lodging & Meals	Engineering	Publicity
Construction (General and Special Contractors)	Personal Services	Architecture & Design	Agriculture Services
	Repair Services	Accounting	Government
	Amusement & Recreation	Education	Armed Services
	Journalism	Trade & Professional Assns.	Publishing
Political Organizations	Labor Unions		Engraving
			Photography

IV DISTRIBUTIVE

Service & Limited Function Wholesalers (Including Importers and Exporters)	Agents & Brokers	Chain Store Warehousing & Storage
	Petroleum Bulk Tank Stations	Chain Stores Mail Order Houses
Manufacturers' Sales Branches and Offices	Assemblers of Farm Products	Industrial Stores Consumer Cooperatives
Communications Facilitating Marketing Agencies	Transportation Incidental Transport Service	Independent Retailers of all Kinds and Types
		Unclassified

* Based, with certain modifications, on the *Standard Industrial Classification*, Executive Office of the President, Bureau of the Budget, Washington, D.C.

CHART I

legitimate human economic activity by industry segmentation, and provides a uniform system for classification which conforms to the existing structure of American industry (see Chart 1).

We have arbitrarily divided all this human activity, as described in the SIC, into *four major brackets*, in this sequence:

1. Extractive Industry
2. Transformative Industry
3. Contributive Industry
4. Distributive Industry

Each of these four major brackets of industry is served by a specialized group of businesspapers.

Businesspapers covering the field of agriculture or of mining, for example, serve particular segments of Extractive Industry.

Papers covering the fields of steel fabrication or of textile manufacture serve segments of Transformative Industry.

Businesspapers on construction, advertising, management, and medicine serve Contributive Industries.

In the fields of wholesaling and retailing, or importing and exporting, which are segments of Distributive Industry, the specialization of the business press is even more highly developed. While there are businesspapers devoted to the entire field of retailing, scores of other businesspapers are concerned with a specialized retail operation such as appliance merchandising or the merchandising of food, automobiles, cosmetics, corsets and morticians' supplies.

Quite simply we can divide all businesspapers into the same four brackets into which industry is divided:

1. Businesspapers covering the fields of extraction
2. Businesspapers covering the fields of transformation
3. Businesspapers covering the fields of contribution
4. Businesspapers covering the fields of distribution

This classification of businesspapers should make it easier for students and teachers of business journalism, business administration, and marketing, and for those in public relations and advertising work, as well as publishers and working journalists, to understand each other's language when they speak of business, or of the business press.

Let us examine the background of these four major brackets of industry served by the business press:

Extractive Industry: This group of industries as a whole is concerned with the drawing out, removal, digging up, growing, and extracting of raw material. The extraction usually requires one or more processes, mechanical or chemical transformation, before it is finished consumers' goods. Other things may have to be added. Some things may have to be extracted or subtracted. In some cases the raw material is itself consumers' goods. In many instances contributive services also enter the extractive picture. There are four major extractive industries: agriculture, forestry, fisheries, mining. Many leading businesspapers are published serving each of the four fields in this bracket. The farm journals are a large and important group. Mining and the oil and gas industries are served by many outstanding businesspapers. Mining and agriculture alone employ 22 per cent of the entire labor force of the United States, or nearly 12 million workers (see Chart 2).

Transformative Industry: The government's Central Statistical Board describes this group as "manufactures." It includes those plants, factories, and mills engaged in the mechanical or chemical *transformation* of organic or inorganic substances into new products. These establishments, characteristically, use power-driven machines and materials-handling equipment. Establishments engaged in assembling component parts or manufactured products also are considered manufacturing, if the new product is neither part of the structure nor other fixed improvement. The final product of a manufacturing establishment may be "finished," in the sense that it is ready for utilization or consumption, or "semi-finished," to become raw material for an establishment engaged in further manufacturing. Example: the product of a copper smelter is a raw material used in electrolytic refineries; refined copper is a raw material used by electrical equipment manufacturers to make, let us say, an electric toaster or an automatic blanket. Copper wire is also sold in hardware stores to the consumer.

Materials processed by manufacturing or transforming establishments may be purchased directly from the producers or the extractors; or obtained through customary trade channels; or transferred from the source to the manufacturing plant under the same ownership. Example: The Aluminum Company of America owns and operates bauxite ore deposits (Extractive); aluminum plants (Transformative); maintains research laboratories (Contributive); and has a steamship line (Distributive). Alcoa is the trade name on aluminum ingots sold to cooking utensil producers including its own subsidiary, the Aluminum Cooking Utensil Company. The latter, in turn, sells the finished product, "Wearever" aluminum pots and pans, to wholesalers and retail establishments which sell to the consuming public (Distributive).

Approximately one-fourth (13 million) of our entire labor force is in "manufacturing" (see Chart 2). Scores of businesspapers serve each of the many important fields in this bracket such as food, textiles, chemicals, etc. The 1940 Census gives "manufacturing" an annual volume of $57 billion and 9,600,000 workers.

Contributive Industry: Management, construction, finance, engineering, journalism, advertising, sales promotion, design, education, government, heat, light and power utilities, all the professional and semiprofessional classes and other groups compose this important third bracket of industry which contributes its talents and facilities to make those in the three other main brackets function efficiently.

It is important to understand why construction is classified as a Contributive Industry. There are three broad types of construction: building, engineering projects, and special trade construction (plumbing, wiring, carpentry, for example). The contractors in this group construct industry's *lines* of transportation and communication: railroads; highways; docks, piers, bridges, aqueducts, and tunnels; airports; pipelines; water power; sewage disposal; drainage systems; wells, mains; steel ovens; kilns; mines; silos; grain elevators; telephone, cable, and telegraph systems; radio stations; radar; motion-picture equipment; printing presses; etc. Once the transportation or communication system has been constructed, it becomes an instrument for the distribution of goods and services. The instrument itself, therefore, falls into the category of Dis-

THE NATION'S LABOR FORCE OF 54,000,000 PERSONS IN LATE 1941

This Nation, with about 7% of the world's population, leads the world in factory output and in national income!
About 40% of its population comprises its "LABOR FORCE." In what fields of occupation are these "bread winners"?
What changes have occurred in employment groups from the peace-time spring of 1940 to the national-emergency fall of 1941?
As seen below, unemployment has declined from 9 to 4 million persons. "MANUFACTURING" is the Nation's foremost occupation, with 3 million
new workers added to its total in 1939 of almost 10 million workers. "AGRICULTURE" is the second largest employer if family workers are included;
it produces the wheat, cotton, etc., which "MANUFACTURING" then processes
This is the first of a series of 10 "INDUSTRIAL AMERICA" charts. They endeavor to portray in graphic, summarized form a picture of the
relationship of associations to all major phases of the National Economy

THE "LABOR FORCE" IN RELATION TO POPULATION IN LATE 1941

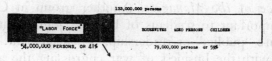

133,000,000 persons

"LABOR FORCE" — 54,000,000 PERSONS, OR 41%

HOUSEWIVES   AGED PERSONS   CHILDREN — 79,000,000 persons or 59%

OCCUPATIONS OF THE "LABOR FORCE" OF 54,000 000 PERSONS

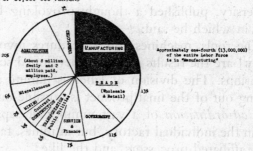

Approximately one-fourth (13,000,000)
of the entire Labor Force
is in "Manufacturing"

THE "LABOR FORCE" IN LATE 1941 (see above chart) AS COMPARED WITH EARLY 1940:

	U.S.A. POPULATION	Housewives, Children, etc.	"LABOR FORCE" (Employed & Unemployed)	Manu-facturing	Agri-culture	Trade	Govern-ment	Service & Finance	Transpor-tation & Pub.Util.	Contract construc-tion	Mining	All other	Unemployed
IN THE FALL OF 1941	133 million persons	79	54	13	10	7	6	4	3	2	1	4	4
Spring of 1940	132 " "	79	53	10	10	6	4	4	3	2	1	4	9
CHANGES	1 million increase	-	1 increase	3 increase	-	1 increase	2 increase	-	-	-	-	-	5 decrease
THE 3,100 ASSOCIATIONS NAMED IN THIS DIRECTORY --	1,100		150	410	85	400	160	30		45	most of the remaining 720 are professional associations

*Of the 54 million "Labor Force", 41 million are males, 13 million are females. Of the 79 million other persons, 29 million are housewives; 31 million are
children under 14; 9 million are students over 14; and 10 million are aged, etc., persons.
Of the 54 million "Labor Force", 39 million are employees at work, 4 million persons are still unemployed, 7 million are farmers, and 4 million are owners
of stores, factories, and other business and professional enterprises. For data on employment and income in each of the 48 states, see Exhibit 20 (page 306)
Source: Employment reports of the Departments of Commerce, Labor, and Agriculture, and the Works Progress Administration; see Exhibit 20.

*Trade and Professional Associations of the U S., 1941 Edition," U S Dept. of Commerce.

CHART 2. THE NATION'S LABOR FORCE

Contributive and Distributive Industry employ a greater number of people than
Transformative Industry.

tributive Industry. Those who manage and use the lines fall into the Contributive bracket. We refer, for example, to the collectors and purveyors of intelligence, such as editors and reporters, correspondents, columnists, newscasters, commentators, writers, lecturers, playwrights, authors, educators, etc. The instruments of communication and symbol multiplication simply transport information and ideas from where they originate to where they are needed.

Importance of the Managers: Another group in Contributive Industry, important to students of business journalism because it is their future "public," or readership, is management.

In 1941, with the business of war engrossing the attention of the entire business world, Professor James Burnham, of New York University, published a thought-provoking book about management in which he said:

"The tools, machines and procedures involved [in modern industry] are the results of highly developed scientific and technical operations. The division of labor is minute and myriad; and the turning out of the final product is possible only through the *technical co-ordination* of a vast number of separate tasks, not only within the individual factory, but in mines, farms, railroads, steamships, affiliated processors, and the like."[3]

Professor Burnham pointed to a wide gap in skill, training, and type of function, between the average worker and those in charge, on the technical side, of the modern process of mass production and organized distribution.

He emphasized three types in Contributive Industry which require lengthy training:

1. Those in industries like Construction, "which have not yet been organized with modern methods . . . but which could be, to increase the relative number of skilled workers."

2. Those who function directly in industry "such as highly trained chemists, physicists, biochemists and engineers."

3. Those concerned with the tasks of technical direction and co-ordination (or management) of the processes of production. Professor Burnham said: "This task is itself a highly specialized

[3] *The Managerial Revolution,* by James Burnham. John Day, New York, 1941.

function. Often it, also, requires acquaintance with the physical sciences (or the psychological and social sciences, since human beings are not the least among the instruments of production) and with engineering."

The managers, as we have said, are the reading public of the businesspaper. They are known by many titles: they are called operating executives, administration engineers, superintendents, supervisory technicians, personnel engineers, traffic managers, sales managers, merchandise managers, advertising managers.

Editors are managers, usually assisted by managing editors. Lawyers, doctors, and accountants are managers. Chemists, bankers, and architects are managers. Labor union leaders are managers.

In government, the managers are chairmen or chiefs of bureaus and committees, commissioners, administrators, secretaries, cabinet officials, consuls, ambassadors. Presidents and vice-presidents are managers, whether in political government or in business government.

Industry's managers in early times were the capitalists themselves. Today in most corporations the managers are no longer the capitalists. They work for capitalists. Professor Burnham's thesis is that someday the capitalists will work for the managers.[4] Managers took control of industry in the emergency of World War II, such men, for example, as Donald Nelson of Sears, Roebuck, who became head of the War Production Board, and Chester Bowles, an advertising agency executive, who became head of the Office of Price Administration.

The urgent need for highly trained managers, in World War II, led to the creation of the "National Roster of Scientific and Specialized Personnel," in the Office for Emergency Management to help the War Manpower Commission. Leonard Carmichael, director of the Roster, in 1943, divided his roster into seven categories: (1) administration and management; (2) agricultural and biological sciences; (3) engineering and related fields; (4) humanities; (5) medical sciences and related fields; (6) physical sciences;

[4] See *The Modern Corporation and Private Property*, by A. A. Berle, Jr., and Gardiner Means. New York, 1933. For specialized treatment see *Advanced Management*, quarterly journals published by the Society for the Advancement of Management, 29 East 39th Street, New York.

(7) social sciences. Journalism, as such, was overlooked, in listing the social sciences, although three important groups of managers had been drawn from journalism by the government to help the prosecution of the war effort. These were the Office of Censorship, headed by the well-known journalist, Byron Price; Office of War Information, headed by the noted Washington correspondent, Elmer Davis; and the Business Paper Editors' Advisory Council, appointed by Donald Nelson right after Pearl Harbor, headed by a businesspaper journalist, Paul Wooton. Two other important groups in Contributive Industry omitted from the National Roster, advertising and public relations, were nevertheless heavily drawn upon to aid the war effort. Subsequent to the issuance of the National Roster, the War Manpower Commission transmitted a memorandum to Selective Service Bureaus including editors and managers of "technical publications" in the essential activity list.

Distributive Industry: The 16th Decennial Census (1940) of the United States recorded 6,096,799 farms, 13,000 mines, and 430,000 oil and gas wells, in Extractive Industry, with 184,000 factories engaged in Transformative Industry—transforming the extracted raw material into producers' goods and consumers' goods. Reference to Chart 1 will show a partial list of the different groups in that fourth bracket of industry which we call Distributive, whose function it is to *move* the product of our ever-expanding agricultural and industrial plant from where it is to where it is needed or wanted. This process is carried on by distributors, wholesalers, retailers, agents, assemblers, and brokers of many kinds, using every modern means of communication and transportation to deliver goods and services to the customer.

The transportation lines distribute goods and people, and include the enterprises that operate railways, seaways, highways, waterways, skyways, pipeways.

The communication lines distribute the intelligence by which our modern complex economy is sustained and include enterprises that furnish communication services, audibly or visually, by wire or wireless: cable, telephone, telegraph; radio broadcasting and television; radiotelephone, radio telegraph, radar; teletypewriter and ticker tape service; facsimile, telephoto, and phototransmission; quotation services recording or reporting price and volume of transactions on security and commodity exchanges; news syndicates and press associations; publishing, printing, and allied industries.[5]

Distributive Industry—Wholesale Trade: Wholesale trade, as defined by the S.I.C., includes all establishments or places of business engaged primarily in selling merchandise to retailers, to industrial or commercial users, or to other wholesalers, or acting as agents in buying merchandise for or selling merchandise to such persons or companies. The principal types of establishments included are service wholesalers (wholesale merchants, industrial distributors, voluntary-group wholesalers, and exporters and importers); limited-function wholesalers (cash and carry, drop shippers, wagon distributors, and retailer-co-operative warehouses); sales branches and sales offices (but not retail stores) maintained by manufacturing enterprises apart from their plants for the purpose of marketing their products; converters; auction companies; agents, merchandise or commodity brokers, and commission merchants; petroleum bulk tank stations; and assemblers, buyers, and co-operative marketing associations of farm products (grain elevators, packers, shippers); and chain store warehouses.

The chief functions of establishments included in wholesale trade are selling goods to trading establishments or to industrial users maintaining inventories of goods; extending credit; physically assembling, sorting, and grading goods in large lots; breaking bulk and redistributing in smaller lots; and bringing buyer and seller together. Other service activities include delivery, refrigeration, and various types of promotion, such as advertising, label designing, etc.

An establishment is classified in wholesale trade if its predominant activity is marketing merchandise to retailers, to industrial

---

[5] The S.I.C. bulks together printing, publishing, and allied industries as a "manufacturing" group, failing to make a clear distinction between the functions of gatherers, conveyers, and purveyors of news information and editorial opinion, and those establishments which simply do commercial publishing and printing, typesetting, engraving, bookbinding, or perform other functions necessary in the process of completing communication from one point to another.

users, or to other wholesalers, whether or not it is engaged in auxiliary manufacturing or retailing.

The 1940 Census shows that $55 billion worth of goods was sold at wholesale. The 200,573 establishments of the Wholesale Census were owned by 145,000 concerns and employed 1,562,000 people. The largest 7,901 companies (5 per cent) had 48 per cent of the nation's total wholesale trade. There are 250 wholesale trade associations.

Distributive Industry—Retail Trade: Out of some 3 million separate business establishments of all kinds in the United States, retail trade ranked first,[6] with 1,770,335 establishments and 4,600,-200 employees. There are 160 larger retail trade associations serving the retail trade. The total annual volume at retail is $42 billion. Wholesale and retail trade alone employs 13 per cent of the entire peacetime labor force of 54 million persons, or more than 7 million workers. Mostly small businesses, the independent retailers and wholesalers, together with the 184,000 small, independent manufacturers, are called the bone and sinew of the country. Business-papers are their bibles. They buy and sell, work and live, by their businesspapers.

The U.S. "Labor Force": Our labor force consists of 54 million persons, which is 41 per cent of our population. The balance, 59 per cent, comprises housewives, students, disabled and unemployed, aged persons and children. Of our entire labor force, reference to the Chart 2 will show Contributive and Distributive Industries are the largest employers of manpower. Construction takes 4 per cent, transportation and public utilities use 6 per cent, service and finance 7 per cent, trade 13 per cent, and government employs 11 per cent. With the professional classes added, there is a possible total of almost 47 to 50 per cent, which is the largest unit of the labor force. Many people have the mistaken idea that the great bulk of our labor force is in farming, mining, and manufacture and believe, to use a common expression, that "production has made our country great." Production has, indeed, made our country great. But those who contribute and distribute also have made our country great. Without them, production would dry up.

[6] 16th Decennial Census (1940).

NEW ERA OF ORGANIZED DISTRIBUTION

As America started tobogganing into the world depression of 1933, a banker, Paul Mazur, wrote a book in which he observed:

The importance of consumer goods in our present day social economy has not received anything like the recognition which it unquestionably deserves. A Nation counts its wealth, assets and property in the smoking chimneys of its factories, the whirling wheels of its machines, the profusion of its mines and the statistics of its production. The shops, large and small, that fill the wants of the population seem but adjuncts to these elements, mere agencies that take little part in the thoughts of big business. This attitude is maintained in spite of the fact that *it is this retail business for which men work and by which they live*; in spite of the fact that, if it is the prime function of an economic system to provide its people with the necessities and reasonable luxuries of life, retail business is the *basis* of a nation's economic existence; in spite of the fact, too, that retailing represents a turnover of capital that overshadows any other business. [See Chart 3.]

Capitalism has converted the production mechanism into a gigantic machine, super-modern in form and functioning, but at the same time has allowed consumptive devices of the social economy to remain in their archaic form. Capitalism has failed to evaluate equitably two equally vital and important factors of economic life—production and consumption.[7] [Italics are author's.]

Rightfully, the consumer stands in the center of the social economy. The home is the pivot point of daily existence. All industry directs its effort toward the consumer and the consumer's home. The consumer is the biggest of all purchasing agents. The home is the largest "factory" in the country (see Chart 4).

As a single example, in our country of 40 million homes, housewives bake, cook, refrigerate, preserve, clean, launder, and garden. They produce something like 120 million meals every day. All the functions of the extractive, transformative, contributive, and distributive industries must be brought into play before sufficient quantities of food, of power, and of equipment are ready for the comparatively simple task of "getting dinner."

[7] *New Roads to Prosperity*, by Paul Mazur. Viking Press, New York, 1931.

ALL DEPENDS ON THE RETAIL SALE

A great merchant once said: "Everything that goes on in my store, and in the entire nation's business, depends on what takes place between the salesperson and the customer, with the goods between them."

Prepared for the Committee for Economic Development in 1944 by the Association of Consulting Management Engineers

CHART 3. IMPORTANCE OF RETAIL TRADE

The main and usually the only personal contact point between industry and the consumer is the counter of a retail store.[8] More people pass up and down the aisles of our retail stores than all the magazines or newspapers published in our country can match in

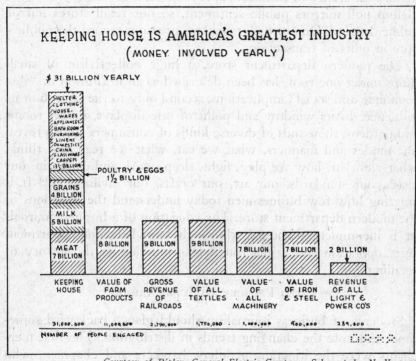

Courtesy of Ripley, General Electric Company, Schenectady, N. Y. 1935

CHART 4

total readership. Only the radio has as intimate a contact with the consumer.

It is true that businesspapers are not designed for the consumer, nor seen by the consumer. Nevertheless, the consumer controls the destiny of the business press as surely as he controls the destiny of the consumer press or the radio. For the consumer is the *leitmotiv* of business. The world's work is done to satisfy him. He is the laborer; he is the capitalist; he is small business; he is big busi-

[8] Exceptions are the house-to-house salesmen.

ness; he is industry; he is the taxpayer; he is the voter; he is the investor; he is the soldier; he is the public.

The retail counter is where you meet and talk with the *public*, intimately, face to face. One retail executive, addressing the National Conference of Business Paper Editors, observed: "Just as the Gallup poll mirrors public sentiment, so our retail stores mirror public demand. On our cash registers our stores record the public's vote in units of transactions."[9]

The modern department store, a huge collectivism of small shops under one roof, has been described as an institution of "vast economic and social" implications, second only to the church in its influence. In its window and point of sale displays, model rooms and gardens, thousands of diverse kinds of consumers' goods reveal our modes and manners, what we eat, what we read and think, what we wear, how we play, fight, sleep, work and entertain, our tastes, our standards, our art, our crafts, our civilization.[10] It is amazing how few businessmen today understand the functions of the modern department store. The education of a business journalist is incomplete without a thorough knowledge of department store operation and a generous backgrounding in the history of retailing.

From Peddler to Supermarket

Students of business journalism should glance backward sometimes and note the changing trends in distribution. The first merchants were the itinerant peddlers, hawkers and chapmen, who brought the goods to the people. Then came the medieval fairs, Oriental bazaars, and trading posts[11] where shrewd traders brought

[9] O. C. Thompson of the Associated Merchandising Corporation, New York, 1943.

[10] "Today's department store is an institution of vast economic and social importance, far greater indeed than most of us would ever realize unless we were deprived of its services. Its very size gives it significance—the large building required for its operations, the army of people employed to conduct its business, the crowds of customers who throng its aisles, and the enormous quantity of merchandise that it sells"—from *History of Macy's of New York 1858-1919*: chapters in *The Eovlution of a Department Store*, by Ralph M. Hower, assistant professor of business history, Harvard University. Harvard University Press, Cambridge, 1943. (See Chart 3.)

[11] Adam Gimbel had a trading post in Vincennes, Ind., in 1842. Later he and

the people to the goods. These were crude beginnings and the changes that followed happened because someone had a better idea. The peddler bought a horse and wagon. It increased his cost of distribution, but it also increased his volume of business. He sold more goods. The trader built a permanent shop. This increased his cost of distribution, but made it possible for him to sell more goods than the peddler.[12]

Then came the department store embracing many shops under one roof. New services and new ideas for styling and promotion further increased the *cost* of distribution, but also have increased the distribution of goods. (Chart 5). The pattern of changing distribution trends includes the specialty shop, the mail order chain, installment selling, manufacturers' outlets, commissaries, company stores, cooperatives, credit stores, service stations, roadside industries and supermarkets.[13]

The story of retailing is a great unfinished chapter in the history of business which is intimately interwoven with the history of business journalism and closely fused with the history of mankind.[14]

The general store, like the trading post, had no one-price system to begin with. The proprietor charged what traffic would bear, or he bartered with the customers. Rum, molasses, linen, wool, and

his brothers moved to New York and opened a general store from which sprang the great Gimbel organization.

The trading post, usually at the headwater of a stream, or near a frontier, traded supplies for pelts. The posts lasted until 1850. Indeed, some still exist in the Arctic Circle.

[12] The peripatetic human "businesspaper" of colonial America was the Yankee peddler. For a century he had packed a portable variety store on his back or pushed a cart up and down dirt roads and cowpaths or along the riverbanks. He brought farm in contact with factory, kept farmers' wives in touch with city fashions. He told New England manufacturers about public demand as he got it straight from the public and he showed manufacturers how to improve consumers' goods; see *Hawkers and Walkers in Early America*, by R. Wright; "The Old Wholesale Peddler and His Team," *New England Magazine*, 1933.

[13] "Airport Bazaars and glorified filling stations will offer serious competition." "The Postwar Battle Royal in Distribution," by Godfrey Lebhar, *House Furnishing Review*, July and August, 1944.

[14] See *Retailing*, by Professor Norris A. Brisco (Prentice-Hall, New York, 1937); *The Outline of Man's Work and Wealth*, H. G. Wells, Chap. VI (Garden City Publishing Co., New York); Edward A. Filene's works.

hardware were the main lines, but local products, accepted in lieu of money, also were sold.

Specialty stores grew from the public demand for variety of lines of merchandise and for more complete assortments in each line from which to make selections.

Department stores, to render extra services to the customer (credit, delivery, advertising, display, and lower prices), assembled groups of specialty shops under one roof and one management. The department store, in 1880, firmly established the one-price system and the policy of the cash transaction.

In 1900, the growth of new types of retail outlets was rapid: mail order (selling from catalogues, mailed to consumers); chains[15] (syndicates of stores); co-operatives (syndicates of consumers); and supermarkets[16] (self-service stores, chiefly dealing in foods).

Latest census, prior to 1938, showed there were in the United States 24 leading chain store classifications with more than 110,000 individual chain store units, having a total annual sales volume of $7 billion. Grocery stores lead with almost 50,000 units (stores) and in annual volume of close to $2½ billion.

A phenomenon of modern businesspaper publishing in the field of distribution is *Chain Store Age*, established in 1925. Originally it covered general merchandise, drug, shoe, men's and women's apparel, and other types of chain stores in the one publication. But in 1928 a new policy inaugurated separate editions, such as Fountain and Restaurant, Drug-Gifts, Variety Store, and Grocery editions. An Administration Edition was brought out for chain store executives in all branches of chain store distribution.

Editorial scope of *Chain Store Age* is to treat comprehensively the problems of multiple store operation: personnel, promotion, expansion and construction, traffic and accounting. Regular departments are: (1) Financial and Statistical; (2) Expansion and Construction; (3) New Equipment and Services; (4) News.

[15] Chain store system goes back to China (200 B.C.); Fugger chain stores operated in fifteenth century Germany; Mitsui chain (Japan) in 1643; Hudson's Bay (oldest American chain) in 1670. See *The Challenge of Chain Store Distribution*, by M. M. Zimmerman (Harper & Brothers, New York, 1931).

[16] "Supermarket: Miracle of Modern Merchandising," by M. M. Zimmerman, *Printers' Ink Weekly*, Vol. 185, No. 11.

Nearly 12,000 top executives in all types of chains are claimed as subscribers to the Administration Edition of *Chain Store Age.* Advertising classifications in the Administration Edition include: air conditioning, business machines, illumination, trucks, real estate, store fronts and fixtures, refrigeration, time switches and clocks, typewriters, etc. When chain stores were threatened with legislative extinction, the paper's widely traveled editor-publisher, Godfrey Lebhar, used radio time and the public platform, as well as his editorial columns, to successfully defend this type of distribution against discrimination.

Supermarket: The depression of 1929-1933 gave birth to the supermarket, which has eight characteristics: (1) larger space than the average food store; (2) self-service or limited service operation; (3) extensive price concessions advertised; (4) mass merchandise display; (5) free parking facilities; (6) spectacular sales promotion; (7) departmentalization; (8) all goods easily accessible.

There were 1,200 supermarkets in 1936; 3,000 in 1937; 3,637 in 1938, excluding additional 1,500 chain store supermarket units. Supermarket sales total a billion dollars annually.

More than a hundred businesspapers cover the food field and many of them reach the supermarkets. For his own publication, *Supermarket Merchandising*, M. M. Zimmerman (an authority on chain store distribution, who acts as publisher, editor and business manager) reported a net paid circulation of 8,000 (November, 1942) and a controlled (free) circulation of 77,514 (November, 1942) of which food markets, including supermarkets, accounted for 69,331 copies.

DISTRIBUTION COSTS—A TASK FOR BUSINESS JOURNALISTS

The greatest problem facing business today is the cost of distribution, created by the fact that merchandise is manufactured on a horsepower basis, while we still distribute goods on a manpower basis. Mass production methods have made it possible to manufacture greater quantities of goods at lower and lower costs.

Production has become a science. It is taught in schools and colleges as a science. Distribution, on the other hand, is still a hit-

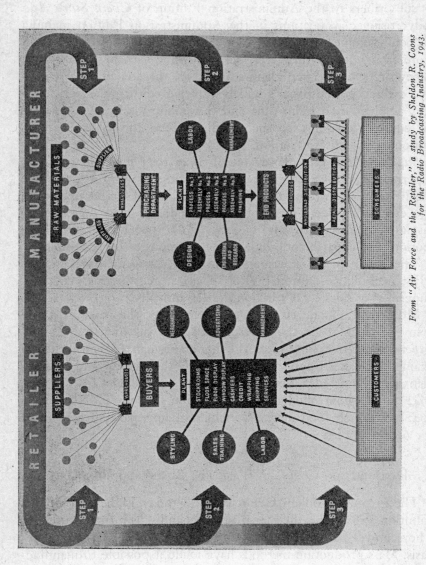

From "Air Force and the Retailer," a study by Sheldon R. Coons
for the Radio Broadcasting Industry, 1943.

CHART 5. THE MARKETING PROCESS

and-miss proposition, an "economic wilderness," to use a phrase of Q. Forrest Walker, Macy's economist. If we are to have more employment and higher standards of living, it is going to be necessary to reduce distribution costs. This is a great opportunity for business journalism. Most of the economies achieved by mass production today are absorbed by the costs of marketing the finished goods, and so denied to the ultimate consumer. This has resulted in restricting both investment and industrial expansion. Study Chart 5 (The Marketing Process). You will observe that in production the costs are cut by decentralizing the plant, putting plants near sources of supply, integrating extractive operations and transformative operations (step 1). Manufacturers' costs are cut also by economies in design, laborsaving improvements, and more efficient plant layout and plant operation (step 2).

Further savings are effected in the channels of wholesale distribution by the proper location and maintenance of factory branches, and so on (step 3).

In the case of the retailer, however, there is little or no control over manufacturing costs and in the majority of cases the average retailer has no opportunity for large-scale or co-operative buying (step 1). Efficiency in his own plant depends on how much merchandise is displayed effectively and moved at a profit by correct use of his available space (step 2). His services to the customers, such as deliveries, charge accounts, returned goods, layaways, telephone and direct mail, advertising, promotion, styling, and other factors besides space, often spiral his costs to new highs (step 3). While production is more or less a *mechanical* job, distribution depends on *consumer acceptance* of goods and services and involves the use of many contributive functions as well as distributive functions, which increase the cost.

It is the task of businesspapers covering the fields of distribution to find and describe ways for increasing *efficiency* in distribution. If you can cut the cost of the finished goods, more people will be able to buy goods and so ensure greater production, higher employment, and more purchasing power (higher standards of living). But purchasing power is not necessarily *wanting* power. All the forces of advertising and selling must be brought into play.

Distribution research used advantageously provides management with the answers to these questions: Who are my customers? Where are my customers? What will they buy? When will they buy? At what price level will they buy freely? At what price level will they buy in limited quantities or not at all? Can I expand my market? How? What improvements in my product will increase its utility or enjoyment?

The businesspaper does not deal in generalities in attacking the problems of distribution costs. The businesspaper deals with precise details of these specific problems: 1) physical costs, such as wrapping, packaging, crating, freight charges, warehousing, storage, trucking; 2) functional costs, such as salesmen's salaries and commissions, travelling expenses, sales executives' salaries, office expenses, advertising expenses, the commissions and expenses of jobbers, brokers and other middlemen.

Know-how to eliminate waste in the costs of distribution is described in carefully documented articles on such subjects as these: more efficient personnel selection and sales training, better division of labor, store front modernization, counter arrangements to improve traffic flow, installation of escalators, new types of display, self-service devices, automatic vending machines, dramatic presentations of goods, and intra-store television.

The businesspaper publishes the findings of continuing studies of cost-accounting methods, credits and collections, use of heat and light, administrative procedure, deliveries, parking facilities, testing laboratories, sales promotion, advertising and public relations programs, the returned goods evil and informative labeling.

Unfair competitive practices are always an editorial target. Competition is the force that compels efficiency in business, but it must be fair competition. We will see, in Chapter III, that to prevent the uneconomic decline of competitive business enterprise, an orderly market is essential.

THE MARKETPLACE AND THE BUSINESS PRESS

THE MARKETING PROCESS

THE modern businesspaper's chief editor, if he is wise, abandons his editorial swivel chair as soon as his publication has been put to bed and *greshams*[1] around his markets, with the rest of his editors. In the chapters that will follow, covering the functions of the managers on a businesspaper, you will find markets described in more detailed and concrete terms, as seen through their eyes. The word "market," by itself and without a referent, is, of course, just an abstract term. We are all buyers; we are all sellers; we are all producers; we are all ultimate consumers.

Trade is the lifeblood of a country: poet, preacher, doctor, soldier, statesman, farmer, philosopher, editor and auditor, teacher and truck driver—all of us (except the criminal and parasite) live by trade. In some market, somewhere, we trade what we have for what we need. The exchange, whether it is money for goods, money for money, or services for money, takes place in a market. There are stock markets, bond markets, money markets, commodity markets. As we all live by trade, so trade lives by *news* of all of us. That necessity, as we shall see in Chapter IV, gave birth to the trade press. The market is any place where each of us brings an excess of his own kind of wealth to swap for someone else's wealth which he wants. Today's markets are trading posts—only more highly *specialized*. The marketplace conditions our lives today just as it did in the days of the Caesars.

The ancient businessman's problem of reaching his widely scattered markets in the shortest space of time, with comparative

[1] Sir Thomas Gresham, see Chap. IV.

safety and the least expenditure of effort, was solved by the device known as the fair (Italian: *feria*; French: *foire*; Latin, *feriæ*: meaning festival, holiday, or day of rest). Many fairs were held under the auspices of the church and the fairgrounds, being sacred, made it possible for merchants to trade in safety. The church got a commission on the business done. In some cases churches were banks, or repositories of gold. Priests were custodians of trade treaties and other documents for traders and provided a place for the "money-changers" to operate right in the temples.

The fair is still an important device. Manufacturers and wholesale merchants of our modern world are accustomed to meet buyers or purchasing agents at annual and semiannual markets or fairs. In the United States the big market cities are New York, Chicago, St. Louis, Boston, Pittsburgh, Grand Rapids, San Francisco, Los Angeles, Dallas. Businessmen meet at these cities for one- or two-week periods, chiefly in January (spring market) and July (winter market). Often wholesale and industrial exhibits, trade shows and conventions are staged in large hotels, taking over as many as six to a dozen entire floors for the exhibits alone. Sometimes they are staged in municipal auditoriums or in great mercantile buildings which house permanent display rooms of manufacturers or factory representatives, and wholesalers, such as the Furniture Marts in New York, Grand Rapids, and Chicago, or the Merchandise Marts in Chicago and San Francisco. New merchandise and new merchandising ideas are displayed. Most new goods shown at markets is already in production. Sometimes, however, "original" handmade or mock-up models are exhibited, in order to get the retailer's or wholesaler's reaction on style, utility, design, price, packaging, terms of sale and potential volume, before tools and dies or molds are made, or actual production is begun. As high as 60,000 wholesale and retail buyers from every state in the Union, as well as from other countries, attend these markets in January and July.

Periodically, state, national, and world fairs or expositions are held, usually to signalize some anniversary or some turning point in the progress of industry or civilization. These are open to the consuming public, and glamorize the future of industry and mankind.[2] There are also three famous annual "business" fairs, the Brussels "Sample Fair," the Leipzig Fair, and the great fair at Nijni Novgorod in Russia which attract buyers from all parts of the world. At all these market events, as in early times, producers and distributors exchange views and news while exchanging goods and services; lay plans and schemes for enterprise on a larger scale, and foster a spirit of amity. The market, in any form, performs an important function in an economy.

High-level production, by creating more jobs, simultaneously creates increased purchasing power; but it does not necessarily create a disposition on the part of the public to buy the specific things a manufacturer has produced. Purchasing power has to be translated into *specific demand*, and then into a specific *brand preference*. The consumer has to be *persuaded* to buy more things than he ever had or wanted before. To do that, an entire set of skills and specialized agencies are set into motion, in the contributive field, as we have seen: styling, designing, research, engineering, merchandising, sales training, selling, promotion, publicity, and advertising. Production remains at a high level only when the circular flow is completed by the intelligent functions of those in the contributive and distributive industries. This is the marketing process.[3]

Throughout the history of human activity, and more especially since the birth of the specialized press, there has been a growing desire among businessmen to keep this marketing process orderly, to give it synthesis and objectivity. The marketing process is essentially traffic. Traffic requires orderly controls. Such orderly controls at any given period in human history are known as an *economy*.

An editorial in the New York *Herald Tribune* recently[4] declared the reading of almost any treatise on the social sciences, "a

[2] St. Louis, 1904: open 187 days, covered 1,240 acres, 19,695,855 visitors.
Wembley, 1924: 165 days, covered 220 acres, 27,900,000 visitors.
Chicago, 1933: 329 days, 38,626,546 visitors.
New York, 1939-1940: 340 days, covered 1,216 acres, 44,932,534 visitors.
Paris, 1900: 270 acres, 39,000,000 visitors. (*World Almanac*, 1943.)
[3] Charts 1 and 5.
[4] September 2, 1943.

brain-befuddling exercise" . . . "appalling prose in which professors entangled their thoughts." The editorial pointed out that Carlyle, a century and a half ago, had referred to economics as the "dismal science," and that so it is.

When more people read businesspapers, economics will become less befuddling and dismal. The businesspaper is the accurate, colorful story of economics-in-action. It is a continuous program to improve economic literacy. It employs no "appalling prose." Its pages may seem dismal to the outsider, but to those who understand its language it can be as thrilling as an adventure story. The businesspaper tries to overcome the natural tendency of people to leave economics to economists. Any one may go to a standard dictionary and there discover for himself that the term "economy" is made up of two ordinary Greek words: *oikos*, meaning house, and *nomos*, meaning management. *Oikonomia*, management of the house; *economy*, management of all the houses.

The businesspaper seeks to improve the management of each house as well as of all the houses together. When examination of a businesspaper reveals articles on the elimination of wasteful practices, replacing guesswork with scientific controls, or the incorporation of technological improvement in product, plant, and operation, that is simply *economics-in-action*. The businesspaper editor is constantly challenging business enterprise to be more enterprising.

Between trade shows and fairs, there are permanent "markets" which businesspaper editors cover regularly. These may be the showrooms of manufacturers or their agents, wholesale distributors, jobbers, exporters and importers, and other types of middlemen. Many such markets, particularly in consumers' goods, are concentrated in key cities along the Atlantic and Pacific seaboards. Manhattan, for example, is a great market for textiles and, naturally, for apparel, draperies, floor coverings, and upholstery made of textiles. In California the ingenuity and originality of certain designers and producers has created a great West Coast market for pottery and giftware, outdoor furniture, hand-woven textiles. Hollywood's influence has helped to create this western market.

Businesspaper editors also visit primary and secondary producing centers in the course of their coverage of their markets: farms, stockyards, forests, quarries, fisheries, factories, mills, mines.

Most Sensitive Market in the World

Stock exchanges are the most sensitive primary markets in the modern world. On its famous "big board" in the New York Stock Exchange are listed most of our country's leading private, public, and quasi-public enterprises and the price of a share in any of those enterprises at that moment.[5] Magnified ticker tape records the second-by-second aggregate transactions in securities as they change ownership all over the country. Simultaneously the giant news strip from an automatic typewriter spells out the current events and news developments. Today, as ten thousand years ago, news controls markets, the difference being that the present moment is now world-wide.

Fundamentally, the New York Stock Exchange, which is the feeder to about 600 brokerage houses located in every important city, is a mechanism no different from the marketplace a housewife visits for meat or groceries. It is simply a trading post. As a matter of fact, it started as a trading post in 1792, under a buttonwood tree in front of what is now 68 Wall Street in Manhattan. Its first task in 1792 was to finance those private enterprises of our country which had buckled down to the postwar job of *paying* off the debt of the Revolution. The government had won the war and dropped the victory, as usual, into the laps of the businessmen to keep won! One winter under the sky was enough for the stock traders. In 1793 the exchange moved indoors, into the Tontine Coffee House, corner of Wall and William.[6] Like Lloyd's Coffee House in London, Tontine's in Manhattan was also a favorite news rendezvous of shippers and merchants, and therefore an important business information source. And like Lloyd's, which gave birth to one of England's oldest businesspapers, *Lloyd's List*,

[5] There is also a "curb" exchange and an "over-the-counter" exchange listing securities not registered on the New York Stock Exchange.

[6] The *Exchange*, house organ of the New York Stock Exchange, 150th Anniversary Number, May, 1942.

the Tontine gave birth to the first American businesspaper, *New York Prices-Current* (1795.)

By means of this great primary market, private enterprise has been able to get money needed to build plants, equip those plants with machinery, hire labor, purchase other companies, buy raw materials, design new and revised products, hire men to study markets, plan businesspaper and consumer advertising campaigns, train salesmen, set up better distributive systems, and move more goods.

The stock exchange has played a lead role in financing 150 years of American industrial expansion from the Colonial Revolution to the World Revolution: the steamboats, turnpikes and canals of the 1800's—clipper ships and railroads of the 1830's—steel mills of the 1840's—cable and telegraph of the 1850's—modern banking system of the 1860's—petroleum in the 1870's—telephone in the 1880's—gold as money in the 1890's—mass production—automotive and electrical appliance industries in the 1900's—movies, aviation, radio in the 1930's. Tomorrow: air conditioning—plastics—television—radar—organics—electronics—light metals—cheap housing—chemical substitutes—sulfa drugs—the helicopter—the prefabricated portable house—frozen and dehydrated foods.

*   *   *

In the future, because of the increasing recognition of the economic interdependence of nations, businesspaper publishers will send their editors to visit the markets and trading centers of other countries and continents, and we may expect foreign businesspaper editors to comb our markets for their readers. An "exchange" of business journalists like the exchange of college professors, with other countries, may be desirable.

IMPORTANCE OF THE MIDDLEMAN

Forty centuries before the advent of the Yankee peddler, traveling salesmen for the middlemen of Mesopotamia (2500 B.C.) were already carrying homewares, metal goods, sickles, needles, weapons, wool, spices, ointments, and slaves through the Brenner pass along the Danube and the Elbe, up into Scandinavian markets. The Mesopotamian's caravans and galleys transported cargo to the ancient cities of Uruk and Ur—ancient before Rome was

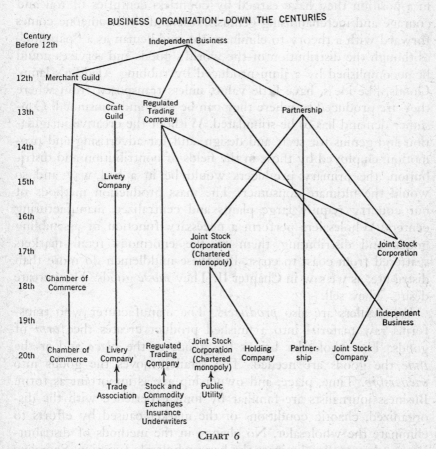

BUSINESS ORGANIZATION – DOWN THE CENTURIES

CHART 6

From *An Introduction to Business* by Prof. Melvin Anshen, Macmillan, New York, 1942; adapted from *Casebook of American Business History*, by Prof. N. S. B. Gras, F. S. Crofts & Co., New York, 1939.

even built. Regulation of market prices, new laws for the conduct of business, and general news, as reported by the news gatherers of forty-four centuries ago, were recorded on clay tablets. These tablets, "filed" in clay jars in the office vaults of buried towns, have been spaded up by modern archaeologists to testify to the antiquity of business journalism.

The middlemen of today (see Chap. II, The Background of Industry Served) serve primary producers and ultimate consumers in a position they have earned by countless centuries of toil and courage and merchandising genius. Now and then someone comes forward with a theory to eliminate the middleman as a "parasite," as though the distribution of the world's goods and services could be accomplished by a jinni produced by rubbing Aladdin's lamp. Goods, like ideas, have little value, unless transposed from where they are produced to where they can be used and consumed. Consumer demand has to be stimulated. Without the creative imagination and genius for style and design, and for advertising and promotion, employed by those in the fields of contribution and distribution, the primary producers would be in a bad way and so would the ultimate consumer. The mass production methods of our country require large plants and centralized manufacturing centers. Wholesalers perform a necessary function of assembling goods and distributing them to the enormous retail markets scattered from coast to coast. But these middlemen do more than distribute, as we saw in Chapter II. They *move* goods. They create desire. They sell.

Wholesalers are also *producers*. The manufacturer who transforms raw material into a finished product creates the *form* of goods. The wholesaler brings the goods to the *place* and at the *time* the goods are needed. The retailer moves the goods into *ownership*. Time, place, and ownership are as important as form. Business journalists are familiar by long experience with the disorganized, chaotic conditions of the market caused by efforts to eliminate the wholesaler. No change in the methods of distributing goods actually eliminate the basic wholesale function. Someone must perform the function.

The wholesaler keeps small manufacturers alive by giving them large enough bulk orders so that they can schedule production programs. He keeps small retailers alive by providing a single source—a stockpile or reservoir—from which they can quickly fill their merchandise needs. The everyday customer of a whole-

saler would find it difficult and uneconomical to send to widely
scattered factories for goods or to interview their thousands of
salesmen. The manufacturer would find it uneconomical to ship
small orders to widely scattered retail establishments or send salesmen to call on thousands of small retail stores. The same holds
true for the industrial distributors for mines, oil wells, farms, the
wholesalers of industrial machinery, equipment, and supplies. The
strength of the wholesaler is his service to both manufacturer and
retailer.[7] That is what we mean when we say that organized mass
distribution is as important to the whole economy as organized mass
production.

From the Phoenicians, Mesopotamians and Mercatores, down
the ages to the Yankee peddler of early New England days, and
on to the contemporary distributor and wholesale jobber, exporter,
and importer, the middleman always has been the *key man*—the
man to be reckoned with in all economic history. He is the ful-
crum on which civilization can swing over from narrow national-
isms, leading to depressions and trade wars, to economic world
order. That is why the middleman is the eternal opponent of the
doctrine of scarcity. He is the promoter of *abundance* in production because he wants to distribute ever-greater volume of goods
in ever-wider markets of the world in order to keep more people
employed all over the world.

[7] Butler Brothers, Chicago wholesalers, furnish more than 2,000 retail stores with
complete lines of merchandise and an over-all management service, including
accounting, advertising, window display, and miscellaneous promotional material.

CHAPTER IV

THE DEVELOPMENT OF THE TRADE PRESS

. . . there are not more useful members in a commonwealth than merchants. They knit mankind together in a mutual intercourse of good offices, distribute the gifts of nature, find work for the poor, add wealth to the rich, and magnificence to the great.
—THE RT. HON. JOSEPH ADDISON (1711)

JACOB FUGGER THE RICH: FIRST GREAT BUSINESSPAPER PUBLISHER

Neues Zeitungen, "News Tidings" of the House of Fugger, was a business journal well known to merchants during the fifteenth, sixteenth, and seventeenth centuries. The mercantile House of Fugger, at its peak, lavishly supplied the exchequer of the Holy Roman Empire, shaped the policies of the Hapsburgs, financed foreign kings, worked intimately with princes and popes, owned and operated mines, banks, chain stores, and its own business news service. In a world without multiple printing or electrical communication, the Fuggers devised an elaborate chain newsletter system, organized their own news-gathering services, and kept their world-wide clientele remarkably well informed on trade and politics, both local and international.

Jacob Fugger the Rich[1] operated his vast industrial empire from his countinghouse in Germany.

Scribes sent daily newsletters about German business conditions to all Fugger branches even in China and South America. Others translated daily newsletters as they arrived from Fugger foreign offices, and in turn sent copies to other branches, written in the language of each country. Thus the *Zeitungen* chain brought

---

[1] *Fugger* (2 vols.), edited by Victor von Klarwill. John Lane, The Bodley Head, Ltd., London, 1924.

Jacob Fugger news information gleaned from all the world's marketplaces. They also kept him informed of the activities of his chief competitors, the Welsers. As this news information was organized and analyzed, Jacob Fugger made his *decisions*. Those

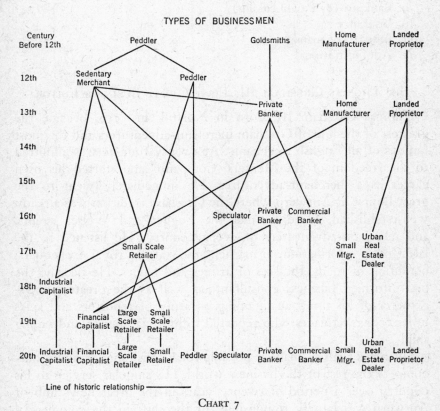

TYPES OF BUSINESSMEN

CHART 7

From *An Introduction to Business* by Prof. Melvin Anshen, Macmillan, New York, 1942; adapted from *Casebook of American Business History*, by Prof. N. S. B. Gras, F. S. Crofts & Co., New York, 1939.

decisions set into motion a dozen important functions practiced by this sedentary merchant-capitalist.

1. Importing
2. Exporting
3. Manufacturing

4. Wholesaling
5. Retailing
6. Warehousing
7. Communication
8. Transportation
9. Banking (or Pawnbroking)
10. Insurance
11. Investment management
12. Administration

Sir Thomas Gresham III: First Great Business Editor

Thomas Gresham III, born in Norfolk in 1519, became the greatest of the line of Gresham merchant-adventurers and the most famous of all English merchants. At twenty-four he was admitted to the freedom of the Mercers' Company[2] and started his own career as a merchant-adventurer. He immediately went to the great Bourse at Antwerp where the Gresham tradition was already well-established. Here he met the Fugger and Welser agents, and merchant-adventurers of every country. He listened to the latest news information on markets, the state of royal exchequers, condition of roads, the size of armies and navies. He became the best-informed business consultant, as well as the greatest news-gatherer of his times, maintaining an army of reporters and spies in lesser marketplaces who reported to him via courier and sailing ship.

His news analysis made it possible for English merchants to out-compete the rest of the business world. His singular service to his country over a period of twenty years in the great news hub of Antwerp was largely responsible for the shift in the commercial center of the world from that Flemish city to the city of London. One might say the British Empire reached a top position in sixteenth century world affairs because one man, in that critical period of history, appreciated the importance of organized busi-

[2] First of the twelve great Livery Companies of London. Latin root *merx* gives the origin of several basic business terms: *mercis*, merchandise; *merces*, reward or wages; *mercer*, merchant, mercenary; *mercari*, to traffic; *mercatus*, to barter; *Mercury*, Roman god, messenger of intelligence; *merceries*, originally included small wares and drugs as well as cloth and apparel.

ness intelligence, gathered at its source and consistently transmitted to the point where it would do the most good.

Sir Thomas Gresham III built a great personal fortune out of his ability to recognize and analyze news events and forecast trends. One of his monuments[3] is the Royal Exchange (1569), where, as Gresham explained, "merchants could meet and trade instead of walking in the rain when it raineth, more like pedlars than merchants." He induced a group of 750 leading London businessmen to subscribe £4,000 sterling which paid for the ground. Out of his own personal funds Sir Thomas built the Royal Exchange on this land.

Miriam Beard says of Gresham: ". . . he united in his single person functions which we today distribute over a variety of agencies: the Associated Press; the Diplomatic and Consular service; the Secret Service; the Board of Estimates. He was spy, ambassador, consul and councillor . . ."[4]

ADAM SMITH: FIRST GREAT MARKET ANALYST

"First notable recognition," said Jesse Neal, "that there was anything in business worthy of public discussion was the publication by Adam Smith of *The Wealth of Nations*."[5] Like Gresham, this Scottish professor of economics was one of the great business investigators of his day, and the modern world's first great market analyst.

Adam Smith attacked the mercantilism of his times: the theory that the producer is more important than the consumer. He advanced the counter theory that competition works only where there is an approximate equality of *bargaining power*. He challenged the isolationist idea that a nation gained by a favorable balance of trade (excess of exports over imports) either (1) by exploiting its own colonies as suppliers of raw materials and pur-

[3] Another is "Gresham's law," that bad money will drive good money out of circulation.

[4] *History of the Business Man*, by Miriam Beard. Macmillan Co., New York, 1938.

[5] "A Review of Business Press History," by Jesse H. Neal, executive secretary, the Associated Business Papers, Inc., in *N. W. Ayer's Newspaper Annual & Directory* for 1922.

chasers of finished goods or (2) by exploiting other foreign markets. "Consumption," Smith wrote, "is the sole end and purpose of all production . . . but in the mercantile system the interest of the consumer is almost constantly sacrificed to that of the producer."[6]

The American Revolution was, in a way, a revolt against British mercantilism as expressed by such tyrannical directives as the Stamp, Sugar, Molasses and Navigation acts. In England, the elder Pitt and other Whigs led the revolt against mercantilism, which Adam Smith had precipitated. These movements were part of a greater development: the Industrial Revolution, the beginning of the struggle for wider and freer markets in which to sell the increased production of factory labor. Adam Smith's *Wealth of Nations* is a good handbook for every student of business journalism. It will prepare him for a better understanding of the industrial and mechanical revolutions, which gave birth to the modern business press (see Chart 8).

Dynamic freedom of the market defeated the static ideas of the isolationists and England entered a period of great technological and economic progress.

The genesis of the businesspaper may be traced through four modern revolutionary stages as shown on Chart 8. In the Copernican Revolution, sedentary merchants used such devices as newsletters, trade fairs, merchant guilds and livery companies, cities and city leagues, as collectors and purveyors of business news. In the Industrial Revolution the business press was formalized. The familiar contemporary format of the trade journal made its appearance with the advent of commercial printing. With the Mechanical Revolution came specialization: better organized news multiplication and technological know-how. Electrical communication. Industry began to be served by the modern businesspaper.

Nourished in the soil of the free market and supported by competitive private enterprise, the specialized press owes something to Messrs. Fugger, Gresham, and Smith. They taught three basic concepts of business journalism: (1) gather news information at its sources methodically and meticulously; (2) sift, or-

---

[6] *An Inquiry Into the Nature and Causes of the Wealth of Nations*, by Adam Smith, LLD., FRS. Strahan and Cabell, London, 1776.

FOUR MODERN REVOLUTIONS
Affecting Business Communication

1. *Copernican Revolution* (15th century). Beginning of modern thought. First successful attack on bigotry and isolationism. Proof that the earth was NOT the center of the universe. Exploration and discovery. New trade routes. New communication lines. Advancement in man's control over his physical environment. Struggle for free markets. Business newsletters.

2. *Industrial Revolution* (18th and 19th centuries). A social and financial development, stemming from the division of labor (factory system) in the Scriptorium; the guilds and city leagues. Foundation of the merchant-capitalist administrator or sedentary merchant. Changeover of production from home workshops to large factories. Changing mode of thinking. Changing methods of production. Changing pattern of living. Struggle for free market. Multiple business communication. Coffeehouse bulletins.

3. *Mechanical Revolution* (19th century). Organized science. Organized news intelligence. Mechanization of extractive, transformative, contributive and distributive industries. A new complex society, with new social, political, economic, and moral problems. Struggle for free markets. (Mechanical and industrial revolutions were going on simultaneously.) Birth of the specialized business press.

4. *Philosophical Revolution* (20th century). Time span shortens. Globe shrinks. Technics destroy space and time at greater speed. Ideologies clash. Huge concentrations of wealth threatened. Dignity of the individual at stake. Communication failure. Struggle for free markets employing submarine and dive bomber. Civilization building on cheap mechanical power instead of cheap human slavery. Two problems: labor and management. Private enterprise challenged. Cradle-to-grave social security. Trade barriers down. Emergence of the world community. World highway-skyway. Three-dimensional images, in natural color, televised. Integrated business journalism.

CHART 8

ganize, and interpret it carefully; (3) purvey it directly to the points where it is needed and show readers how to use news for profit to the greatest number.

BRITISH BUSINESS PRESS

In 1845 there were 24 British businesspapers. In 1937 the number had increased to more than 600.[7]

A Collection for the Improvement of Husbandry and Trade is believed to be one of the earliest business magazines published in England. Many copies are preserved in the Sell collection (Sells Limited, London). No. 182, dated Jan. 24, 1694, specialized in the corn market and contained miscellaneous shipping reports.

Another early businesspaper in England (one of its most important today) is *Lloyd's List*, which was started as *Lloyd's News* (1696-Current), published by Edward Lloyd. Instead of going out to its readers at first, the readers came to it: *Lloyd's News* was posted up in Lloyd's Coffee House on Lombard Street in London. The bulletin reported shipping intelligence, war news, and other items having a bearing on the business of merchants who frequented this coffeehouse. Many coffeehouses became similar news centers just as barbershops once were and still are news centers. Lloyd's had become, at the turn of the century, the central clearinghouse for news information of all kinds in London.

In 1728, Mr. Thomas Jemson organized a syndicate of coffee men to pool the news they collected at their respective coffeehouses and issue a morning and evening paper. Nothing came of this project but it is supposed to have given Mr. Jemson or his associates the idea of a specialized news sheet or businesspaper. Mr. Jemson died in February of 1734, and *Lloyd's List* appeared the following April as a weekly. In 1737 it was published bi-weekly.

Subscribers paid 3 shillings a quarter at the bar of Lloyd's Coffee House. Many of the subscribers were underwriters. *Lloyd's List* maintained correspondents at all the ports and paid an annual

[7] *Trade Journal Operation and Management*, by Cyril E. Matthews. The Technical Press, Ltd., London, 1937.

gratuity to the post officials for prompt delivery of shipping lists to their messengers and for exemption from postal charges, which were a much heavier item in those days than they are now.

Today *Loyd's List* covers the fields of transportation, commodity markets, money and stocks, coal and fuel oil trades, aircraft, wireless, maritime, and commercial law.

Other well-known eighteenth century British businesspapers were the *Public Ledger* (1759), a daily, covering agricultural products; *Morning Advertiser* (1794), which was the daily businesspaper of the "Friendly Society of Licensed Victuallers"; *Bells Weekly Messenger* (1796), an agricultural paper, and at the turn of the nineteenth century, a paper for the book trade, *Bent's Literary Advertiser* (1802).

The *Cabinet Maker*, first published in 1880, started the firm of Benn Brothers, Ltd., famous contemporary publishers of British businesspapers. Nine others of Benn's many businesspapers also were started in the nineteenth century: *Hardware Trade Journal* 1874 (*Ironmongery* was merged in 1900); the *Electrician*, 1861; the *Gas World*, 1886 (in the seventies it was called *Lights* and in 1884, *Gas and Water*); *Fruit Grower*, 1895 (originally *Green Grocer, Fruiterer and Market Gardener*); *Timber Trades Journal*, 1873; the *Miller*, 1875; *Leather Trades Review*, 1867; *British Trade Journal and Export World*, 1863 (editions in Portuguese, Dutch, Italian, Chinese, and Russian)—*British Trade Journal* incorporates *Aeronautics*, founded in 1907, *Export World*, founded in 1907, and *Commercial Intelligence*.

The international character of many of the Benn business publications was due to the British policy of extending its markets. Sir Ernest Benn, widely traveled himself, followed a wise policy of requiring all his editors, advertising sales managers, and heads of departments to refresh their minds and methods by periodic visits to countries overseas. His oldest son, John Benn, studied at Princeton in New Jersey, and his second son, Glenville Benn, worked on the New York *Times* in Manhattan.

King George V, sent his congratulations in 1930 to Sir Ernest Benn, chairman of Benn Brothers, Limited, on the occasion of the publisher's Golden Jubilee. The king's message expressed "the hope that every success may attend the efforts of your publishing house for the development of British trade." The British business press hailed this statement as a royal sanction of the businesspaper's claim to national status. It was a landmark in the history of British trade journalism.

The Benns, incidentally, have played important roles in the social, artistic, political, and military life of England. John William Benn was chairman of the London County Council, knighted in 1905. Sir Ernest Benn was created a baronet in 1914. Captain Oliver Benn died in action at Gallipoli in 1915. In 1929, the Right Honorable Wedgwood Benn, D.S.O., member of Parliament, became Secretary of State for India. Benn businesspapers, in World War II, began writing glorious chapters in businesspaper history in behalf of their country's war effort.

National Trade Press, Limited, was privately organized in 1917 to acquire the *Organizer*, a general trade publication. It was discovered later, however, that there was little or no effective support from business for the general business publications, that specialization was essential to success. The *Organizer* was discontinued. Specialized papers were promoted, such as the *Drapers' Organizer, Footwear Organizer, Furnishing Trades Organizer, Style For Men, British Shoeman* and *Laundry Journal*. These were successful.

This firm (N.T.P.) also acquired five papers which had been founded in the nineteenth century: *Confectionery News*, 1887; *Dyer and Textile Printer*, 1879; *Cigar and Tobacco World*, 1888; *Laundry Record*, 1890; *Watchmaker Jeweler and Silversmith*, 1875. A number of yearbooks and trade directories also are published as services to their trades.

N.T.P. has achieved notable leadership in all the various fields covered by its papers. The *Drapers' Organizer* inaugurated the first artificial silk exhibition ever held in any country, at Holland Park Hall, London, in 1926. The exhibit ran five years, until it merged with the British Industries Fair. This was also the first British businesspaper to issue fashion shade cards to its readers, which resulted in the formation of the British Colour Council.

Fashion parades were staged under its sponsorship at the May Fair Hotel.

Several N.T.P. publications inaugurated well-known design competitions. The *Furnishings Trades Organizer* in 1927 organized a competition for "modernist" furniture which was then little known in England: £500 was distributed in prizes.

Another British businesspaper known the world over is *International Textiles* published by I.T. Publishers, Ltd.

Industrial Newspapers, Limited, another British publishing firm, counts among its publications such well-known British businesspapers as *Iron and Coal Trades Review, Foundry Trade Journal, Coal Merchant and Shipper, Fish Trades Gazette, Tobacco, The Decorator, Sheet Metal Industries, Confectioner Baker, Metal Treatment, Ryland's Directory, Tobacco Trade Year Book and Diary, Smoker's Handbook (Retail Prices), Decorator's Trade Reference Book & Diary.*

A famous nineteenth century British businesspaper which enjoys an international circulation is the *Linen Trade Circular* of Belfast, Ireland, founded in 1851, now published by H. R. Carter & Son. It is a direct descendant of the personal newsletters of the seventeenth and eighteenth centuries. Sir Robert Baird, Ulster's Northcliffe, set the paper's type by hand in his youth as a printer's apprentice. Great-grandfathers of the present Irish linen generation used to call for the *Circular* in person every Monday, after dining at their favorite tavern nearby. In the same year *Dundee Prices Current*, a jute paper, was founded. Other important British businesspaper publishers[8] include *Iliffe*, Temple Press, W. Reed, Ltd., Morgan Bros., Ltd., the Nema and St. Margarets Press. Hundreds of independent technical papers cover the fields of British industrial enterprise. The textile field has some 35 businesspapers, among its leaders being the *Draper's Record* which boasts the largest businesspaper circulation in the world; transport has 31; shipping, 16; liquor, 8; machinery, 9; printing, 17; engineering, 47; building, 25; commerce, 23; publishing and financial, 13 papers.

---

[8] The author is indebted to two of his own correspondents, Robin Walker, Scotland, and Alfred S. Moore, North Ireland, for information on the British business press.

Greater specialization in businesspaper publishing, stimulated by the success in the United States, was just beginning to blossom in Britain when World War II broke out in 1939. The *Periodical Trade Press and Weekly Newspaper Proprietors Association Ltd.*, London (P.T.P. & W.N.P.A.) is the leading British businesspaper association, corresponding to the Associated Business Papers, Inc., in the United States and Canada.

GERMAN BUSINESS PRESS

Impetus given to multiple communication by Johannes Gutenberg at his press in Mainz, in 1450, resulted in the outcropping of scores of printing presses throughout fifteenth century Germany. Hundreds more of improved presses sprang up everywhere in the sixteenth and seventeenth centuries. The products of these presses —books, magazines, newspapers and businesspapers—provided a great stimulus to industry, to scientific research, and to the growth of the professions. In 1837, Germany had about 200 businesspapers; in 1888, about 2,725; in 1907, about 5,715; and by 1931, the German business press had reached its peak with 7,475 specialized businesspapers being published.[9]

By 1937, the Nazi program of confiscation and concentration of ownership, as well as state control of the press, had cut down the businesspaper total in Germany to 5,800. Of this total, the largest field in number of papers, strangely enough, was theology, with a total of 640 publications. Medicine came next, with 330; "technic" papers, 500. In 1907, there were 71 military trade journals; in 1937, there were 58. By comparison, there were published, in 1937, only a dozen businesspapers in the United States for the military profession.

One of Germany's oldest businesspapers of modern times was founded in 1749, *Physikalisch-Oekonomische Wochenschrift*

[9] The author is indebted to Dr. Leo Lion, now living in New York, former head of the businesspaper division of the House of Ullstein, for a wealth of information on the German business press, which space limitations prevent him from using. For the story of this great publishing house destroyed by the Nazis see *The Rise and Fall of the House of Ullstein*, by Herman Ullstein. Simon & Schuster, New York, 1942.

(Physical-Economic Weekly), published at Stuttgart. The oldest businesspaper still in existence in 1937, according to Dr. Leo Lion, was *Dingler's Polytechnisches Journal*, established in 1820 in Berlin.

By 1940, the German business press had become a small, unknown quantity to the outside world, tightly controlled by Propaganda Minister Goebbels and permitted to print nothing except what the military censors or the propaganda bureau ordered or approved.[10]

EARLY AMERICAN BUSINESSPAPERS

Tremendous gains in power conversion, mass production of iron and steel, the textile era, and the railway age marked the three decades preceding the opening of the twentieth century. These last thirty years of the nineteenth century were the formative period of the American business press. From the founding of the first independent businesspaper in the United States, *New York Prices Current* (1795-1920), to report market news, until the Civil War (1861-1865) more than 30 businesspapers came into existence covering such industries as iron and steel, gas, coachmaking, leather, telegraphy, photography, printing, dry goods, mining, meat packing, shipping, pharmacy, science, railroads, banking, medicine, dentistry, insurance. Many of these pioneer businesspapers have survived to this day and in their time have absorbed other leading businesspapers.

Scientific Group: The period known as post bellum, following the Civil War, was a flourishing one for specialized businesspapers. By the twentieth century there were few industries or professions which did not have at least one leading businesspaper.

American interest in things scientific was stimulated by the startling discoveries and inventions here and abroad after the Civil War. Scientific journals sprang up everywhere. Business journalism was prolific on "mechanics." The Centennial Exposition in

---

[10] In contrast, United States businesspaper editors were placed on their honor not to divulge information useful to the enemy and only required to submit articles of a military nature for censorship during World War II.

Philadelphia, in 1876, and the World's Fair in Vienna, in 1873, further stimulated scientific interest.

Rufus Porter, shoemaker's apprentice and house painter, started the *Scientific American* in 1845. He had been a peddler of a "revolving almanac" of his own invention and had many other devices to his credit: fire alarm, signal telegraph, fog whistle, camera obscura, washing machine, rotary plow, portable house, corn sheller, flying ship. In 1840 he was editing the New York *Mechanic* and experimenting with electrotyping when he founded the *Scientific American, The Advocate of Industry and Journal of Mechanical and Other Improvements.* It was bought in 1846 by Orson Desaix Munn (whose grandson, Orson D. Munn, is the present publisher) and Alfred Ely Beach, son of Moses Y. Beach, editor and publisher of the New York *Sun.* These men were patent lawyers. To the *Scientific American* came A. B. Wilson with his model sewing machine and Thomas A. Edison with his talking machine for "write-ups." Also to its editorial office came Samuel F. B. Morse, Elias Howe, Captain John Ericsson, Dr. R. J. Gatling, Peter Cooper Hewitt, Samuel P. Langley, and Glenn Curtiss. Its editorials fought fakers and quacks persistently. From a purely technical businesspaper it expanded into a popular consumer magazine about 1875.

Agricultural Group: McCormack's reaper (1831-1851) crowned King Wheat. In 1844, the *Price Current-Grain Reporter* appeared. Mechanized processes and steam power were applied throughout industry. Farming methods were transformed. Population in the United States jumped from 5 million in 1800 to 25 million in 1850. In the same period businesspapers increased from a single paper to 10. Population jumped from 25 million in 1850 to 75 million in 1900. Businesspapers increased from 11 to 800.[11]

In 1850 the value of United States manufactured products was $1 billion. In 1900 it was $13 billion, several times the value of agricultural products. In 1929 the value of manufactured products was $70 billion; population neared 130 million, and businesspapers had multiplied to about 1,500.

[11] *American Newspaper Directory*, 1900 Edition. In 1922 this directory listed 1,400 businesspapers.

Iron Industry Group: In the middle nineteenth century most bloomeries, forges, and blast furnaces converting ore into iron were located in the country because the basic fuel was charcoal. The owner of the mill ran a country store. Workers were paid in truck. In the 1850's, with high tariffs reaching even 100 per cent ad valorem, our crude iron production was not large enough to fill domestic needs. Foreign ore and iron was imported. In 1826 there were 7 rolling mills in the Pittsburgh area. The *Pittsburgh American Manufacturer* was started in 1838. *Iron Age* was started in 1855 as a 3-sheet paper. *Hardware Age* was started. Ironmasters did not erect their own blast furnaces in Pittsburgh until 1859. The Civil War really inaugurated the Iron Age of American industry. Orders for rails, armor plate, cannon, shot and shell, and other items poured in from the Ordnance Departments.

Meat Industry Group: Quartermasters of the Union Army during the Civil War also sped up the integration of the meat and packing industry. Financed by government contracts, groups of men like Nelson Morris, Jacob Dold, and Phil Armour began to assemble all the functions of slaughtering and packing under one roof. They set up stockyards and plants to utilize waste products. The *National Provisioner*, a businesspaper for the meat-packing industry did not materialize, however, until 1889. A lapse of 81 years exists between the start of this paper and the other leading nineteenth century meat publication, *Butcher's and Packer's Gazette* (1808).

Railroad Industry Group: In January, 1832, when the *American Rail-Road Journal* (now *Railway Mechanical Engineer*)[12] started to publish, canal expansion was over. The railroad by 1850 was emerging as a long-distance contender instead of just a feeder for canal and waterway traffic. When the *Railway Gazette* (later *Railway Age*) started in 1856 there were little more than 9,000 miles of railroad. In 1860 there were 20,000 miles more. The Railway Era of America was destined to make the Iron Age a great one. It is not generally known that public capital, rather than

[12] "It is the object of this Journal to record the observations and suggestions of gentlemen of experience in the construction and use of railroads here; and to afford the whole at so cheap a rate, as to be within the reach of every person taking an interest in the subject"—from the January 2, 1832, issue.

private capital, played the pioneering role. According to Louis M. Hacker,[13] Baltimore & Ohio, first state-chartered railroad in America, in 1828, received $500,000 from Maryland, and in 1836 got $3,200,000 additional, which Maryland raised in the English money market. Massachusetts gave the Western Railway of Massachusetts $4,300,000 which had been raised in England. States gave public lands to private railroad companies. Cities built their terminals for them. In 1850, the federal government made generous grants from the public domain to the railroad promoters. For example, as a bonus for building the Illinois Central the promoters received generous public land grants. It took six years and cost $16,500,000 to build its 700 miles of railroad. The same promoters realized $25,000,000 from the sale of these public lands. One can begin to understand what is meant when it is said that a public utility is affected with a "public interest."

Railroads were the biggest customer of the extractive and transformative industries from 1868 to 1872, and founded the fortunes of several pioneer businesspaper publishers.

PIONEER BUSINESSPAPER PUBLISHERS

E. A. Simmons, of the Simmons-Boardman Publications, left public school in 1889 to help support his mother, and started in business for $1.50 a week at the bargain counter of A. D. Matthews' Sons Department Store in Brooklyn. In six months he was earning $5 a week reading exchanges for the *Railway Age-Gazette*, whose president was W. H. Boardman. In 1892 he took charge of their Chicago office and got married (on $12 a week). In 1894, when he was earning $20 a week as an advertising salesman, *American Engineer* offered him $40 "with regular increases and a quarter interest at the end of ten years." He submitted this proposition to Boardman, who countered by selling Simmons fifty shares at par in *Railway Gazette* for $5,000. Simmons's bank account had only $50 in it, but he borrowed the rest and bought into the business. In 1911, when Boardman was suddenly deprived

---

[13] *Triumph of Capitalism*, by Louis M. Hacker.

of part of his faculties, Simmons paid a quarter million dollars for Boardman's holdings in the company.

In the seventies, the *Railway Gazette*, singlehandedly pioneered the fight for a uniform width for railroad tracks. Some tracks were five feet apart and others only three and a half feet between rails. George Westinghouse came into this famous businesspaper's editorial offices with a model of the airbrake under his arm. One of its great editors, M. N. Forney, pioneered the adoption of standard threads for bolts and nuts. Consider what these three contributions alone meant to railroad progress.

Another editor, Colonel Prout, won a ten-year fight (1893-1903) for the Isthmian Canal to be cut across Panama instead of Nicaragua. The Nicaragua project, had it been successful, would not have been large enough for a modern cruiser, let alone a battleship, to pass through. *Railway Age* (1876-current) and *Railway Gazette* (1856-1908) were merged in 1908 and called *Railway Age-Gazette*.

Horace M. Swetland, like James H. McGraw, Sr., was a schoolteacher who gave up that vocation for something more resultful. He sold advertising space for the American Railway Publishing Co., later becoming manager of the firm, which published *Power*, *Street Railway Journal*, and *American Journal of Railway Appliances*. James Herbert McGraw, Sr., sold subscriptions for the same company during his summer vacations from schoolteaching. Later McGraw joined the firm as a full-time subscription solicitor and then became an advertising space salesman like Swetland.

Both Swetland and McGraw became part owners of the company. McGraw disagreed with some of his other publishing partners on the question whether motor power would supplant horses on street railways. McGraw and Swetland thought it would. The other partners are long since forgotten men.

The circulation of *Street Railway Journal* was partly to veterinarians and partly to engineers. Which readership to build up? That was the question.[14] Advertisers of feed, wheelbarrows, and

---

[14] Baltimore, on Aug. 28, 1830, witnessed a race between Tom Thumb, first locomotive built in the United States and a horse and buggy. The horse was the winner.

hay pressed for a decision. It was up to the editors to denounce the electric streetcar. The firm finally split up on which way the world would go, and·McGraw got the two railway journals/and the composing room.

Swetland got *Power*, which back in 1880 had been called *Steam*. For a time it was *Power-Steam* but in 1892 it was again *Power*. In 1908 it absorbed the *Chicago Engineer* and became *Power and the Engineer*. It absorbed nine or ten other papers and is currently *Power*.

McGraw Sr. envisioned the electrical era, just as his four sons who succeeded him have envisioned the air era.[15] *Street Railway Journal* was renamed *Electric Street Railway Journal*. The senior McGraw fought for electrified street railways, employed trained electrical engineers for his editorial staffs, and bought other electrical businesspapers. Swetland had faith in the automotive field. He sold *Power* to John A. Hill and bought automotive publications. When he wrote the first textbook[16] on the business press he was president of United Publishers Corporation.

John A. Hill, a fireman on the Denver & Rio Grande Railroad started a daily newspaper in Pueblo, Colo., in 1885, but sold it soon afterward to go back to the railroad. His correspondence for *Locomotive Engineering* brought him to the attention of the publishers, who gave him a place on the staff and eventually the editorship. Later he sold his half interest in that paper to become publisher of *American Machinist*. Hill built a large organization, publishing, in addition to the *Machinist, Coal Age, Engineering and Mining Journal*, and *Engineering News*. He acquired Swetland's *Power*.

The *American Journal of Mining* (1866) was the ancestor of the *Engineering and Mining Journal* (1869). Edited by G. F. Dawson, it remained a weekly until 1929. Its many absorptions included *Mining Review* (Chicago), *Mining Journal* (Michigan), *Mining & Scientific Press* (California), *Coal & Iron Record*, *Mining & Engineering World*.

[15] *Aviation* was started in 1916.
[16] *Industrial Publishing*, by H. M. Swetland. New York Business Publishers Association, Inc., 1923.

After Hill's death in 1916, the McGraw and Hill publishing houses joined forces and the McGraw-Hill Publishing Co. was launched, with nine strong businesspapers. *Engineering Record* and *Engineering News* were combined. Expansion took place in many industries such as food, textiles, photography, aviation, electronics. *Power* became a McGraw-Hill paper.

D. Kimball Minor, part owner of the New York *American*, a daily, started the pioneer railroad businesspaper, as a weekly, in 1832. He called it the *American Rail-Road Journal* and gave the town wits quite a laugh. Why not a "Turnpike Commentator" or an "Aqueduct Chronicle"? they asked. Publisher Minor saw a vision: "iron roads superseding the canals" (*American Rail-Road Journal*, Jan. 2, 1832). There were half a dozen or more railroad journals in 1832 although the 12 railroads at that time had only 200 miles of road, and 9 relied on horsepower. Only 3 had locomotives! Some of these journals were published in New York, Boston, Philadelphia, Cincinnati, Chicago. They all fought editorially for the transcontinental railroads to the Pacific. Minor moved the *Journal* to Philadelphia in 1846, but in 1848 it returned to New York as the property of John H. Schultz. Its new editor was Henry V. Poor. Poor, on the side, started a yearly reference work, *Poor's Manual*. In 1862, Poor resigned as editor to devote full time to the *Manual*, which was destined to become an institution in industry. Schultz took over as editor until 1879.

Van Nostrand's Electric Engineering Magazine (1869-1887) was merged with the *American Rail-Road Journal* in 1887.

James Artman, head of the Trade Publishing Co., founded one of the oldest automobile businesspapers, originally called *Cycle Trade Journal*, in June, 1896. In the next three years he was bitten by doubts whether the bicycle would be a serious rival of the horseless carriage in the twentieth century. In 1899, he was wisely calling his paper, *Cycle and Automobile Trade Journal*. That same year two men joined forces with Artman. They were George H. Buzby and C. A. Musselman. In 1901 the firm name was changed to Trade Advertising and Publishing Co. with Artman as president, Buzby as vice-president, and Musselman as secretary-treasurer.

In 1907 the Chilton Printing Co., which printed the *Cycle and Automobile Trade Journal*, was purchased and the publishers took the name of Chilton for their company. It was not learned until 1913 where the name came from. It seems the owners of the Chilton Printing Co., Mr. Deputy and Mr. McFarlan, did not like each other's names, so they got a list of the families who came over on the *Mayflower*. One of the names was Chilton. They liked it. The source of the name was discovered when a Senator Chilton of North Carolina decided to look up his family tree. In December, 1923, the Chilton Co., of Philadelphia and the Class Journal Co., of New York, which it already owned, were merged by the United Publishers Corp., who took over all the capital stock.

Messrs. Artman and Buzby retired from active business. H. M. Swetland, founder of the Class Journal Co., remained as president of U.P.C. A. B. Swetland became vice-president of the Chilton Co. and remained as manager of the Class Journal Co. Upon the death of H. M. Swetland in 1924, C. A. Musselman became president and general manager of the subsidiary, Chilton Class Journal Co., with Joseph S. Hildreth as vice-president. Some years later, the U.P.C., for purposes of simplification of title, changed its name to Chilton Co. and the Class Journal subsidiary became the automotive division of U.P.C. Mr. Hildreth headed up this division with Julian Chase and G. Carroll Buzby as vice-presidents. In addition to publishing businesspapers in the steel, automotive, aviation, insurance, and consumers' goods industries, Chilton Co. own an equal interest with McGraw-Hill in Business Publishers International Corp., which publishes overseas editions.

In the consumers' goods field one of the foremost publishers of businesspapers, sometimes described as "merchandising" papers, is Andrew J. Haire, descendant of three generations of dry goods merchants. Fifty years earlier his father had operated one of the first chains of stores (four units) in Connecticut. Eighteen years later Mr. Haire's two sons, A. P. and Andrew Jr., started the Haire Publishing Co. A. P. Haire died in 1920. Mr. Andrew J. Haire acquired 33 businesspapers in the succeeding two decades. Many were consolidated. He now publishes nine consumers' goods magazines and two papers in the field of aviation, *Aviation Equipment* and *Airports* (formerly *American Pilot*). The three oldest of the consumers' goods papers are *Crockery & Glass Journal* (1874), *House Furnishing Review* (1892), and *Home Furnishings Merchandising*, formerly *Decorative Furnisher* (1878), each representing several mergers. Arthur I. Mellin is Haire's senior editor.

One of the oldest businesspaper publishers was Isbon B. Scott, who died at the age of ninety in August, 1944. He had served on the U.S.S. *Constitution* as a boy. As a young man he worked on the old New York *Post*. He joined Clifford & Lawton, a businesspaper publishing house, in 1891. Under the name Clifford, Scott & Lawton, this firm published the *Upholsterer*, *Wall Paper News*, and *Shoe & Leather Review*. In 1892, Scott sold out his interest and started *House Furnishing Review* in Philadelphia, as an independent venture. At that time "house furnishing goods" was scattered on every floor of a department store selling such goods. To seventy-five department store owners of that era, whom he had contacted, Scott promised that he would cover the entire field for news and new products if they would put all the miscellaneous "house furnishing" merchandise on one floor under one buyer and subscribe to his magazine. Thus was born the housewares department which now flourishes in thousands of department stores. In 1909, Scott sold *House Furnishing Review* to the Trade Magazine Association. In 1927, it was acquired by Simmons-Boardman Co. who sold it, in 1932, to the Haire organization. Other pioneers in businesspaper publishing were Henry Lord of *Textile World*; W. H. Ukers of *Tea and Coffee Trade Journal*; Ed Shaw of *Power Plant Engineering*; John B. Nind, *Furniture Record*; Charles T. Root, head of the Root Newspaper Association, and Charles G. Phillips of *Department Store Economist*; John Williams, founder of *Iron Age* and his son, David Williams. One of the foremost contemporary businesspaper editors is president of *Iron Age*, John H. Van Deventer.

PIONEER BUSINESSPAPER EDITORS

One of the deans of businesspaper editing is H. C. Parmelee, editor of the *Engineering and Mining Journal*, oldest of the McGraw-Hill businesspapers. A graduate chemist and metallurgist and past president of the Colorado School of Mines, "Doc" Parmelee has served in the businesspaper field for over thirty-three years.

When *Railway Gazette* and *Railway Age* finally merged in 1908 as *Railway Age-Gazette*, W. H. Boardman, long editor and publisher of the *Gazette* continued as chief editor until 1911, when E. A. Simmons bought him out. Simmons made Samuel O. Dunn chief editor. Mr. Dunn had specialized in railway journalism as an editorial writer on the Chicago *Tribune*. He joined the staff of *Railway Age* in 1907. In 1931 editor Dunn became chairman of the board of Simmons-Boardman, who are publishers of five leading contemporary railroad businesspapers. He is a past president of the Associated Business Papers and of the National Conference of Business Paper Editors.

Simmons-Boardman Co. bought the pioneer *American Railroad Journal* in 1911 and Roy V. Wright became its editor. In 1916 the title *Railway Mechanical Engineer* was adopted. Mr. Wright, who is an M.E., University of Minnesota, and Dr. Eng., Stevens Institute of Technology, had worked for two midwestern railroads. He was mechanical engineer of the Pittsburgh & Lake Erie Railroad when he became editor of *American Engineer and Railroad Journal* in 1904. He is past president of the American Society of Mechanical Engineers, and editor of various editions of Cyclopedias in the locomotive- and car-building fields. He is a past president of the Associated Business Papers and the National Conference of Business Paper Editors. His background indicates the training, experience, and achievement required of editors in every field of businesspaper activity.

Julian Chase is probably the dean of American businesspaper editors. He has been associated with the automotive industries since the turn of the century. Graduating from Brown in 1899, he engaged in designing, building, and selling automobiles as background for his first editorship, in 1906, of an automotive and marine businesspaper. In 1915 he was managing editor and part owner of *Horseless Age*, first automobile publication in this country, founded in 1895.

In 1899, the *Automobile and Motor Review* was started. In

1903, the *Automobile Horseless Age* was absorbed, and *Automotive Industries* became the foremost of Chilton businesspapers. Mr. Chase was on the War Department's General Staff, in 1918, organizing training centers for transport drivers. In 1933 he became directing editor of all Chilton automotive papers, which include *Automobile Trade Journal*, descendant of *Cycle Trade Journal* (1896). The "Cycle" was not dropped from the title until 1912. He is a vice-president of the Chilton Co.

Another great businesspaper editor was the late Paul I. Aldrich, editorial director for thirty-two years of *National Provisioner*. He was president of the Associated Business Papers, Chicago Business Publishers Association, Chicago Business Editors Association, and National Conference of Business Paper Editors. Founder of the Institute of American Meat Packers, he wrote many textbooks for his industry. He died in 1943.

Henry Bridgman, apothecary and druggist, in 1857 founded and edited the *Druggists Circular and Chemical Gazette*. He was a courageous enemy of nostrums, adulteration, and quackeries. The *Circular* published annual trade directories for forty years.

The *American Miller* (1873-current), an amalgamation of eight other milling businesspapers, is the oldest in that industry, founded by Samuel S. Chisholm in Chicago. Its circulation is international.

Without a break (even during Prohibition) the *American Brewer* has been published since 1867 by the Schwarz family. The president-editor, Robert Schwarz, is a grandson of the founder, Anton Schwarz.

The *U.S. Army and Navy Journal and Gazette of the Regular Volunteer Forces*, like its name, has had a long record of service in a field which some regard as a business and others as a profession. Founded in 1863, it became *Gazette of the Land, Sea and Air* in 1926, and today is the *Army and Navy Journal*. A young soldier who fought with "War-is-hell" Sherman, Captain William C. Church, was the first editor and co-owner with Silas Casey. Church and his brother Francis, also an owner, were sons of a Baptist preacher, the Rev. Pharcellus Church, who ran a sectarian newspaper, New York *Chronicle*.

Electrical World (1874-current) sprang from a local telegrapher's businesspaper in New York, the *Operator*, founded in 1874. As the application of electricity broadened, the name was changed to the *Operator and Electrical World*. Among the papers absorbed in its history is the *American Electrician* (1882-1899), whose editor was F. L. Pope. Known in 1884 as the *Electrician and Electrical Engineer*, it was called *Electrical Engineer* when it was merged with *Electrical World* in 1888.

W. D. Weaver who left the editorship of *Electrical World* to become editor of *American Electrician* was described as "one of the few really great engineering editors of the day" by the publisher, James H. McGraw, in a lecture in May, 1929, before the Princeton School of Engineering. "His reputation grew until many of the leading electrical engineers, not only of America, but of the world, came to his office to seek his advice and listen to his judgements," Mr. McGraw said.

In 1944 the contemporary editor of *Electrical World*, Samuel Baker Williams, had the distinction of being elected president of the Illuminating Engineering Society. He has a graduate degree in electrical engineering from Princeton and had been active for many years in trade association work in his professional field. He also served as chairman of the New York Business Paper Editors in 1941. He joined the staff of *Electrical World* in 1914.

Factory started in 1882[17] as *Review of the Telegraph and Telephone*; then it became *Electrical Review* (1883-1921); *Industrial Engineering* (1922-1931); *Maintenance Engineering* (1931-32); *Factory Management and Maintenance* (1932-current). In the process of finding itself, *Factory* absorbed several other businesspapers. A pioneer editor was Charles W. Price (1891-1921). The contemporary editor, L. C. Morrow, is a widely respected mechanical and management engineer, with twenty-four years' experience. He is a world authority on factory management.

Textile Industry Group: As late as 1830 household woolen production was greater than factory production in the United States, and did not become really negligible until 1870. Cotton textiles adopted the factory system earlier but it was about 1845 before it

[17] The publishers of *Factory* give 1891 as the founding date.

was going strong. Sam Slater used automatic machinery in 1791 at Pawtucket, R.I., for spinning yarn (with child labor), but weaving was done by the parents in their own cottages.[18] Wage payments were in truck (groceries) from the company-owned stores. At Waltham, Mass., in 1815, the first industrial community for cotton textiles started with automatic weaving and spinning machinery; first complete factory system in our country. By 1868, when *Textile World* started as *Manufacturer's Review* and *Industrial Record*, textiles had already piled up quite an industrial record. Textiles had become the backbone of the dry goods store, which in 1846 began reading its own businesspaper, *United States Economist and Dry Goods Reporter*, founded by W. B. Burroughs and Robert Boyd. Later it was called *Dry Goods Reporter & Commercial Glance*. Then *Dry Goods Economist* and now *Department Store Economist*. The National Retail Dry Goods Association was organized in the editor's office in 1911. William M. Thackeray in a letter to Leigh Hunt, described a copy of the *Dry Goods Reporter* which he came across on a coffeehouse table in Glasgow.

Another veteran publisher in the consumers' goods field of textiles is E. W. Fairchild, who started in business as a grocery and yeast salesman in Chicago during the nineties. On the side he picked up news items for a friend who ran a grocery tradepaper. In this way Fairchild became acquainted with the printer of this grocery paper. One day the printer found himself the owner of an apparel tradepaper he printed, called *Chicago Herald Gazette*; the owner, John B. Waldo, could not pay his printing bills. He promptly sold the *Gazette* to Fairchild. The name was changed to *Chicago Apparel Gazette* and in 1890 Fairchild entered the businesspaper field as a publisher. In 1896 an eastern edition was issued as *Men's Wear* and soon the western edition adopted the same name. *Men's Wear* has since become one of the apparel industry's leading businesspapers.

At the Chicago World's Fair in 1893, Fairchild distributed a mimeographed daily news bulletin for visiting textile buyers. When

[18] See *Abraham Lincoln: The Prairie Years*, by Carl Sandburg (Harcourt, Brace & Co., New York, 1926), for this transition period in our country's history.

the Fair ended this bulletin was moved to New York and transformed into a daily trade newspaper (tabloid size) called *Daily News Record*. Its present editor, Harry Riemer, has served the paper for 25 years and is one of the best known textile editors in the country.

During the great ladies' garment strike in New York, in 1910, the *Daily News Record* published a special page covering news of union attempts to organize that industry. Special reprints of this page were distributed free in the Garment Center. Out of these daily pages *Women's Wear Daily* evolved in 1910.

In 1929, *Retailing-Executive* was started as a weekly (suspended in 1941) and in 1931 *Retailing-Home Furnishings* commenced publication. Fairchild's hold the Associated Press wire service franchise.

E. W. Fairchild was joined by his brother, L. E. Fairchild in the publishing venture, in 1892, and later by a third brother, Arthur. "E.W." and Arthur are retired. Louis Fairchild, son of "E.W." is general manager in charge of editorial and advertising and a second son, Edmund Fairchild, has charge of the headquarters in Chicago. Edgar Fairchild, son of "L. E." is in charge of publishing administration.

Thumonnier's sewing machine[19] (1829) revolutionized clothing and shoe industries. In 1851, *Shoe and Leather Reporter* was founded. In 1868, *Textile World*. Eli Whitney's[20] cotton gin had made cotton king.

William L. Terhune canvassed the leading shoe manufacturers and jobbers of Boston's famous market, in 1882, with his dummy for a proposed trade paper, to be called *Boot and Shoe Recorder*. Like Isbon Scott, first publisher of *House Furnishing Review*, Mr. Terhune was also an ex-newspaper journalist. After working on several Newark (N.J.) papers and the Auburn (Me.) *Herald*, Terhune had become editor of the *New Hampshire Independent*. In 1870, he was manager of a family magazine, *Merry's Museum*.

Terhune's first advertising order came from Goodyear & McKay

[19] It was 44 years before the founding of *Sewing Machine Journal* (1873-1893).
[20] Eli Whitney, as early as 1807, was working on the principles of standardized parts and interchangeable mechanisms. These were first applied to firearms and clocks, later to textile and farm machinery.

Sewing Machine Co. for one inch of space, three insertions, at a cost of $4. *Boot and Shoe Recorder* had materialized. Everit B. Terhune, son of the founder, is an official of the Chilton Co., and present publisher of *Boot and Shoe Recorder*. The contemporary editor, Arthur D. Anderson, has served the paper for 27 years. He is the author of *Shoe and Leather Lexicon*.

From post-Civil War days the business press crawled over a long, tortuous road in the United States before reaching in 1895 a fair level of respectability or importance in the eyes of "business." Business itself during this period had not enjoyed any too good a reputation.[21] Forward pace of American industry from 1868 to 1872 dropped off in 1873 with a panic in September of that year and a depression that slowed down all industries, particularly those depending on construction.

Professional Group: Journals of medicine, law, finance, and agriculture, too numerous to give space to in detail in this book[22] sprang up all over the country in this period. There were specialized journals devoted to livestock, poultry, and horticulture.

By 1885, *Jones Index* listed 43 legal journals. Oliver Wendell Holmes, Jr., edited the *American Law Review*, founded in 1866.

In 1869, *Rowell's American Newspaper Directory* listed 40 medical journals, which had grown by 1885 to some 400. Seventeen "homeopathic" journals enjoyed brief existences.

Two of the oldest medical papers were *American Journal of the Medical Sciences*, of Philadelphia, and the *Boston Medical and Surgical Journal*, founded about 1850.

The outstanding contemporary editor in the field of medicine is Dr. Morris Fishbein, editor since 1924 of *The Journal of the American Medical Association*. He succeeded a famous editor, the late Dr. George H. Simmons. Dr. Fishbein, who is also editor of of *Hygeia*, the lay publication of A.M.A., has become the recognized spokesman for organized medicine, in spite of the fact that he never practiced medicine. He writes 15,000 words a week, makes 100 speeches a year and reads 3,000 manuscripts that are

[21] *Our Times*, by Mark Sullivan. Scribner's, New York, 1927.
[22] Students who wish more details should read *History of American Magazines*, by Frank Luther Mott, Vols. I, II, III, Harvard University Press and D. Appleton & Co., New York, 1930.

submitted annually for the medical journals. In addition, he turns
out a daily syndicated newspaper column called "Family Doctor"
and is a contributor to other businesspapers here and abroad.
Average issues of the *Journal* of the A.M.A. carry 48 pages of the
most carefully selected advertising at $408 a page. Net earnings in
1937 were $670,000. Articles in the *Journal* are abstracted from
1,400 foreign and domestic medical publications. The net paid
circulation is over 100,000.

In finance, one of the most notable businesspapers described by
Professor Mott is *Thompson's Bank Note and Commercial Reporter*, founded in 1836. Later it was called *Thompson's American Bank Report* and in 1877 became the *American Banker*. Judge
Thompson, the editor, laid the foundation of the current business
magazine of banking by issuing a daily bulletin on rates of currency exchange. In 1863 he was the first man in New York to
organize a national bank, First National Bank, and in 1877 he
founded the Chase National Bank, now the world's largest. Salmon
P. Chase, after whom it was named, was Editor Thompson's close
friend and coworker. Charles Dow and Edward Jones founded the
Wall Street Journal in 1882.[23]

Manufacturers had eliminated much of the drudgery of hand
toil, at the turn of the century. The United States was harnessing
mechanical power in a big way and becoming the top-rank producer of iron and steel. The inventiveness of the American Yankee
caused Edward Everett to write an essay called "The Inevitable
March of Improvement."

Inventors, protected by patent laws, were hard at work destroying time and space. Ducos had a motion picture machine (1864),
perfected by Marly (1882) and Edison (1889-1893). Scholes was
writing on a typewriter (1867). Swift had built a refrigerator car
(1875). Bell was talking through his electric telephone (1876).
Edison played tunes on a phonograph (1877) and worked by his
own incandescent light (1878). Mergenthaler operated a linotype
(1884) and Leviston a monotype (1887). Eastman carried a hand
camera (1886). Hertz was describing electromagnetic waves
(1887). Marconi and Metchikoff were signaling with radio teleg-

---

[23] See Chap. V for biographical sketch of the *Wall Street Journal*.

raphy (1896). In rapid succession came the steam turbine, electric railroad, elevator, flying machine, movies, internal-combustion engine, electric furnace (making commercial aluminum possible), adding machine, phonograph, diesel engine, rayon, Xray. Thus were scattered the seeds of new industries. New businesspapers were ready to spring into being to nourish and keep those industries informed of even newer inventions, improvements, schemes, devices, merchandising ideas, and plans for promotion and expansion.[24]

Machinery of distribution was likewise improving, but less quickly. Communication, transportation, transmission of power, of goods, of facts and ideas, had begun to wrap up the United States into a group of packaged regional markets: New England, Middle Atlantic, South Atlantic, East North Central, East South Central, West South Central, Mountain, and Pacific states.

Insurance Group: The great Chicago fire was a blessing to the insurance business in New York. The total capital of New York companies was $10 million while their income was $40 million and their risk $1,600 million. The Chicago fire put 57 companies out of business (one-third of New York's and three-fourths of the Illinois companies with a total loss of $85 million, far, far, in excess of their aggregate capitalization.[25]

The *Spectator*, a leading insurance journal, which had started in 1868, hailed the catastrophe: it made possible higher rates and a flood of business. It also cut down the competition and it has been held down ever since. Today five life insurances companies control more business than all the rest of them.[26] *New York Underwriter* led in circulation, but many insurance businesspapers flourished in dozens of key cities. Twenty founded after the Civil War lasted half a century and nine are published currently. Several

[24] Note that inventions are often patented long before they can be practicably used; on the other hand, they are often ready for use long before industrial enterprisers are willing to take advantage of them. Thus, the founding dates of American, British, and German businesspapers are a better guide to the birth of new industries than is the Patent Office (see Appendix I).

[25] The editor of *Nation*, Jan. 26, 1871, Vol. XII, tr. 54.

[26] Report of The Temporary National Economic Committee, Document 35. Washington, D.C., March, 1941.

big insurance companies published powerful house organs in the 1870's.

The oldest insurance businesspaper currently published is *American Insurance Digest & Insurance Monitor*, which took over the old *Insurance Monitor* founded in 1853. Second oldest is *Weekly Underwriter* (1859). Other old-timers still being published are the *Standard* (1872), *Insurance Index* (1870), and *Rough Notes* (1853).

The late Carl Avery Werner for 46 years was editor of *The Tobacco Leaf* as well as a poet, novelist and short story writer. He started his career as a reporter on the Watertown (N.Y.) *Daily Times* and entered the businesspaper field in 1899. He was an authority on the tobacco business and founded the New York Tobacco Table, a trade association. He died in 1944.

Foreign-Language Business Press: Many businesspapers are published for export and import trade. The Business Publishers International Corp., through its affiliation with the Chilton Co. and McGraw-Hill Co., publishes businesspapers in Spanish and Portuguese for Middle and South America. *American Exporter*, founded in 1877, is one of the largest export businesspapers. Its "Industrial Supplement" carries messages in English and Spanish. Claiming "a New Industrial Revolution second in importance to the Industrial Revolution in 18th century England," the *American Exporter* published a brochure[27] in 1943, showing the rapid industrialization of agricultural and pastoral countries such as Australia, New Zealand, India, South Africa, Middle and South America.

HOUSE ORGAN: ANCESTOR OF THE BUSINESSPAPER

Ancestor of the businesspaper and also of the general magazine were the court circular papers published by feudal lords in China during the Han Dynasty (200 B.C.). In the Tang Dynasty (7th century A.D.) they became official gazettes. The house organ flourished in Germany of the Middle Ages in the form of newsletters. *Neues Zeitungen* of the House of Fugger has already been

[27] "The New Industrial Revolution," *American Exporter*, New York.

described, as well as the famous house organ of Lloyd's of London.

Ben Franklin's Print Shop in eighteenth century Philadelphia issued *Poor Richard's Almanack*, first house organ in North America and popularly but erroneously supposed to have been the ancestor of the *Saturday Evening Post*.[28]

Factory News, published by National Cash Register Co. in June, 1891, was one of the earliest bona fide house organs in the United States.

Many book publishers started house organs which eventually became independent consumer magazines, such as *Atlantic Monthly*, *Harper's*, and *Scribner's*.

Printers' Ink was the house organ of the George P. Rowell Advertising Agency. *Scientific American* was the organ of a firm of patent attorneys, Messrs. Munn & Co. Southern Pacific Railway started *Sunset* magazine.

Other notable house organs are *Dun's Review* (Dun & Bradstreet) and *Fashions of the Hour* (Marshall Field & Co.).

House organ editors are organized. They call themselves "National Council of Industrial Editors" and among the important subsidiary groups is A.R.M.E.A.—"American Railway Magazine Editors' Association," organized in 1922. The editors represent 28 railway employee publications which in 1943 had a total readership of 1,554,770 railroaders and their families in the United States.

Biggest house organ publisher in the United States is probably the General Electric Co. which publishes two groups: (1) Internal papers, for their own stockholders, firm members and employees, such as *G-E Monogram*, 17,000 monthly; *General Electric Review*, 6,000; *Work News*, 175,000 weekly. (2) Numerous other

[28] The *Saturday Evening Post*, actually, is a lineal descendant of *The Universal Instructor in All Arts and Sciences and Pennsylvania Gazette*, a weekly, first published in Philadelphia on Dec. 24, 1728, by Ben Franklin's former boss, Sam Keimer, who stole the idea from Ben. "An idea for a newspaper" is usually not worth a nickel without the idea's parent, which proved to be the case ten months later when poor Ben Franklin bought the *Gazette* with its 90 subscribers from Keimer for a song. Shortened to the *Pennsylvania Gazette*, it became the best-known paper in the colonies, while its editor and publisher, Ben Franklin, lived. In 1897, when Cyrus H. K. Curtis bought it for $1,000, it was called *Saturday Evening Post* and was gasping its last breath. Today, $1,000 buys one-half column of advertising, one time, in one of its weekly issues. The circulation of the *Post* in February, 1944, was 3,205,166 paid subscribers.

magazines and newspapers for external distribution, to dealers, wholesalers, customers, and prospects, including the utilities: *G-E News Graphic* for the appliance field; *Light* for lighting engineers; *G-E News-Digest*; and *General Electric Review*, an ABC paper which disseminates information from its various laboratories and engineering departments to utilities, consulting organizations, colleges and trade schools, and other electrical concerns.

Editors of *G-E Work News* have their offices in the eight largest G-E factories. A general manager in the Schenectady plant co-ordinates the work of these eight editors and their staffs, syndicates various editorials, cartoons, and news on general company matters.

Monsanto (St. Louis) and duPont (Wilmington) also publish well-known house magazines in the chemical industry. General Motors and Westinghouse are runners-up to General Electric as large house organ publishers, on one hand, and heavy supporters of the business press, on the other.

Some house organs, like *General Electric Review* and *Combustion Engineering*, carry the advertising of other manufacturers.

Aggressive promotion by the independent business press and the results obtained by industry through consistent advertising in the business press have practically eliminated the reason for most house organs, except the employee type. Expenses of printing house magazines, maintaining competent editorial staffs on full-time pay, keeping alive large mailing lists, cost of postage, and other subsidies involve more money and manpower than a businesspaper advertising campaign would cost, in most cases. Using an independent medium, however, involves more important considerations than the "costs."

Any news of a business concern is much more readily accepted on its face in the columns of an independent businesspaper than in the columns of a subsidized house organ whose editorial policy is controlled by a manufacturer. Moreover, a businesspaper can maintain rigid standards for evaluating readership as well as news.

House organs do not enjoy second-class mailing privileges, since they cannot meet these qualifications required of a businesspaper: (1) bona fide list of subscribers who pay more than a nominal (gratis) price for the paper; (2) paid distribution; (3) not primarily for advertising purposes; (4) publisher cannot be the chief advertiser; (5) must conform to government regulations, such as regular publication date, etc.

Tide, a business magazine of the advertising and marketing professions, estimated there were 1,500 house organs being published in the United States at a total cost to their owners of $10 million annually.[29] *Sales Management* recently claimed there were 4,000 "kept publications" published in the United States. The money spent for this kind of advertising is estimated by other authorities between $15 and $22 million annually. It is also estimated that the annual casualties are 30 per cent.[30]

Many firms engaged in war work, with vastly increased personnel, saw need for maintaining sound employee relations during World War II. *Printers' Ink* Directory of House Organs[31] listed 5,100 company magazines published by 4,016 different concerns, the largest list ever compiled.

"STUFFED CLUB" PUBLICATIONS

The independent business press is constantly faced with the dubious competition of trade association organs and "souvenir" booklets, the latter carrying paid advertising and often promoted by questionable persons for uneconomic purposes.

"It is a moot question," says Dr. Hugh Agnew, "whether maintaining a publication, wholly or partly supported by advertising is ever a legitimate activity of an association."[32]

The *Bulletin* of the National Wholesale Grocers' Association is cited by Dr. Agnew. Declared the Grocers' Association in one issue:

Even for advertising space in the *Bulletin* we cannot in justice to the manufacturer or to ourselves accept money; we represent the

---

[29] March, 1940, *Tide*.
[30] *Advertising Media*, by Hugh Agnew & Warren B. Dygert. McGraw-Hill, New York, 1938.
[31] October, 1944.
[32] *Op. cit.*

wholesale grocer and the wholesale grocer alone and we feel that we must be free to act at all times in the wholesale grocer's interest without obligation of any kind to anyone other than our own members. Some day, in the constant upward course of business practice, this view will be crystallized into something more tangible than ethics.

Sales Management, in an editorial, criticized this form of competition with the independent business press in similar vein:

We understand that the American Association of Manufacturers has embarked on an ambitious program to build up its organ, *American Industries,* into a second *Nation's Business.*[33] It would seem to us that there ought to be other ways that the secretary of the American Association of Manufacturers can secure revenue without going into the publishing business in competition with the legitimate business publications.

It seems strange, to say the least, that an organization which boasts of the good influence it exerts upon the ethics of industry should stoop to this sort of thing. Not only is it eminently unfair for an association, which is maintained by subscription, to employ its funds to finance a subsidized publication, but it encourages other associations to follow the example. As it is, there are about 4,000 "kept" publications in this country—that is to say, publications that are printed and distributed regardless of whether they are wanted or not.

Nearly all of these publications use the "stuffed club" to sell advertising space. With a few exceptions none of the advertising space is worth what it costs, and millions of dollars annually are charged against selling expense, when they should have been charged to charity. There is the church paper, the high school annual, the iron puddlers' union program, the local Order of Wild Cats' souvenir program, etc. Whenever funds are needed, the first thought is to sell advertising in something or another—it makes no difference what.

This condition is growing worse instead of better. It is already a heavy tax on business. It seems to us that the American Association of Manufacturers should turn their influence against such practices, instead of endorsing them as they are doing with *American Industries.*

[33] *Nation's Business,* published in Washington, is the official mouthpiece of the United States Chamber of Commerce, headquarters for thousands of chambers, big and little, in cities and towns of our country. Washington Chamber is the national spokesman for management and employers of management. The organ had an ABC circulation in February, 1944, of 391,025 readers.

CHAPTER V

FLOWERING OF THE SPECIALIZED PRESS

JUST as a new businesspaper, specializing in coverage of a specific industry, gives status and solidarity to that industry, so three businesspapers founded within a few years of each other, in the eighties, gave status to the specialized businesspaper publishing industry.

Editor & Publisher: VOICE OF PUBLISHING

The *Journalist*, founded in 1884, was the first businesspaper to gain a foothold in the field of United States journalism. In 1907 it was purchased from its founders and the name changed to *Editor & Publisher*. It became the leading professional service paper edited for newspapers. In 1912 the late James Wright Brown, Sr., purchased a controlling interest. In 1925 he purchased *Newspaperdom*, which had started in 1888, and *Advertising*. Both papers were consolidated with *Editor & Publisher*. The *Fourth Estate*, founded in 1894, was purchased and merged a year later.

Issued weekly, *Editor & Publisher* today specializes in serving the newspaper field in all its phases. A monthly section, *Equipment Review*, is devoted to the mechanics of newspaper production. Its readers are 4,794 newspaper executives and employees (April, 1943, figures) and 1,394 advertisers and employees, 280 advertising agents, 228 newspaper representatives, 530 other periodicals, 361 schools of journalism, 169 students of journalism; libraries and miscellaneous, over 2,000.

The *Editor & Publisher*, in 1912, advocated uniform sworn, audited statements of newspaper circulation. In October of the same year the Bourne law was passed, establishing the practice of publishing semiannual statements of ownership and circulation in newspapers. This practice is now required, under the postal regulations, of all periodical publishers.

Printers' Ink: VOICE OF ADVERTISING

George Presbury Rowell established *Printers' Ink* in 1888 and for more than half a century it was the familiar pocket-size bible of the advertising profession. Mr. Rowell's original publication was *Advertisers Gazette*, founded in 1867. The *Gazette* changed its name in 1871 to the *American Newspaper Reporter* which functioned chiefly as a house organ for Mr. Rowell's advertising agency business.

The editorial content of *Printers' Ink*, Rowell's new name for the publication, was designed "to serve, without fear or favor," the best interests of the advertising profession and the men who used advertising to promote their business interests. Its publishers describe it today as "an open forum of interchange of method and experience among business concerns, together with editorial guidance on moving merchandise more effectively from factory to consumer." Many papers were launched in imitation of *Printers' Ink*, but few survived. The same editorial formula, however, adopted by businesspapers in other branches of industry helped those papers to survive the decades.

John Irving Roemer (editor in 1908 and later president) was stirred by the epidemic of fraudulent advertising. He engaged the services of a well-known corporation lawyer, Harry D. Nims[1] who drew up a *Printers' Ink* Model Statute on false advertising. Roemer began to plug this statute in his editorials and eventually put it over. Today, twenty-five states, or more, have incorporated the *Printers' Ink* Statute into their laws. Enforcement of this statute by district attorneys and Better Business Bureaus has saved literally millions of dollars a year previously lost by the public through fake advertising.

In 1919, *Printers' Ink Monthly* was started, to deal with "human interest phases" of marketing, employing what the promotion

[1] Author of a textbook on *Unfair Competition*.

manager called "a dramatic format," the larger page size. Twenty-three years later, in 1942, the familiar pocket-size weekly disappeared and *Printers' Ink* was issued every week in regular magazine size, combining both publications.

The Wall Street Journal: VOICE OF PRIVATE ENTERPRISE

Instantaneous distribution of news "without fear or favor" by means of an electric ticker was the revolutionary service introduced by the famous financial businesspaper, the *Wall Street Journal*, in 1897. Fifteen years before, in 1882, Charles H. Dow and Edward D. Jones, reporters for Kiernan News Agency, the leading financial news organization in Wall Street, set up their own agency, Dow, Jones & Co. They began publishing "Customers' Afternoon Letters" with a dozen subscribers. On July 8, 1889, Vol. 1, No. 1 of the *Wall Street Journal* appeared.[2] When its famous editor and publisher, Clarence W. Barron, who had bought the *Wall Street Journal* in 1902, died in 1928, his own tickers reeled off the news of his demise in 140 cities in the United States and Canada and in its Pacific Coast edition.

In addition to the New York paper, there is the Philadelphia *Financial Journal* and Boston *News Bureau*, owned by the same organization. Subscription rate to the *Wall Street Journal* is $18 a year. Dow-Jones news ticker service costs stockholders, financiers, and other decision-making, policy-forming business executives $100 a month ($200 on Pacific Coast) in cities were Dow-Jones offices are located. This instantaneous news is gathered by special correspondents in 123 of the world's cities and is the largest of all news organizations serving news to business.

PUBLICATION DIRECTORIES

One important function of businesspaper publishers is amassing, analyzing, and classifying market data. In 1667 "A Collection of the Names of Merchants" was published in London, one of the

[2] A "Wall Street Journal," published 1852 to 1875 by John Hillyer, at 14 William Street, New York, is unrelated to the present journal.

earliest known directories. Benjamin Franklin published a directory of Philadelphia in 1785. George P. Rowell, in 1869, issued *The American Newspaper Directory*, first attempt to list periodicals and give their circulation figures. In his directory there were just 56 publications listed under the headings "Commerce & Finance" and "Mechanics." Forty medical journals were listed. Eleven years later, in 1880, the first edition of N. W. Ayer & Sons' *American Newspaper Annual* listed 323 publications under the heading "Commercial, Financial and Trade"; 110 under "Fashion"; 28 under "Insurance"; 38 under "Legal"; 18 under "Real Estate"; 53 under "Mining"; 32 under "Music"; 22 under "Railroad"; and 19 under "Typographic"; making 669 periodicals which, with the exception of some of those in the musical and scientific lists, were regarded in those days as "business" papers. There were also listed about 1,000 professional and so-called "class" publications of various kinds, medical, educational, agricultural, religious, etc. There were nine foreign-language lists in 1880, including 11 languages and 19 secret society lists.[3] Rowell's directory was merged with the N. W. Ayer directory in 1880.

Today there are five types of directories: (1) Trade or business; (2) population; (3) professional; (4) social; (5) telephone. Trade directories list trade-marks, names of manufacturers, jobbers, selling agents, mill and factory representatives, classifications of merchandise, retail stores and the names of their executives, buying personnel, and other related information.

Standard Rate and Data Service

Started in 1932, *Standard Rate and Data Service* publishes five sections monthly: Its Business Paper Section is found in every advertising agency and in every publisher's office. Price is $20 a year. Other sections are Newspaper, Magazine, Farm, Radio. In 1932, S.R.D.S. listed 1,544 businesspapers in the United States and 151 in Canada. In 1935 (postdepression), S.R.D.S. listed 1,387 in

---

[3] *Ayer's Newspaper Annual & Directory* for 1922, "A Review of Business Press History," by Jesse H. Neal, executive secretary, the Associated Business Papers, Inc.

the United States and 131 in Canada. In 1940, the list had grown to 1,528 in the United States and 146 in Canada. In 1943, there were 1,542 United States and 153 Canadian businesspapers listed.

In the past half century many businesspapers have been consolidated with leaders in the same fields. Indeed, mergers among businesspaper publications seem to have been more frequent than in the case of newspapers or general magazines. Some businesspaper publishers adopt the practice of buying out competitive papers started by opportunist publishers who might lower publishing standards or develop into serious competitors.

PRESS ASSOCIATIONS

In 1887, in Rochester, 51 newspaper publishers met and established the American Newspaper Publishers Association (A.N.P.A.), primarily a newspaper trade organization, to adjust conflict of viewpoint and practice between advertiser, agent, and publisher.

In 1888, the Association of General Newspaper Agents was formed in New York, the first organized advertising group.

In 1890, the Business Writers Association was started in Detroit as a social group.

In 1894, the Agate Club was formed in Chicago by magazine advertising representatives and claims to be the oldest advertising club in the United States.

In 1895, sixty farm paper publishers, editors, and business managers formed the Agricultural Press League of Chicago.

In 1896, the Sphinx Club was formed in New York to bring together advertisers, agents, publishers, and men in related activities.

THE RISE OF "MERCHANDISING" PAPERS

Two natural desires on the part of manufacturers of consumers' goods brought about a change at the turn of the century: a desire to tell the world about their own business and a curiosity to learn more about their competitors' business. The manufacturer was beginning to feel proud of his own accomplishments. He wanted a vehicle in which he could glorify himself and his business to other businessmen. He wanted to reach his market more regularly. He did not want all his eggs resting in the drummer's sample trunk. He wanted wider distribution for his product.

The day of specialized businesspaper publishing had begun. In turning to the specialized business press as a vehicle to reach these goals, the manufacturer sought circulation without waste: he wanted the readers of his message to be either potential or actual buyers of his products or services. He wanted a direct approach to his own customers which was not possible in a daily newspaper. His advertising circulars seemed to lack authority. He wanted the authority of independent publishing auspices for his product news, in a publication whose chief interest was his kind of business and whose readers were his buyers or prospects.

He wanted his message "next to reading matter," but *legitimate* reading matter. Even today many advertisers in the business press will order a half page next to legitimate news columns or next to the carry-over of a feature article in preference to a full-page advertisement in the front or the back of the magazine.

Much of the advertising in businesspapers of this era, however, failed to pull because the copy played up the vanity of the advertiser and ignored the problems of the reader.

Printers' Ink,[4] perhaps the most authoritative historian of this transition period in the history of the business press of the United States writes:

The old-time business man [prior to 1895] believed in maintaining a veil of secrecy over all his movements. He was extremely jealous of competitors and the idea of publishing news concerning the flow of business was not at all relished. The pioneer business publishers had no easy time.

In the very earliest days the business periodical was represented by a handful of journals of broad editorial scope. A single paper, for example, would cover all phases of mechanical matters, another every type of manufacturing product. Lists of topics were comprehensive.

Then came new papers which addressed themselves to some specific

[4] Fiftieth Anniversary Issue, July 28, 1938, which is recommended to students of business journalism for its complete and authentic survey of the past half century of business from the advertising, merchandising, and sales promotion viewpoint.

branch of business which seemed inadequately served by the more general publications. . . . The specialized businesspaper was the outgrowth of an endeavor of the "wholesale man," or manufacturer, to find his customer in a more direct manner than was possible through the daily newspapers, and it took the rudimentary form of putting his wares under the customers' eyes in an advertising circular to which was attached a thread of reading matter on some subject that might interest the readers. In other words, it was simply a house organ.

Some few newspaper men, usually of limited means and experience, took up the idea of publishing papers of their own. The conditions were not favorable for attraction of the best talent and the possibilities of the field were not recognized. Business journals were looked upon as a luxury and support was to be had only through cultivating the vanity of manufacturers. Facts were ignored in favor of windy write-ups given in return for advertising contracts. The businesspaper was still a house organ, though published by proxy.

Gradually these publishers, or wiser men who succeeded them, came to learn the practical disadvantages of servility and slowly the fawning clipsheet gave way to the paper that stood on its own independent feet. It was seen that success depended upon *bona fide* circulation, which in turn rested with favoring the reader in terms of progressive and fearless news-gathering methods. Though the publisher who remained with his face turned toward the advertiser was still in the majority in 1890—and has not entirely disappeared to this day—the businesspaper which stood as the exponent of progress and guardian of sound practice in the trade it represented had made its mark.

As early as 1898, manufacturers, in their consumer advertising, were warning women against an allegedly "dangerous" practice among storekeepers: substituting something just-as-good for a nationally advertised brand. Sometimes the retailer or dealer openly advocated a private brand when a customer asked for X brand. Many inferior counterfeits were palmed off on the gullible public. This is not to say, however, that many inferior items were not palmed off on the gullible public under the shield of national advertising in the nineties.

Retailers had started a practice of selling well-known national brands below cost as "loss leaders" to bring traffic into their stores. This uneconomic practice continued until World War II.

In consumer advertising, appearing in general magazines and large city newspapers at the turn of the century, the retail trade was bitterly attacked by manufacturers for these practices.

On his side of the fence, the retail merchant resented having trade-marked goods or national brands arbitrarily shoved down his throat with orders to shove it down his customer's throat.

Important retailers, large department store proprietors particularly, considered their store name more important in their own communities than any manufacturer's trade-mark. Their customers seemed content to buy unknown goods on the recommendation of the retailers. In some cases this position was justified. Retailers had built local institutions on foundations of integrity and service. Their buyers were good judges of quality. The store brand was often better than a national brand, and usually better known locally.

As early as 1909 the merchandising businesspapers in consumers' goods began to play an important part in resolving the difficulties that existed between manufacturers, who were their prospective advertisers, and retailers, who composed the bulk of their readership. Editors of businesspapers in these fields had been for some time painfully conscious of the many defects in the system of distribution of both goods and information about goods. They pointed out to manufacturers that the retailer was interested chiefly in his *own* problems and that manufacturers would be well-advised to study those problems and write their businesspaper advertising copy in terms of the retailers' problems—in a language the retailer was accustomed to speaking—instead of employing self-glorification copy, illustrated with pictures of factories.

Manufacturers were also advised what retailers wanted and urged to satisfy those wants. Surveys showed that retailers wanted definite kinds of sales promotion aids, sometimes called dealer helps: advertising displays to fit the size and suit the needs of their interiors, counters, and their windows rather than to suit the aesthetic tastes of some advertising agency's art director. They wanted direct mail material which talked the same language they used in their own newspaper advertising copy, not an agency copywriter's literary effusions.

Manufacturers found the retail dealer or merchant had problems of stock control, sales training, slow turnover, price-lining, returned goods, markups and markdowns, warehousing, shipping, deliveries, and storage; and problems of anticipating style trends and seasonal demands. They discovered, to their amazement, that retail promotions were planned 60 to 90 days ahead of the event, in large stores, that retail merchants had to know in July what a manufacturer intended to offer in September in the way of merchandise or promotional ideas as well as what kind of advertising copy consumers would read in September magazines or hear on the air.

The manufacturer found that the best place to *merchandise* his consumer advertising campaign, his forthcoming promotional plans, his new styles, or colors, or designs, or packaging, or other ideas, was in columns of the merchandising businesspaper reaching his particular type of buyers, well in advance of the release of similar news to consumer media. His salesmen began to request such businesspaper advertising to pave the way for their calls on the trade, and to help move goods after they had sold it to the wholesale or retail trade.

While the consumer advertising exerted *pull* on customers in the direction of retail store counters, businesspaper advertising copy, by educating dealers on the merits of national brands and the services of producers, exerted a *push* on the goods itself. As a result, goods moved over counters and off floors into consumer homes at a rapid rate of turnover.

Manufacturers began to publish lists of their dealers in each trading area, in their consumer magazine advertising, and particularly in newspapers having coverage in the area in which large groups of dealers were located. They began to discover that retailers wanted fair treatment in the matter of price maintenance, uniform rather than special discounts, and that they demanded loyalty from the manufacturer as the price of loyalty from the retailer.

Some manufacturers adopted a system of selective distribution:

one dealer to a given territory, eliminating the cutthroat competition that follows when, for example, three stores in the same neighborhood, carrying a similar brand, start to outpromote each other by price reductions.

Manufacturers began to allocate more of their advertising funds for market studies and dealer surveys. Advertising managers and agency men, including copywriters, put on their hats and departed from their ivory towers to visit the market and learn its problems at first hand.

New processes in printing and engraving made it possible to furnish retailers with direct mail material, bearing the store imprint, that reflected credit on both the store and the product. Better types of matrices and electrotypes carrying a higher quality of copy and illustration were prepared for retail newspaper advertising.

Businesspaper publishers in merchandising fields began to survey their fields to prove that their readership was as good as they had been claiming it was. Many began issuing audited circulation statements.

Federation of Trade Press Associations

"Something else that had been holding up businesspaper growth was the unpeaceful state of affairs existing between agents and publishers," *Printers' Ink* reported. "The former complained of cut rates, uncertain circulation and lack of commissions. The large majority of papers paid no agent's commission. The publishers, on the other hand, resented the slight regard which the agents accorded the businesspaper as an advertising proposition and felt, often rightly, that the agent was unable to handle technical accounts intelligently. About 1913 both sides began to take steps to compose the differences and two years later the Federation of Trade Press Associations established an agency relations committee to confer with agents and establish a basis for mutual cooperation."

The first trade press associations were formed early in the twentieth century when less than 150 businesspapers were functioning.

One association operated in New England, one in Chicago, one in St. Louis, and one in New York.

The Federation of Trade Press Associations in the United States was formed in 1906. In 1913 the federation took active steps to effect a closer organization and in 1914 adopted "Standards of Practice"[5] for businesspapers. The same year similar standards were endorsed by the Associated Advertising Clubs of the world, which had been organized a year previous as the American Federation of Advertising Clubs.

Associated Business Papers, Inc.

However, it was not until 1916 that a new constitution was adopted and the new name, Associated Business Papers, Inc., was taken. The purpose, as stated in its constitution and by-laws was "to foster the best interests of the business press and to secure the proper solution of problems common to trade, class and technical papers."

The A.B.P. barred from membership "organs or mouthpieces of any house or combination of houses to further its or their special interest as against the joint interest of the trade."

The job faced by charter members of the Associated Business Papers was no small one. Through their efforts the businesspaper division of the Audit Bureau of Circulations was brought into existence. The charter members of A.B.P. drew up standards of practice in 1916 in pursuance of a new theory: *that businesspapers should be edited for the reader, not the advertiser.* For many years this original code of 1916 stood as a publishing guide for every businesspaper member or nonmember which operated to render a real service to subscribers and advertisers.

However, new business and publishing concepts developed during the next two decades. In 1939, the Associated Business Papers unanimously adopted a "Revised Code of Ethics and Standard of Practice" (see Chart 32, Chap. XI, "Function of the Editor"). Each A.B.P. member publication pledges itself to observe these high professional standards. The membership of A.B.P. is limited

[5] See Chart 32.

to businesspapers with paid circulations which are also members of the Audit Bureau of Circulations.

NATIONAL BUSINESS PAPERS ASSOCIATION

For businesspapers which are members of the Controlled Circulation Audit, there is the National Business Papers Association (N.B.P.). Organized in New York in June, 1940, its purposes, according to Rex W. Wadman, president, are "to serve as a medium for the interchange of ideas" . . . "to gather and disseminate statistical information" . . . "to foster a better understanding of the function and usefulness of these publications by those who can and should benefit by their use." Papers in this association do not have paid subscribers. The method of distribution is free circulation. For more on the "Controlled Circulation" paper see Chapter IX.

AMERICAN ASSOCIATION OF ADVERTISING AGENCIES

Called the "4A's" in publishing circles, this organization was an amalgamation, in 1917, of New England, New York, Philadelphia, southern and western advertising agency associations. Executive headquarters of its 133 member firms who operate more than 251 offices all over the country (June, 1943, figures) is 420 Lexington Avenue, New York. Purpose, as stated to the author:

One of the major aims of the association is to keep advertising agency practices on a high level,[6] in order that it may be most useful to the advertiser, most helpful to the publisher and respected by businessmen.

Through its various committees, it seeks to improve agency technics in media selection, art, mechanical production, radio broadcasting, and other functions, and endeavors to standardize financial and accounting practices for the better conduct of the agency business. It also offers members a clearinghouse of infor-

[6] Any connection with or interest in an advertising medium, printing, engraving or other business supplying material to its clients, or a part ownership by an advertiser disqualifies an agency from 4A membership. Rebating of commissions also is considered unethical.

mation at headquarters on any subject that pertains to advertising, marketing, or the advertising agency business. It engages in scientific research of circulations, markets, and technics, and participates in joint research work done co-operatively by advertiser, agency, and media owners, such as the Advertising Research Foundation, the Traffic Audit Bureau, and similar bodies in the publication field.

The association takes an active part in guiding and defining the public relations of advertising, involving consumer education, constructive legislation, and helpful contacts with the government.

A fusion of organized communication agencies in advertising and publishing resulted in the formation of the Advertising Council during World War II. This council provided effectively organized contact with the war effort, and a chance, particularly for advertising agencies, to make a direct and substantial contribution[7] toward winning the war.

NATIONAL INDUSTRIAL ADVERTISERS ASSOCIATION

For years the extractive and transformative industries had neglected or ignored the merchandising function in selling to other processing industries. As so-called "industrial" buying became more and more discriminating, these extractors and semifinished goods manufacturers recognized the great need for better advertising and marketing technics and practices. Small groups which had met regularly in several cities, in 1922 established N.I.A.A. with organization headquarters in Chicago, and district chapters in key industrial cities.

District chapters of N.I.A.A. meet once or twice a month for clinical or round-table sessions or to listen to outside speakers. Annual conferences are held. Advertising, sales promotion managers, agency account executives, businesspaper and service organization executives make up the membership. Investigations are

[7] Chester La Roche, chairman of the Advertising Council, and consultant of the Office of War Information, declared, July 14, 1943, in an NBC broadcast: "Advertising agencies have contributed 4 million dollars worth of time and skill—the radio industry 100 million dollars of time and talent—to the war effort."

conducted on advertising and marketing, budget procedure, standard records and contracts, direct mail and catalogue practice, public relations, United States census activities, publishers' statements, and phases of distribution.

The "Publisher's Statement" of the N.I.A.A. (See Chart 19) is an analytical form which, when filled with the requested information, provides a check for users of businesspaper space. Another form is provided for users of catalogues and directories and for publications issued by charity and political enterprises. A bulletin, *How and Why to Use the NIAA Publisher's Statement*, is also issued.

ASSOCIATION OF NATIONAL ADVERTISERS

This association in 1943 represented over 300 national advertisers, many of whom were among the largest in the country. These advertisers included firms in virtually every classification of industry, from makers of food to makers of steel. They spend over $300,000,000 a year for advertising, and their individual budgets range in size all the way from a few thousands to several millions.

In June, 1910, advertising managers of 17 of the largest companies in the United States met in a hotel in Detroit to discuss their current problems. At that time there was no organization composed of, or acting in the interests of, buyers of advertising. These men decided that what they needed most was a forum where the problems of advertisers could be discussed intimately and impartially, a place where one could hear and profit from the experience of the others, an organization which would express the voice of them all and would become a power for protecting their mutual interests and increasing the efficiency of their advertising expenditures. So they founded the Association of National Advertising Managers, later to be changed to the Association of National Advertisers, Inc.

The association aims to eliminate experiment in the buying of service, space, printing, and in formulating sales and merchandising plans as much as possible. It fosters the practice of scientific principles in advertising, gathers fresh and accurate sales and advertising information, and co-operates with other organizations in the advertising and sales field.

Many of the organizations and facilities on which all advertisers now depend with confidence and often take for granted, including the Audit Bureau of Circulations, the Advertising Research Foundation, the Co-operative Analysis of Broadcasting, the Traffic Audit Bureau and others, originated as activities of, or through the efforts of, the A.N.A.

ADVERTISING FEDERATION OF AMERICA

Advertising, spark plug of business, began to think of itself nationally in 1905. In Chicago that year the various advertising clubs of key cities organized as the American Federation of Advertising Clubs, a year later changing their name to Associated Advertising Clubs of America. In 1911, the "Truth-in-Advertising" movement was launched. In 1914, the name was changed to Associated Advertising Clubs of the World and a year later the first educational program was launched. In 1916, the first Women's Advertising Club was founded. In 1922, a speakers' bureau began operating. In 1926, the name was again changed, to International Advertising Association, and in 1928 a bureau of research and education was established. In 1929, the present name was adopted. Advertising agents, journalists, publishers, radio broadcasters, publicity men, advertising managers for manufacturers, retail stores, utilities and railroads and trade association officials make up its board of directors. Prime objective of A.F.A. is:

"To help make advertising increasingly effective as an instrument of distribution" and "to preserve freedom of individual enterprise in America."

MARKET PUBLICATIONS

Market Data Book (Industrial and Consumer Annual Edition) is published by Advertising Publications, Inc., which also publishes *Advertising Age* and *Industrial Marketing*. It contains a wealth of valuable market information and analyses, useful in planning an advertising campaign.

Brad-Vern's Reports

Purchased in 1943 by *Printers' Ink*, a valuable annual study of businesspaper advertising schedules was started in January, 1939, by the energetic Van Diver family: Vernon H. Van Diver, advertising manager of Union Carbide & Carbon, his wife and their two sons, Bradford (15) and Vernon Jr. (17), whose combined names gave the service its name. The 1942 report reflected the advertising schedules of about 25,000 concerns using some 516 businesspapers. Brad-Vern helps a buyer of businesspaper space to estimate the amount of advertising being done by his competitors and contemporaries and judge what papers lead their field in volume of advertising. Some businesspapers, however, do not submit reports to this service. The figures are given quarterly and reflect seasonal variations, but are intentionally not accurate with reference to smaller than page units of space. The reports are issued annually and the last one (1942) cost $12.50 a copy.

Dotted Line Clubs, New York and Chicago

In New York and Chicago the salesmen of A.B.P. papers are organized in Dotted Line Clubs. Membership is restricted to the salesmen on A.B.P. member papers, and the desire of salesmen with nonmember companies to join such clubs and attend the meetings bears witness to their value. Meeting monthly and working together on common problems, they are enabled to do a better job of selling. Each meeting yields tangible, worth-while, workable ideas for the salesmen who participate. A.B.P. absorbs the cost of this activity; no special fees or dues are involved.

Promotion and Circulation Round Tables

Also for the exclusive benefit of the promotion managers and circulation managers of A.B.P. members are the Promotion and Circulation Round Tables conducted in New York and Chicago. In separate meetings, promotion managers and circulation managers gather periodically to discuss their common problems. As a result, each man carries back to his desk new ideas which others have found successful in the promotion and circulation departments.

NATIONAL CONFERENCE OF BUSINESS PAPER EDITORS[8]

For the exclusive benefit of the editors of A.B.P. papers, the A.B.P. trade association sponsors the National Conference of Business Paper Editors. This conference meets periodically in Washington for shirt-sleeve, off-the-record interviews with important government officials, from the President down. Congressmen and members of the diplomatic corps are included in these conferences. More than 90 businesspaper editors crowded around President Roosevelt's desk at a White House conference during the strenuous war days of June, 1943. The President was in his shirt sleeves, puffing a cigarette in an ivory holder which jutted from the side of his mouth at a cocky angle. He was in fine fettle. News of the capture by the Allies of the island of Pantelleria in the Mediterranean, steppingstone to Sicily and the continent of Europe, had just reached him. The president of the Conference of Editors, Paul Wooton, started his introductory remarks:

"Mr. President, there are so many of us this morning, we will dispense with the usual handshaking and introductions. Before you commence your off-the-record remarks I would like to say that the business press has done a pretty good job in the war effort to date and—"

PRESIDENT ROOSEVELT (interrupting): "Are you trying to sell me the business press, Paul? I'm sold. Go no further!"

MR. WOOTON (smiling): "I simply wanted to say—"

THE PRESIDENT (interrupting again): "You are not going to say anything this time. *I'm* going to be the spokesman for the business press today! I'm going to tell *you* what they think of *you* and what I think of you! I have been waiting for this opportunity for years."

---

[8] See Chap. XI, "Function of the Editor," for a description of activities of the National Conference in wartime. See also Appendix III, "Agenda of Three Wartime Editorial Conferences."

Smiling broadly at Wooton's astonishment and discomfiture, the President reached into his desk drawer and brought out a gold watch and a slip of typewritten manuscript. He read aloud the copy of the engraved inscription on the watch:

Presented to Paul Wooton by President Franklin D. Roosevelt on behalf of The Associated Business Papers, in appreciation of his outstanding service to the business press in time of war. June 11, 1943

These conferences, held over a long period of years, have made official Washington conscious of the vital importance, power, and influence of the business press. The editors of the National Conference also meet in other key cities for off-the-record sessions with industrial leaders.

UNIVERSITY SPEAKERS BUREAU

Alarmed by the fact that the marketing courses in colleges and universities were devoted almost exclusively to general magazine, newspaper, and radio advertising, A.B.P. several years ago established an Educational Committee for the purpose of inducing college instructors to describe the functions of businesspapers in their lectures on advertising and marketing and journalism. Members of the Educational Committee deliver class lectures in more than a score of colleges each year, but as it is incidental to the editor's overcrowded routine, it cannot be described as a major activity at present.

NEW YORK AND CHICAGO BUSINESS EDITORS LUNCHEON CLUBS

Two large publishing centers of the business press are New York and Chicago. Each of these cities has an organization of editors and assistant editors of businesspapers. They meet at monthly luncheons for shop talks or to listen to speakers in their own and related fields. The sessions are well-attended and the groups act as clearinghouses for new ideas and methods of business journalism practice. These groups act also as personnel placement centers.

BUSINESS NEWS SERVICE

In October, 1943, a much-needed news service, modeled along the lines of the United Press, was organized by Ray Bill, publisher of *Sales Management*, in New York City. It is called Business News Service (B.N.S.). Mr. Bill is president and the member publication circulation at the end of 1944 was in excess of 658,000. Maintaining a staff of reporters in its Washington office, B.N.S. furnishes its member papers with a number of news services, and an editorial and monthly feature article by "big name" writers and authors in the fields of business economics.

ANNUAL BUSINESSPAPER AWARDS

Two awards are made every year, one for the best editorial accomplishment and one for the best industrial advertisement. The editorial award is given by G. D. Crain, publisher of *Industrial Marketing*, Chicago. The advertising competition, originated by the Chicago Business Papers Association, was turned over, in 1943, to the Associated Business Papers, who now sponsor it as a national event. Appropriate recognition of good editorials and good advertisements acts as a stimulant to improve the standards in both fields.

CHAPTER VI

TRADE ASSOCIATIONS AND THE BUSINESS PRESS

Modern Trade and Professional Associations

The specialized business press maintains a close and intimate contact with the trade and professional associations. These contemporary associations are important sources of news and statistical information for businesspapers. Conversely, the business press is itself utilized by trade association officials, both as a carrier and as a source of information. But more than this, the trade association provides the framework for industrial self-government, in which business journalists are deeply interested.

It is not uncommon for businesspaper publishers and chief editors to assume presidencies and directorships of trade and professional associations. Trade associations are sometimes born in the offices of businesspapers.[1] Publishers and editors of businesspapers constantly participate in the programs of trade and professional associations.

The trade association and the chamber of commerce are often regarded as modern business instruments for organizing specialized trade information and disseminating it to the membership and to related fields of interest. Both are old devices.[2] Their prototypes were the Merchant Guilds (Gilda Mercatoria) of the Middle Ages (see Chart 6) which survived the first four centuries of modern times. These early trade associations were news-clearing

[1] National Retail Dry Goods Association was created in the office of the editor of *Department Store Economist*; Linen Trade Association, dormant 25 years, was revived in the editorial offices of a new business magazine, *Linens & Domestics*; American Society of Mechanical Engineers was founded in the office of *American Machinist*; American Society of Chemical Engineers started in the office of the progenitor of *Chemical and Metallurgical Engineering*.

[2] Guild of Shang-Kieu merchants existed in China in 1686 B.C.

Exhibit 4.

RELATIVE IMPORTANCE OF THE 20 GROUPS OF MANUFACTURING INDUSTRIES (1939), AND NUMBER OF NATIONAL AND INTERSTATE TRADE ASSOCIATIONS IN EACH (1941)

"MANUFACTURING" is the largest single field of employment and of national income in the United States. In 1939 (latest Census of Manufactures) there were over 9,600,000 employees in the more than 184,000 factory establishments. Factory products were valued at $57,000,000,000. For 1939-41 trends in manufacturing, see Exhibit 5.

There are approximately 1,100 national and interstate trade associations of manufacturers. Data on each are given in Section 2.

Shown below is the relative size of each of the 20 major groups into which the Census Bureau divides "Industrial America" (ranked according to value added by manufacture), and the number of larger trade associations in each. The names of a few larger associations in each group, as to size of paid staff, are also given.

As is seen below, the "FOOD" group was the largest as to value added by manufacture—but "TEXTILES" was first as to number of employees. "IRON AND STEEL" was first as to amount of payroll (and during war years is usually first as to number of employees).

Value added by mfr. (billions)	GROUP	Value of products (billions)	Number of— Employees*	Number of— Establishments	A FEW LARGER NATIONAL TRADE ASSNS. (as to number on staff)	Approx. no. of Trade Assns. (see Sec.7)
$3.6	FOOD	$10.6	937,000 (1,132,000)	51,448	American Meat Institute (55 staff) National Canners Assn. (55)	150
3.0	IRON & STEEL	6.6	1,063,000 (1,127,000)	8,994	American Institute of Steel Construction (30) American Iron & Steel Institute (35)	120
2.0	MACHINERY (Exc. Electrical)	3.3	630,000 (680,000)	9,506	Machinery & Allied Products Institute (10) Nat. Machine Tool Builders Assn. (15)	100
1.9	CHEMICALS	3.7	350,000 (404,000)	9,203	National Fertilizer Assn. (25) National Paint, Varnish & Lacquer Assn. (40)	70
1.8	TEXTILES	3.9	1,138,000 (1,162,000)	6,444	Cotton Textile Institute (30) National Federation of Textiles (55)	70
1.8	PRINTING & PUBLISHING	2.6	468,000 (553,000)	24,878	American Newspaper Publishers Assn. (50) Lithographers National Assn. (15)	70
1.4	APPAREL	3.4	812,000 (845,000)	20,206	National Coat & Suit Industry Recovery Board (85)	90
1.3	AUTOMOBILES (& Equipment)	4.0	445,000 (440,000)	1,133	Automobile Manufacturers Assn. (80)	10
1.0	ELECTRICAL MACHINERY	1.7	314,000 (335,000)	2,014	National Electrical Mfrs. Assn. (75)	20
0.9	STONE, CLAY & GLASS	1.4	321,000 (328,000)	7,024	Portland Cement Assn. (450)	70
0.9	PAPER	2.0	296,000 (315,000)	3,279	American Paper & Pulp Assn. (20)	60
0.8	NONFERROUS METALS	2.6	263,000 (282,000)	5,600	Copper & Brass Research Assn. (15)	40
0.7	PETROLEUM & COAL	3.0	125,000 (143,000)	989	American Petroleum Institute (80)	20
0.6	FURNITURE, ETC.	1.3	320,000 (345,000)	8,457	National Assn. of Furniture Mfrs. (6)	50
0.6	LUMBER	1.1	385,000 (459,000)	11,520	National Lumber Mfrs. Assn. (50)	50
0.6	LEATHER	1.4	352,000 (382,000)	3,508	Tanners Council of America (25)	20
0.5	TRANSPORTATION EQUIP. (Exc. Auto.)	0.9	185,000 (189,000)	968	Aeronautical Chamber of Commerce (25)	30
0.4	RUBBER	0.9	123,000 (128,000)	595	Rubber Manufacturers Assn. (25)	5
0.4	TOBACCO	1.3	88,000 (88,000)	765	Tobacco Merchants Assn. (15)	5
0.7	MISCELLANEOUS	1.2	337,000 (357,000)	7,699	- - -	60
$24,682,918,119		$56,843,024,800	8,935,174 (9,022,923)	184,230		1,110

Top figures are total wage and salaried employees engaged in manufacturing, plus salaried officers. United States totals were: 7,886,567 wage earners; 909,257 manufacturing salaried employees; 139,350 salaried officers; a total of 8,935,174. In addition, there were 687,749 construction and repair employees, salesmen, etc., of manufacturing companies; making a grand total of 9,022,923. The bracketed figures include these 687,749 additional employees.

Source: Trade assn. data—U. S. Department of Commerce, Trade Association Section; other data—U. S. Department of Commerce, Bureau of the Census.

*Trade and Professional Associations of the U. S., 1941 Edition,**U. S. Dept. of Commerce.
(10)

CHART 9

houses, pressure groups, sometimes monopolies, and also social clubs. Members, for their fixed dues[3] (*gild* or *geld*, Anglo-Saxon; *gilde*, Danish and Low German; meaning contribution) were afforded not only protection and fellowship, but business news information much more accurate and timely than they could secure in any other way. In Chapter IV we described how one merchant-adventurer, Sir Thomas Gresham, operated to gather business news for the guidance of his associates in the Mercer's Company and later for his sovereign.

The "guild" idea is even more important in contemporary business life and destined to play a much greater role in the future.

Of the 3 million or more individual business enterprises in the United States, the overwhelming majority hold membership in one or more of our 12,000 co-operative business groups. There are about 8,000 trade and professional associations, 4,000 chambers of commerce, and numerous other types of community development and business organizations. Unofficial estimates place the total membership at more that 2 million units.[4]

Since 1913, the Department of Commerce has issued 11 directories of trade and professional associations. The current one (1942) contains a wealth of information about these national and interstate business associations of our country: size of staff, membership, and principal services offered to members. It is a useful handbook for the businesspaper editor.

There is a distinction—not always clear—between trade and professional associations.

---

[3] Dues in modern U.S. trade associations are collected by seven methods, in the following order of popularity:

Volume of business	38.8%
Flat rate	26.7
Unit of product	16.4
Number of employees	4.3
Capital investment	2.1
Agency rating	1.8
Payroll	1.4

From *Financing a Trade Association*, Chamber of Commerce of the United States, Washington, D.C.

[4] Considering the 12,000 associations as a whole, New York leads with 2,100 and California is second with 1,200.

A trade association, as defined by C. J. Judkins, trade association specialist of the U.S. Department of Commerce,[5] as "a voluntary non-profit organization of business competitors (usually in one branch of the manufacturing, distributing or service fields), the objective of which is to assist its members and its industry in dealing with mutual business problems in several of the following areas: accounting practices, business ethics, commercial research, industrial research, standardization, statistics, trade promotion, and relations with the Government, with labor, and with the general public."[6] This definition excludes such single-purpose associations as credit bureaus.

Some of the difficulties in drawing a line of demarcation between a trade association and a professional association, in certain cases, are discussed in the National Industrial Conference Board's Report on "Trade Associations: Their Economic Significance and Legal Status" (1929). The board points out:

". . . One of the distinguishing characteristics of a trade association is to be found in the fact that its membership is ordinarily limited to persons or firms engaged in a particular trade or industry—to the producers, or distributors, or both, of a particular product or generic class of products."

"On this basis, such 'general business organizations' as the Chamber of Commerce of the United States or the National Association of Manufacturers, or corresponding local organizations, cannot be classified as trade associations. . . . On the other hand, those associated in the operation of commodity exchanges for the marketing of the staple products of agriculture which are subject to accurate grading may be deemed to be organized into a special type of trade association. Trade associations do not themselves produce, buy, or sell goods for profit . . ."

The Cotton Textile Institute is a trade association (business competitors in one industry).

The American Arbitration Association is a business association

---

[5] U.S. Dept. of Commerce *Directory of Trade and Professional Associations*, 11th Edition, Washington, 1942, by C. J. Judkins.

[6] National Institute, founded in 1921, is the only annual summer school for executives of associations and chambers. The 1944 seminars were conducted at Northwestern University, Chicago, Ill.

composed of businessmen, but *not* a trade association, under this definition.

Professional organizations are not regarded by the National Industrial Conference Board as trade associations. "The professional societies are composed of *individuals*, united primarily by a common *intellectual* interest in a particular field." Trade associations, on the other hand, the board holds, are "organizations of *business units*, which may be corporations, partnerships, or individual enterprises, and the common interest of the membership is primarily *economic* rather than intellectual."

CHAMBERS OF COMMERCE

One of the earliest business associations in our country is the Chamber of Commerce of the State of New York, organized in 1768. Similar associations of traders were formed soon afterward in Boston and Philadelphia, and in 1773 a Chamber of Commerce was established in Charleston, S.C.

American chambers of commerce are corporations concerned with purely local or community affairs. They are represented in Washington by a federated association, called the Chamber of Commerce of the United States, which publishes a monthly news magazine, *Nation's Business*.

FEDERATED TRADE ASSOCIATIONS

By 1900 there were about 100 national and interstate trade associations. By 1920 there were more than 1,000. By 1942 there were about 8,000 trade and professional groups, and a great many "federated" trade associations.

World War I (1917-1918), the National Recovery Act (NRA) 1935-1937,[7] and World War II stimulated the growth of the trade association movement just as they stimulated labor and farm organization movements. In extreme emergencies, businessmen tend to band together and seek the advantages of co-operation and common action with their competitors. When times are lush they have

[7] Some 300 "national" associations, formed during 1935-1937, disbanded in 1938-1941.

a tendency to fall apart, and forget the advantages of co-operation.

Bernard Baruch, who was chairman of the War Industries Board in World War I, paid high tribute to the assistance he received from trade associations.[8] In World War II, Donald Nelson, of WPB, leaned heavily on trade associations for help in the battle of production.

Among the largest trade associations, from the standpoint of membership, is the National Association of Retail Grocers with 60,000 members and a staff of 20. Food industry tops the list in number of associations (see Chart 9).

The Portland Cement Association, with a staff of 450, has only 75 members (see Chart 9).

Names of trade associations can be misleading. Many associations employ the use of the term "national" although their influence is purely local or regional. The word "national" is no guarantee that an association is national in scope or even the voice of its industry. The word "association" is no indication that an organization has more than a half dozen members, all that is required to incorporate as an "association." "National" and "federal" and "American" are often propaganda words employed in the names taken by small pressure groups. Some full-purpose trade associations use such a word as "bureau," "institute," "conference" or even "guild," as part of their name. Some private companies use the word "association" or even "industries" for their peculiar purposes. The businesspaper editor must have no false illusions about any group he is dealing with or giving publicity to. He should *know* its size, structure, and objectives, and its officers.

Many changes in the structure of trade associations, in order to present a united front to the government, took place after the enactment of the National Industrial Recovery Act in 1933. The Federated Trade Association came into being to co-ordinate the functions of numerous trade associations in the same industry, representing different geographical districts or different products.[9]

The National Association of Retail Grocers is a horizontal fed-

[8] *American Industry in the War*, by Bernard Baruch.
[9] *Federated Trade Associations*, a booklet published by the Chamber of Commerce of the United States, 1939.

eration of state associations. Each state grocers' association sends one delegate for each 50 members to the national conclaves.

The National Lumber Dealers Association is another federation of state, regional, and metropolitan associations or groups of retail lumber dealers. Individual dealers are not eligible.

Some of these associations are *vertical*, like the Better Vision Institute, Inc., which serves such groups as the Optical Manufacturers Association, Optical Wholesalers Association, and the Guild of Dispensing Opticians.

Other examples of the federated vertical setup are the Associated Wool Industries organized by the National Wool Trade Association, the National Association of Wool Manufacturers, and the National Wool Growers Association.

A typical horizontal association is the National Electrical Manufacturers Association which has more than 100 "product" divisions.

INDUSTRIAL SELF-GOVERNMENT

The purpose in providing this trade association background material for students of business journalism is to show that a framework and pattern of experience exists for industrial self-government. As the antidote for bureaucracy in government, business journalists are constantly advocating that business develop its own capacity for self-government. The reasons why the trade association has often failed in this respect will accumulate as we proceed with this chapter.

President Franklin D. Roosevelt's "New Deal" administration attempted to utilize the country's trade associations, in 1933, as working units in a broad program for business recovery, under the National Industrial Recovery Act. A year later Donald R. Richberg, an administration spokesman, expressed keen disappointment in the kind of business statesmanship he had found in the then existing trade associations. Mr. Richberg, who was the first chief of NRA,[10] told a convention of the National Association of Manufacturers:

"We found few trade associations truly representative of an entire trade or industry, and even in the best of them the capacity

[10] National Recovery Administration.

for self-government was pretty weak. Probably in the long years of intermittent and uncertain enforcement of the anti-trust laws,[11] it could not be expected that strong trade associations would develop. It was the early vision of the NRA that when trades and industries were integrated under codes of fair competition, a voluntary coordination of their activities could be worked out in the second stage of NRA through some sort of a national industrial council, which might attract to its deliberations the elder statesmen of business. Now we know that there is a long road to travel before we reach that stage of economic progress. . . . *We found that business men were theoretically opposed to government interference, but practically anxious to wield political power in the disciplining of their recalcitrant competitors. Thus, as usual, political power was beloved by those whom it favored and denounced by those on whom it frowned.*"[12]

Businessmen often deride the ineptitude of Congress, but in drafting rules of conduct for their own industries, in 1934, trade association executives got themselves as hopelessly involved as congressmen sometimes do when drafting national legislation. As a result, from 1934 to 1941 there was a steady trend toward industrial government by federal bureaus, which reached a peak in World War II.

Since there is no agreement among businessmen or among congressmen as to what constitutes legal or illegal "restraint of trade," there is today no clean line of demarcation between "co-operation" and "conspiracy" in trade association activity. Some clarification would serve as a guide for postwar industrial self-government. This is a problem which will bear close watching and study by business journalists and students of business administration.

PROBLEM: CONCENTRATION OF ECONOMIC POWER

An important point for students of business and business journalism to fix in their minds is that the consumer and small business

[11] *Does Trade Need Anti-Trust Laws?* by Alexander Levene. Ray Long and Richard H. Smith, Inc., New York, 1931.
[12] Annual Convention, National Association of Manufacturers, Waldorf-Astoria, New York, December, 1934. See also *Government & Business Tomorrow* by Donald R. Richberg. Harper & Brothers, New York, 1943.

can be protected only by *compelling* competition.[13] Thus, the
Sherman Antitrust Act, after more than half a century, is still one
of the most important economic and political issues in our country
which, by the way, is the only country with a comprehensive
written statute against monopoly and restraint of trade. No student of business or of business journalism, when he joins a firm or
a businesspaper, can hope to understand clearly all that is going on
in his particular field unless he knows the background and philosophy of antitrust legislation. No field of business is immune to its
influence. One reason for the contention that industrial self-government has failed may be found in the fact that in some industries a *few* companies, by reason of their great business volume,
huge capital assets, physical size and economic power, tend to
dominate the activities of all other members of their trade association.[14]

The 6,000 "large" factories of the United States have an average value of production, per factory, of $5 million, or 53 per cent
of the total output, while 157,000 "small" factories averaged $76,-
000 per factory, or 21 per cent of the total output. World War II
greatly increased this concentration of economic power in industry so that by 1943, 200 large concerns controlled 70 per cent of
the total industrial output.[15]

TRADE PRACTICE CONFERENCE

The Federal Trade Commission Act, passed in 1914 and amended
in 1938, set up the FTC as an agency to deal with competitive
conditions in industry, to act to prevent unfair methods of competition and unfair practices in interstate commerce, and to pro-

[13] *Theory of Monopolistic Competition*, by Edward Chamberlin. Harvard
University Press, 1938.

[14] Document No. 35, Investigation of Concentration of Economic Power,
Final Report of TNEC, p. 641. See also TNEC Monograph No. 38, Study of
Construction and Enforcement of Federal Antitrust Laws.

[15] There are about 184,000 manufacturing establishments in the United States.
Before World War II, 100 corporations had 30 per cent of the industrial output
and the remainder had 70 per cent. In 1943, during the war, 200 top corporations,
through 1,400 subcontractors in the upper brackets, had 70 per cent of the industrial output. The figures were given by Tom Clark, assistant attorney general of
the United States, in a radio forum on WOR.

tect the public interest. To do this, rules of fair trade practice are established under what is known as the *trade practice conference* procedure, a plan which has been in operation for more than twenty years. The FTC has conducted more than 200 such conference proceedings and has established rules for fair enterprise in as many industries.

The "public interest" guides the FTC. Trade practice conference proceedings are authorized only when it appears that the public interest will be substantially served. The conference is initiated by application from industry itself, usually through a trade association which can show that its membership in annual volume of business, number of employees, and total capital investment is representative of that industry. Conferences are then held, where interested parties, including representatives of the trade association, the industry, labor, and the consumer, participate with the commission in promulgating competitive standards of business practice. Harmful and unfair trade practices, as well as good practices, are defined and catalogued, and methods for eliminating the bad and sanctioning the good practices are provided.

The essence of the plan is to organize and encourage voluntary co-operative effort, or industrial self-government, to end unfair trade abuses, banish monopolistic practices which restrict private competitive enterprise, to create official, recognized standards, afford guidance respecting the requirements of the law, and to maintain the free and constructive functioning of the competitive economy.[16] In actual practice, the present setup of the Federal Trade Commission for regulating fair trade practices has many weaknesses, some of which are inherent in the trade associations themselves. As we said, it is not easy to draw a clean line between co-operation and conspiracy or between the areas of permissive and prohibitive activities under the changing meaning of "restraint of trade." Joseph J. O'Connell, Jr., special assistant general counsel, Department of the Treasury, testifying before the Temporary National Economic Committee on March 7, 1941,[17] asked that

[16] See Monograph No. 34, Report of the Federal Trade Commission to the Temporary National Economic Committee, U.S. Government Printing Office, Washington, D.C., 1941.

[17] Document No. 35, Investigation of Concentration of Economic Power, Final Report of TNEC, p. 641.

body to recommend to Congress the passage of legislation requiring all trade associations to register with an appropriate federal agency, file periodic reports of their activities, and sworn copies of their minutes, keep open files, and adhere to certain other rules of conduct, as follows:

(a) Use of registration statements and filed reports to facilitate proof of background facts in antitrust litigation.

(b) All files accessible to the government to expedite investigation.

(c) Open covenants openly arrived at by full disclosure and required publicity.

(d) Periodic reports to disclose the initiation of each type of concerted activity and permit the government to take action, if unlawful, before the activity becomes the established practice of the industry.

Mr. O'Connell also recommended that the Federal Trade Commission and the Department of Justice be furnished with more of the "sinews of war," meaning increased appropriations, larger staffs and additional sanctions, to maintain fair competitive enterprise in industry in the public interest and to prosecute illegal monopolistic practices.[18]

BUREAU OF INDUSTRIAL ECONOMICS

President Franklin D. Roosevelt recommended the creation of a Bureau of Industrial Economics, endowed with powers to supplement and supervise the collection of industrial statistics by trade associations. This bureau would function for business the way the Bureau of Agricultural Economics functions for farmers: to disseminate over-all information on market conditions, issue warnings of temporary overproduction and excessive inventories or against the dangers of shortages and bottlenecks. The bureau would also study trade fluctuations, credit facilities, monopolistic trends, and endeavor to keep small business as well informed as big business, in the interest of an orderly and competitive marketplace.[19]

[18] TNEC Report, Joseph J. O'Connell, Jr., special assistant counsel, Department of the Treasury.
[19] S. Doc. 173, 75th Congress, 3rd Session.

FEDERAL RESEARCH LABORATORY

In 1943, Senator Harley M. Kilgore of West Virginia proposed the creation of a national laboratory for industrial research where promising products could be perfected and the knowledge presented to all industry. The facilities of such a laboratory would be at the disposal of small business concerns who cannot afford the expensive modern laboratory equipment maintained by large private corporations. The national laboratory might attract graduate students of scientific schools and independent inventors not interested in joining private laboratories or assigning their patents to large private corporations and to cartels.[20]

Peacetime progress, as well as the effective prosecution of war, require full development and co-ordination of our country's scientific and technical resources. Such a national laboratory, according to its proponents, could promote the most advanced technics for the benefit of all segments of industry, protect the enterprise of inventors and scientists, develop substitutes for strategic and critical materials, and expand free enterprise by making the benefits of scientific discovery available to smaller business. It would break up what is now called a "corner in experimentation" or too tight control of know-how and freedom of enterprise.

AMERICAN ARBITRATION ASSOCIATION

Man's faith in man, in the business world, is not theoretically discussed, but actually *tested* in 1,600 communities of North and South America by the tribunal known as the American Arbitration Association. The late Charles L. Bernheimer, founder of the Arbitration Foundation, and Moses Grossman, founder of the Arbitration Society, amalgamated the two groups in 1926. Today there are branch tribunals in thirty key cities. Headquarters are in New York, in Rockefeller Center.

This tribunal is destined to play a very heavy part in industrial self government of the future. A national panel of 7,000 arbitrators drawn from all walks of life arbitrate a multitude of business

[20] Science Mobilization Act, S.702, 78th Congress, March 30, 1943.

disputes out of court. The records show that in only two per cent of the cases was resort made to the courts for legal enforcement of one of the tribunal's awards or agreements.

The arbitrators are not theorists but men who daily write and execute the terms of thousands of business contracts, who risk their own possessions in competitive enterprise, and therefore have wide and deep experience in economic controversy and business ethics. Many disputes between labor and management were settled during World War II by the tribunal with minimum delay and cost.

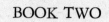

BOOK TWO

THE ORGANIZATION OF A BUSINESSPAPER PUBLISHING BUSINESS

We have traced, in the foregoing chapters, the ancestry, development, integration, and magnitude of American business journalism. We have shown the vital part this specialized business press has played in building industrial America, the influence of the middleman in the marketing process, the role of the trade association, and the vital importance of businesspapers in the new era of distribution.

It was noted that, prior to the twentieth century, industrial inventions did not immediately produce industries, nor did new industries immediately create a specialized business press to serve them. The twentieth century, however, witnessed a change in tempo. Now, new inventions quickly bring new businesses and new businesspapers into existence; and the appearance of a businesspaper quickly gives a new field of business activity the *status* of an industry: cohesion, integration, a desire for standards of practice, and pride in the product.

What has caused this? Simply the *service* the modern businesspaper is now able to perform in providing authentic, specialized news coverage, know-how information, and an articulate voice for the new industry. The businesspaper is at once a conscientious critic, a spokesman, a defender, an interpreter, and an enthusiastic promoter of the new industry. The businesspaper provides a *vehicle* that members of the industry can use to carry their advertising messages to buyers and sellers. It provides a *forum* where buyer and seller can discuss their mutual problems. It is an unending chain of currently new textbooks to help the new industry improve technics and processes. It is market analyst and public relations counsel to industry.

The remainder of this book is chiefly devoted to the way all this work is done: the actual way in which the business press functions to serve industry through its different divisions.

A businesspaper publishing house has three main divisions, which are so closely articulated that no one division could exist without the other divisions: editorial, circulation, advertising.

All three of these divisions are on the fighting front. All other divisions in a businesspaper publishing house operate to back up the men in these three fighting divisions. All the divisions of a businesspaper publishing establishment, taken together, become a versatile, flexible, highly expert, and technically trained army, producing an entirely *new end product* every day, or week, or month —the businesspaper. The specifications of this product, or its final ingredients, are not *certainly* or *completely* known, sometimes, until a few hours or minutes before the deadline—just before the product goes to press.

From the time a businesspaper goes to press and until the next deadline, certain basic functions are performed by the publishing house with machinelike precision. Efficient preparation is made for another new product—tomorrow's or next week's or next month's issue of the businesspaper. Reporters, market editors, correspondents, and contributors are busy traveling routine avenues for news and product information, but always ready and eager to go down unbeaten tracks for news. Circulation managers and their staffs are busy with subscriptions, deliveries, readership studies. Advertising, production, research and promotion managers, auditors, and publishers also are functioning.

There must be paper, ink, type, plates, presses, manpower, finances, to produce a businesspaper. The cost of gathering, publishing, and delivering business intelligence can be paid for only out of the revenues from advertising. Advertising is attracted to a businesspaper by reason of that paper's circulation *in the right markets*. Circulation penetration is the result of the *force* of editorial presentation.

What are the precise functions of the publisher, the editor, and the sales managers of circulation, advertising, and promotion divisions? What do these functions require in the way of duties and abilities? The chapters that follow describe these divisions of labor in a modern businesspaper publishing house, with this major objective: to make it easier for the young man or woman who enters the field of business journalism in a subordinate capacity to qualify for rapid advancement in one of these divisions.

CHAPTER VII

FUNCTION OF THE PUBLISHER

"Freedom of the press" is a right *inherent in the readers; it is only a* privilege *in the hands of a publisher which he earns by his continuity of effort.*

Why Do We Publish?

"Do you know why we publish the *Ladies' Home Journal?*" the diminutive publisher of that great consumer magazine, Cyrus H. K. Curtis, once asked a group of advertising men. "The editor thinks it is for the benefit of the American women. *That is an illusion but a very proper one for him to have.* But I will tell you; the *real* reason, *the publisher's reason,* is to give you people who manufacture things that American women want and buy a chance to tell them about your products."[1] (Italics are the author's.)

The editor of the Cleveland *Plain Dealer,* on the other hand, speaking before the Cleveland Advertising Club, bluntly said:

"I am told you do not like the *Plain Dealer.* I don't care whether you do or not; in plain language I don't give a damn what kind of paper you like. I don't like the *Plain Dealer* very well myself. If I were editing it to please myself I'd make a very different publication, but I am editing it for 150,000 people who live here. You advertising men like their business, and the only way I can help you get it is to give them the kind of a newspaper they will read. If they read my paper, they will also read your advertising."[2]

The editors of the *Ladies' Home Journal* followed the philosophy of the editor of the *Plain Dealer* and built up a profitable and highly successful publishing property for Mr. Curtis.

[1] *Advertising Media*, by Hugh E. Agnew and Warren B. Dygert. McGraw-Hill, New York, 1938.
[2] *Ibid.*

They helped raise the status of the American home and the American housewife who was their reader. Once they held fast her interest and her confidence, there was no problem for the makers of carpet sweepers and electric irons. This preconditioned audience was ripe for any manufacturers who could afford Mr. Curtis's advertising rates.

To the expressions of the magazine man and the newspaperman on *why a publication is published*, let us add the expression of a businesspaper publisher. On the fiftieth anniversary of his entrance into the publishing business, the dean of businesspaper publishers, James H. McGraw, Sr., at a dinner in his honor voiced these convictions:

"Businesspapers, so far as I know, were the first group to voluntarily set up a *code of fair practice*. While these standards may not be as high as some of us would have liked to have made them, it should be remembered that when they were formulated it was a remarkable achievement to have set up *any* yardstick by which to measure the standards of an industry. The mere setting up of standards did not, of course, 'make saints out of sinners' over night and never will, but the constant emphasis on right and wrong methods of publishing has raised the level of the business press immeasurably and today we have publications that we are all proud of. We recognize that we still have a long way to go to reach our ideals."[3]

BUSINESSMEN CRAVE LEADERSHIP

"I suppose that first and foremost we are all of us looking for profits in our business and most Americans regard profits as the measure of success," Mr. McGraw told his fellow publishers. "But it seems to me that back of the money success there must have been something else in our business, and something more than money-making must be our objective if these papers of ours are to continue to hold and expand the influence that they have had on

[3] James H. McGraw, Sr., before the Associated Business Papers' annual convention, Hot Springs, Va., May 4, 1935. See Chart 32, Canons of Business Journalism.

American industry. We must make our papers not only so useful and informative, but so attractive and readable that it is not merely a duty, but a pleasure to the average business man to read the papers that we prepared for him with so much care and labor. But the mere presentation of business material that is 'worth printing' is not enough. Other competitors for our readers' interest can present readable material, too. It seems to me that we, better than any one else, know how and where to find the 'hard-to-get' material which only experts can discover. Our editors must have the instinct of perceiving what it is that their readers *want to know* before the readers are themselves conscious of it and they must present to them the kind of original material and facts that come only from fundamental research and fact-finding and study which lifts our papers out of the competitive rut. When we present *that* kind of material in an attractive way, we need not fear losing our place as an important factor in industry. More than ever, business men are craving leadership. Most of our leaders are industrially minded and our job can be and should be one that will point out the direction which their effort should take and help convert individual thinking into the desired group trend. Some of our papers are doing this and reaping the reward that comes from acknowledged leadership."[4]

For half a century the senior McGraw published businesspapers on the theory that the interest of the *readers* was paramount; and he permitted his editors to determine what was in the best interests of the readers. For many years businesspaper publishers like McGraw regarded their chief function as an educational one.

But after a half century of publishing, Mr. McGraw said: "The chief function of a businesspaper today—a new function—is *to advance the status of the industry it serves.*" . . . "In fulfilling this function, which is really a leadership job," Mr. McGraw added, "the businesspaper requires a new relationship to its field, different to that it bore when it was primarily a teacher. It becomes both a *protagonist* and a *critic* of its industry. The former role is easy; the latter one is a real job. *It is necessary to differ with one's indus-*

[4] *Ibid.*

try from time to time. This necessitates guarding against a bumptious editorial attitude, but at the same time sticking to one's guns.

"And here is the important point: Industries may kick about this criticism, but actually they will 'take' much more from their businesspapers today than formerly. In fact, they really want critical leadership and the paper which refuses to supply it may escape the bricks which its more aggressive competitor gets, *but it will also forfeit the real respect of its field.*

"In so far as governmental relationship is concerned, obviously the businesspaper must fight its industry's battles with government. But it should fight these battles only when it is sure its industry's side is right. It must show its industry just what is right and what is wrong.

"Writing an editorial *against* something usually makes better 'copy' and is easier than writing *for* something. That, I believe, is why a negative attitude creeps too often into editorial writing. A businesspaper of today, in my opinion, has a greater opportunity for constructive, *positive* leadership than ever before."[5] (Italics are the author's.)

Solvency Is Important to Independence

While the businesspaper is not a private commercial enterprise in the sense that a hardware store is, or that a manufacturer of motors or frying pans is, still the business of producing a businesspaper is in one respect like any other business in a private enterprise system: it must be solvent; it must make a profit. Indeed, in so far as it is solvent and a profitable enterprise, because of efficient management in turning out the commodity it sells, to that degree can it be independent of subsidy and free from pressures. The businesspaper must hold its readers and increase the number of its readers; it must sell its advertising space at a profit and increase the number of its advertisers and the volume of space units sold to them. By efficiently managing its finances and operating expenses it should have funds for emergencies and depreciation,

[5] *Ibid.*

ample reserves for expansion, and a surplus like any other well-managed business enterprise. Control of these factors comes within the domain of the publisher.

Most businesspapers are financed by means of a publishing corporation, although there are some individual proprietorships and some partnerships. The corporate structure has the advantage that it is not limited to the lifetime of the owner, or necessarily to his own capital; and the business risks are less in case of failure. In the corporation, individuals (sometimes the members of one family) unite for the common purpose of publishing. Membership in the corporation may be changed without dissolution.

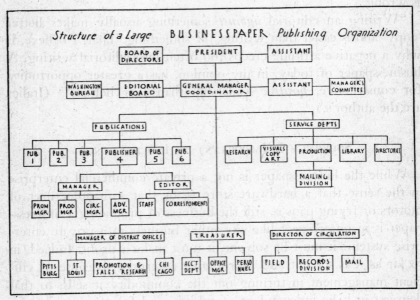

CHART 10

In the chapters that follow, describing the functions of the circulation manager and of the advertising manager, it will become clear that in the business office the businesspaper must be looked upon as a commodity—a product to be turned out at reasonable cost without sacrificing either the *quality* of the contents, attractiveness, or service utility. It also will become plain that there is little or no profit in the sales to the subscribers. The business-paper's use as a *carrier* of specialized information is what is profitably sold in units of advertising space—to those who want to reach the reader-audience under the independent publisher's auspices. The *use* of the carrier must be ably promoted and vigorously sold at the best price to ensure a fair profit in the open field of fair competition. Since the businesspaper might pay well on the basis of its use-function to the advertiser and lose heavily in many of its other functions, the publisher, or president, or general manager is chief supervisor of all those functions, including the actual mechanics of producing and distributing the businesspaper.

The chart (No. 10) showing the structure of a large business-paper publishing house serves equally well to illustrate the functions of a publisher in a small organization, publishing several papers or perhaps only one businesspaper. His two chief executives are an editor and a manager. The manager may be a vice-president or a general manager. He may also be treasurer. As treasurer he has charge of the accounting department, the direction of office routine, record keeping, personnel, and general traffic. As general manager he serves directly under the publisher (who may be president) and directs (1) publications and (2) service departments. Under the general manager, in larger organizations, certain executives may be designated as "publishers," usually men with long service in either the editorial or the advertising department. These men will control all functions on one, two, or several publications with related or common interests. The sales manager, under such a subpublisher, has charge of four major departments: advertising, promotion, circulation, production. Each of these departments, in turn, is in charge of a manager specializing in a single function, as, for example, a circulation manager.

There are no hard and fast rules for conducting a successful businesspaper, but an important body of laws and rules for the efficient discharge of the functions of publishing executives has been established, largely through the efforts of one man, J. K.

Lasser, C.P.A., who for a number of years has been consultant to the Associated Business Papers, Inc. His firm also serves many leading publishing houses.[6] Mr. Lasser's summaries of records for the control of publishing costs are given in this chapter.

A study in 1941 of salary ranges of 297 editorial workers on 11 businesspapers (see Chart 11) showed the following:

16 received $ 25 to $ 37 weekly
34 " 37 to 50 "
37 " 50 to 62 "
40 " 62 to 77 "
65 " 77 to 100 "
51 " 100 to 135 "
22 " 135 to 150 "
32 " 150 and up "

Of the total of editorial workers studied in this survey of 11 businesspapers, 22 per cent were paid from $77 to $100 a week and 17 per cent from $100 to $135 a week. About 54 per cent received $135 a week or better.

Comparative figures on newspaper editorial workers for the same period are undoubtedly much higher than the latest figures we have, which are for 1933 (American Newspaper Publishers Association). The 1933 figures for newspaper editorial workers follow:

42.64 per cent—$32 to $60 weekly
20.04 " —$20 a week
19.7 " —less than $20 a week
20.04 " —$20 to $32 a week
42.64 " —$32 to $60 "
13.38 " —$60 to $100 "
4.22 " —$100 and up "

American Newspaper Guild claim the average reporter with 20 years' experience gets $38 a week.

[6] J. K. Lasser & Co. Mr. Lasser is author of the perennial best seller, *Your Income Tax* (Simon & Schuster, New York). He is also Blue Network commentator on taxes; Editor, *Handbook of Accounting Methods*; Editor, "The Tax Clinic" in *The Journal of Accountancy*; Lecturer, New York University.

CHART 11

STUDY OF MONTHLY SALARY RANGES IN ELEVEN BUSINESS PAPERS WHEN THE ORGANIZATION EMPLOYS OVER 40 PEOPLE

(As of September 1, 1941)

	Number of People in Each of the Following Monthly Salary Ranges									
	$50 to $75	$75 to $100	$100 to $150	$150 to $200	$200 to $250	$250 to $300	$300 to $400	$400 to $500	$500 to $600	Over $600
ADVERTISING DEPARTMENT										
Business Managers					1	1	6	2	4	34
Salesmen		1	9	12	18	16	31	24	35	93
Promotion Men			9	6	9	12	20	9	8	4
Artists, Retouchers, etc.			4	11	2	3	5		1	
Production Men		3	21	22	7	2	9	2		
Stenographers, Secretaries	4	47	95	14		1				
Typists		14								
Clerks	22	48	24	1	1		1			
EDITORIAL DEPARTMENT										
Editors		1	16	34	37	40	65	51	22	32
Artists			4	7	4	3	3			
Production Men		1	4	11	2	3	3			
Stenographers, Secretaries	2	23	61	9						
Typists		4	2							
Clerks	6	9	17	4						
CIRCULATION DEPARTMENT										
Salesmen		38	12	48	24	19	49	10	2	3
Promotion Men				1	6	6	11		4	
Stenographers, Secretaries	8	11	16	1			1			
Typists	2	33								
Clerks	38	116	29	4						
GENERAL										
Management				10	4	2	1	1	4	21
Accounting Department Heads			1	2	7	1	4	1	1	1
Assistants	4	7	8	13	5		1			
Typists	2	4	2							
Clerks	7	13	21	1						
Credit Men				1	1		1		1	
Stenographers, Secretaries	1	10	12	6	3	1				
Typists		7								
Clerks	12	35	22							
Cut Boys, Messengers	32	15	1	1						
Others	3	6	11	1	1					
TOTAL	143	446	402	220	131	111	210	100	82	188

From *Cost Committee Report*, Associated Business Papers, Inc., November 14, 1941. The study covered 2,033 employees.

Fortune (February, 1937) stated that Associated Press reporters averaged $40 to $75 weekly and that the average salary of chiefs of Associated Press bureaus was $100 weekly.

PUBLISHING CONTROLS

Installation of controls is the function of a publisher. Administrative controls fall into five major divisions:

1. Organization. Every publishing house should have a graphic organization chart or diagram which clearly indicates the flow of authority, and prevents buck-passing, uncertainty, and confusion. The chart should specify the responsibility of each function of management. It should prevent managers from working at cross-purposes or performing overlapping duties.

2. Policies and Procedure. Manuals defining policy and explaining the specific duties of managers and assistant managers in both editorial and business departments should be kept up to date. Definition and channeling of duties make it possible for many problems to be solved by routine operation.

3. Cost Finding. A modern system for keeping costs under constant observation, controlling costs, fixing blame where costs are excessive, is an important function in publishing.

4. Budgets. Adequate budget control is necessary in order for management to operate and plan.

5. Operating reports. Periodic reports enable the publisher to compare actual costs and budget allotments in each department and avoid decisions based on intuition or snap judgment.

Cost controls fall into four major divisions:

1. Control of Mechanical Costs
2. Control of Advertising Costs
3. Control of Editorial Costs
4. Control of Circulation Costs

Cost clinics held in Chicago and New York in 1941 and 1942 and surveys of current publishing practice, under the sponsorship of a Cost Committee of the Associated Business Papers, Inc., provided a wealth of up-to-date information for the guidance of publishers of businesspapers. J. K. Lasser & Co. arranged the material, which was privately published as a manual in 1942.

Four summaries of this information follow:

CHART 12

SUMMARY OF RECORDS FOR THE CONTROL OF MECHANICAL COSTS

Element	Records for Control	Detail of Record	Its use in Control

Composition Costs	Card File—By Issues Monthly statistical reports	Advertising
		  Number of advertisements segrated by sizes
		  Number of standing pages (including furnished plates)
		  Total advertising pages
		  Cost of corrections
		  Total composition costs
		  Average cost per page
		Editorial
		  Number of pages by type sizes
		  Total editorial pages
		  Cost of corrections
		  Cost of killed matter
		  Total composition costs
		  Average cost per page
			Reduction of costs by
			1. Planning to reduce costly corrections
			2. Elimination of frills
			3. Intelligently budgeting future operations
			4. Decrease in quantity of killed matter
			5. Improvement in quality of copy submitted
			6. Comparison of costs with those of other operators

Presswork	Card File—By Issues Monthly statistical reports	Press Run
		Total Pages
		Size and number of forms
		  Regular
		  Extra Colors (number of color pages in each form)
		Cost of regular forms
		Cost of extra color forms
		Cost of covers
		Cost of extras (in detail)
		Total cost of presswork
		Cost per M copies
			Economies may be obtained as a result of
			1. Reduction in number of copies printed
			2. Decrease in use of bleed and other costly form
			3. Improved scheduling to eliminate overtime
			4. Comparison of costs with other publishers
			5. Decrease in acceptance of late material

Binding and Mailing	Card File—By Issues Monthly statistical reports	Size and number of signatures Number of copies mailed Cost of extras Total binding and mailing costs Cost per M copies	Costs can be reduced by 1. Review of "special" costs in light of income collected 2. Binding in maximum size signatures 3. Change from envelopes to wrappers
Paper, Wrappers, Envelopes, etc.	Perpetual Inventories	Kind of stock (size and weight) Quantity purchased and received From whom purchased Price per pound Quantity used and cost (by issues) Quantity on hand and cost Cost per M copies	Reduction of costs by 1. Switching from envelopes to wrappers 2. Larger purchases resulting from precise knowledge of requirements 3. Reduction in allowance for waste on part of printer 4. Change in texture or finish of paper 5. Decrease in sheet size for trim requirements

Prepared by J. K. Lasser & Co.
March 25, 1942.

CHART 13

SUMMARY OF RECORDS FOR THE CONTROL OF ADVERTISING COSTS

Element	Records for Control	Detail of Record	Its use in Control
Prospect Lists	Card Files	Name and address of prospect Business Products or lines Financial rating Name and title of person to see Best time of day, week or month to see him Next date to call or write Competitive paper advertising volume Potential volume obtainable Complaints or reason for refusal to advertise	Direction of Salesmen's activities through 1. Routing 2. Calls to be made weekly 3. Arming him with sales argument 4. Budgeting his production 5. Budgeting his traveling expense
Salesmen's Performance	Monthly Reports	For each salesman Sales by issue Sales by month Sales quota Compensation of salesman Travel expense of salesman	Measure of salesmen's worth by 1. Comparison with quota or budget 2. Comparison with previous record 3. Comparison with competitive publications 4. Relation of cost to income 5. Study of the method of compensation 6. Comparison with other publishers
Salesmen's Expenses	Weekly Expense Reports Weekly Record of Calls	Itemize in minute detail Cities visited Prospects called upon and sales made Railroad fare Hotel charges Meals Pullman Taxis Telephone and telegraph Valet and laundry, if allowed Entertainment, including person entertained and reason	Justification of the expense through 1. Elimination of backtracking and useless traveling 2. Comparison with calls budgeted 3. Relation of sales to calls 4. Careful scrutiny of the reasonableness of the expense item 5. Comparison with budget 6. Comparison of cost to income produced 7. Comparison with other publishers
Promotion	Monthly reports of cost	Statement of costs by kind of promotion Surveys of markets Advertising in other publications Industry analysis Salesmen's kits Presentations to advertisers Speculative copy Promotional mailings Salaries of employees	Maintenance of proper balance by 1. Budgeting the expenditure 2. Computing the cost per call or contact 3. Comparison with previous record 4. Relating sales to promotion where possible 5. Obtaining prospect reaction 6. Comparison with other publishers

CHART 13

SUMMARY OF RECORDS FOR THE CONTROL OF ADVERTISING COSTS—*Continued*

Element	Records for Control	Detail of Record	Its use in Control
Copy service	Monthly reports of cost	Statement of costs by advertisers Salaries on time basis Artwork and supplies Telephone calls or telegrams to secure late copy	Eliminate waste by 1. Billing full cost where possible 2. Reducing advertisers' abuses
Full Advertising Costs	Monthly reports	Salesmen's salaries and commissions Other salaries Social security taxes Traveling expense Telephone (toll calls) and telegraph Branch office expenses Promotion costs Attending conventions Dues and subscriptions Stationery and supplies Postage Artwork, cuts, etc. not billed Bad debts	Hold these in line by 1. Maintaining balance to income produced 2. Comparison with budgets and previous experience 3. Close scrutiny of each item of expense 4. Comparison with other publishers

Prepared by J. K. Lasser & Co.
March 25, 1942.

CHART 14

CONTROL OF EDITORIAL COSTS[1]

EXECUTIVE CONTROL

1. Are editors making the required calls, interviews, and answering correspondence properly?
    A. Are they really abreast of their industry?
    B. Do they encourage reader contributions?
    C. Are they originating new material?
    D. Are they turning in sufficient matter?
    E. Have you checked their production against that in the industry?
2. Do you maintain protective checks against wastes in purchase of contributions? Art work? Engravings? Traveling expense?
    A. Do you make sure that editors understand production costs?
    B. Is there lack of control of content by editors who do not understand budgets? (For specific items see Mechanical Department Control.)

COMPENSATION

1. Have you checked salaries against those of other profitable papers? Are they too low or excessive?
2. Are contribution costs high even though you are paying fair salaries to your staff?
3. If you are paying for quality in editorial content:
    A. Is it reflected in your renewal percentage?
    B. In reduced circulation costs?

CONTRIBUTIONS

1. Have you thought of the following savings in connection with editorial matter?
    A. Have you considered the possibility of economies from adopting standard rates of payment for contributions and photographs?
    B. Elimination of payment for contributions to editors on a salary?
    C. Elimination of purchase of contributions, photos, and engravings, long in advance of publication.
    D. Are contribution rates greater than those in the industry?

TRAVELING

1. Are too many people going to too many conventions?
    A. Are necessary visits intelligently planned?
    B. Could some required data be obtained from advertising or circulation fieldmen if suitably organized?
2. Can you eliminate editorial visits to your printer?

OTHER COSTS

1. Are expenditures too high for photos, art work, and cuts as compared to the industry?
    A. Are there excessive illustrations when other methods will accomplish the same results?
    B. Are clipping bureau costs excessive?
2. Are telephone and telegraph charges in excess of similar bills by others?

RECORDS

1. Do you keep usable records of manuscripts, photographs, maps and art work, etc., on hand?
    A. Do these records provide a check on wastes?
    B. Do you keep a record of the cost per editorial page?

[1] *Control of Business Paper Costs*, prepared by J. K. Lasser & Co., for the Associated Business Papers, Inc., March 25, 1942.

2. Does the number of editorial pages bear the profits relation to the other factors?
3. Have you used the "marked copy" method for graphic illustration of editorial costs?
   A. Do you mark each cut with the cost of photo, art work, and engraving?
   · B. Mark each contribution with its cost?
   C. Mark each article with the name of the editor who wrote it?
   D. Mark an occasional copy with the composition, bleed, extras, and authors' alterations cost?

CHART 15

SUMMARY OF RECORDS FOR THE CONTROL OF CIRCULATION COSTS

Element	Records for Control	Detail of Record	Its use in Control
Prospect Lists	Card File or Stencils	Name and address of prospect Business title of prospect Former subscriber Source of name Date added to list	Direction of promotional activities through 1. Testing list before adding to files 2. Check off of names found to be dead through salesmen's reports or mail returns 3. Preserving "dead" names to prevent their addition to list when new lists are purchased 4. Classification of list to facilitate rifle shot appeals, etc. 5. Budgeting orders to be secured 6. Budgeting expenses

Mail Promotion	Monthly Reports	Number of pieces mailed
		Copy appeal used
		Keyed appeals
		List or lists used
		Direct costs of campaign
		  Paper
		  Processing
		  Mailing
		  Postage
		  Premiums
		Results of campaign
		  Subscriptions secured-new and renewal
		  % to total pieces
		  Cost per subscription
			Reduce costs and improve results of future campaigns by
			1. Elimination of unsuccessful copy
			2. Elimination of unsatisfactory names from active lists
			3. Information as to success or failure of
			  a. Kinds of paper
			  b. Methods of reproduction
			  c. Cards vs. letters
			  d. Stamps vs. meter machines
			  e. Mailing dates
			  f. Premiums
			4. Analysis of costs to determine saturation points (diminishing returns)
			5. Comparison with previous campaigns
			6. Budgeting the expenditure
			7. Comparison with other publishers

CHART 15

SUMMARY OF RECORDS FOR THE CONTROL OF CIRCULATION COSTS—*Continued*

Element	Record for Control	Detail of Record	Its use in Control

Salesmen's Performance	Monthly Reports	Number of subscriptions-new and renewal
		Dollar volume-new and renewal
		Quality of subscriptions secured
		  Term of subscriptions
		  % from preferred list
		  % from miscellaneous sources
		Compensation of salesmen
		Expenses of salesmen
			Measure of salesmen's worth by
			1. Comparison with quota or budget
			2. Comparison with previous record
			3. Relation of salesmen's cost to income
			4. Comparison with cost of mail
			5. Analysis of quality of subscriptions secured
			6. Comparison with other publishers

Salesmen's Expenses	Weekly Expense Reports Weekly Report of Calls	Itemize in minute detail Cities visited Prospects called on and sales made Railroad fare Hotel charges Meals Pullman Taxis Telephone and telegraph	Justification of the expense through 1. Elimination of back tracking and useless traveling 2. Comparison with calls budgeted 3. Relation of sales to calls 4. Careful scrutiny of the reasonableness of the expense items 5. Comparison with budget 6. Comparison of cost with income produced 7. Comparison with other publishers

Full Circulation Costs	Monthly Reports	Subscriptions sold by salesmen—new and renewal
		Subscriptions secured by mail—new and renewal
		Gross income per order
		Cost per order (full cost)
		New subscriptions
		Cancellations
		Total circulation income
		Total circulation expense
		Expenses separately for mail, field and record keeping—
		  Salaries and Commissions
		  Promotion
		Premiums
		  Stationery and Supplies
		  Travel and Entertainment
		  Conventions
		  Postage
		  Telephone and Telegraph
			Hold these costs in line by
			1. Maintaining balance with income produced
			2. Comparison with budget
			3. Comparison with previous results
			4. Comparison with other publishers
			5. Comparison of costs of mail and field force efforts with results—taking long term renewal results into consideration
			6. Comparison with other publishers

Prepared by J. K. Lasser & Co.
March 25, 1942.

Control of Business Paper Costs, a manual published by the Associated Business Papers, Inc., New York, 1942, prepared by A.B.P. Cost Committee consisting of William A. Barber, the Chilton Co., chairman; Edward A. Becker, Industrial Press; E. S. Gillette, Gillette Publishing Company; and B. R. Putnam, McGraw-Hill; with the co-operation of J. K. Lasser & Co., consultants to A.B.P.

CHAPTER VIII

FUNCTION OF THE ADVERTISING SALES MANAGER

*The Trade of Advertising is now so near to perfection that it is
not easy to propose any improvement.*
— DR. SAMUEL JOHNSON (1759)

DEFINITION OF ADVERTISING

YOU DO not know what advertising is. No one in the advertising business knows what advertising is. No advertiser knows for certain what advertising is. If you want to know, tell this messenger that I should come up. I'm waiting in the lobby downstairs.

The above message, addressed to Albert D. Lasker,[1] in 1910, brought "the father of the modern advertising concept" up the elevator to the advertising agency of Lord & Thomas, which Mr. Lasker headed. Years later Mr. Lasker described the event: "It was six o'clock when I asked the messenger to tell the writer of the note to come up . . . I left the building at three o'clock the next morning. I sat continuously with him throughout that time. And when I went home I knew what advertising was . . . *salesmanship in print.*"[2] The man's name was John E. Kennedy.

In 1914, a group of businesspaper publishers paid John E. Kennedy $25,000 to show advertising agencies and their clients how they could get a greater return for dollars invested in businesspaper space.

In his now famous monograph[3] Mr. Kennedy compared businesspaper advertising space to a small garden which must be intensively cultivated. "I would rather spend one dollar to make one

[1] Chairman, War Shipping Administration, World War I.
[2] From a speech by Mr. Lasker, "Fundamentals of Advertising," delivered before the Advertising Federation of America in 1935.
[3] *Intensive Advertising*, by John E. Kennedy, reprinted by the Associated Business Papers, Inc., New York, April, 1940.

TOOLS
MATERIALS
PARTS
ACCESSORIES

AVIATION EQUIPMENT

DESIGN
PRODUCTION
OPERATION
MAINTENANCE

1170 Broadway, New York, N.Y.

RATE CARD No. 2   Effective April 15, 1943

AVIATION EQUIPMENT is a monthly reporting medium devoted solely to factual descriptions of new and improved tools, products, materials and accessories for aircraft design, production, operation and maintenance. It covers the aviation industry completely and thoroughly, and is sent free to the men in this industry who influence or specify the purchase of equipment.

1—GENERAL ADVERTISING

(a) Rates

	12 times	6 times	3 times	1 time
1 Page	$185	$210	$225	$240
½ Page	110	125	130	135
¼ Page	75	80		85

(b) Preferred Positions: 12 times, non-cancellable — rates upon request.
(c) Minimum space ¼ page.
(d) Color rates — $60. per color.
   Standard Colors — Red - Yellow - Blue - $40. per color.
(e) Bleed pages or borders — 15% additional.
(f) Cancellations accepted after closing date.
(g) Space used will be short-rated at earned rate.

2—COMMISSIONS and DISCOUNTS

(a) Agency commission to recognized agencies only — 15%
(b) Cash discounts — 2%

3—CIRCULATION — National Distribution — 15,000 minimum — (CCA).

4—MECHANICAL REQUIREMENTS

(a) Plate sizes — 1 page: 7"x10"; ½ page: 3⅜"x10", 7"x4⅞";
   ¼ page: 3⅜"x4⅞";
   Trim size: 8½"x11¼"
(b) Bleed size: 8¾"x11½"
(c) 110 screen preferred
(d) Closing date: 10th of month preceding date of issue

5—MISCELLANEOUS

(a) All copy subject to approval of publisher.
(b) Published monthly.
(c) All copy and cuts should be sent to "Aviation Equipment," 1170 Broadway, New York, N. Y.
(d) Advertising representatives:
   New York, N. Y. — F. Hyde, 1170 Broadway
   New York, N. Y. — W. F. Becker, 1170 Broadway
   Connecticut — Alan Gibson, 1170 Broadway
   Mass. & R. I. — R. J. Weeks, 1170 Broadway
   Eastern Pa. — R. Hanson, 300 W. Willow Grove Ave., Phila., Pa.
   Western Pa. — B. C. Nebo, 5535 Centre Ave., Pittsburgh, Pa.
   Middle West — F. A. Lederle, 1411 Merchandise Mart, Chicago, Ill.
   Ill.-Ind.-Wis. — G. P. Grant, 1411 Merchandise Mart, Chicago, Ill.
   Ohio — A. Hawley, 326 Bulkley Bldg., Cleveland, Ohio
   Michigan — F. Pickrell, 314 Stephenson Bldg., Detroit, Mich.
   Missouri — I. Wright, 915 Olive St., St. Louis, Mo
   West Coast — L. B. Chappell, 427 West Fifth St., Los Angeles, Calif.

ALL PROVISIONS REGARDING THIS CONTRACT ARE EXPRESSED HEREIN.

Name _____   Space _____

Address _____   Rate _____

AVIATION EQUIPMENT, 1170 Broadway, New York City, _____ 194__

You are hereby authorized to insert our advertisement in AVIATION EQUIPMENT beginning
_____ 194__   to occupy space of _____   page each month for _____
consecutive months or in months indicated as follows:

In consideration of which we agree to pay you _____ Dollars ($_____)
per month as issued. If copy is not supplied by the 10th of the month preceding date of issue, last advertisement, in the event this contract is not completed, rate reverts to that on reverse side for number of insertions used. All bills due 10th of following month.

We agree to accept the above order and to publish this advertisement for the period mentioned and at the rate specified, beginning _____ 194__ and thereafter, in accordance with the terms of the contract.

for AVIATION EQUIPMENT

Signed _____

By _____

CHART 16. TYPICAL RATE CARD

sale than spend one dollar to half-make two sales," he declared. "Advertising," he wrote, "is nothing more than *salesmanship* multiplied mechanically by the printing press . . . but good advertising is salesmanship intensified . . . With the salary of a single salesman, it is now possible to reach 1,000 probable customers for every individual that salesman could have reached personally . . . with the selfsame selling talk. But for all this, it does not *supplant* the personal salesman. It *increases* his value instead."

ADVERTISING REVENUE AND A FREE PRESS

Sales of advertising space units—not subscriptions—are the chief source of revenue on the independent businesspaper. The subscription fee is usually absorbed in the cost of getting the subscription. On the free circulation paper, where it is not subsidized by any group or association, sales of advertising space units are, obviously, the only source of revenue. It is the *primary* function of the advertising sales manager of a businesspaper to increase that revenue by selling more and, if possible, larger units of space to more producers whose commodities are being used, can be used, or should be used, by the readership of his businesspaper.

Critics of the press are continually jabbing at the "dominance" or "influence" the advertiser exerts over editorial policy because he supplies the revenue. The advertising manager would be naïve indeed to take a blind stand that this criticism is entirely unfair. It is, in many cases, well-founded criticism, and often well-documented by its critics.[4]

On the other hand, there would be no free press without revenue earned by private enterprise in the publishing business.[5] Subsidy, if it is big enough, means concentrated control by those who furnish the subsidy. The subsidizers can withdraw the major financial support of a publication in one quick move. This makes the

[4] *Lords of the Press*, George Seldes. Julian Messner Inc., New York, 1938.
American House of Lords, Harold L. Ickes. Harcourt, Brace & Co., New York, 1939.
The Tragedy of Waste, Stuart Chase. Macmillan Co., New York, 1924.
[5] See "Freedom of Advertising and a Free Press," A. D. Lasker, *Vital Speeches Magazine*, Vol. 1, Oct. 8, 1934.

Standard Order Blank for Publications
(Standard Conditions 1933. *See Over*)

(*Member of A.A.A.A.*)

FULLER & SMITH & ROSS INC.
NEW YORK CLEVELAND

OUT

Advertising

BCN

1501 EUCLID AVENUE CLEVELAND OHIO

REPRESENTATIVE: 1411 Merchandise Mart, Chicago, Illinois

TO PUBLISHER OF House Furnishing Review, 1170 Broadway,
ORDER NO. 17187

CITY AND STATE New York, New York
DATE December 14, 1942

PLEASE PUBLISH ADVERTISING OF [advertiser] Westinghouse Electric & Mfg. Company
FOR [product] Full Line

SPACE	TIMES		DATES OF INSERTION
1 page 2 colors	One (1)	1943	January 1 page 2 colors

POSITION
COLORS: Any standard colors

COPY	KEY	CUTS
To come later		To come later

ADDITIONAL INSTRUCTIONS

RATE
$195.00 per page plus $50.00 for color (3 time)

LESS AGENCY COMMISSION	PER CENT ON GROSS	LESS CASH DISCOUNT	PER CENT ON NET
15%		2%	

Subject to standard conditions on back hereof.

FULLER & SMITH & ROSS INC. Wm. J. Staab

A copy of each issue in which the advertising appears must be sent to the advertiser and to the office of this agency.
Copy for advertiser should be addressed to:

Mr. Roger Bolin,
Westinghouse Elec. & Mfg. Co.,
Mansfield, Ohio

This order can be canceled by Fuller & Smith & Ross Inc. at any time before forms are closed for any given issue.

1. No advertisements should be inserted to apply on this contract except when covered by specific insertion order.
2. In case contract is returned for revision, no insertions should be made until mutual agreement is reached.
3. The prompt receipt of proof of publication assures prompt payment of your invoice.

Member of
AMERICAN ASSOCIATION OF ADVERTISING AGENCIES

Standard Order Blank for Publications "A.A.A.A. Form." Copyright 1933. American Association of Advertising Agencies. Blank No. 1 (*OVER*)

Chart 17. Advertising Agency Publication Order

threat of withdrawal always a powerful influence on the publisher and even the editor.

If the sale of an advertising space unit, say a half page or a page, is also to be considered a subsidy, then in a given issue of a businesspaper there are at least from fifty to several hundred such small "subsidies."[6] No one advertiser or group of advertisers controls enough of the paper's advertising revenue seriously to menace its life or to dictate its policies by wholesale withdrawal or threat of withdrawal of the advertising. The laws against combinations in restraint of trade take care of those who conspire to withdraw advertising support in order to influence or "punish" a publication.

The independent businesspaper cannot support itself on subscription revenue alone. It is conceivable for a publication covering a wide or unbounded field of interest, such as *Reader's Digest* serves, and with a correspondingly wide field of readers from which to draw its subscribers, to operate without advertising revenue, supported solely by its subscription fees. But even the businesspaper of general subject matter as, for example, the *Journal of Commerce*, finds its field limited and the revenue from that limited readership even at its peak insufficient to pay for the kind of publication its readers will expect, and to which they will be entitled by the subscription price.

The safety and independence of the free press lies in *numbers* of advertisers, who make it independent of a single subsidy. In the

[6] To be entirely realistic, it must be noted that newspapers and general magazines, and to a much smaller degree businesspapers with paid subscriptions, do enjoy a government subsidy. In ten years it amounted to over $1 billion. This subsidy is the "second-class" mailing privilege, originated in 1851 and amended in 1887, "so that education and enlightenment may flourish in a democracy." Using the figures for the fiscal year ending 1937, the then Postmaster General, James A. Farley, revealed that it cost the U.S. Post Office $38 million that year to deliver daily newspapers (for which privilege the newspapers paid only $9 million.) The full figures for 1937 follow:

	Post Office handling cost	Payments by Publications	Loss to Post Office
Daily Newspapers	$38,001,739	$8,999,158	$29,002,581
All other newspapers	14,293,411	2,999,241	11,294,170
Magazines	33,583,007	9,246,108	24,336,899
Philanthropic, Fraternal papers	18,512,038	1,903,590	16,608,448
Papers from County	7,906,711	None	7,906,711
Total Government Loss			$89,148,809

On January 16, 1939, Secretary of Interior Harold Ickes, during a Town Meeting of the Air debate with Frank E. Gannett, chain newspaper publisher, referred to the "enormous subsidy to the press in the form of less-than-cost postage rates" which amounted to "$90 million" for the "last fiscal year," which would be 1938.

final analysis, however, that safety and freedom of the press will depend on the character, courage, and vigilance of its owners, publishers, editors, and other executives: in how highly they look upon their functions, how well they are guided by the interests of the readers rather than the advertisers.

ADVERTISING AND MERCHANDISING

Division of Industrial Advertising Budgets in 1941

	SALES VOL. LESS THAN $200,000		SALES VOL. $200M TO $500M		SALES VOL. $500M TO $1 MIL.		SALES VOL. $1 MIL. TO $2 MIL.		SALES VOL. $2 MIL. TO $5 MIL.		SALES VOL. $5 MIL. TO $10 MIL.		SALES VOL. $10 MIL. TO $50 MIL.		SALES VOL. OVER $50 MIL.		NO SIZE CLASSIFICATION		TOTALS	
	No. of Co's	%	No. of Co's	%	No. of Co's	%	No. of Co's	%	No. of Co's	%	No. of Co's	%	No. of Co's	%	No. of Co's	%	No. of Co's	%	No. of Co's	%
(1) Display Advertising A-Tech. & Indus. Publs.	9	42.22	13	40.54	17	44.35	50	31.23	55	34.72	34	28.88	49	27.68	10	25.90	2	33.60	239	32.62
B-Gen. Bus. Publs.	3	55.33	..	.....	6	21.80	10	10.18	14	9.44	9	10.51	25	11.94	6	12.15	..	.....	73	13.65
C-Prod. Costs on A&B	5	11.00	9	6.56	17	10.26	40	7.90	54	8.00	30	7.67	4	7.17	9	.02	2	10.29	212	8.01
(2) Publish. Cons. Cat'ls. A-Space only	7	22.29	8	6.94	15	4.55	35	4.06	35	2.08	25	2.82	39	2.99	6	1.56	2	1.11	172	4.03
B-Production Costs	1	2.00	7	.87	9	1.54	19	1.22	23	.94	12	1.48	20	.49	1	.31	1	.30	93	1.02
(3) Adv. to Gen. Public A-Magazines	1	10.00	1	50.00	1	40.00	4	19.75	10	15.28	6	18.42	13	22.98	5	25.20	1	6.00	42	20.79
B-Radio	..	.....	..	.....	..	.....	..	.....	1	2.00	2	3.20	2	1.39	2	2.90	..	.....	7	9.82
C-Other Medium	..	.....	2	5.45	1	7.00	2	2.30	3	11.83	5	19.90	8	2.63	3	15.17	..	.....	24	9.34
D-Production Costs	..	.....	1	10.00	2	1.00	3	4.42	7	2.85	7	1.66	9	2.96	5	3.80	1	1.00	35	2.95
(4) Cat's & Prod. Liter.	11	16.45	11	24.72	19	19.15	50	23.05	52	18.69	31	15.57	43	17.07	9	13.84	2	7.73	228	18.85
(5) Direct Mail	8	14.44	10	23.50	21	18.98	47	42.40	44	12.63	30	14.30	40	9.59	9	3.72	2	14.41	211	13.14
(6) House Organs	1	6.00	2	1.00	4	6.65	17	9.11	14	6.61	13	14.19	18	8.83	6	14.10	1	19.40	76	8.81
(7) Editorial Publicity	1	1.00	3	.68	3	1.13	17	1.45	25	2.43	12	2.15	25	1.23	5	1.33	1	.53	92	1.69
(8) Motion Pict. Stills, Etc.	..	.....	..	.....	4	4.05	12	2.52	11	4.25	8	1.79	17	3.53	4	1.50	..	.....	56	3.10
(9) Conventions & Exhibits	3	10.00	5	6.00	10	6.23	31	6.15	33	4.52	23	6.45	42	3.82	10	4.83	1	14.70	158	5.28
(10) Traveling Expense	1	16.00	3	1.67	6	2.15	12	1.63	25	1.75	17	.95	22	1.15	5	1.40	2	1.37	93	1.60
(11) Market Research	..	.....	..	.....	2	.90	3	1.00	6	3.37	4	1.18	13	1.83	..	.....	..	.....	28	1.91
(12) Sales Promotion & Educational Liter.	2	22.50	4	2.63	10	3.81	19	4.50	28	5.91	16	5.98	22	6.34	3	4.08	1	.73	105	5.64
(13) Administrative Expense	2	7.00	7	17.57	13	14.12	39	12.74	46	13.54	27	10.28	37	14.97	8	9.58	1	17.17	180	13.14
(14) Miscellaneous	2	9.50	7	3.21	13	6.76	32	3.84	33	3.34	21	6.81	33	6.35	4	2.86	1	1.69	146	4.99
(15) Contingency or Reserve	2	1.75	4	2.13	6	5.72	14	3.45	17	3.51	10	2.84	18	3.57	5	4.40	1	1.50	77	3.51

SCHEDULE 11
—*National Industrial Advertisers Asso.*

CHART 18

Division of Industrial Advertising Budgets (1941)

The "press" is comprised of many private enterprises but, unlike other types of business, it is affected with a public interest. It is, in a way, a quasi-public utility. As such it bears a distinction which earns for it certain privileges (and also certain restrictions) not placed on ordinary private enterprise.[7]

In direct ratio to the financial growth of a businesspaper will its

[7] Discussed at length in the final chapter, "Future of Business Journalism."

independence of editorial interference gain. But financial growth on the press is—or should be—the reward for service.

These observations are trite but also basic, and the advertising sales manager must keep them always in the foreground of his selling. He will not always be selling to seasoned buyers of business-paper advertising space units, or to men of balanced judgment or understanding. Sometimes it becomes his function to teach and educate new manufacturers, new advertising directors, and new agency account executives; sometimes he is called upon to defend the independent press and the high standards it has pledged itself to uphold.

Like his coworker, the circulation sales manager, the advertising sales manager cannot afford to remain a swivel-chair expert. He must get out on the front lines, visit men at work in the industries where the products his readers buy are made or transformed. He must visit advertising agency executives and space or media buyers and review with them the editorial program of his publication in a critical light. He must visit the readers too. He must become expert in problems of the producer or manufacturer, the distributor, and the retailer and thoroughly understand the relations of these three classes to each other and to their salesmen and employees, to stockholders and the public. He must discuss problems of distribution with distributors; of production with producers, of public relations with publicity men. He must take a particular interest in all kinds of salesmen.

In the chapter on the circulation manager, which will follow, we show how industrial advertising managers and businesspaper space buyers fortify themselves with numerous devices to check and prove not only circulation claims and reader interest, but also *reader usefulness.*

The advertising agency space buyer, in recommending a businesspaper advertising space schedule to his client, must be prepared to prove to those who will approve the advertising budget that the money is judiciously invested.

Legal advice and medical service are still bought largely on faith, but not businesspaper space. Proof of reasonable return on the investment is demanded. It is the function of the advertising sales manager to furnish some proof or measure of the advertising's effectiveness.

THIRTEEN SUCCESS FACTORS

A successful advertising sales manager on a businesspaper must *know* these things:

1. The role of communications, which is the keystone of a free society.

2. The importance of the specialized business press as an integrated whole: its dominant role in the business economy as compared with other media today, and some concept of its future role.

3. The importance of business itself, the contribution it now makes and the greater contribution it can make to human progress.

4. The importance of the *field* in which he is trying to sell—thorough knowledge of its interrelationship with the other fields of human activity. He must be able, on occasion, to glorify his own field: dramatize the importance of its men and markets, its factories or farms or oilfields or retail stores and shops.

5. The advertiser's or the advertising prospect's business, his markets, his methods of production and distribution, his objectives, and as much as possible about the product itself.

6. The prospect's advertising history, his agency, the agency account executives, the kind of copy he has used. The advertising sales manager must be prepared to suggest the kind of copy the prospect should use for the particular market *his* publication reaches. He must sell proper use of his publication by stressing the advantage of the "tell-all" technic instead of the constant use of general or prestige copy. He should turn down copy he knows will not produce results.

7. The functions of his own paper, its readership as a *market* for the prospect's products or services.

8. His editors, their education and training, their background of accomplishment, their abilities, their leadership in the field. He must win appreciation and support for the merit of the editorial page. He must know his paper's *objectives*.

9. He must be able to justify the point that comparatively

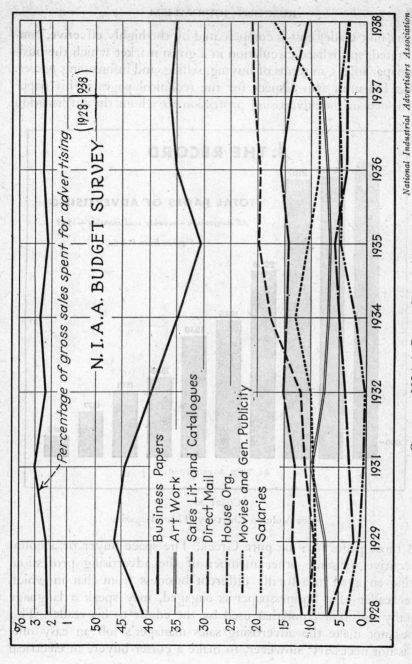

CHART 19. N.I.A.A. BUDGET SURVEY (1928-1938)

higher unit reader cost is compensated by the highly effective, concentrated, specialized circulation in a given market which the businesspaper offers, in terms of buying, selling, and influencing *power*.

10. He must win respect for the technical pages in his paper from men in the advertising profession to whom the information

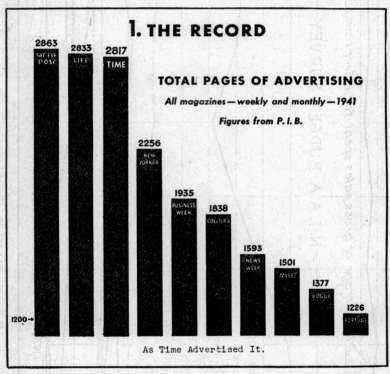

1. THE RECORD

TOTAL PAGES OF ADVERTISING

All magazines — weekly and monthly — 1941

Figures from P. I. B.

2863 SAT EVE POST
2833 LIFE
2817 TIME
2256 NEW YORKER
1935 BUSINESS WEEK
1838 COLLIER'S
1593 NEWS WEEK
1501 ALLEE
1377 VOGUE
1226 FORTUNE
1200 →

As Time Advertised It.

CHART 20

Sales Volume Chart by *Time* Magazine

on those pages may be pure Greek. The space buyer or account executive or some other member of the advertising profession, being engaged in a totally different business from that in which the reader of a businesspaper is engaged, may speak a language totally different from that used by the editor to his reader. This does not make the advertising sales manager's job an easy one. It is not necessary, however, to make a corset buyer, an electrical engineer, or a transportation manager, out of the agency space buyer; it is necessary only to show him how your paper helps *its readers* to do a better job. The advertising sales manager must demonstrate why the subscriber is willing to pay for the paper, why he devotes the time to reading it, or why he wants it to keep coming, if it is a "free circulation" paper.

11. He must keep his thinking in pace with the changing business world and give proper significance to the competition, not only of papers in his field but to new competition of general or horizontal business magazines that serve industry. His publisher has no *special franchise* to serve the field exclusively.

12. He must be able to speak with knowledge and intelligence —and pride—about his publishing organization—the owners, and his associates.

13. He must be able, in short, to build a convincing case for business, for the business press as a whole, for advertising as a whole, for his field as a whole, and finally for the place of his own publication in that field.

What Is a "National" Magazine?

Among the general consumer publications which go gunning for advertisers in specialized fields (particularly the extractive and transformative), which leading businesspapers once considered their exclusive territory, are such publications as *Saturday Evening Post*, *Collier's*, *Time*, and *Life*. The advertising sales manager of a businesspaper often encounters the argument, advanced by these big general magazines, that the advertising prospect should select a "national magazine" in preference to a businesspaper. Most businesspapers are themselves national magazines that actually grew up with the nation and helped build our country into the world's leading nation. Often businesspapers are more truly "national" in character than the general consumer paper.

In 1942, *Time* published a chart in one of its advertisements in the advertising businesspapers, in which it appeared to rank *third* in number of pages of advertising carried by leading national magazines in 1941 (see Chart 20). The business press was quick to scotch this *Time* advertising message by publishing a similar chart in which seven national businesspapers outranked *Time* and *Life* and fifteen businesspapers outranked *Saturday Evening Post* and twenty-three outranked *Collier's* as carriers of national advertising. The leader, *Iron Age*, a weekly with 17,000 readers, carried 5,360 pages of advertising as against *Time's* 2,817 pages, for the year 1941 (see Chart 21).[8]

In 1941, with only 125 member publications, the A.B.P. recorded a total of 120,012 pages of advertising carried with a gross revenue of $22,885,537 (see Chart 22).

The *Standard Rate & Data Service*, in its February, 1943, issue listed 1,695 businesspapers, of which 153 were Canadian. It is estimated that some 200 additional businesspapers exist that are unlisted. The total volume of advertising pages and the gross total revenue of the American business press is variously estimated. According to A.B.P., the total volume of advertising and subscription revenue of the entire business press, 1929 to 1942 inclusive, excluding the year 1932 for which no figures were available, was $796,400,000. Volume of advertising in page units for the same period was 4,917,450 pages.[9] These figures do not include the agricultural press.

The *Wall Street Journal* in its Aug. 19, 1943, issue reported:

> While general magazines and newspapers were showing a loss of approximately 5 per cent in advertising lineage, 11 leading trade magazines accomplished a 22 per cent increase. And in the first 6 months of this year, 103 of the industrial group of trade magazines experienced a 19.39 per cent gain. War is directly responsible for much of the soaring circulation and advertising shown by the trade magazines. Under intense industrial activity they have become more valuable than ever to their readers. This increased interest, plus greater demand for industrial equipment, improves the position of the [business] magazine as advertising media.

[8] In 1942, *Iron Age* was an even greater champion, carrying 6,640 pages of advertising to the steel trade alone, against *Life's* 2,966 pages and *Saturday Evening Post's* 2,372 pages, Runner-up was *American Machinist*, with 5,529 pages of advertising in 1942.

[9] Postwar studies, based on 1940 prices, estimate that businesspaper annual volume will be somewhere between $88 million and $140 million.

WHAT PRICE AGENCY SERVICE?

The problem of agency commission turns up periodically in publishing circles. The Federal Trade Commission, in 1923, filed a complaint in which certain publishers' associations[10] were

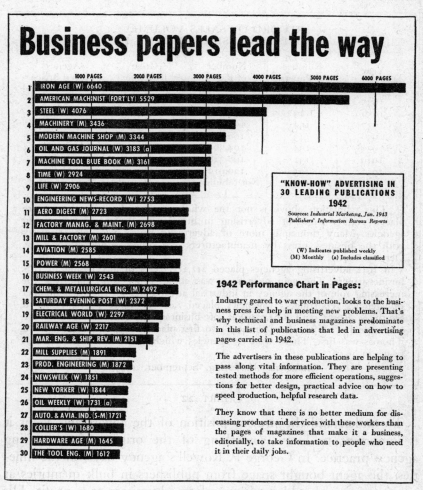

Business papers lead the way

		1000 PAGES	2000 PAGES	3000 PAGES	4000 PAGES	5000 PAGES	6000 PAGES
1	IRON AGE (W) 6640						
2	AMERICAN MACHINIST (FORT'LY) 5529						
3	STEEL (W) 4076						
4	MACHINERY (M) 3436						
5	MODERN MACHINE SHOP (M) 3344						
6	OIL AND GAS JOURNAL (W) 3183 (a)						
7	MACHINE TOOL BLUE BOOK (M) 3161						
8	TIME (W) 2924						
9	LIFE (W) 2906						
10	ENGINEERING NEWS-RECORD (W) 2753						
11	AERO DIGEST (M) 2723						
12	FACTORY MANAG. & MAINT. (M) 2698						
13	MILL & FACTORY (M) 2601						
14	AVIATION (M) 2585						
15	POWER (M) 2568						
16	BUSINESS WEEK (W) 2543						
17	CHEM. & METALLURGICAL ENG. (M) 2492						
18	SATURDAY EVENING POST (W) 2372						
19	ELECTRICAL WORLD (W) 2297						
20	RAILWAY AGE (W) 2217						
21	MAR. ENG. & SHIP. REV. (M) 2151						
22	MILL SUPPLIES (M) 1891						
23	PROD. ENGINEERING (M) 1872						
24	NEWSWEEK (W) 1851						
25	NEW YORKER (W) 1844						
26	OIL WEEKLY (W) 1731 (a)						
27	AUTO. & AVIA. IND. (S-M) 1721						
28	COLLIER'S (W) 1680						
29	HARDWARE AGE (M) 1645						
30	THE TOOL ENG. (M) 1612						

**"KNOW-HOW" ADVERTISING IN
30 LEADING PUBLICATIONS
1942**

Sources: *Industrial Marketing, Jan. 1943
Publishers' Information Bureau Reports*

(W) Indicates published weekly
(M) Monthly   (a) Includes classified

1942 Performance Chart in Pages:

Industry geared to war production, looks to the business press for help in meeting new problems. That's why technical and business magazines predominate in this list of publications that led in advertising pages carried in 1942.

The advertisers in these publications are helping to pass along vital information. They are presenting tested methods for more efficient operations, suggestions for better design, practical advice on how to speed production, helpful research data.

They know that there is no better medium for discussing products and services with these workers than the pages of magazines that make it a business, editorially, to take information to people who need it in their daily jobs.

CHART 21.   COMPARATIVE ADVERTISING CHART

[10] American Association of Advertising Agencies, Newspaper Publishers Association, Southern Newspaper Publishers Association, American Press Association, and the Six Point League.

charged with "unlawful conspiracy" to prevent advertisers who were placing business direct from receiving the same commissions that publications paid advertising agencies. After seven years of litigation, the Commission ruled that the matter was outside its jurisdiction.

RECORD OF SALES VOLUME[1]
ASSOCIATED BUSINESS PAPERS, INC.

Year	Number of Papers	Number of Pages	Gross Revenue	Agency Placed Space
1935	135	88,667	$14,413,717	Not tabulated
1936	149	118,516	19,500,436	60.0%
1937	152	135,565	22,025,341	61.0%
1938	143	106,484	18,811,446	61.8%
1939	134	104,360	18,640,078	62.0%
1940	131	108,318	20,132,367	67.7%
1941	125	120,012	22,885,537	64.0%
1942	122	Not tabulated	24,059,026	Not tabulated

[1] This tabulation above is not the whole picture. In 1941 there were placed 213,831 pages of advertising in businesspapers by 504 advertising agencies. Many thousands more of advertising pages were placed direct with the business press by manufacturers and others. (*Advertising Age*, Oct. 19, 1942.)

In 1942 advertising agencies placed 212,232 pages of advertising in U.S. businesspapers. The gain over 1941 was about 7 per cent, reflecting the increasing role of the agency in industrial advertising. Of the total number of agencies reporting, 57 agencies placed 1,000 or more pages. Fuller & Smith & Ross, with 6,054 pages of businesspaper advertising in 1942, advanced from fifth place (in 1941) to first place in 1942. In 1941, Lord & Thomas was first. There were 65 agencies which placed from 500 to 1,000 pages in 1942.

(*Industrial Marketing*, September, 1943.)

CHART 22

To understand the present position of the advertising agent it is important to know something of the origins of advertising agency practice. In George P. Rowell's agency days, in the nineties, the agent bought space from publishers in bulk quantities at a low price and sold it piecemeal to advertisers at a profit. His commission was 25 per cent plus 3 per cent cash discount. Rowell stood personally responsible for the publisher's bill and guaranteed payment whether or not he got his money from the advertiser.

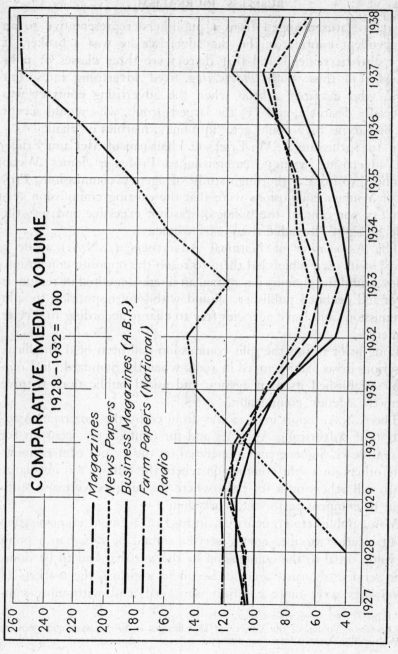

CHART 23. COMPARATIVE MEDIA VOLUME

Rowell's status changed from a publishers' representative to an independent contractor. To the advertiser he was a broker. It must also be remembered that there were three classes of publishers: (1) those with *undeviating* fixed advertising rates; (2) those who *deviated a little* when the advertising contract was especially desirable; and (3) the largest group, who would accept the best terms they could get, "in money, marbles or chalk."[11]

In 1932, the late A. W. Erickson, chairman of McCann Erickson advertising agency, commissioned Professor James Webb Young,[12] to make a thorough study of agency commissions. Professor Young's conclusions were that the existing commission system (15 per cent of the billings) was not excessive and was the best "in sight" for advertising as a whole.

The Association of National Advertisers (A.N.A.) made a study of its own which led them to reach the opposite conclusion. They found the commission system an illogical method of remuneration and declared publishers should withdraw opposition to split commissions and leave agencies free to charge according to service rendered.

Long prior to this the split commission had been held unethical. A serious crisis had occurred in 1909, when the Standard Oil Company established its own agency and asked publications to give them the agency commission.

The A.N.A. report in 1932 was disputed by the American Association of Advertising Agencies and the controversy went on for several years. Some agencies operated on the 15 per cent commission, others on a split commission where the billings ran into large sums, still others on a fee basis where the billings were not sufficient to compensate for the work done.

Many publishers argued that, instead of a cut in compensation to fit inferior service, agency service should be *raised* to a point of value equal to the commission or the job that had to be done. The service of many agencies began to improve, the markets of advertisers were more carefully surveyed; and with more con-

[11] *Printers' Ink* Anniversary Issue, July 28, 1938.
[12] Professor Young, of the University of Chicago, is now market consultant to J. Walter Thompson advertising agency.

scientious surveys came greater appreciation on the part of both agency and client of the services rendered by the business press.

WHAT COMPENSATION FOR BUSINESSPAPER SPACE?

Stanley Knisely made this statement to the National Industrial Advertisers Association (N.I.A.A.) in 1939, when he was advertising manager of Republic Steel Corporation:[13]

"The low cost per advertising page is the most potent and insidious sleeping potion the industrial advertiser ever had to combat . . . too many of us judged its value by its price. Ten lean years were needed to give us a new respect and higher regard for the advertising dollar and the unit of white space."

The average page cost of advertising in a businesspaper runs from $200 to $300.[14] A 15 per cent agency commission on this space, $30 or $45, was once regarded by agencies as hardly worth bothering about. To employ the services of high-priced copywriters and visualizers, expensive artists and high salaried account executives on a "trade paper" account was unthinkable.

The commission on a black-and-white page costing $8,500 in a consumer magazine like the *Saturday Evening Post*, $1,200, was more like it. You could do things with such a commission. In four colors it cost $12,000 (1943); agency 15 per cent commission, $1,800. The result was that many advertisers missed the advantages which carefully prepared businesspaper advertising might have gained for them in their primary and secondary markets by merchandising the costly consumer advertisement to the trade. To the agency, $45 was peanuts compared to $1,800.

This unfortunate attitude has gradually dispelled in the advertising field although businesspaper advertising rates are still too low. The agency commission is now incidental, in any case. Intelligent agency executives realize today that from small business-

---

[13] *The Ten Lean Years*, by S. A. Knisely, president of the N.I.A.A., before the annual conference, Hotel New Yorker, Sept. 20, 1939. Mr. Knisely is now executive vice-president and director of the Associated Business Papers, Inc.

[14] Highest rate for 11 leading businesspapers was $360 a page for a single insertion in *Factory Management and Maintenance*, circulation (1942) 30,968. *Iron Age* charges $153 a page (1943); *American Machinist*, $240 (1943).

BUSINESSPAPERS GET *ONE* PER CENT
OF NATIONAL ADVERTISING DOLLAR

*NATIONAL ADVERTISING VOLUME** (1939)

Magazine Adv.	$112,000,000
Radio Adv.	80,000,000
Newspaper	152,000,000
Dealer Display	50,000,000
Direct Mail	75,000,000
Miscellaneous	50,000,000
Total	$519,000,000

BUSINESSPAPER VOLUME (1939)

A.B.P.	$ 18,640,000
C.C.A.	9,000,000
Others	7,000,000
Total	$ 34,640,000

20% from national
advertisers $6,928,000, or 1% of total

Chart prepared by Arnold Friedman of *Chain Store Age*, chairman of Merchandising Papers Clinic, Convention of the Associated Business Papers, Inc., Hot Springs, Va., May 2, 1940.

Industrial Marketing, Oct. 25, 1942, reported advertising expenditures for space and time alone in a "normal year" exceed $1 billion, to which must be added $150 million for preparational costs (15%) and another $150 million for administration costs (15%). Here are the estimates:

Magazine Adv.	$165,000,000
Radio Adv.	155,000,000
Newspaper Adv.	650,000,000
Outdoor	40,000,000
Car Cards	15,000,000
Direct Mail	100,000,000*
Businesspapers	50,000,000
Farm papers	20,000,000

* Not the total volume of advertising; does not include premium advertising or direct mail done by local department stores or by manufacturers to their own customers. Direct mail estimates run as high as $250,000,000.

CHART 24

paper accounts grow great consumer advertising accounts. They also know it is necessary to "merchandise" consumer advertising to the trade, since it is the trade that will be expected to sell and promote the advertised product to the consumer. The biggest consumer advertisers, excluding perhaps food and drugs, if they had to make a choice, would hesitate a long time before giving up their businesspaper advertising.

Where the commissions from the consumer advertising do not cover an agency's cost of primary market operation, the agency charges service fees for trade activity, which often includes copy pretesting and checking, surveys and studies, in connection with preparation of the businesspaper advertising campaigns.

As between addressing a consumer audience and a businesspaper audience, the latter requires the better talent in the preparation of advertising copy. The businesspaper reader is a technician. He is in the *salaried* class. He is trained. His mind is conditioned. You have to know the language of his business in order to establish any successful communication. The businesspaper reader cannot subsist on glittering generalities. He wants useful information of the know-how kind. "Tell-all" technical copy must deal with *his* problem as well as with the advertiser's product. It requires the best brains in the advertising agency to turn out a successful businesspaper campaign.

In the foreword to Mrs. Hanford's book,[15] which was published in 1938, Roy Durstine, then a partner of the Batten, Barton, Durstine & Osborne advertising agency (now head of his own agency), emphasized the low agency commission as "an economic problem for which no one has found the answer."

"How," Mr. Durstine asked, "can an agency afford to prepare an advertisement for a businesspaper in which the page rate is so low? Even a moderate fee charged above the 15 per cent commission now almost universally paid rarely compensates the agency for the specialized study and careful writing necessary to intelligent preparation. Should the businesspapers increase their commission scale or raise their page rates? Or both? Either of these reme-

[15] *Advertising and Selling Through Business Publications*, by M. P. Hanford. Harper & Brothers, New York, 1938.

dies would seem only to penalize the advertiser without justification. Should the agency employ only low salaried youngsters to write the copy and resign itself to doing a superficial, slap dash job. Obviously, this would not service the advertiser's interests. Should the advertiser prepare his own businesspaper advertising within his own advertising department, depending on the agency for counsel and criticism?"

In the six years since Mr. Durstine posed these questions, some approaches to that problem have been made:

(a) Businesspaper publishers prepare thousands of advertisements every year on their own premises; they maintain high-priced research staffs, copywriters, visualizers, layout men, artists, photographers and typographers, for that purpose. (Indeed, some have done it for many years.) Many businesspaper advertisers start without benefit of advertising agency. They are not usually picked off by an advertising agency until they are "ripe" for consumer advertising, or in the big money. Businesspapers nourish small accounts on the little-acorn-big-oak principle.

(b) Businesspaper advertisers, in some cases, maintain large advertising departments of their own, for the preparation of businesspaper campaigns and direct mail promotion, with a special manager in charge.

(c) Agencies, in cases where the commission on consumer advertising does not cover the expense, charge not "moderate" but *proportionate* service fees for the preparation of businesspaper advertising. In all cases, fee or no fee, the agency bills the client all preparational costs on businesspaper advertising the same as he does on consumer advertising. In some instances the cost of preparing copy and plates for a $200 page in a businesspaper will amount to ten times the advertising space unit cost.

(d) Where consumer advertising schedules run into big money,[16] so that a 15 per cent commission to the agency is also big money, advertising agencies often maintain a staff of half dozen or a dozen expensive executives *on the premises of the*

---

[16] Fifteen per cent commission on a "million dollar advertising account" usually provides an advertising agency with ample funds to do a trade advertising job without thought of the space-commissions from businesspapers.

manufacturer, to co-operate with the manufacturer's own advertising department, in the necessary studies incident to the preparation of businesspaper advertising.

There is one final solution to Mr. Durstine's "economic problem": recast the page rates of businesspapers. Businesspaper advertising rates were arbitrarily established years ago on *numbers* of readers, which is perhaps all right for a consumer publication. The advertising rates for a businesspaper should be based on *power*, not *numbers* of readers—*purchasing, selling, advertising, and influencing power of the individual reader.*

A discussion of *Saturday Evening Post* and *Printers' Ink* advertising rates, in Professor Agnew's chapter on Business Publications,[17] reveals some interesting comparisons to prove the fallacy of buying businesspaper readership by numerical size. The circulation of *Printers' Ink*, in 1938, was 17,000 and the page rate $155, or $9 per page per thousand readers. The *Post* was 3 millions and the page rate $8,000, or $2.66 per page per thousand readers. Besides, the *Post* page was twice as large in physical size. The advertiser, N. W. Ayer Advertising Agency, used both media to reach the prospects who were some 4,000 firms from whom they could hope to get a reasonable number of profitable advertising accounts. It costs N. W. Ayer $8,000 to reach them in the *Post* and $156 in *Printers' Ink*. The cost per prospect was $2 in the *Post* and 3 cents in *Printers' Ink*.

Printers' Ink readers spend $1 billion a year in advertising. The average *Printers' Ink* reader, therefore, invests $65,000 a year in advertising. The same average reader's investment in chewing gum or cigarettes is so small that it would be profligate folly for Wrigley or Lucky Strike to concentrate on *Printers' Ink*. But the *Post* remains a magnet for every firm that can bring itself to spend $8,500 to $12,000 for a single shot of advertising.

In selecting 4,000 firms (who spent over $10,000 a year for advertising) as Ayer's "prospects," Dr. Agnew's argument reveals a slight fallacy. At least five persons in each firm will have some influence on the *decision* as to which agency should get the account. That would be 16,000 more executives. Of course, these

[17] *Advertising Media*, Agnew and Dygert, McGraw-Hill, New York, 1938.

agency executives may not all read the *Post*, but even if they do, 20,000 readers from 3 million still leaves a lot of waste circulation.

It is rare for a businesspaper's circulation to exceed 50,000. More often it is 10,000 or 20,000. On the basis of *numbers*, the advertising rate is often called "too high." On the basis of buying and selling power and influencing power the advertising rates now charged are ridiculously low in most cases.

If businesspaper advertising rates were increased on the basis of *power* of the reader, the advertiser's interests would not be injured. He would be paying a fair price for value received. The advertising agency's commission problem would be automatically solved. The publisher, with a better income, could pay attention to streamlining his businesspaper: using even better talent in layout, art, typography. He could pay better salaries to the editorial staff and increase their budgets so that they could pay for a better class of contribution. There are Bernard Shaws, Sinclair Lewises, Somerset Maughams, and Ernest Hemingways in the fields of business economics, if businesspapers could only afford to pay them.

With better writers, the advertiser and his customer—the reader—would get a better magazine. The status of both industry and the business press would advance. In time, on the theory that financial strength brings independence from outside interference with editorial policy, one might expect to see an even more courageous business press, better geared to come to grips with economic problems on all sides, without fear or favor.

THE ADVERTISING DEPARTMENT

The advertising sales manager may have his own solicitors, copywriters, research men, visualizers, and artists or he may utilize the department of his organization which provides those services (see Chart 10); he may use outside service agencies where his own organization does not have a department rendering the services he requires as, for example, for art work or research. The advertising sales manager and his assistants, to be effective in their own work, have to co-operate closely with the editorial, circulation, promotion, and production or mechanical divisions of their organization.

"Copy" for an advertisement usually follows these routine steps: (1) A contract for advertising is secured, checked for credit, and accepted by the publisher. (2) Arrangements for space, size and position, and date of issue are made with the production department which schedules the advertisement. (3) Advertiser provides copy or copy is prepared by his advertising agency, or by the businesspaper in collaboration with the advertiser. (4) If publication prepares copy, such copy and layout are submitted to advertiser for O.K.; necessary changes are made in copy. (5) Copy is set in type, plates are made (if any), and proofs of complete advertisement are submitted for final O.K. to the advertiser or his agent, or both. Any changes at this stage involve expense. (6) The advertisment is published according to schedule. (7) checking copies of the publication are provided to the advertiser and/or his agency. (8) The accounting department bills the advertiser or his agency for the cost of space and preparation, if preparational expenses were incurred in the publication office. (9) Reprints or preprints are sometimes furnished to the advertiser.

CHAPTER IX

FUNCTION OF THE CIRCULATION SALES MANAGER

The reader is the unit of a publication's survival.
—ARTHUR KROCK, Washington correspondent,
New York *Times*.

CIRCULATION, to a businesspaper, is like circulation to the human body: necessary to life. A sluggish circulation is a danger sign in either case.

Nothing is so lifeless as a businesspaper still in its wrapper or envelope on a reader's desk; nothing so inert as its unread contents. The contents may be inspired but it remains static until it meets the eye or ear of someone who can do something about it: *the logical reader.* It is "live" circulation that stirs the contents into action. Action is life.

What makes circulation "alive"? And what is "circulation"? To different people circulation means different things. It was not until 1618 that Harvey discovered circulation of the blood. Scientists even today find out startling things about the blood stream.

To some circulation sales managers circulation is (far too often) only a drawerful of stencils, a card file of names of people who have exchanged a subscription fee, or mere promise to read, or nothing of value, for a periodical copy of the publication. This is *distribution*, not circulation. The circulation begins when the businesspaper is read.

DEFINITION OF CIRCULATION

To a *successful* circulation sales manager, circulation is a group of alive human beings, the right group, about whom he knows a great deal, but never enough, who are *reading* his publication and translating its contents into action.

To the editor of the businesspaper, the circulation is his *readership*—his audience, very real and human individuals of varying degrees of intelligence, who *read*, applaud, condemn, or never read his editorials, who study or ignore the articles he publishes, who write telegrams and letters, or telephone, or call in person on him; who tell him what he should or should not do and say; people who buy and sell something, or influence others to do so; people who read not only his paper but other publications, people who think (in more or less degree), who act or fail to act, who get promoted, shifted, fired, retired, or interred.

To the advertising sales manager of a businesspaper, the readership is the *market* he delivers (sometimes in a compact package, sometimes loose like a barrel of sugar) for a valuable consideration, to a *logical* advertiser—someone who has something to sell this particular market. The valuable consideration is the price of the advertising white space. Under the terms of the advertising contract, he sells the advertiser certain units of white space for his business message *addressed to this market.*

To the manufacturer and his advertising manager, and their advertising agent, the circulation is also penetration of a *market* —a group of buyers or prospective buyers or purchasing agents of the manufacturer's product: people who will consume it, use it, perhaps transform it into something else, perhaps display it, re-advertise it, promote it, resell it, and, naturally, order more of it from the advertiser.

To the press agent, circulation is the *organized*, preconditioned public. Without access to it, he's like a preacher all by himself on a desert island.

To the businesspaper publisher the true circulation is his stock in trade. Without it he has nothing but the registered title of a magazine (goodwill) and a staff of technical experts. Without it he is like a congressman minus a constituency. To make money, he must possess faithful *readership* that will act upon what his editors and advertisers say.

To the promotion manager the circulation is a composite conception. He must and should know everything about it, in order to eliminate the guesswork in buying and selling it.

Nothing in a publication office is more important than the circulation. Neglect it, ignore it, mistreat it, and it dies, or transfuses with some abler publication's circulation.[1] To keep circulation alive, healthy, responsive and faithful, requires eternal vigilance on the part of publisher, editor, advertising sales manager, circulation sales manager, and promotion manager; and equal vigilance on the part of advertiser and his agency. Particularly the advertiser: in a fast-moving world of shifting markets and methods, the manufacturer and his advertising agency cannot afford to have any of their valuable conveyers or carriers—whether information carriers or commodity carriers—get out of order and out of business. The businesspaper is an information railway and, like the mechanical railroad, it is affected with a public interest. It is a quasi-public institution in which manufacturers and advertising agencies have a heavier investment than they sometimes realize. It is to their interest to see that all branch lines of industry's information railways are properly circulating and vigilantly attended.

Technically defined, the distribution of a businesspaper is the number of copies printed and delivered, by mail or other means, to a given list of readers; the penetration is the number of *readers*; what use readers make of the paper is *readership*.

The sale of space, or the purchase of space, in a businesspaper, according to some authorities, is the sale or purchase of a service: the delivery to a definite audience of a specific number of sales messages in a given medium of the reader's indicated or optional choice, which medium is primarily designed to transmit organized and useful know-how and news intelligence from where it is to where it is needed.

The businesspaper, like other periodicals, is referred to as a medium, or communication *line*. *Media*, to an advertising man, are vehicles or carriers for transmitting or conveying business messages to logical buyers or users of certain kinds or types of commodities or services. Radio is a *medium*. The mailing piece and the billboard likewise are *media*.

Ben Duffy, a vice-president of the advertising agency, Batten,

---

[1] Publishers of strong businesspapers are constantly buying and merging and thus eliminating weaker competitive businesspapers which have lost their readership and eventually their advertisers.

Barton, Durstine & Osborne, which is a heavy purchaser of businesspaper space for its clients, splits all media into two groups on the basis of circulation.[2]

1. Those with *indicated* reader interest
2. Those with *optional* reader interest

Indicated: where the reader initiates some action to show that his desire for the publication is more than superficial; best evidence of that desire being the exchange of money (a paid subscription fee). The newsstand is Mr. Duffy's example of 100 per cent "indicated interest."

Optional: where no exchange of money for the publication takes place to indicate the reader's desire. Typical of this group of media are the radio, posters, car cards, billboards, skywriters, direct mail (circulars and catalogues), and free circulation businesspapers. "Here," says Mr. Duffy, "the medium simply furnishes the right audience."[3]

The circulation sales manager in a small organization, publishing several businesspapers, generally has charge of circulation matters relating to all of them. In a large businesspaper publishing organization (see Chart 10) the circulation sales manager is concerned with only one publication's circulation and works under the supervision of a director of circulation, who is concerned with the circulation of several publications. The director has charge of four working groups: (1) his own field force; (2) his own mail force; (3) a records division; (4) an outside circulation sales agency.

While the circulation sales manager is responsible for the subscription sale (if paid) and distribution of a given publication, that is not the end of his responsibility. The basic function of the circulation manager is, and always will be, *market analysis*: day-by-day study, definition, classification, and clarification of his publication's readership, in terms of their buying, selling, promotional, and influencing *power*.

An independent, paid-circulation businesspaper has but two

---

[2] *Advertising Media & Markets*, Ben Duffy. Prentice-Hall, New York, 1931.
[3] Advertising sales managers for media of this type will challenge Mr. Duffy on this statement.

chief sources of revenue: sales of subscriptions and sales of units of advertising space.[4] Since nearly all businesspapers operate in circumscribed and limited fields of specialization, their readerships are definitely limited *in numbers* of readers. They could not operate profitably on subscription revenue alone.[5]

The *chief* source of revenue is, therefore, from the sale of advertising space units. Because sales of advertising space units are dependent on *facts* about readers or subscribers: who they are, how many, where located, what they do, how much buying, selling, promotional, and influencing power they have, their habits, their intelligence, their training and experience, their interest in a given publication, and other factors (all embodied in the word "circulation"), the manager of that circulation is a very important man, indeed, to the sales manager of the space units. The circulation sales manager is the logical man to provide all the correct answers. He is the diagnostician and the physician of ailing circulation. He is the *analyst* of that circulation which the advertising sales manager and the advertising agent call a "market." He must wrap up into a compact "package" the known values for the business office to sell. This package is readership.

There is another package the circulation manager must wrap up. This package is something he himself sells to the readers. It is the work the editor and his staff are doing and are planning. One of the functions of the circulation manager is to constantly sell the newsworthiness and editorial leadership of his publication to its *present* readers as well as to *prospective* readers. Every reader becomes a prospective reader as his paid subscription lapses and comes up again for renewal. Space buyers are keenly aware that the subscription *renewal percentage* is a reliable index of healthy circulation. Keeping it high is largely the circulation manager's responsibility. No matter what induces a reader to subscribe to a businesspaper, the real test is to induce him to *renew* the subscription. He has to like the publication, get something worth while out of it, to say, "Yes—here's my three dollars—keep it com-

[4] Many businesspaper publishers also sell books, manuals, directories, mailing lists, and other services.

[5] By contrast, *Reader's Digest* coverage is universal and is, therefore, profitable although adless.

Class. 67: House & Home Furnishings — **Business Papers—November, 1944**

67—HOUSE and Home Furnishing Goods

CCA

CURTAIN AND DRAPERY BUYER and DRAPERY PROFITS

Published by Clifford & Lawton, Inc.
373 Fourth Ave., New York 16, N. Y., Murray Hill 5-1716.
Rates effective May 1, 1944.
Agency commission 15%; cash discount 2%—10 days from invoice date.

General Advertising

	1 ti.	2 ti.	4 ti.	6 ti.	12 ti.
1 page	175.00	162.50	150.00	142.50	137.50
1/2 page	100.00	95.00	87.50	80.00	75.00
1/4 page	62.50	57.50	52.50	50.00	45.00
1/8 page	37.50	35.00	34.00	32.00	30.00

Special Positions and Colors Rates on request.
Colors
Standard colors, per color, extra 75.00
Inserts
Furnished by advertiser, charged as two pages according to contract. Must be furnished complete ready to insert. Size 6-1/8 inches by 9-1/4 inches; trim size 6 inches by 9 inches.
Bleed Pages
Extra 10%
Tip-ins
Extra 25.00
Classified
Position Wanted .05 word, minimum charge 1.00.
Help Wanted or For Rent .10 word, minimum charge 3.00.
For Sale or Business Opportunities .10 word, minimum charge 5.00.
Advertisements in all capital letters, double above rates. Cash with order.
Contract and Copy Requirements
All advertising copy subject to approval.
Mechanical Requirements

	Width	Depth	Width	Depth
1 page	5	7-3/4	—	—
1/2 page	5	3-3/4	2-3/8	7-3/4
1/4 page	—	—	2-3/8	3-3/4
1/8 page	—	—	2-3/8	1-3/4
Double spread	11	7-3/4	—	—

Page is 2 columns, each column 2-3/8 inches wide.
Halftones 120 screen.
Can use electrotypes. Cannot use mats.
Author's alterations will be charged for.
Mortising, mounting, art work, or other work on cuts or drawings, will be charged for.
Issuance and Closing Dates
Published monthly; issued 5th of publication month.
Last forms close 25th of preceding month.
First forms close 20th of preceding month. Where proofs are required for O.K. copy should be received before first closing date.
Personnel
Advertising Manager—C. J. Potter.
Representatives
Chicago — MacIntyre & Simpson & Woods, 75 E. Wacker Drive, Central 1716.
Atlanta—E. A. Hunter, 2246 E. Lake Road, N.E.

CIRCULATION—C.C.A. 6-30-44

Established 1935. Single copy .25; per year 2.00.
Total controlled circulation (6 mos. aver.) 4,150
Advertisers, agencies, exchanges, adv. prospects 259
All other distribution 176
Total distribution (6 months average) 4,585

TERRITORIAL DISTRIBUTION

Net controlled, June issue 4,273

New England	349	West South Central	288
Middle Atlantic	1,080	Mountain States	132
South Atlantic	414	Pacific States	286
East North Central	1,059	Canada	45
East South Central	199	Miscellaneous and	
West North Central	362	Foreign	59

TRADE DISTRIBUTION

(This issue is 2.9% above average for period.) Department stores 2,907; furniture stores 369; drapery shops 408; New York resident buyers 66; dry goods wholesalers 89; jobbers of decorative fabrics 67; cutters-up 28; manufacturers and converters 295; manufacturers' salesmen (bulk) 40; designers 4.

Home Furnishings Merchandising

A Haire Specialized Trade Magazine

Published by Haire Publishing Co.
1170 Broadway, New York 1, N. Y., Murray Hill 3-3800.
Rates effective October 1, 1944.
Agency commission 15% to recognized agencies on business originated by, or placed through, them; cash discount 2%—10 days to recognized agencies only.

General Advertising

	1 ti.	3 ti. as wanted	3 cons.	6 ti. as wanted	6 cons.	12 ti. as wanted	12 cons.
1 pg	280.00	265.00	240 00	235.00	212.75	203.00	185.00
3/4 pg	240.00	229.00	208.00	202.50	184.00	176.00	160.00
1/2 pg	165.00	157.00	143.00	139.00	126.50	121.00	110.00
1/4 pg	90.00	86.00	78.00	76.00	69.00	66.00	60.00
1/8 pg	57.00	54.50	49.50	48.00	43.75	42.00	38.00

1/16 page (sold for 12 consecutive issues only) 20.00
1/32 page (sold for 12 consecutive issues only) 12.00
Rate holder 1/8 page.
Covers and Special Positions—Non-cancellable
Rates on request.
Colors
Per color, extra 60.00
Inserts
Rates on request.
Size 9-3/8 inches by 12-1/2 inches; trim size 9-1/4 inches by 12-1/4 inches; stock not heavier than 25 x 38—70 lbs.
Bleed Pages
Extra 15%
Tip-ins, extra 10%
Plate size 9-3/8 inches by 12-1/2 inches; trim size 9-1/4 inches by 12-1/4 inches.
Reprints
Full page— 500 .... 7.00
Full page—1,000 .... 10.00
Reverse Plates
Reverse plates not accepted unless Ben Day or stippled background is used.
Classified
Miscellaneous, help and situation display want ads—2.50 per inch per insertion. Cash with order.
Reading Notices Not accepted.
Contract and Copy Requirements
All copy subject to publisher's approval.
Publishers reserve the right to refuse any advertisements and to cancel advertising contracts for reasons satisfactory to the management.
All rebates earned by advertiser using more than contracted space are paid in advertising space to be used within 60 days after expiration of contract.
Mechanical Requirements

	Width	Depth	Width	Depth
1 page	8-5/16	11-1/4	—	—
3/4 page	6-1/8	11-1/4	—	—
1/2 page	8-5/16	5-1/2	4-1/16	11-1/4
1/4 page	4-1/16	5-1/2	2	11-1/4
1/8 page	4-1/16	2-3/4	2	5-1/2
1/16 page	—	—	2	2-3/4
1/32 page	—	—	2	1-1/4

Page is 4 columns, each column 2 inches wide.
Halftones 120 screen. Composition—no charge.
All cuts must be blocked, mortised and notched. Mechanical operations necessary on engravings will be charged to advertiser at cost.
Issuance and Closing Dates
Published monthly; issued 29th of preceding month.
Last forms close 14th of preceding month; five days earlier for proofs.
Cancellation for run of book advertising not accepted after 5th of preceding month.
Publisher will not be responsible for errors in advertisements due to failure to return proofs in time to make corrections.
Personnel
Publisher—Andrew J. Haire.
General Manager—John J. Whelan.
Representatives
Chicago 54—F. A. Lederle, Western Manager, 1411 Merchandise Mart, Whitehall 5875.
Los Angeles 13—Loyd B. Chappell, Pacific Coast Manager, 427 W. Fifth St., Michigan 9849.
New England—D. V. O'Connell, 10 Palfrey Road, Belmont, Mass., Belmont 1090.
Pittsburgh 6—B. C. Nebo, Jr., 5535 Centre Ave., Schenley 7080.
St. Louis—Fred J. Wright, 915 Olive St., Chestnut 1965.
Atlanta 3—H. F. Cogill, 1722 Rhodes-Haverty Bldg., Walnut 8113.
Philadelphia 18—Rodman Hanson, 300 W. Willow Grove Ave.

CIRCULATION

Established 1901. Single copy .35; per year 2.00.
After three requests publisher has failed to furnish recent sworn circulation statement in accordance with S.R.D.S. requirements.

Advertisement

"Home Sweet Home" is the keynote of all post war thinking. To develop the maximum of service of retailers to their own customers is the object of HOME FURNISHINGS MERCHANDISING. It is the only monthly magazine that covers the entire homefurnishings field. Our audience: Retail furniture and floor covering stores, small, medium and large. Home furnishings divisions of department stores. Merchandise Managers. Buyers. Store coordinators and manufacturer's stylists. Copywriters. Display departments. Salespeople. Manufacturers will pay close attention to HOME FURNISHINGS MERCHANDISING because they will want their staffs to know what is going on in the retail scene . . . and we know the consumer press will cast an approving eye our way because we are helping them, too. Now, with a larger format (see listing), our new editorial staff, headed by Esther Skaar Hansen and Gladys Miller, two of America's leading authorities in the home furnishings field, will have ample opportunity to present and illustrate their ideas in appropriate graphic form.

ABC ABP

House Furnishing Review

A Haire Specialized Trade Magazine

Published by Haire Publishing Company.
1170 Broadway, New York 1, N. Y., Murray Hill 3-3800.
Rates effective July 1, 1944.
Agency commission 15% to recognized agencies on business originated by, or placed through, them; cash discount 2%—10 days to recognized agencies only.

General Advertising

	1 ti.	3 ti.	3 cons.	6 ti.	6 cons.	12 ti.	12 cons.
1 pg	265.00	250.00	227.50	221.50	201.25	192.50	175.00
2/3 pg	210.00	200.00	182.00	177.00	161.00	154.00	140.00
1/2 pg	147.00	140.00	127.50	124.00	112.75	108.00	98.00
1/3 pg	115.50	110.00	100.00	97.50	88.50	84.75	77.00
1/4 pg	84.00	80.00	73.00	71.00	64.50	61.50	56.00
1/6 pg	68.00	64.50	58.50	57.25	52.00	49.50	45.00
1/8 pg	52.50	50.00	45.50	44.25	40.25	38.50	35.00

Covers and Special Positions—Non-cancellable contract only Rates on request.
First cover subject to publisher's approval.
Colors
Per color, extra 60.00
Inserts Rates on request.
Size 8-1/4 inches by 11-1/2 inches; trim size 8-1/8 inches by 11-1/4 inches; stock not heavier than 25 x 38—70 lbs.
Bleed Pages
Extra 15%
Tip-ins, extra 10%
Plate size 8-1/4 inches by 11-1/2 inches; trim size 8-1/8 inches by 11-1/4 inches.
Bleed 2/3 page size 5-1/16 inches wide by 11-1/2 inches deep, which allows 1/8 inch trim on top, bottom, and outside edge; trim size 4-15/16 inches wide by 11-1/4 inches deep.
Reprints
Full page— 500 .... 7.00
Full page—1,000 .... 10.00
Reverse Plates
Reverse plates not accepted unless Ben Day or stippled background is used.
Gadgets and Where-to-Buy
2-1/4 inches by 1-1/8 inches on 12 time contract only—12.00 per insertion. (Not a rate holder.)
Classified
Want ads 2.50 per inch. Minimum one inch. Cash with order.
Reading Notices Not accepted.
Contract and Copy Requirements
All copy subject to publisher's approval.
Publisher reserves the right to refuse any advertisements and to cancel advertising contracts for reasons satisfactory to the management.
All rebates earned by advertisers using more than contracted space are paid in advertising space to be used within 60 days after expiration of contract.
Mechanical Requirements

	Width	Depth	Width	Depth
1 page	7	10	—	—
2/3 page	4-5/8	10	—	—
1/2 page	7	4-7/8	3-3/8	10
1/3 page	4-5/8	4-7/8	2-1/4	10
1/4 page	—	—	3-3/8	4-7/8
1/6 page	—	—	2-1/4	4-7/8
1/8 page	2-1/4	3-11/16	—	—

Page is 2 columns, each column 3-3/8 inches wide, or 3 columns, each column 2-1/4 inches wide.
Halftones 110 screen.
All cuts must be blocked, mortised and notched. Mechanical operations necessary on engravings will be charged to advertiser at cost.
Issuance and Closing Dates
Published monthly; issued 3rd of publication month.
Last forms close 18th of preceding month; five days earlier for proofs.
Cancellations for run of book advertising not accepted after 10th of preceding month.
Publisher will not be responsible for errors in advertisements due to failure to return proofs in time to make corrections.
Personnel
Publisher—Andrew J. Haire.
General Manager—John J. Whelan.
Business Manager—J. J. Dubro.
Representatives
Chicago 54—F. A. Lederle, Western Manager, 1411 Merchandise Mart, Whitehall 5875.
New England—D. V. O'Connell, 10 Palfrey Road, Belmont, Mass., Belmont 1090.
Pittsburgh 6—B. C. Nebo, Jr., 5535 Centre Ave., Schenley 7080.
St. Louis—Fred J. Wright, 915 Olive St., Chestnut 1965.
Los Angeles 13—Loyd B. Chappell, Pacific Coast Manager, 427 W. Fifth St., Michigan 9849.
Atlanta 3—H. F. Cogill, 1722 Rhodes-Haverty Bldg., Walnut 8113.
Philadelphia 18—Rodman Hanson, 300 W. Willow Grove Ave.

CIRCULATION—A.B.C. 6-30-44

Established 1892. Single copy .25; per year 2.00.
Total net paid excluding bulk (6 mos. aver.) 4,030
Total net paid including bulk 4,067
Advertisers 282
Advertising agencies 135
Samples to prospective advertisers 67
All other unpaid distribution 273
Total distribution (6 months average) 4,824

TERRITORIAL DISTRIBUTION

Based on total net paid of May issue 4,088
(Mail 4,061; single copy sales 27)

New England	433	West South Central	140
Middle Atlantic	1,448	Mountain States	73
South Atlantic	264	Pacific States	338
East North Central	934	Canada	77
East South Central	69	Foreign	53
West North Central	233	Miscellaneous	26

BUSINESS ANALYSIS OF SUBSCRIPTIONS

Retail dealers in house furnishings (department stores, furniture stores, independent retailers, purchasing organizations and public utilities), including executives, merchandise managers, buyers and other employees 2,394; wholesalers and exporters, executives and employees 377; manufacturers' representatives and employees 354; manufacturers, executives and employees 686; libraries, colleges, government bureaus and associations 48; miscellaneous 118; unclassified 84. Unpaid distribution (6 mos. aver.—not analyzed) 757

Advertisement

HOUSE FURNISHING REVIEW, for more than a half a century, has been faithfully serving the great and prolific housewares and household appliance markets. Wherever these products are bought and sold, HOUSE FURNISHING REVIEW is helping dealers with its helpful, constructive editorial services.

The day is not far distant when manufacturers of housewares and appliance merchandise will again be free to produce in volume for civilian consumption. Billions of dollars worth of goods will be made and released for distribution and plans are now being completed for that selling era. Competition will be keen—merchandising will be intense.

In such a market, the right kind of advertising in HOUSE FURNISHING REVIEW will reflect directly in sales and distribution.

HOUSE FURNISHING REVIEW, from coast to coast, is received and acknowledged as the unquestioned leader by all prominent buyers of housewares and appliances in department stores, hardware stores, furniture stores, chain and mail order houses and buying groups. These buyers control the purse strings of billions of dollars worth of buying power.

This is the entree and market that HOUSE FURNISHING REVIEW offers to manufacturers of housewares, kitchen equipment and electric, gas and oil appliances for the immediate future. A Haire Specialized Trade Magazine.

ABC

INTERIORS

11 E. 44th St., New York 17, N. Y., Vanderbilt 6-2954.
See listing under Classification No. 73.

Page 260

CHART 25. STANDARD RATE AND DATA

ing." Space buyers in advertising agencies want to know what percentage of the total paid readership on a publication is renewed automatically: 50 per cent, 60 per cent, 70 per cent? When a businesspaper or any other publication reaches 70 per cent renewals it is clicking with its readership.

Changes in position, by promotion, resignation, retirement, and death create casualties in circulation lists which the manager must replace, and quickly. A large staff is required to keep a list "alive."

To get *new* readers, the circulation manager must show that old readers get something valuable out of his publication. This requires the submission of proof—not just mere assertion—to a prospective reader.

The advertising sales manager is selling white space units in his publication as sites or locations for advertising messages, the theory being that the reader will be interested enough in these advertising messages to read them and act upon their suggestions, just as he reads and acts upon the editorial messages. This presupposes that the reader is really reading the editorial columns. The prospective advertiser will require factual proof that this is so.

It is easy to see, therefore, that advertising sales managers and circulation sales managers have no clear line of demarcation in their functions. They both sell reader interest and both must *prove* reader interest.

The circulation sales manager proceeds, therefore, to arm himself with facts to sell the editorial contents to prospective readers as something of *value* to them in the conduct of their business. He is required to arm the advertising sales manager with factual information of value about the reader-subscribers and their special interests in the publication, which information will, in turn, be passed on to prospective purchasers of the white space.

All of which brings into sharp relief this important point: the circulation sales manager cannot be a swivel-chair artist. He cannot look complacently upon the readers as a drawer of stencils, or a card file, or a mailing list of names and titles, and expect the records division and mailing staff to keep that circulation alive and healthy. He must live among these human beings who read his publication whenever he can and as often as he can. He must be alive, himself. He must interview readers, see them at work, attend their meetings, get their reactions and criticisms, listen to their troubles. He must also attend meetings of the advertising sales department, to be conversant with the difficulties advertising space salesmen encounter in selling the readership to manufacturers.

The circulation sales manager must maintain close liaison with editors, not only intelligently to transmit news of editorial activities to readers who are up for renewal, and to prospective readers, but also to relate plans of future editorial activity. He must talk to manufacturers' distributors and salesmen, who are selling goods to his readers, for their reactions and experiences.

From all these sources comes the vital information about the readership which he must know and impart to the advertising sales manager, the promotion manager, the editor, and the publisher.

The circulation sales manager should be constantly engaged in devising more graphic and more dramatic ways of presenting the circulation or "market picture" to those who want to see that true, living, and ever-changing sector of industry which is referred to as a publication's "circulation."

FALLACY OF "NUMBERS" OF READERS

Will Rogers used to say, "Numbers don't mean nuthin': it's people that count."

In his book on advertising media,[6] Dr. Hugh Agnew, emeritus professor of marketing at New York University, on the same point, cites a remark by Dr. Emil Ludwig, the well-known biographer. Dr. Ludwig had received a telegram from the editor of a consumer magazine asking him to name his price to write a thousand words on immortality for that magazine's "million readers." Dr. Ludwig wired his answer:

I am not interested; but I would be glad to write a million words on the same subject for a magazine with a thousand readers.

Let us compare a consumer publication with a business magazine in order to see the difference between mere *numbers* of readers and *power* on the part of readers to do things.

[6] *Advertising Media* by Hugh Elmer Agnew and Warren B. Dygert. McGraw-Hill, New York, 1938.

Ladies' Home Journal is a monthly consumer magazine which is purchased, as the title suggests, chiefly by housewives and home-makers. Each reader of *Ladies' Home Journal* has a definite pur-chasing power for the type of merchandise advertised and featured in it. A woman whose husband earns $25,000 a year may be a reader; a woman whose husband earns $2,500 a year may be a reader. The publishers of *Ladies' Home Journal* keep an accurate and timely picture of the size, wealth, location, and habits of their consumer audience. To any manufacturer interested in advertising his products in *Ladies' Home Journal*, the publishers will under-take to deliver this well-defined readership, which in 1941 had a numerical strength of more than 3½ million readers.

House Furnishing Review, on the other hand, is a business maga-zine also published monthly; but unlike *Ladies' Home Journal*, it is not published for consumers. The *Review* is published for whole-sale and retail distributors of consumers' goods: sales managers, merchandise managers, their buyers, advertising and selling per-sonnel.

Consumers' goods in the field of house furnishings fall into three major classifications: (1) Housewares: utensils for preparing, cooking, canning, refrigerating, freezing and dehydrating foods; kitchen china and glassware; unpainted, painted, and metal furni-ture for house and garden; garden and workbench tools, hardware, and miscellaneous gadgets. (2) Appliances: refrigerators, ranges, heating and air-conditioning equipment, washing machines, vacuum cleaners, small appliances. (3) Bath Furnishings: shower curtains, toilet seats, scales, hampers, vanity sets, and accessories. The *Review*'s audience is shown in the Publisher's Circulation State-ment (Chart 26).

Manufacturers of house furnishing merchandise advertise their products in *House Furnishing Review* in order to secure distribu-tion in department, furniture, hardware, electrical dealer, variety and specialty stores, chain stores, and by mail order and premium houses and public utilities.

In a given city, let us say New Haven, Conn., there are nearly 15,000 readers of *Ladies' Home Journal*. In this same city of New Haven, there are two large wholesale jobbers of house furnishings, four department stores with eight buyers of house furnishings; a dozen hardware, furniture, and electrical dealers and a public utility, who are subscribers to *House Furnishing Review*. Twenty-two of these readers are retail buyers.

But these 22 retail buyers stock most of the housewares, appliances, and bath furnishings which will be purchased subsequently by the majority of the 15,000 New Haven women who read *Ladies' Home Journal*.

These 22 house furnishing buyers, obviously, have a far greater buying power than the combined purchasing power of the 15,000 *Ladies' Home Journal* readers. There are 50,000 families in New Haven. The local house furnishing stores are purchasing agents not only for New Haven, West Haven, North Haven and Hamden, which is known as "Greater New Haven," but also for 27 other thriving communities in the New Haven *trading area*. The 84,000 families in this greater shopping area, of course, read various other consumer magazines and daily newspapers, and listen to radio commercial broadcasts. Many read foreign-language newspapers, and undoubtedly some heads of families cannot read at all. The total retail buyers of New Haven undoubtedly also read other businesspapers: *Electrical Merchandising, Electrical Dealer, Hardware Age, Hardware Dealer, Retailing, Department Store Economist*—to mention some competitors in this field. These 22 buyers who subscribe to and presumably read the *Review* are *purchasing agents*, when it comes to house furnishings, for a large part of the 84,000 families.

No consumer magazine can ever hope to offer as much buying power to a manufacturer as can a good business magazine concentrating on that manufacturer's market, because no consumer magazine or daily newspaper or radio station, or all three combined, reaches the maximum purchasing power of all trading areas or any one of them.

In this connection it will be of passing interest to note that a black-and-white page in *Ladies' Home Journal* costs an advertiser $8,500 and a black-and-white page in *House Furnishing Review* costs an advertiser $225 (1941).

One must not get the impression, however, that the consumer

magazine does not deliver full value, when it delivers so important a national audience as the 3½ million readers of *Ladies' Home Journal* to an advertiser. The best testimony of the value of the consumer magazine's influence is the impressive list of advertisers of everything from automobiles to soap who use consumer magazines year after year to impress the quality of their products, their trade-marks, and their brand names upon the public consciousness.

Our point is: beware of the trap into which many advertisers and advertising agencies have fallen in buying advertising space in businesspapers: the fallacy of numerical strength, the mistake of confusing "how many readers?" with "how much buying and selling *power* for my product?"

Businesspaper publishers are likewise trapped, for they, too, often sell their readership numerically. The average businesspaper page advertising rate runs from $150 to $300. The average circulation is 5,000 to 10,000. Numerically those are high rates to pay for readership. In point of *power* purchased, it is, in most cases, dirt cheap.

As demonstrated, a circulation of 22 readers may represent more buying power than a circulation of 15,000 readers. The geographical distribution of people with buying power in our country is such that 80 per cent of the United States families in normal times live in 24 states, and 84 per cent of the retail sales are made in these 24 states.[7]

SELLING POWER—THE EXTRA VALUE

Another point to keep in mind about the specialized business magazine's readership is this: The store buyer, in addition to *buying* power, has *selling* and *promotional* power which is important to the manufacturer. The store buyer uses such selling tools as window displays, departmental displays, cooking schools, contests, concerts, lectures, newspaper and magazine advertising and publicity, direct mail (catalogues, booklets, letters), sales clerks, the

[7] Purchase Survey released in 1941 by the Departments of Labor and Agriculture.

telephone, radio broadcasts, and even house-to-house canvassing to move the goods from retail counters into homes.

This selling and promotional power is in itself a tremendously important kind of consumer advertising for national brands—a point which many manufacturers and their advertising agencies are sometimes prone to overlook when they plan consumer advertising schedules. *More women pass the windows and walk down the aisles of retail stores than the combined circulation of all consumer magazines and newspapers.* The point is that advertising in consumers' goods businesspapers, can be used efficiently to promote the use of dealer helps[8] which are a most valuable form of consumer advertising. A *House Furnishing Review* reader survey[9] asked these questions on store traffic and sales transactions:

"How many shoppers pass through your housewares and appliance departments or sections daily?"

"What is the average number of sales transactions in your housewares and appliance department daily?"

That is what the *Review* learned:

"2,905,100 shoppers pass through the housewares and appliance departments of our retailer-subscribers *every day*" (about 3,000 stores).

"1,584,000 individual sales transactions take place *every day* in these departments."

Birth of Audited Circulation

The circulation liar began to worry honest publishers and advertisers as early as 1889. The California legislature in 1893, largely through the efforts of the San Francisco *Examiner* finally passed a bill (introduced three years earlier) enabling an advertiser who had any reason to doubt the circulation of a periodical to bring the publisher into court and make him produce proof. This act had a sobering effect on circulation liars. So did the clamor for standardized and uniform advertising rates. The pressure of advertisers and

---

[8] Window and counter display material, newspaper matrices, booklets, sales training manuals, radio scripts are types of "dealer helps" furnished by producers and wholesale distributors.

[9] "Meet Our Merchants," by the Haire Publishing Co., New York, 1941.

Publisher's Statement – Business Paper
PERIOD ENDING DECEMBER 31, 1944

1. HOUSE FURNISHING REVIEW
2. Haire Publishing Co., Inc.
3. 1170 Broadway, New York, N. Y.
4. Established 1892
5. Published Monthly
7. Class, Industry or Field Served — The House Furnishing, Retail and Wholesale Industry covering specifically Houseware, Major and Minor Household Electric Appliances, Bathroom Furnishings and Allied Products.

HOW MANY COPIES ?

8. Averages for 6 months ending December 31, 1944:

Mail Subscriptions—Individual	4,112	**TOTAL NET PAID includ. Bulk**		4,508
Net Single Copy Sales	24	Unpaid Distribution		
Mail Subs. Special Par. 25	336	Advertisers	360	
		Advertising Agencies	153	
		Correspondents		
		Samples to Prospective Advertisers	75	
		Exchanges, Complimentary, Subscription		
		Salesmen, Samples & Employes	218	
		Credit Subs. Canc. for Nonpayment	23	
TOTAL NET PAID exclud. Bulk	4,472			
Term Subscriptions in Bulk Par. 26.	8			
Single Issue Sales in Bulk Par. 26.	28	**Total Unpaid**		829
TOTAL NET PAID includ. Bulk	4,508	**Total Distribution**		5,337

HOW MANY OF EACH ISSUE ?

9. NET PAID CIRCULATION INCLUDING BULK BY ISSUES FOR PERIOD STATED IN PARAGRAPH 8:

Date	Copies	Date	Copies	Date	Copies	Date	Copies
July	4,230						
Aug.	4,403						
Sept.	4,552						
Oct.	4,564						
Nov.	4,627						
Dec.	4,676						

WHO READS IT ?

10. BUSINESS ANALYSIS OF SUBSCRIPTIONS based on November, 1944, issue:

NOTE—Total subscription circulation of this issue was 2.90% greater than average total subscription circulation for period.

CLASSIFICATION		PERCENTAGE
1. (a) Retail Dealers in House Furnishings (Department Stores, Furniture Stores, Independent Retailers, Purchasing Organizations & Public Utilities) including executives, Merchandise Managers, Buyers & Other Employes	2,559	55.79%
(b) Wholesalers & Exporters, Executives & Employes	479	10.44%
2. Manufacturers' Representatives & Employes	400	8.72%
3. Manufacturers, Executives & Employes	783	17.07%
4. Libraries, Colleges, Government Bureaus & Associations	51	1.11%
5. Miscellaneous	151	3.29%
6. Unclassified	164	3.58%
TOTAL	4,587	100.00%

WHERE ARE READERS LOCATED ?

11. NET PAID CIRCULATION INCLUDING BULK BY STATES: *(See reverse side of this page)*

CHART 26A. PUBLISHER'S CIRCULATION STATEMENT (A.B.C.)

(ABC) AUDIT BUREAU OF CIRCULATIONS   **House Furnishing Review**

165 WEST WACKER DRIVE · CHICAGO I, ILLINOIS

[This statement is subject to audit by the Audit Bureau of Circulations. For Audit Report refer to latest white paper form.]

12. AUTHORIZED PRICES for sale of this publication during period stated in Paragraph 8:

(a) Basic prices: Single Copy 25¢. Subscriptions 1 yr. $2.00; 2 yrs. $3.00 ....

(b) Prices higher than basic: In Canada, 1 yr. $3.00; 2 yrs. $5.00. Foreign, 1 yr. $4.00; 2 yrs. $7.00 ....   **1,775**

(c) Combination sales prices: Prices for combination sales of this publication with other publications varied from 50% to 83-1/3% of combined basic prices of publications in combinations. Combination sales prices ranged from $2.50 to $25.00 in actual amounts **38**

(d) Combination or basic prices: Publisher unable to identify, also see Par. 16(c) ....   **None**

(e) Prices established for sales in quantities: Lots of 5 or more subscriptions 1 year $1.00 ....   **231**

(f) Group organizers' prices for this publication alone: ......   **None**

(g) Association subscription prices: ....   **None**

(h) Special reduced prices: 1 yr. $1.00, 15 months $2.00 ....   **None**

    TOTAL SUBSCRIPTIONS SOLD IN PERIOD   **2,044**

(i) Collection stimulants: ....   **None**

13 & 14. (See Note Par. 28)

ANALYSIS OF NEW & RENEWAL SUBSCRIPTION SALES
For Period Stated in Paragraph 8.

15. CHANNELS OF SUBSCRIPTION SALES:

(a) Subscriptions direct to publisher by mail **1,678**

(b) Catalogue & newspaper subscription agencies, & other publishers **172**

(c) (1) Publisher's own field selling organization **146**

    (2) Other field selling organizations **48**

(d) Independent individual subscription salesmen reporting direct to publisher ....   **None**

(e) Organizers of groups (not combinations) ....   **None**

(f) Associations ....   **None**

(g) All other channels ....   **None**

    TOTAL SUBSCRIPTIONS SOLD IN PERIOD   **2,044**

16. COMBINATION SUBSCRIPTION SALES:

(a) Known combination sales ...Par. 12(c)...............   **38**

(b) Known not to be in combination **2,006**

(c) Through intermediaries authorized to sell subscriptions either singly or in combination, therefore unable to determine accurately whether in combination or not ..:   **None**

    TOTAL SUBSCRIPTIONS SOLD IN PERIOD   **2,044**

17. PREMIUMS:
(In (a) below, the premiums were offered by publisher or with his knowledge.)

(a) Subscriptions sold with premium .Par. 28(a)..........   **8**

(b) Subscriptions sold without premium **2,036**

    TOTAL SUBSCRIPTIONS SOLD IN PERIOD   **2,044**

18. SUBSCRIPTION SALES BY PRICE CLASSIFICATIONS:
(See Par. 12)

19. DURATION OF SUBSCRIPTIONS SOLD:

(a) For five years or more ....   **None**

(b) For four years or more but less than five years ....   **None**

(c) For three years or more but less than four years **8**

(d) For two years or more but less than three years **842**

(e) For one year or more but less than two years **1,180**

(f) For six months or more but less than one year **14**

(g) For less than six months ....   **None**

    TOTAL SUBSCRIPTIONS SOLD IN PERIOD   **2,044**

20. (See Note Par. 28)

---

21. MISCELLANEOUS CIRCULATION CONDITIONS

ARREARS & EXTENSIONS:

(a) Subscriptions carried in arrears as of November, 1944, issue: Up to 3 months 4.19%. Is above representative of condition of list for all other issues covered by this statement? No. Other issues varied from 3.35% to 3.88% for up to 3 months.

22. RENEWALS OF SUBSCRIPTIONS:

(a) Subscriptions Other than Bulk
Thru October 31, 1944, there were 1,818 renewals received on expirations May, 1943 thru April, 1944. The number of expirations possible of renewal was 2,374 ..   **76.58%**

(b) Term Subscriptions in Bulk
Thru October 31, 1944, there were 35 renewals received on expirations May, 1943 thru April, 1944. The number of expirations possible of renewal was 39 ......   **89.74%**
A renewal is considered one received and paid for within six months after expiration.

23. ALL OTHER CHANNELS EXPLAINED: *(Items 2% or more only)*
None

24. THIS PUBLICATION is not an official organ of any association.

25. MAIL SUBSCRIPTIONS SPECIAL:
Represents copies served on yearly subscriptions sold to retail merchants and manufacturers at $1.00 per subscription in lots of 5 or more, for branch stores and employes, mailed in individual wrappers direct to names and addresses furnished by purchasers.

26. BULK SUBSCRIPTIONS & SALES:
Term Subscriptions in Bulk represents copies served on yearly subscriptions sold at half yearly price, mailed in bulk to purchasers for redistribution.
Single Issue Sales in Bulk represents copies sold in bulk at 12½c and 15c per copy, distribution being made by purchaser.

27. (See Note Par. 28)

28. EXPLANATORY:
NOTE—Gaps in paragraph numbers in form are due to two causes: (1) desirability of retaining familiar paragraph designations regardless of dropping of obsolete paragraphs as revisions have been made during course of years; (2) co-ordinating of similar paragraphs in various types of Publisher's Statement forms.

a) Paragraph 17(a):
8 subscriptions sold with Pots & Pans Manual as a premium.

We hereby make oath & say that all statements set forth in this statement are true.

ALBERT C. ESSER   JOHN J. WHELAN
   Circulation Manager   General Manager

Subscribed & sworn to before me this 23rd day of January, 1945.

                     BEATRICE G. STAHL
My commission expires March 30, 1945.   Notary Public

CHART 26B

advertising agents for lower rates put it up to the publisher to prove that he deserved his present or higher advertising space rates.

Another impetus to verified circulation statements was the publication directory. One of the earliest was issued in 1869, the *American Newspaper Directory*. By 1878 it was guaranteeing the accuracy of the circulation statements reported in its columns. George Presbury Rowell,[10] pioneer advertising agent who was the publisher of this directory, invited publishers to submit "signed statements" of their circulations, on the theory that they would avoid appending their signatures to fraudulent figures. Rowell also offered $100 reward to any one who could disprove the figures he published. (The reward was claimed and paid five times in one year.)

Rowell's directory differed from Mitchell's *Directory of the Newspapers of Great Britain* in two ways. Mitchell's sold for a shilling and Rowell's for $5. Mitchell's was silent on circulation. "I was often told that it would not be allowed in England," Rowell says in his autobiography, ". . . an effort made in London about two years ago to bring out a directory on a plan so long in use by us was promptly squelched by the courts."

Other American advertising agents, N. W. Ayer and Lord & Thomas, for example, soon began publishing directories, and by 1890 14 directories were being published.

A transition in the functions of the advertising agent are worth noting at this point. The advertising agent started out originally as the agent of the publisher, who paid his commission. His equipment included a list of good publications, a pretty accurate guess of their *actual* circulation figures, plus an aggressive bargaining power to get the lowest possible rates (before rates were fixed and standardized) for an advertising prospect. Armed with this equipment the agent sallied forth to "pick up ads." He placed the orders, mailed the copy, and checked insertions for the advertiser. Whether the copy was right and what results the advertiser obtained were not the agent's problems. By 1900 the agent's loyalty was reversed—he had become, in effect, part of the advertiser's organization rather than the publisher's. Sometimes he received

---

[10] *Founder of Printers' Ink. Forty Years An Advertising Agent*, by G. P. Rowell, Franklin Publishing Co., New York, 1926.

large fees from advertisers not only for preparing their copy but for setting up and training their sales organizations and even for analyzing markets for their products or services.

Guesses, estimates, and publishers' signed but still doubtful statements of circulation eventually became unacceptable to most advertisers and advertising agents. They wanted a more accurate measure of circulation. That meant one thing: the advent of the independent professional auditor of circulation.

In the spring of 1899 representatives of some 30 advertisers met in New York City and formed the Association of American Advertisers with Frederick L. Perine of Hall & Ruckel as first president. In three years the AAA (known as the 3-A's) audited 400 publications (chiefly consumer) and made "inspection reports" on 57 cities. Similar auditing work was started by a western organization, American Society of National Advertisers, headed by C. W. Post, which subsequently merged with the AAA.

The Association of American Advertisers, by 1912, had examined more than 1,000 separate circulation statements but never was able to get more than a handful of advertisers to underwrite the expense of this type of work. By 1913 things were pretty bad. Lawsuits were filed against publishers, demanding circulation rebates. In a speech that year one publisher said, *"Circulation liars humiliate honest publishers."*[11]

Two new movements started in 1913 aimed at accomplishing what the 3-A's had failed to achieve. One was the Association of National Advertising Managers in New York, which had changed its name to the Association of National Advertisers. The other was Western Advertising Agents' Association, a Chicago group of advertisers and agency men, headed by Stanley Claque, who had been backers of the 3-A movement.[12]

Finally, the same year (1913), an "Advertising Audit Association" was formed in the West, and a "Bureau of Verified Circulation" in the East, to tackle this problem of audited readership and forestall a threatened collapse of the entire advertising structure.

[11] *Printers' Ink*, Anniversary Edition.
[12] For detailed histories see also *ABC Anniversary Edition*; *Advertising Age*, October, 1934, and *Scientific Space Selection*, by O. C. Harn, published by the Audit Bureau of Circulations, Chicago, 1921.

A proposal was made to President McChesney of the Association of National Advertising Managers by O. C. Harn. Mr. Harn was the advertising manager of the National Lead Co., New York. He proposed that the group organize a new auditing body admitting publishers to membership. The publishers would provide most of the income; the advertiser-members would hire and control the auditors. A "circulation audit committee" was appointed, with Mr. Harn as chairman, and L. B. Jones and G. B. Sharpe as members.

Invitations to a conference on April 22, 1913, at the Hardware Club, New York, brought together representatives of many publishing and advertising associations with businesspaper associations playing a dominant part. A permanent organization was recommended with three representatives from each of the following organizations: Federation of Trade Press Associations, Grocery and Allied Trade Press Association, Technical Publicity Association, Farm Press Association, American Newspaper Publishers Association, Quoin Club, Periodical Publishers Association, New York Advertising Agents' Association, Association of National Advertising Managers, and Association of American Advertisers. The Bureau of Verified Circulations was organized.

First organizations to adopt the plan were the Grocery and Allied Trade Press Association and the Association of New York Advertising Agents. Only the 3-A's openly opposed the plan. Their Mr. Bert M. Moses suggested merger with the 3-A's. This was rejected. That summer the 3-A's collapsed, owing several thousand dollars. The members blamed the Bureau of Verified Circulations in the East for their downfall and turned for help to Mr. Clacque's Western Advertising Agents' Association of Chicago, which group had not been invited to the New York conference of April 22.

Mr. Claque drew up a new plan and an "Advertising Audit Association" was formed at the La Salle Hotel, Chicago, in September, 1913, headed by Claque, Colonel Emory Mapes (Cream of Wheat Co.), and Jason Rogers. This group paid off the indebtedness of the AAA. In October, 1913, the organizers of the Bureau of Verified Circulations went to work. On their board was F. R. Davis of

General Electric, representing Technical Publicity Association; A. W. Erickson, representing New York Association of Advertising Agents; O. C. Harn, Association of National Advertising Managers; M. C. Robbins of *Iron Age*, representing the Federation of Trade Press Associations of the United States; George M. Rogers of Cleveland *Plain Dealer* representing American Newspaper Publishers Association; George Von Utassy, of *Cosmopolitan* magazine representing Periodical Publishers Association, and Wm. H. Whitney, Farm Press Association.

After several meetings with representatives of both eastern and western groups, the bodies consolidated as the "Advertising Audit Association and Bureau of Verified Circulations"—headquarters in New York and Chicago.

On Aug. 21, 1914, the Audit Bureau of Circulations was duly incorporated, the first president being Louis Bruch of American Radiator Co., Chicago; Erickson and Davis were vice-presidents. To A. W. Erickson, an advertising agency executive, acting as temporary chairman, must go credit for successfully engineering the merger of these two groups in 1914.

The Audit Bureau of Circulations (ABC), the Canadian Circulations Audit Board (CCAB), and the Controlled Circulation Audit (CCA) are the three public accounting organizations now existing for buyers of advertising space, to enable them to verify the statements which publishers make concerning their circulations. The vital information in the ABC, CCAB reports and in the CCA reports become a basis for judging the *quality* as well as the quantity of a businesspaper's circulation.

The Audit Bureau of Circulation

Known by the symbol "ABC" the merger in 1914, which we have described, brought together 400 advertisers, advertising agencies, and periodical publishers into the now internationally famous public accounting organization known as the Audit Bureau of Circulations.[13] Co-operative and nonprofit, the purpose of ABC is to

[13] By 1942, ABC membership embraced every leading publication of paid circulation in the United States and Canada as well as the leading advertising agencies and the leading advertisers. The British ABC, founded in 1931, is the

collect and verify *paid* circulation data, establish uniform methods of auditing paid circulations and to disseminate information among its members by standardized reports.[14] Its establishment provided the first adequate yardstick to measure the value of publication media. This yardstick of values is found in the standards and audits of the ABC. The ABC Publishers' Statements,[15] sworn to by the publisher, are issued in printed form every six months. Regularly employed, experienced ABC auditors are sent once each year to each publisher's office to make an exhaustive investigation and audit of the circulation. These findings are embodied in the ABC Audit Report, which is issued annually in mimeographed form (Chart 26). If the previously issued publisher's statement was in error, the Audit Report points it out.

It is noteworthy that, while the ABC is financed chiefly by sellers of space (the publishers), the control of its policy rests with the buyers of space (advertisers and their advertising agents).

The rules and regulations of member publications are the strictest and the severest with regard to methods of getting new subscriptions or receiving expirations. Many premium practices used by non-ABC papers are strictly forbidden.

The ABC[16] is an important example of industrial self-government and the will to conduct business honestly and aboveboard.

In 1942 more than 41 per cent of the total average net paid cir-

---

largest in Europe. The French ABC, founded in 1923, is the second largest. Belgium, Switzerland, Holland, Norway, Sweden, and Australia have similar Audit Bureaus of Circulation. It will cause no surprise to know that Italy and Germany got along without audited circulations. Germany, however, in 1933 passed a law requiring publishers to keep authentic records.

[14] "The objectives of the founders of the Bureau were to define and provide standards of definition for paid circulations . . ." from *Self-Regulation in the Advertising and Publishing Industry*, a pamphlet published by ABC in 1942.

[15] The CCA do not issue "publishers' reports."

[16] *Advertising and Selling*, in 1934, published the standing of ABC businesspaper membership as follows: A.B.C., 15.9 per cent; non-A.B.C., 84.1 per cent. Thus a gain is indicated since 1934. The ABC report of 1942 showed an increase of over 25% in businesspaper memberships:

Business Press A.B.C.	41.4%	Non-A.B.C.	58.6%
Dailies A.B.C.	87.7%	Non-A.B.C.	12.3%
General Magazines A.B.C.	82.5%	Non-A.B.C.	17.5%
Farm Papers A.B.C.	81.7%	Non-A.B.C.	18.3%

These are the figures of publication memberships—not readers. As of March, 1942, membership included 1,151 newspapers, 215 consumer magazines, 56 farm papers, 273 national businesspapers, 431 advertisers and advertising agencies.

culation of businesspapers was ABC.[17] But the comparisons, *being based on net paid circulations of publications with at least 50 per cent net paid*, exclude a lot of publications and a lot of circulation.

A proposal that all publications in good standing with either the Audit Bureau of Circulations or the Controlled Circulation Audit should be admitted to membership in The Associated Business Papers was made late in 1944.

Here is the way businesspapers listed in the July, 1944, issue of *Standard Rate & Data Service* lined up on circulation audits.[17]

All Papers	Number		Circulation	
	No.	%	Copies	%
A.B.C. and A.B.P	126	10.12	1,381,486	7.73
A.B.C. but *Not* A.B.P	172	13.83	3,064,690	17.16
Sworn paid circulation	553	44.42	7,398,036	41.43
C.C.A.	159	10.36	3,523,147	19.72
Sworn controlled circulation	235	18.87	2,491,198	13.95
	1,245	100.%	17,858,557	100.%
No circulation information	374		?	
Total Papers Listed	1,619		?	

Percentage of papers that are audited

	Paid		Controlled	
Audited papers	298*	35.02	159*	40.36
Unaudited papers	553	64.98	235	59.64
Total	851	100.%	394	100.%

Percentage of audited papers that belong to an association

	Paid		Controlled	
Members	126	42.28	78	49.06
Non-members	172	52.72	81	50.94
Total	298	100.%	159	100.%

* Without an examination of the facts that follow, the figures above have little real significance. As an indication of trends in the businesspaper publishing industry, here are four facts:

A.B.C.—Organized 1914. Businesspaper Membership in December, 1944, at an all time high, 280.

A.B.P.—Organized 1916. Membership all time high, December, 1937, was 158; in December, 1944 was 127.

C.C.A.—Organized 1931. Membership at all time high was 170 in December, 1944.

N.B.P.A.—Organized November, 1940. Membership was at all time high, 78 in December, 1944.

C.C.A.B.—(Canadian Circulations Audit Board). Membership in December, 1944 was 101. Eleven Canadian businesspapers are A.B.C. but not C.C.A.B. Remaining 172 Canadian businesspapers have no independent circulation audit.

[17] From an analysis, *Should the A.B.P. Admit Free Circulation Papers to Membership?* issued December 14, 1944, by E. F. Hamm, Jr., Traffic Service Corp., Chairman of the Committee on Memberships.

The A.B.C. reports 280 businesspaper members. This differs from S.R. & D.S. count because some papers classified by A.B.C. as general magazines, are listed as businesspapers in S.R. & D.S. and because some papers with one membership in A.B.C. covering several editions list their editions separately in S.R. & D.S. The result of this is that A.B.C. showing here is a little inflated. On the other hand, if an A.B.C. figure was used A.B.P. would make a little better showing. The C.C.A. reports 170 members, this difference being due to new members. In analyzing trends the current figures are used.

Controlled Circulation Audit

During the depression following World War I, the business-paper publishing field discovered that even with the best-edited businesspapers it was economically impossible to sell much more than 50 per cent of the buying power in many industries. To get as much as 60 per cent of the buying power in some fields usually costs 1½ times the subscription price.

By 1930, high-pressure selling, according to some authorities, had become necessary in order to get circulation. Expensive mail effort was supplemented by the use of premiums and sheet writers. The sheet writer is an independent subscription solicitor who usually collects the full subscription price or more, as his fee. He sells groups of businesspapers. Sometimes, he gives away premiums as an inducement. Even with all this effort, it was impossible for some businesspapers to attain more than 50 or 60 per cent coverage of their buying power.

The Controlled Circulation Audit, Inc., was formed by Frank L. Avery in 1931 to supply verified information about business-papers which were being circulated *free of charge* in widely scattered areas and in fields where it was claimed to be difficult to obtain paid subscriptions in large numbers. By 1930 the number of such free circulation papers had increased to about 100. Many of these papers had cut the size to 5 x 7 to save postage and were blanketing the fields their advertisers sought to sell. Most of these papers claimed "practically 100 per cent" or blanket coverage.

Released for Publication February 24th, 1943.

CCA

FOR SIX MONTHS ENDING

December 1942

(This form to be used only in accordance with Article IV of the Rules and Regulations. Use or reproduction in any other manner is prohibited.)

CONTROLLED CIRCULATION AUDIT REPORT – 1971

THIS REPORT HAS BEEN AUDITED BY THE CONTROLLED CIRCULATION AUDIT, INC.
420 Lexington Avenue, New York, N. Y.

1. MILL & FACTORY
   (Name of Publication)
2. Conover-Mast Corporation
   (Name of Publishing Company)
3. 205 East 42nd Street, New York, N.Y.
   (Address)
4. 1927
   (Year Established)
5. Monthly
   (Frequency)

6. Class, Industry or Field Served __ General Industrial

7. AVERAGE TOTAL DISTRIBUTION FOR PERIOD COVERED BY THIS AUDIT

Total Controlled Circulation Mailed in Individual Wrappers	29,118	Advertisers, Agencies, Exchanges,	1,468
		Advertising Prospects	145
Total Controlled Circulation Bulk	422	Other Samples Spec.order & Dist.Nov.issue	1,330 See #15
		Unclassified	141
		Show	
		Office, Files, etc.	642
AVERAGE TOTAL CONTROLLED CIRCULATION	29,540	AVERAGE TOTAL EDITION	33,274

8. NET CONTROLLED CIRCULATION BY ISSUES, INCLUDING BULK

Date 1942	Number Receiving Every Issue	Number on Rotated Lists	Total	Date 1942	Number Receiving Every Issue	Number on Rotated Lists	Total
July	28,923		28,923	November	30,923		30,923
August	29,127		29,127	December	29,802		29,802
September	28,990		28,990				
October	29,475		29,475	TOTALS	177,240		177,240

9. ANALYSIS OF CONTROLLED CIRCULATION AS TO TYPE OF READERS BASED ON ISSUE

This issue is 2.45% or 722 copies below   average for period.   OF   June 1942.

	TOTAL	PERCENTAGE
Company subscription	16	.05%
Plant operating Men..............................	25,074	87.00%
(a) Factory managers, production managers, superintendents, company officials, owners and managers.........................14,752		
(b) Assistant plant managers, assistant superintendents, mechanical, electrical and maintenance superintendents, master mechanics, department heads and other operating executives.................. 7,109		
(c) Engineers-Production, design construction, consulting, etc..............3,213		
Educational organizations and officials............	168	.59%
Libraries, trade associations, etc..	70	.24%
Distributors and distributor salesmen..............	1,655	5.75%
Miscellaneous.....................................	703	2.44%
Titles Unknown....................................	901	3.13%
Bulk..	231	.80%
TOTALS.............................	28,818	100.00%
Average for Period...............	29,540	

9a. WHAT IS THE NUMERICAL EXTENT OR LIMIT OF THE FIELDS AND WHAT IS THE SOURCE OR AUTHORITY FOR THIS INFORMATION?

Classification or Group   Number   Source (Including date of authority)

Publisher knows no other statistics showing extent of this field.

Form Copyright 1938 Controlled Circulation Audit, Inc., New York N. Y.

CHART 27A

The restricted type, or controlled circulation, is described by Mr. Avery as "the outgrowth of the blanket type." The CCA lists five types of "restricted or controlled circulations" which claim to deliver a "demonstrable 70 per cent" of the buying power of a given field. Example of what is meant by "demonstrable": An advertiser knows that the purchasing agent for office equipment is an

10 . CIRCULATION BY STATES, based on the _____ December 1942 _____ issue.

STATE	Receiving Every Issue	Number on Rotated Basis	TOTAL	STATE	Receiving Every Issue	Number on Rotated Basis	TOTAL
Maine	178		178	Minnesota	204		204
New Hampshire	110		110	Iowa	242		242
Vermont	184		184	Missouri	604		604
Massachusetts	1,489		1,489	North Dakota	10		10
Rhode Island	271		271	South Dakota	20		20
Connecticut	1,172		1,172	Nebraska	159		159
New England	3,404		3,404	Kansas	201		201
				West No. Central	1,440		1,440
New York	3,015		3,015				
New Jersey	1,488		1,488	Arkansas	80		80
Pennsylvania	2,638		2,638	Louisiana	326		326
Middle Atlantic	7,141		7,141	Oklahoma	235		235
				Texas	962		962
Delaware	110		110	West So. Central	1,603		1,603
Maryland	535		535				
Dist. of Columbia	82		82	Montana	16		16
Virginia	514		514	Idaho	33		33
West Virginia	401		401	Wyoming	48		48
North Carolina	565		565	Colorado	150		150
South Carolina	332		332	New Mexico	28		28
Georgia	749		749	Arizona	129		129
Florida	469		469	Utah	141		141
South Atlantic	3,757		3,757	Nevada	30		30
				Mountain	575		575
Ohio	2,431		2,431				
Indiana	984		984	Washington	240		240
Illinois	2,032		2,032	Oregon	266		266
Michigan	2,001		2,001	California	840		840
Wisconsin	890		890	Pacific	1,346		1,346
East No. Central	8,338		8,338				
				Bulk	237		237
Kentucky	349		349	United States	29,633		29,633
Tennessee	635		635				
Alabama	611		611	U. S. Territories	32		32
Mississippi	197		197	Canada	6		6
East So. Central	1,792		1,792	Foreign	131		131
				Miscellaneous			
				Grand Total	29,802		29,802

Average for Period   29,540

11. If rotational method is used for part or all of list, give below a comprehensive statement showing number of names rotated, period in which rotated and if not periodic, then explain rotational system used.

NOT ROTATIONAL

CHART 27B

office manager. Thus, if a businesspaper covering that type of equipment can show that it has 70 per cent of the office managers

12. Give below a comprehensive statement as to source of supply of names on lists and provisions made for keeping lists up-to-date.

Practically the entire circulation is built and maintained by a syndicate of mill and machinery supply distributors located in all of the principal industrial trading areas throughout the United States. These distributors, through their salesmen, supplied the publisher with lists of the individuals in their territories whom they identified from personal contact as doing the specifying and buying for their organizations. Magazines are mailed to these lists in individual wrappers by the publisher, and a charge is made to distributors for all copies mailed to their lists.

Lists are kept up-to-date by constant supervision on the part of the distributors' salesmen, who report changes in personnel, new companies, etc. All changes are made promptly by the publisher.

Each month, letters are sent to portions of the list calling the recipient's attention to the magazine, describing what it is doing for him editorially, and asking for his cooperation in keeping his address correct.

Mailing wrappers carry a request to postmaster to notify publisher of change of address. All notifications are taken up with the distributors, who "okay" the change of address if the reader still occupies a position of specifying and buying authority, or give replacement names if he does not.

13. NUMBER OF NAMES REMOVED FROM AND ADDED TO LISTS DURING PERIOD COVERED BY REPORT

1942 DATE	REMOVED	ADDED	1942 DATE	REMOVED	ADDED
July	274	379	November	307	536
August	267	471	December	49	147
September	534	397			
October	147	632	TOTALS	1,578	2,562

Publisher may report by months or issues, or give totals only.

14. If same grade and weight of stock are not used in entire edition, state quantity of each in each edition and give reason for this policy.

Same grades and weights of stock used throughout each edition.

PUBLISHER'S AFFIDAVIT

State   New York

County New York

We hereby make oath and say that all statements set forth in the three pages of this report are true.

C.R. Gordon, Asst. Secty.   E.H. Howard, Circ. Mgr.

(At least one of above signatures must be that of an officer of the publishing company)

Subscribed and sworn to, before me, this   30th   day of   January   , 194 3

Geo. P. Vallar

Notary Public.

CHART 27C

on its list, it has demonstrated[18] that it has 70 per cent of the buying power, according to Mr. Avery.

[18] Strictly speaking, it has only demonstrated that it has 70 per cent of the names on its list. Ten per cent of all the office managers may actually represent 50 per cent of the buying power. But proving that 10 per cent *read and act* is a different matter altogether.

15. Space below is reserved for remarks or comment by auditor.

The sample figure average of 1,330 copies shown in Paragraph #7 reflects a total of 8,020 copies of special November "Know How Handbook" issue which was sold to advertisers at 50¢ per copy and to others at $1.00 per copy. These sales are not allowed by C.C.A. as regular controlled distribution since they involved only a single issue.

The office, file figures average of 642 shown in Paragraph #7 includes a total of 2,683 copies of the November issue reserved for future sales.

The analysis shown in Paragraph #9 is based on the June 1942 issue which is 2.45% below the average for the six month period ending December 1942. This percentage indicates normal industrial growth due to increased manufacturing activities.

AUDITOR'S AFFIDAVIT

State .... New York ....

County .... New York ....

I hereby make oath and say that I have personally examined the records of the publication subject of this report and that all the statements set forth in the four pages of this report are true to the best of my knowledge and belief.

T. R. Avery
Auditor

Subscribed and sworn to, before me, this ___19th___ day of ___February___ 1943

.... Wm. J. Horne ....

Notary Public.

C. C. A. AUDITING METHODS

Circulation facts and figures in this report have been verified in the following manner:

The auditor has examined all available records pertaining to circulation. Post Office receipts, vouchers, and ledger records have been examined. Bills for supplies, service, paper, printing and addressing have been checked and compared with bookkeeping records.

Stencil files and other lists have been counted, sampled and tested to verify qualitative analyses of circulation.

Officers and employees concerned with circulation have been questioned with regard to the work or records in their charge

The auditor has compared and cross-checked data from these various sources and has conducted direct samplings and other tests considered essential to the complete and accurate authentication of this report.

CHART 27D

1. *Financial type:* The circulation here is determined:

   (a) By financial ratings
   (b) By titles
   (c) By annual volume of sales

(d) By floor space or its equivalent (the length of counters or some other measure of buying volume)

2. *Geographical type:* Here the circulation is not national coverage. It may be all the cotton mills south of Mason and Dixon's line or all the coal mines, or all the meat markets in Metropolitan New York.

3. *Zone type:* This circulation is national coverage but offers to sell an advertiser space on the basis of zone units. His advertising will appear in a national magazine but is distributed only in the zone or zones which he selects. Thus he gets the coverage he wants, without waste circulation, at a lower cost, according to CCA. By a familiar printing operation, four-page forms designed only for the readers of certain zones are bound in certain specified numbers of the zone type national magazine by the printer and left out of others.

4. *Supply-house controlled type:* Where the neck of the bottle is controlled by a relatively few supply houses or wholesalers in a given field of distribution, these supply houses or wholesalers furnish lists of their customers (sometimes dealers, sometimes machine shops, etc.) to the publisher. In return, the supply house or wholesaler will obtain a page of advertising or a cover or a part of a cover or will have his folder or flier inserted or bound in the magazine. The manufacturer who supplies a well-known product to a given wholesaler or supply house is then induced to take advertising space in this controlled circulation paper to one or more of the hand-picked fields which are the known customers of certain wholesalers or supply houses. *Mill and Factory* has the supply-house type of controlled circulation. Although there are 1,200 mill supply houses in the United States, *Mill and Factory* has only 70 of these supply houses. These 70, however, are the largest, and their lists of customers make up part of the controlled circulation list of *Mill and Factory*. Other publications of supply-house type are *Medical Economics, Dental Survey, Paper Progress*, and *Welding Industry*.

5. *Rotated type:* At the same time the other restricted types of controlled circulation were originated, the rotated type was in-

vented, so that the majority buying power in a given field could be reached regularly while a minor portion was reached consistently but irregularly. Thus, a manufacturer selling equipment in the aviation field might find it valuable for his advertising message to reach airplane pilots every two or three months. The rotated type of circulation would send copies of the aviation magazine at irregular intervals to this minor type of circulation at lower cost.

The controlled circulation is versatile enough to cover almost any requirement of the advertiser in a businesspaper, as to both page rates and types of buying power desired, according to CCA.

Unlike ABC, there are no paid subscription receipts and no sales records. Here the auditor checks the amount of money paid to cover post-office mailing permits (which may not be used except for mailing the publication),[19] invoices for paper purchased and printing costs, and the actual mailing stencils are also checked, as 95 per cent of the list must be kept on stencils. Audits are made semiannually. *Standard Rate & Data* recognizes the CCA and publishes circulation reports of its member-papers. In May, 1943, the CCA membership was 150 publications, or about 85 per cent of the business publications listed as controlled circulation papers in *Standard Rate & Data.*

The total number of controlled circulation papers in July, 1944, was 395. CCA membership rose steadily in twelve years from 37 in September, 1932, to 170 in December, 1944.

The total circulation of 298 ABC businesspapers in July, 1944, was 4,446,176. The total circulation of 159 CCA businesspapers in July, 1944, was 3,523,147.

[19] There is nothing in the post-office rules which requires a publisher to mail a publication under a given post-office permit. This is the loophole through which crooked publishers ride their team of horses. Some crooked publishers are known to have secured a third-class mailing permit in the name of the company. They would then mail out three different publications under this same permit at one time, getting one post-office receipt. A copy of each of the three publications would then be weighed individually. By dividing the weight of each of the three copies into the one total, they would "prove" tremendously high distribution for all three papers, when, as a matter of fact, it was the total distribution of the three papers collectively instead of individually. As the post office will not give information about another company's mailing permits, the difficulty of checking is apparent.

Audits of circulation are as important to advertising and circulation executives in exercising their functions today as law reports are to an attorney.

THE CASE FOR CONTROLLED CIRCULATION PAPER[20]

1). Payment of money for a subscription is no evidence of reader interest, if as an added inducement something else is given: many publishers of paid circulation businesspapers resort to (a) discounts, (b) clubbing offers, (c) high-pressure selling, and (d) premiums. Premiums are sometimes expensive books or fountain pens. Five-year subscriptions are often given for the price of an 18-month subscription by subscription salesmen who keep the subscription price they collect, although they are on salaries.[21] "Sheet writers," high-pressure independent subscription salesmen, are employed, who collect the entire subscription price plus an extra bonus per subscription.

2). Economy—a lower rate per thousand readers.

3). Economy—greater and more complete coverage—less economic loss.

4). Economy—selectivity of audience—elimination of waste circulation.

5). Economy—duplication in three or four competing paid circulation papers in the same field is avoided by confining effort to the over-all free paper.

6). Economy—flexibility by rotating the selected audiences on a seasonal, geographical, editorial, or occupational basis.

[20] "An Analysis and Appraisal of Controlled Circulation Among Business Papers" (a thesis), by Oscar Dystel, B.C.S. (New York University), M.B.A. (Harvard Graduate School of Business Administration), was published by the Controlled Circulation Audit, Inc., New York, 1938.

[21] While there is no question that a crooked salesman could do this (he could give away the magazine for nothing), it would undoubtedly be caught by an ABC verification audit. Under ABC rules the maximum one can sell a magazine for on a special offer is 50 per cent of the established one-year rate. If the subscription salesman is operating under the ABC rules, therefore, he could not legally sell a 5-year subscription for less than the price of a 2½-year subscription. On a paper selling for $3 a year, a 5-year subscription would cost $15 at full rates. The least a publisher could legally sell it for under ABC rules would be $7.50.

7). Reader interest, like listener interest, depends on editorial content, which must be proved on some other basis than subscription.

The radio listener does not subscribe to the program he receives, but there are other ways of proving the high interest or popularity of radio programs. Free circulation proves its readership by product-information inquiries mailed to the publishers, by surveys, letters, advertiser testimonial, and reader testimonial.

8). Even paid circulation papers maintain a free circulation list.

9). The Modern Tempo—new discoveries and inventions create new industries overnight. Old-fashioned attempts to give coverage to these fields by the slow method of building up a paid subscription would be an economic loss to manufacturers, who want this market at once. The CCA device makes this possible.

THE CASE FOR PAID SUBSCRIPTION PAPERS

1). The overwhelming majority of periodicals in this country have paid subscribers.

2). The exchange of cash for subscription is proof of *indicated* reader interest.

3). The subscription renewal is tangible evidence of *definite* reader interest, especially where a high subscription renewal percentage can be shown.

4). Most controlled circulation papers are catalogues containing the product information of many instead of one manufacturer, distributed free in the catalogue tradition. Since the sole income is from those whose advertising matter is thus distributed free, the publisher becomes in effect an agent for the manufacturer.

5). The "100 per cent coverage" claim of free circulation papers cannot be substantiated. Surveys show that three out of ten in any given industry read no businesspapers; two out of ten prefer some other paper. Even with a "100 per cent coverage," a paper cannot claim more than 50 per cent readership of any field—paid or free.

6). The CCA paper's "list" of readers is vulnerable. Every list is vulnerable.[22] Statistics show 35 per cent of the men in any field change jobs, retire, die, get promoted, transferred, or released every year. The paid circulation paper provides an automatic list-cleaning service, by cutoffs for cancellation or nonrenewal of subscription, which no free paper can duplicate.

7). The CCA paper can use a list ten years old without being questioned by its auditors. The ABC paper's list, when it accumulates deadwood, automatically throws the paper out of the ABC membership.

8). The free paper's publisher selects the issue to be audited by CCA; but the ABC auditor, not the publisher, selects the issue of the paid circulation paper he wishes to audit.

9). Editorial leadership, the best guarantee of readership and reader interest, is the result of years of upbuilding, crusading, winning reader confidence, fighting for better standards of practice.

THE FIELD FORCE

As one circulation manager[23] says: "Our object is to deliver the greatest value to the advertiser by finding all the worthwhile outlets in the field for his commodity. To do this we use 1) mail selling, as a shotgun, scattering our shots broadly through the field, 2) field selling, as a rifle, aiming straight for what we want."

This manager employs a full-time field staff of 250 trained men under 16 district managers who call on half a million executives and engineers. They are paid 25 cents for every plant unit report they send in. These reports give full information on operating per-

[22] A large businesspaper publisher showed these records of circulation changes in titles, addresses, replacements from January, 1938, to July 1, 1941:

1938—first 6 months	....	55,023
1938—second "	....	51,342
1939—first "	....	58,299
1939—second "	....	50,390
1940—first "	....	74,660
1940—second "	....	65,948
1941—first "	....	77,913
Total for 3½-year period	....	433,575 changes

"Business Publications" by Roger L. Wensley, president, G. M. Basford Co., advertising agents, *Advertising & Selling*, February, 1942.

[23] James E. Blackburn, Jr., circulation director and vice-president, McGraw-Hill.

sonnel and management executives, and form the basis for subscription sales effort. The field salesman sells management the idea that the key men in the establishment should read businesspapers. The field salesman sells the advantages of the reading habit to the prospect. He sells the prospect dissatisfaction with present methods and present equipment. He sells the idea of making better profits by reading his businesspaper. He does a real missionary job for the advertiser.

"Ten salesmen in the field getting ten interviews a day is 350,000 subscription sales talks a year, selling dissatisfaction with obsolete methods of work, of selling, advertising, promoting, displaying, dissatisfaction with old or incomplete stocks of merchandise," he says. "Thus you are doing a real job for the advertiser." He adds:

"We do not permit high pressure canvass: this means grief in renewals and cancellations on half-sold or over-sold subscribers. The standard sales story and the standard prospectus are the best method. Each man gets a manual and book of rules."

The greatest problem in field subscription selling is control of salesmen. The manager we have quoted pays his field salesmen as follows: (quoting)

1. A salary in order to hold them loyal to us.

2. Plus a commission to make them hustle and prove they are as good as they think they are.

3. Plus a bonus to make them do the job our way, send in daily reports, use our manual.

This circulation manager spends $35,000 a year for 100,000 questionnaires mailed to the industries covered by his publications eight times a year, to keep up with personnel changes.

Many authorities argue that the method of distribution of a businesspaper, whether paid or free circulation, makes little difference in the quality of the readership. *The degree of circulation control*, according to Roy Eastman,[24] whether paid or free, is the important thing.

According to his surveys: "The average businesspaper has approximately three active readers per copy. (That is about one less

[24] The Eastman Research Organization, New York, N. Y. Mr. Eastman was former head of research for McGraw-Hill.

than the average claimed by the salesmen. That is because the salesmen talk in terms of the number of readers who see the paper at any time, while our figure is based on the average number of actual readers of each issue).

"If it is a paid paper, obviously only one reader out of three can have any cash investment in it."

(Eastman surveys have shown that approximately one-half of the paid subscriptions, on an average, were paid for by the company or firm; therefore, only one-sixth of the readers of the average paid paper had made a personal investment in it.)

". . . All of that" declares Mr. Eastman "may sound like a brief for controlled circulation, but here is the other side of the picture. It is just as tough, and just as expensive a job, inherently, to build and maintain a valid controlled circulation as it is to build and maintain a valid paid circulation.[25] But the point is that the paid publication *must* maintain at least this degree of control: someone has to pay something for the paper.

". . . While the free circulation publisher, if he has no conscience, can get away with murder. And some do, much to the disgust and distress of the upright controlled circulation publishers.

"On the other hand, a paid circulation does not guarantee, per se, a higher quality of readership. Measured by meticulous standards, we have found controlled circulations with an enviable readership, and paid circulations that were woefully lacking.

"True circulation control, with either paid or free papers, is dependent equally on circulation management and editorial effectiveness. And neither of these can be supplied in the degree that it is needed to insure stability and advertising results without authentic and critical readership."

SUBSCRIPTION RENEWAL POTENTIAL

Before a high percentage of subscription renewals on a paid circulation businesspaper can have real meaning the current turnover in the field covered by the publication must be a considered

---

[25] Most circulation authorities will disagree with Mr. Eastman on this point. Controlled circulation can be built to a maximum in months or even weeks, while paid circulation requires *years* of confidence-building through service and editorial leadership.

factor. In some distributive fields the turnover of business is greater than in others. The turnover in jobs in industry is tremendous. In construction the turnover is always greater than in the utility field. Roy Eastman points out that when a publication is not trying to expand circulation it will have a greater renewal percentage than when it is putting on a drive to increase it. Mr. Eastman says:

The job of a publication is to keep abreast of the movement of its market—physically as well as mentally—circulationwise as well as editorially. The market never stands still, but publications sometimes do.

Incidentally, this problem of keeping abreast of the market movement applies just as sharply to the controlled paper as to the paid. The controlled circulation isn't "controlled" unless there is effective machinery to keep the turnover of the list well tuned to the current turnover of the market.

As a matter of fact the renewal percentage of any paid paper doesn't mean a thing and can't mean a thing until it is compared with the "renewal potential." And we know of no other way to get at this vital figure except through field research.

We go at it this way: First we take the "cut-offs" for a given period from our client subscription list. Then we go into the field to find WHY these losses have occurred. First we find a certain number of "Disappearances"—people who have just vanished and left no trace. If our men can't find them, it's a cinch the postman or circulation salesman won't.

Then we find cut-offs have actually renewed, sometimes up to 5 to 10 per cent, but haven't gotten into the record because renewed under a different name or address or renewed subsequent to the cut-off.

Next we find lapses for unavoidable reasons, like death, retirement, loss of job, change of job or interest.

Finally we get at the proportion of lapses for avoidable, or at least theoretically avoidable, reasons. This is really the net loss, or attainable renewals. Thereby we arrive at two important figures; first, the inevitable turnover; second, the attainable renewal potential.

Renewal performance in the light of this sensible bogie is often a totally different story than the bald renewal percentage indicates.

Another important thing in this connection is the extent to which loss of subscriptions means loss of readers. Both publishers and advertisers frequently forget that the great majority of readers of any publication are non-paying passengers.

UNFINISHED BUSINESS

There is a vast "twilight zone" of entirely unaudited business-papers being supported by the advertisers of this country—largely the big industrial advertisers.[26] Ralph Leavenworth, one-time advertising manager of Westinghouse Electric & Manufacturing Co., cautioned in a speech[27] to his associates: "There are too many businesspapers; too many weak ones, living on the careless buying habits of advertisers; parasites sapping the strength of the better papers, the needed ones, by diverting a sizable proportion of the advertising money which the better ones could use to make themselves still better."

To some extent this condition has been corrected but there still remains a wide field for improvement. Above all other enterprises, the press should offer nothing for sale to which any doubt attaches. Circulation larceny should be placed in the same category with window larceny. *Printers' Ink* Statute in New York State makes misleading advertising a criminal offense. In a long editorial crusade several years ago *Linens & Domestics* successfully tested this law by securing the arrest and conviction of a Fifth Avenue linen specialty shop proprietor for "window larceny." The specific charge was labeling cotton handkerchiefs as "pure linen." The merchant used his windows as bait to attract inside and victimize wealthy women. Window larceny, until his conviction, had proved a profitable racket for a number of fly-by-night merchants. Circulation larceny also is profitable for unscrupulous publishers.

In July, 1944, issue of *Standard Rate & Data Service*, 1619 businesspapers were listed. Of this number, 1162, or *more than 70 per cent*, permitted no outside audit of their circulation figures. Indeed, 374 refused to give any circulation information. This is

[26] "The Auditor's Viewpoint," by Frank L. Avery, *Industrial Marketing*, October, 1935.
[27] Address before the National Industrial Advertisers Association, Sept. 20, 1935, published in *Industrial Marketing*, October, 1935.

THE NATIONAL INDUSTRIAL ADVERTISERS ASSOCIATION, Inc.
100 East Ohio St., Chicago, Ill.

Request for information on circulation, etc. of Reference Media

☐ Consolidated Catalog   ☐ Directory
☐ Reference Manual   ☐ Year Book

1. Date of Statement............................   2. Name of Publication............................
3. Date of first issue............................   4. Name and Address of Publisher............................
     (If a charity or political organization, fill out completely the supplementary form for the purpose.)
5. Is this the original publishing company?................If not, explain briefly............................
6. State if there have been any mergers?................If so, with what publications and when?............................
7. Has this publication always been published under the present name?................If not, trace name changes............................

8. Other periodicals, directories, etc. published by the publisher............................
9. Associations of which publisher is a member............................
     a. If listed in the Standard Rate and Data Service and not a member of an auditing bureau, do you agree to furnish complete circulation reports on Post Office receipts *issued in the name of above named publication* to this service *regularly upon distribution of each issue?*............................
     b. If eligible for, and not a member of, the A. B. C. are there any reasons to prevent your joining it?................Describe your reasons briefly............................
     c. If eligible for, and not a member of, the C. C. A. are there any reasons to prevent your joining it?................Describe your reasons briefly............................
     d. Will you allow outside auditors selected by us to audit your circulation records?................If not, what form of proof of circulation will you furnish?............................
10. Is publication officially sponsored by any association?................Name it............................
     a. Do association membership dues include subscription price?................ b. If so, is subscription compulsory?................Voluntary?................
11. Frequency of publication............................ a. State whether or not published continuously at same frequency since first issue............................
     If not, please explain............................
12. Class, industry, or field served............................
13. Subdivision of class, industry or field or type of individual to which publication particularly appeals............................

14. Average circulation per-issue-per-year and advertising rate, for the preceding fifteen years: (See Note 1)

Year	Circulation Paid (A.B.C. of Item 16)	Circulation Not paid (D. of Item 16)	Page Advertising Rate on basis of one page per each issue throughout one year	Rate per thousand, based on item A.B.C. and D of paragraph 16.	Year	Circulation Paid (A.B.C. of Item 16)	Circulation Not paid (D. of Item 16)	Page Advertising Rate on basis of one page per each issue throughout one year	Rate per thousand based on Item A.B.C. and D of paragraph 16.

     a. Please explain any changes in rate during above period............................
15. Total (paid and not paid) circulation per issue for the twelve months' period ending............................and date each issue's mailing was begun and completed. If twelve months do not cover at least two issues, give information on last two issues. (See Note 1).

Date	Circulation Paid (A.B. and C. of item 16)	Circulation Not Paid (D of item 16)	Date mailing was Begun	Date mailing was Completed	Date	Circulation Paid (A.B. and C. of item 16)	Circulation Not Paid (D of item 16)	Date mailing was Begun	Date mailing was Completed

CHART 28A. N.I.A.A. REQUEST FOR INFORMATION

To assist advertising space buyers to determine eligibility of a businesspaper for a place on their advertising schedules.

16. Average total distribution for period stated in Item 15. (See Notes 1 and 2)

A. Subscriptions — addressed to individuals or attention of individuals ....

B. Subscriptions — addressed to firms ....

C. All other paid circulation (such as net single copy sales, and single issue sale in bulk) ....

E. Advertisers ....

F. Miscellaneous circulation of no direct benefit to advertisers, such as correspondents, advertising agencies, exchanges, complimentary, subscription salesmen, samples, employees of publisher, etc. ....

D. Total average number of copies mailed regularly without charge to individuals or firms for whom publication is edited ....

  a. Copies addressed to individuals or attention of individuals ....

  b. Copies addressed to firms ....

  c. If rotational method is used for part or all of list, append a comprehensive statement, showing number of names rotated and state period of rotation; if not periodic, append explanation of rotational system used.

17. Qualifications, if any, determining eligibility to receive publication regularly—include only circulation under A, B, and D, Item 16; (See Notes 1 and 2) a. Functional or occupational qualifications ....

  b. Financial or business-volume qualifications ....

18. Information regarding section D, of Item 16.

Give a comprehensive statement as to source of supply of names ....

A. How many questionnaires were mailed out in the last twelve months to secure individual names?......................How many replies were received?......................How many individual names were added to your circulation as a result of these questionnaires?......................

B. What is your policy in placing names on your circulation list?......................How do you determine the number of copies mailed to a large or small company?......................

C. Number of names removed from and added to circulation list during period covered by this report. Added.................. Removed..................

19. Authorized prices for sale of this publication during period stated in paragraph 15 (See Note 2)

a. Regular prices: Single copy, Regular issue......................Special issue......................

      Subscription, 1 yr...................... 2 yrs...................... 3 yrs...................... 5 yrs......................

b. Special subscription offers, all prices for various periods, including renewal and extension offers (not in combinations)......................

c. Combination sale prices for clubs including this with other publications......................

d. Group organizers' price for this publication alone......................

20. Annual subscription expirations, renewals, and percentage of renewals, for the preceding five calendar years (See Note 1)

Year	Expirations (A subscription is to be considered expired with the date of the last issue for which payment was originally made—or upon renewal.)			Renewals (A subscription is to be considered renewed if paid for within six months of expiration date and provided such renewal is dated back to actual expiration date.)			Percentage of Renewals (Renewals divided by expirations equal percentage.)		
	1st Term Subscriptions	Subsequent Term Subscriptions	Total	1st Term Subscriptions	Subsequent Term Subscriptions	Total	1st Term Subscriptions	Subsequent Term Subscriptions	Total

21. Analysis of subscription sales for the preceding five calendar years. (See Note 1)

Period	Year	Subscriptions direct to publisher by mail	Catalog and Newspaper subscription agencies and other publishers	Publishers own field selling organization	Other field selling organization	Associations (Explain)	Other Channels (Explain)	Total
1st 6 Mos.								
2nd 6 Mos.								
1st 6 Mos.								
2nd 6 Mos.								
1st 6 Mos.								
2nd 6 Mos.								
1st 6 Mos.								
2nd 6 Mos.								
1st 6 Mos.								
2nd 6 Mos.								

CHART 28B

the situation prevailing some 30 years after the ABC was founded, and founded largely through the efforts of businesspaper publishers, who were intent on curbing circulation larceny.

Manufacturers who would not think of buying raw material

21A. PERIOD (for period stated in Item 15—See Notes 1 and 2)
    Less than one year ....
    One year or more but less than two years ....
    Two years or more ....

21C. PREMIUMS (for period stated in Item 15—See Notes 1 and 2)
    (In sales listed below as subscriptions sold with premiums, the premiums were offered by publisher or with his knowledge)
    a. Subscriptions sold with premium ....
    b. Subscriptions sold without premium ....
    TOTAL SUBSCRIPTIONS SOLD IN PERIOD ....

21B. COMBINATION SUBSCRIPTION SALES
    (for period stated in Item 15—See Notes 1 and 2)
    a. Known combination sales ....
    b. Known not to be in combination ....
    c. Subscriptions received from intermediary unable to determine whether sold in combination or not ....
    TOTAL SUBSCRIPTION SALES, COMBINATION AND OTHERS ....

22. Average number and percent of subscription-in-arrears per issue for preceding five calendar years for classifications A and B in paragraph 16 — by periods: up to 3 months, 4 to 6 months, over 6 months.

Period	Year	Arrears Up to 3 Months Number	%	Arrears 4 to 6 Months Number	%	Arrears 6 Months and Over Number	%	Total Number	%
1st 6 Mos.									
2nd 6 Mos.									
1st 6 Mos.									
2nd 6 Mos.									
1st 6 Mos.									
2nd 6 Mos.									
1st 6 Mos.									
2nd 6 Mos.									
1st 6 Mos.									
2nd 6 Mos.									

    a. Was there any change in subscription rates in any way affecting the above figures?................. If so, explain.

23. Breakdown of circulation into states and counties; Canada; individual territorial possessions; and individual foreign countries — covering circulation under classifications A, B, and D only, in paragraph 16 (Circulation in any county amounting to less than 1% of total for state may be grouped with circulation in other such counties under head "Other Counties.")............

24. Breakdown of circulation by industrial classifications, — covering total circulation under classifications A, B, and D only, in paragraph 16. (Publications concentrating in one or more major classifications, such as food industries or process industries, should subdivide such major classifications.) ....

25. Breakdown of circulation by occupational functions (job interests) — covering total circulation under classifications A, B and D only in paragraph 16. ....

ADDITIONAL INFORMATION

26. Average number of pages of editorial matter per issue during the last five years, exclusive of special issues
    19............   19............   19............   19............   19............

27. Average number of pages of paid for advertising per issue during the last five years, exclusive of special issues. (Not including advertising by publishers, donated space, space paid for with due bills, space paid for with merchandise, and advertising exchanged with other publications.)
    19............   19............   19............   19............   19............

28. What percentage of your advertisers have been with you for more than one year?................What percentage of your advertising volume does this represent?................

CHART 28C

without some measure of the quality and strict conformity to certain specifications are buying space in hundreds of unaudited businesspapers and thus making a blind date with the readership.

There is justifiable suspicion of any circulation that cannot stand

29. Who comprise the Editorial Staff and what special fitness have they for addressing your particular field?.......................
....

30. What percentage of your editorial space was used during past 12 months for
    a. Original staff articles...   e. Material reprinted from other publications...................
    b. Original contributed articles, paid for.....................   f. Syndicated material (news releases, etc.).................
    c. Original contributed articles, not paid for..............   g. News items.................................
    d. Organization proceedings.......................................   h. Miscellaneous (new equipment data, catalog listings, personal
                                    notes, obituaries, etc.).................
31. What material do you provide for your subscribers which they cannot obtain from any other publication?....................
....

32. Do you maintain a Buyer's Directory?........................In each issue?........................In a special issue?...............
33. What are the rules governing the number of listings given each advertiser?.......................
....

34. What marketing cooperation do you give advertisers? (advance business tips, literature distribution, etc.)..................
....

35. Do you maintain a copy or photograph service for advertisers?............... 36. What charge, if any, is made for this service?.............
37. Give complete information on rates, commissions and discounts ....

38. Agency discount................................. 39. Cash discount and general terms of payment.....................
40. Is any allowance made for complete plates, involving no typographical expenses on the part of the publisher?...............
41. Do you guarantee uniform rates to all advertisers using the same amount and kind of space?...............Do you make any concessions from
    regular advertised rates listed in Item 37?...............If so, explain.......................
42. Publication and mailing dates.......................
43. List of special issues to be published during coming twelve months.......................
44. Forms close, with proofs ....without proofs...............
45. Will you accept unblocked electros of full plated advertisements?.......................
46. Columns per page: Advertisements ....Editorial...............
47. Page sizes: (Show only dimensions in space units regularly sold)
    Page (trimmed) Wide........High........ Quarter Page (type) Wide......High...... Sixteenth Page (type) Wide......High......
    Page (type)   Wide.....High..... Sixth Page (type) Wide......High...... Front Cover (type) Wide......High......
    Two-thirds Page (type) Wide.....High..... Ninth Page (type) Wide......High...... Bleed Size (plates) Wide......High......
    Half Page (type) Wide.....High..... Twelfth Page (type) Wide......High...... Other fractional space: Wide......High......
    Third Page (type) Wide.....High..... Fifteenth Page (type) Wide......High......
    Colors { What are Standard Colors?.......................
           { Cost of Standard Colors ....Cost of Special Colors ....
    b. What are your specifications for inserts, weights, size, etc?.......................
48. If this periodical is not of a size accommodating a 7 x 10 ad on one page or two adjoining pages, what is the reason for the odd size?.........

49. Halftone screen requirements; regulations regarding solid backgrounds, Ben Day screens, electrotypes, etc.......................

50. Is publication as sent to readers printed on same type and weight of stock as samples sent to advertisers and agencies?...............If not,
    explain.......................
    A. Are color pages and black and white pages printed on same type and weight of stock?...............If not, explain ....
51. If publication is a member of ABC give date of Audit statement from which information given in items 11, 12, 14, 15, 16, 19, 20, 21, 21A,
    21B, 21C, 22, 23, 24 and 25 is taken or based.......................
    a. If publication is a member of CCA give date of Audit statement from which information given in items 11, 12, 14, 15, 16, 18, 23, 24, 25
    and 50 is taken or based.......................
52. Miscellaneous rules and regulations of the publisher, if any.......................
....

        Note 1 — On items 14, 15, 16, 17, 20, 21, 21A, 21B, 21C: If information is not available for entire period — explain.
        Note 2 — On items 15, 16, 17, 19, 21A, 21B, 21C: If 6 months period does not cover 6 or more issues, include 3 last issues if
                    bi-monthly, 2 last issues if quarterly, last issue if semi-annual or less frequent.
The foregoing information is the same as is being supplied to the Headquarters Office of the National Industrial Advertisers Association, Inc., and
has been given with the purpose and intent of selling advertising space to manufacturers and/or manufacturers' agents and I hereby make solemn
oath that it is true to the best of my knowledge and belief.

                              (Signature) ....

Notary.......................   Title ....
1242 5M   PRINTED IN U. S. A.

CHART 28D

the searchlight of an independent audit. It seems strangely anoma-
lous that the business press which has fought the philosophy of
caveat emptor in industry for a century should have to warn
buyers today in the sale of its own product! Circulation larceny

should be driven from the businesspaper field as it has been largely driven from the newspaper field.[28]

"There are entirely too many trade papers with a high degree of duplication of circulation," wrote Vergil D. Reed.[29] "*Some are parasitical racketeers having neither an economic nor an ethical justification for existence* and using 'strong arm' methods of forcing circulation" (author's italics).

The sharp division between the paid and the free circulation schools, according to some businesspaper publishers, can only result in undermining the entire businesspaper publishing structure, by destructive competition. These observers maintain that the *type* of circulation which a publisher uses does not of itself provide any monopoly on editorial ability, sales ability or publishing ability, and therefore cannot be an accurate measure of a businesspaper's quality.

On the other hand, certain codes of ethics required in editorial performance (Chart 32) and certain standards of practice required by outside bureaus (whether ABC or CCA) do provide yardsticks by which to measure publishing quality and value.

Many businesspaper publishers believe a greater drive should be made to increase the membership of paid circulation businesspapers in the ABC as has been done in the case of daily newspapers and consumer magazines, in order to strengthen the prestige of the paid circulation businesspaper.

Defenders of the free-circulation businesspaper claim it is "here to stay." They point to the fact that many businesspaper publishers own both paid and free circulation papers. They point, further, to the fact that the business press serving the sales and advertising fields carry the advertising of both ABC and CCA publications. These advocates believe businesspaper publishers should be able to

---

[28] Daily newspapers are 87.7% ABC; general magazines 82.5% ABC; farm papers 81.7% from the 1942 report, Audit Bureau of Circulations. 1943 figures of the ABC show 91% of all daily newspapers audited, or 934 out of 1,753 daily papers (1st six months of 1943). Total circulation of audited newspapers 140,024,-629, as against 3,734,932 for the 819 nonaudited newspapers.

[29] *Advertising and Selling Industrial Goods*, by Vergil D. Reed, The Ronald Press, New York, 1936; Dr. Reed is associate director of research, J. Walter Thompson Company, advertising agents.

set up eligibility rules so as to bring all deserving businesspapers into one strong trade association which would more completely represent the business press, and thereby be capable of rendering a greater service to its members and its patrons.

CHAPTER X

FUNCTION OF THE SALES PROMOTION MANAGER

A medieval motto showed a ship turning back at Gibraltar into the Mediterranean, with the inscription, NON PLUS ULTRA— go no farther.

—Bacon: *The Advancement of Learning*

IN ONE of the largest businesspaper publishing houses in our country there is a position that is held to be as important as that of the director of circulation. It is the post of "manager of district offices" (see Chart 10, Structure of Businesspaper Publishing Organization). This manager of district offices has under his control the selling staffs in all key cities, and a home staff. His function is promotion and sales research. He is the right arm of the general manager, co-ordinator, or executive vice-president in charge of sales, or advertising sales manager, as the case may be; the last title being more frequent in smaller publishing organizations.

By reference again to the chart (No. 10) you will observe that in the large organization each individual "publisher" has a "manager" who in turn directs four activities—promotion, circulation, production, sales,—on one particular publication.

Men in the field, no matter whether they sell advertising space units or subscriptions, can, by improving their research talents, furnish the home office with a wealth of material about the market. This material is grist for the sales promotion manager's mill. Everyone wants facts about markets.

WHAT KIND OF INFORMATION IS WANTED?

Over a hundred advertising agency space buyers, when surveyed some years ago[1] as to the type of promotional material they wanted

[1] Ross Federal Research Corporation, New York (1938).

most from businesspapers, listed these, in the order named: (1) data about readers; (2) number and geographical distribution; (3) editorial setup and policy; (4) methods of getting readers; (5) methods of distribution; (6) reading habits; (7) comparative cost of advertising space; (8) amount of duplication with competitive publications; (9) breakdown of readers by products used; (10) types of products advertised. Half of these wants specified some kind of specific market data.

A curious thing about this survey, to which Mabel Potter Hanford attached importance in her chapter on publication promotion:[2] a new demand on the part of the agency space buyer developed between 1938, when Mrs. Hanford's book was published, and 1940, when the late Loyola Guerin, a popular agency executive, undertook an assignment to address the annual convention of businesspaper publishers on the subject of promotion at Hot Springs, Va.[3] Number One ranking demand of advertising agencies, Mr. Guerin declared, was to know *what advertising results are obtained by advertisers*. The Ross Survey did not even list this point.

Mr. Guerin had made a survey of agencies prior to his appearance at Hot Springs. To prepare himself for his talk to the businesspaper publishers, Mr. Guerin related how he had taken home from his own office "34 pounds, by actual weight, of direct mail promotion," which he said he had received from ABP businesspapers in one month. His analysis of all this material showed:

40 pieces of a general nature (the details were inconsequential)
102 pieces (51 per cent) about "special issues"
22 pieces (11 per cent) contained some marketing data
14 pieces spoke of editorial service
6 pieces were promotional news sheets
4 pieces (2 per cent) contained information about advertising results obtained by their advertisers
2 pieces were new services

[2] *Advertising & Selling Through Business Publications*, by Mabel Potter Hanford. Harper & Brothers, New York, 1938.
[3] *Does Business Paper Promotion Help Agencies?*—a paper by Loyola Guerin of G. M. Basford Advertising Agency before the Associated Business Papers, Inc., Hot Springs, Va., May, 1940.

1 piece announced a rate increase
8 pieces were miscellaneous and nondescript

"A total of 199 pieces, but only 2 per cent devoted to the most important information you can give an agency: *information about advertising results obtained by advertisers*," said Mr. Guerin, "and only 11 per cent containing market information."

In this unusually candid talk Mr. Guerin chided the publishers of businesspapers for being themselves "nonbelievers in advertising." He pointed out that, while they took 60,000 pages of advertising from agencies in one year,[4] "that same year you businesspaper publishers used only 340 advertising pages to promote the merits of your own papers to agencies and industry generally in your own business press covering the advertising and selling fields."

CHIEF FUNCTION IS RESEARCH

A promotion manager's chief function, like a circulation manager's, is research, the kind that will provide needed and accurate market information and proof of advertising results. His next function is to distribute this type of information where it will do the most good: to advertisers and prospective advertisers; to agencies and trade associations; and to consumer magazines and daily newspapers. Not infrequently consumer magazines and newspapers buy the advertising columns of businesspapers to reach specialized markets directly and cheaply (see Chart 29).

SERVICE DEPARTMENT

The promotion manager naturally is a goodwill builder. The type of service department a publication operates is the measure of goodwill (see Chart 10). Readers, by personal call, telephone, mail and wire, want to know where to get something, the names of manufacturers, of certain trademarks, or types of goods, the answers to a variety of problems. Agencies want market statistics;

---

[4] The year previous, 1939, which may be the year to which Mr. Guerin referred, 134 member-publications of A.B.P. published 104,360 pages of advertising for which they were paid $18,640,078. Of this, 62 per cent was space placed by advertising agencies, or 64,703 pages.

CHART 29

Consumer magazine's advertisement in a businesspaper.

manufacturers want sales training, and other kinds of information. Schools and colleges, radio stations, and textbook authors beleaguer the business press for information.

The promotion manager promotes the best interests of his publication in the same way as it is done in many other business organizations: by use of the publicity device. He publishes and distributes books, booklets, pamphlets, and broadsides on the findings of his organization. Sometimes the results of research are used as the basis for advertising copy over his firm's signature in specialized business magazines covering the advertising and publishing fields, or in general business and consumer magazines, and often in the daily newspapers. Sometimes he gets a spot on the radio. Sometimes sales letters are powerful enough for his purpose. Members of his organization use his material in speeches before groups of businessmen in civic and other organizations and before trade associations. He, too, must be able to talk to groups of people. Many promotion managers use slide film and sound movies and develop into expert lecturers.

The promotion manager has discovered that by promoting his industry and soft-pedaling his own publication he often accomplishes best long-range results: he wins the goodwill and support of leaders in the industry he has so promoted; many of them are in a position to use, perhaps do use, and no doubt should use, the advertising columns of his publication to reach the markets he talks about.

Valiant allies of the promotion manager are editors and publishers who (sometimes at the promotion manager's suggestion) create industry achievement "awards" for excellence in selling, engineering,[5] merchandising, advertising, displaying, packaging, or designing; establish clinics, forums, symposiums, sales conferences, retail and wholesale trade associations, scientific groups, buyers' clubs, "round tables," and other well-known devices to promote the industry. Editors are *promoters par excellence* if they are worth their salt. The editorial crusades, special issues, feature

[5] A national award in engineering is made annually by *Chemical & Metallurgical Engineering* at a banquet in the Waldorf-Astoria, for which the entire profession turns out.

CHART 30

WHAT ADVERTISERS WANT TO KNOW BEFORE THEY BUY SPACE IN A BUSINESSPAPER*

Here are some of the things advertising men want to know:

Does your current advertisement include this information?

YES   No

ABOUT YOUR PUBLICATION

1. Establish the name of your publication ....
2. Tell something of your editorial policy ....
3. Tell what your magazine has done in its field ....
4. Tell how your magazine differs from others ....
5. Is there anything unique about your publication? ....
6. Indicate the particular job you do well ....
7. Tell what your publication can do for an advertiser ......

CONCERNING YOUR READERS

8. Where does your magazine go? Who reads it? ....
9. Give information about the type of reader ....
10. Tell something about reader acceptance ....
11. Give an analysis of subscriptions ....

ABOUT YOUR MARKET

12. Give a picture of the market covered ....
13. Tell how your publication fits into the picture ....
14. What specialized field does the magazine cover? ....
15. How thoroughly do you cover the field? ....
16. What specific information have you regarding post-war markets? ....
17. Do you interpret United States Department of Commerce statistics as they apply to your own particular field or group of readers? ....
18. Do you interpret statistics obtainable from various local Chambers of Commerce? ....

ABOUT FIELD PROBLEMS

19. How does your magazine keep in touch with changing conditions? ....
20. Have you told about research you are doing? ....
21. What do you know of your subscribers' wants? ....

ABOUT COPY ANGLES

22. Give factual information in your copy; amplify and prove the statements you have made ....
23. Be more articulate; tell more about the magazine and what you have to offer ....
24. Make your copy attractive enough in appearance to induce reading ....

TOTALS —— ——

*This elementary rating chart, to help member publications rate their own values in selling their businesspaper space to advertisers appeared in Feb. 1, 1944, issue of *A.B.P. Promotion News*, issued periodically to members of the Associated Business Papers.

articles, and new ideas they publish to advance the status of the industry give the promotion manager something to hang a promotion on. On the other hand, market studies conducted by promotion or circulation managers have news value for the readers of a businesspaper and are often published in the editorial columns.

The advertising, circulation, and production departments collaborate in all types of promotional effort. The theory that a better mousetrap will induce people to cut a path through the jungle to your mousetrap factory does not work in a complex world where everyone is promoting what he has to sell and making it easily available to the prospective purchaser.

A publisher cannot relax because he is "producing the best businesspaper in the field." People who get valuable things often fail to appreciate them until they are told or shown, forcefully and dramatically, how good those things are and better ways to use them. The best businesspapers have failed because the publishers did not appreciate how good they were.

Ways and means of winning and holding readers and advertisers, and *increasing* the ranks of both, make up the body of knowledge of the sales promotion department on a businesspaper. Businesspapers specializing in the fields of advertising and publishing devote special departments to promotion. Among businesspaper publishers who are members of the Associated Business Papers, Inc., the Promotion Round Table is one of the most popular monthly clinics and idea clearinghouses for promotion managers.

In serving the business office of a businesspaper the promotion manager's functions may include: space unit analysis, circulation analysis, market analysis, copy and art preparation, maintenance and administration of the library, mailing division, and the production of directories. No interoffice conference should exclude the promotion manager. Certainly he should never miss meetings of the sales staff. He should maintain a library of all the types of promotional literature that he can lay his hands on.

ON-THE-JOB VISITS TO READERS

Promotion men are charged with locating reader headaches. They must delve for reader problems—problems the reader cannot

overcome and problems readers have solved—and how. By bringing this information back to the publication, it can be employed to
improve the *editorial usefulness* of the businesspaper to its readers
and also the *advertising usefulness* to the advertiser. Experience
shows that searching interviews with readers, kept informal, are
the most resultful.

A famous radio character, "Baby Snooks," created by the
comedienne, Fannie Brice, was appropriated as the title for businesspaper "reader problem surveys" in 1943. These surveys were
conducted by a headquarters staff of "Baby Snooksers," as they
dubbed themselves, for member publications of the Associated
Business Papers. Baby Snooks' favorite utterance is "Why,
daddy?" Why? was asked of thousands of businesspaper readers
on field calls made by these investigators, devoting a maximum of
eight weeks and a minimum of four weeks to a member publication. Each fieldman or -woman circulated among the readers with
only one motive: *to help them with their problems.* When these
field problems were brought back to headquarters and analyzed by
the fieldworker in collaboration with the promotion manager and
the editor, it was found that a wealth of ideas and information had
been uncovered which was useful for editorial material and also
for advertising sales promotion. As an illustration, *Power Plant
Engineering's* Baby Snooksers early in 1943 completed 100 on-the-
job calls to dig up firsthand information about wartime operating
problems power engineers were up against. The boiled-down field
interview reports were then published in bulletin form and passed
on to advertisers with suggestions to prepare "timely and informative power equipment advertising that ties in more closely with the
current problems of your customers." Seventeen problems were
described in detail. Here are seven of the subjects:

1. Leaky Soap Kettle Coil Brings Woe to Boilers
2. How Do We Change from Sleeve to Ball Bearings in Motors?
3. Using Cash Rewards to Spur on Shovel-Leaners
4. How Can Overworked Power Drives Be Made to Hang on?
5. Wants Pointers on Carrying Peak Loads with Cheaper Fuels
6. What Factors Enter Future Plans to Install Bleeder Turbine?
7. What to Use in Place of Alloy Steel Bolting?

Versatility is probably the most important qualification of a sales promotion manager, assuming a good educational background. He must be a market research expert, a sales expert, an advertising expert, and a good copywriter. He should be an accomplished public speaker, an organizer, and a publicist. Many promotion managers are frequent contributors to magazines in the fields of advertising, publishing, and journalism. In short, his job is a major function of businesspaper publishing, an important sales tool, never to be placed in the hands of a cub.

CHAPTER XI

FUNCTION OF THE EDITOR

> *. . . not only do we have to picture more space than we can see with our own eyes, and more time than we can feel, but we have to describe and judge more people, more actions, and more things than we can even count or vividly imagine.*
>
> WALTER LIPPMANN

KEY CONCEPT OF A BUSINESSPAPER EDITOR

IT IS not enough for the businesspaper editor to look on at the struggle, conflict, and competition of men all about him and report the events simply as they happen. He must go behind the scenes. He must give events *significance*. He must integrate the news. He will point out trends others do not notice. His formula of successful journalism is to give *understanding* to news events, not just describe them. He must even be anticipative. What is about to happen is more important to men today than what has happened, because men often miss the significance of the happening, unless it is pointed out to them in terms of the future.[1]

"Writers there are galore," declared Adolph Ochs, founder of the New York *Times*. "Every profession offers them. But the editor is a profession apart. It is he who should be able to apply the acid test: is it worth printing, and if so, how best can it be put into printable form, *with its values disclosed* and brought within the *understanding* of the readers?" (Italics are the author's.)

Three important social servants are the investigator, the interpreter, and the administrator. Of this trinity the most important, the one of which there is the greatest shortage, is the interpreter. Sometimes he is all three in one. The world today is congested with

[1] *Public Opinion*, by Walter Lippmann, Macmillan, New York, 1929.

facts (inert matter). We suffer from indigestion of knowledge, most of it disorganized and unintelligible, which the physical and social investigators have dug up. In order to cram even more of this inert matter into people, there are scores of "digests" on the news-stands. The word "digest" is often a misnomer. To boil down information does not necessarily promote its mental digestion. People are becoming too accustomed to predigested mental food

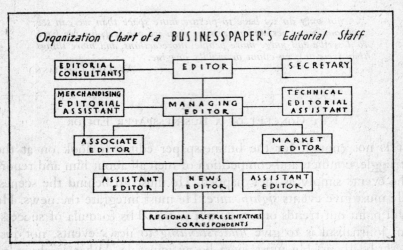

Organization Chart of a BUSINESS PAPER'S Editorial Staff

CHART 31

spooned out to them like cereal to an infant. Where are the read-able interpreters? Where are those who can vitalize this infor-mation, define it, explain it, integrate it, classify it, illuminate it? It is the businesspaper editor's task to make information digestible for those on the receiving end of his communication line. The value of social inventions and scientific discoveries, in the business-paper editor's specialized fields and related fields, depends as much on his intelligent interpretation as on the efforts of the investigative mind. The editor must sense the potentialities of facts and events, inventions and discoveries, in terms of their usefulness and social import. But more than that, he must stimulate the *thinking process* in his reader. Where news calls for action, his duty is to determine and outline the best course of action.

Study in Contrasts: Newspaper Editor and Businesspaper Editor

The businesspaper editor is not the slave of the dramatic headline. His paper does not compete with others on a public newsstand. Few businesspapers are published daily. Most of them are

---

CANONS OF BUSINESS JOURNALISM

Standards of Practice of

THE ASSOCIATED BUSINESS PAPERS, INC.

*A Business Press
Pledge to a Code of Helpfulness
and Fair Dealing*

1) To consider first the interests of the subscriber.
2) To subscribe to and work for truth and honesty in all departments.
3) To eliminate, in so far as possible, his personal opinions from his news columns, but to be a leader of thought in his editorial columns and to make his criticisms constructive.
4) To refuse to publish "puffs," free reading notices or paid "writeups"; to keep his reading columns independent of advertising considerations, and to measure all news by his standard: "Is it real news?"
5) To decline any advertisement that has a tendency to mislead or that does not conform to business integrity.
6) To solicit subscriptions and advertising solely upon the merits of the publication.
7) To supply advertisers with full information regarding character and extent of circulation, including detailed circulation statement, subject to proper and authentic verification.
8) To cooperate with all organizations and individuals engaged in creative advertising work.
9) To avoid unfair competition.
10) To determine what is the highest and largest function of the field which he serves, and to strive in every legitimate way to promote that function.

CHART 32

---

monthlies.[2] There is time to analyze events. The reader gets his businesspaper regularly via the mails. The circulation is fairly constant; it does not rise and fall like a newspaper's. Because the businesspaper circulation is constant, the advertising rate is constant.

[2] Of 1,509 businesspapers surveyed, 1,062 were published monthly; only 18 were dailies (1937), Chap. I.

The circulation manager of the newspaper is forever clamoring for sensational news to hold or boost circulation. The newspaper's advertising manager is not averse to sensational news, either. On the newspaper the advertising *rate* charged for space is based on the circulation figures, which explains the advertising sales department's consilience in sensationalism in the daily press.

Moreover, the newspaper editor's job of interpretation and editorial criticism has been diminished and by-lined: columnists, commentators, special writers, authors of books, humorists, poets, foreign editors, business analysts, Washington and war correspondents, retired admirals and generals, armchair military strategists, politicos, economic pundits, and preachers have taken over his editorial job. Stories from public relations counselors and releases from a wide variety of press agentry, feature articles and even "editorials" from propaganda bureaus and pressure groups relieve him of his job of interpretation. As an interpreter and a critic, it is plain to see that the newspaper editor's importance has been steadily and sadly fading out.

The businesspaper reader does not vacillate in his loyalty. Some *one* businesspaper is the leader in each field. It may have a strong runner-up. The readerships of both papers will remain loyal, even for a lifetime, if these businesspapers continue to merit their positions of leadership.

The businesspaper editor, moreover, practices face-to-face, or personal, journalism. The newspaper editor gave it up long ago, even the small-town editor. The newspaper editor today has too many facilities for bringing the news to his desk to remove himself from that comfortable swivel chair.

The bulk of the news comes to him pre-edited and at second hand, passes quickly from cables and dispatches, from the short wave and from real or pseudo news services, from telephone to rewrite man, and from publicity handout to typesetter.

"Who's Your Editor?" (Personal Journalism)

Few newspaper readers have ever met and talked with the editor of a metropolitan daily, heard him speak, or even know his name.

Newspaper columnists, yes. Via the signed columns in their own big city papers, through the syndicates who sell their columns to hundreds of smaller newspapers, the columnists, with their names and photographs multiplied five to ten million times a day, are better known to the reading public than any newspaper editor, or for that matter any great scientist or many important public officials. Only movie stars challenge the columnists' popularity.[3] Advertisers rarely, if ever, know the newspaper editor or have any particular desire to know him.

The businesspaper editor, on the contrary, is personally known to most of the leaders of his industry and to many hundreds of his readers. Editing a businesspaper is personal journalism, by popular demand.

While not exactly routine, businesspaper editors sometimes descend into the sea in diving suits or ascend into the stratosphere in electrically heated flying suits to get information. A mining businesspaper's editor flew into the Canadian wilderness to talk to men mining pitchblende; a chain store businesspaper's editor got a job behind a retail counter to talk to customers. Businesspaper editors may be found crawling into turbines, balancing themselves on the catwalks of skyscraper scaffolding, wearing tin hats in tunnels under rivers, lunching at the Bankers' Club or in an employees' cafeteria. "*Wear out the soles of your shoes, not the seat of your pants, gentlemen,*" was the oft-repeated admonition of the senior James H. McGraw to his editors.[4]

When confronted by an advertising space salesman, Mabel Potter Hanford, former businesspaper space buyer for one of the country's largest advertising agencies, asked the question: "Who's your editor?" In her book Mrs. Hanford writes:

To my thinking, one of the most serious reflections against editorial influence is the effort of some editors to publish from a swivel chair. The editor who thinks he can understand his reader audience, even though he may have a vast amount of experience behind him, from in front of a desk, has forgotten that readers may read as they run, that

[3] See *Lords of the Press*, by George Seldes. Julian Messner, New York, 1938.
[4] *Teacher of Business*, by G. D. Crain, Jr. Advertising Publications, Chicago, 1944.

publishers have a great ado today to keep abreast of the economics of business conditions and changes, that overnight new factors enter into the picture and the old has given place to the new as the picture was being painted.

An editorial chair might well be empty half the time while the editor is out in the field, talking to his readers, to his advertisers, to the industrial leaders, to the man on the street, the man behind the machine, the clerk in the shop; listening and talking to the leaders in Wall Street, the Government servants in Washington, the harassed manufacturer facing labor and economic problems never faced before, and the laborer not definitely sure where it is all leading. The editor may have a cuff for a note-book, but what he has to say to his readers will be based on what is actually happening in the field of his interest, not what he thinks or hopes is happening.

. . . In the selection of any publication as an advertising medium for a sales message, the standing of the editorial department out ranks every other factor. *Who is your reader* may be quickly established by audited reports on circulation and coverage as soon as *"Who's your editor?"* is made completely and unassailably clear.[5]

Mrs. Hanford has not described half the musts in a businesspaper editor's routine. "When do you get time to put out the paper or write editorials?" is the question most often asked an editor who gets around. Many businessmen feel aggrieved if the businesspaper's chief editor does not show up in person once in a while. He is accused of high-hatting them. To avoid that charge he finds himself, sometimes at the risk of shortening his life span, attending business breakfasts, luncheons, dinners, "stags," cocktail parties, golf tournaments, and smokers; visiting factories, and wholesale showrooms, retail store "previews," fairs and trade shows; visiting conventions, participating in seminars, forums, clinics, and round tables; attending "mass meetings," and sales conferences, and hearings.

The businesspaper editor belongs to many organizations, institutions, and associations. He may be, by training, an engineer, a chemist, or an accountant, a physician or a lawyer. He will find it

[5] *Advertising and Selling Through Business Papers*, by Mabel Potter Hanford. Harper & Brothers, New York. Mrs. Hanford is now research director of *Modern Industry*. Formerly, she was businesspaper space buyer for Batten, Barton, Durstine & Osborne.

necessary to be a mass joiner. He will find it difficult to keep off committees or boards. Sometimes he ends up as trade association secretary or even president (with the consent of the publisher, who decides if it is "good policy"). In the charitable activities of each field he covers he is also expected to take an active part. He serves on governmental advisory committees. He sits in on many intracompany committee meetings in his own organization and in some publishing houses is a member of the board of directors. His duties accumulate. Rarely do they decrease.

To keep up with his own profession or career in journalism, he meets with and often assumes leadership in associations of editors both local and national. Sometimes he accepts assignments to lecture at schools of marketing or schools of journalism in leading universities. He is often a speaker at affairs in his own or related fields. Businesspaper editors are authors of more than 112 standard textbooks.

Here are a few of the publications the editor must keep an eye on regularly himself to be conversant with the broad economics of his own fields: *Domestic Commerce*, *Current Business* (Department of Commerce),[6] *Printers' Ink*, *Tide*, *Advertising Age*, *Advertising & Selling*, *Editor & Publisher*, *Industrial Marketing*, *Modern Industry*, *Sales Management*, *Journal of Commerce*, *Time*, *Newsweek*, *Fortune*, *Journalism Quarterly* and the *Quill* (publication of Sigma Delta Chi, honorary professional fraternity of journalism). If he is an engineer or architect, there are other professional publications for him to keep up with. There are scores of other papers he must read as well as those of his own specialized competitors, particularly in the field of management. He cannot fall behind in knowledge of new economic writers, authors, and lecturers in general fields of knowledge, or his specialized fields.

He will be asked, "Have you read so-and-so's book?" Many new books on economics and world affairs must be appraised and reviewed, as well as novels, biographies,[7] important speeches, papers, and pamphlets.

---

[6] U.S. Department of Commerce also publishes *Foreign Commerce*, a weekly.

[7] The Sinclair Lewis Course: No businesspaper editor's education is complete without having read this trilogy: *Main Street* (small towns); *Babbitt* (businessmen), and *Gideon Planish* ("uplifters, do-gooders, lecturers, professional philan-

He will accompany his publisher or one of the department managers to luncheons of the Advertising Club, the Sales Executives Club, Dotted Line Club, Business Paper Editors Club, Rotary, Kiwanis, Chamber of Commerce, or some other luncheon club, to hear men of the moment take an hour to say it. Program committees think up dinners to take care of his evenings.

The business office expects, and rightly, personal contact with the advertisers. And the advertisers expect it. On this point former businesspaper Editor Woolf writes:

As a general principle . . . the editor has as much to gain from regular contacts with advertisers as with readers. In fact, he often has more to gain because those who sell to his industry are apt to have more original ideas, as a class, than the rest of the subscription list.

Unfortunately, he can't give both groups equal time. In the first place . . . his job is to get out a paper. That's what he's paid for. To do it, he must know what his industry is doing and thinking. His primary field work is with his industry. Also, he must realize that his advertisers are having constant contact with members of his sales staff. He cannot neglect the members of his own industry in order to cultivate men who are spending money on advertising . . . if we had the time to establish that type of relationship with all our advertisers it would be fine. We haven't—nor has any other editor, if he really edits his own paper. He is forced to rely on his technical editors.[8]

BUSINESSPAPER EDITOR AND HIS GOVERNMENT

The agenda of three wartime sessions of the National Conference of Business Paper Editors,[9] (Appendix II), one held in New York City in December, 1942, and two sessions held in Washing-

---

throbbers, committee maniacs, public dinner presiders, organizators, microphone hounds"). "He is," says Van Doren in his biographical sketch of Sinclair Lewis, "a man without a skin . . . all eyes, all ears, all nerves of sense." Like Gresham and Adam Smith, Sinclair Lewis is one of the great investigators and interpreters of his times, employing as his device the novel, rather than the economic book or editorial, to record his findings and criticism.

[8] *The Business Paper Editor at Work*, by Douglas G. Woolf. McGraw-Hill, New York. Former Editor of *Textile World*, Mr. Woolf is now director of the Textile Research Institute.

[9] The professional organization of businesspaper editors affiliated with The Associated Business Papers, Inc., numbering about 150 members (see Chapter V.) It has offices in New York and Washington, D.C.

ton in June, 1943 and June, 1944, will serve to indicate the type of men with whom businesspaper editors confer informally, intimately, and regularly in order to get background material for reporting, interpreting, and anticipating news events and trends in terms of their own industry and in order to guide themselves in planning editorial programs for their readership.

Herbert Hoover, when he was the Secretary of Commerce, suggested that leading businesspaper editors of the United States come to Washington periodically to meet with him. That is how the National Conference of Business Paper Editors came into existence. Being an engineer by profession, Mr. Hoover could appreciate the importance of organized and interrelated business intelligence, transmitted via the business press directly to industrial *management*. He also appreciated that the business press was a two-way carrier; it could bring information he needed to Washington as well as take away information. The many conferences were fruitful. Upon becoming President of the United States, Mr. Hoover wrote this message to businesspaper publishers:

The Business Press is probably the greatest force in making industrial opinion. The schools and colleges have an important place; the trade associations can do much in the fields of production and distribution; the government bureaus that keep in contact with business can help promote sound leadership in industrial and economic thinking. All have an important place, but the business and technical journals are in a unique position and have a unique opportunity. Your great group of journals cannot only recognize and support sound industrial leadership, but you can also initiate it. The field of your opportunity is practically limitless.[10]

The interviews with Secretary Hoover were extended to include President Coolidge, other Cabinet members, Congressional leaders, and the diplomatic corps. The intimate relationship of businesspaper editors with official Washington continued during the administration of President Hoover and his successor, President Franklin D. Roosevelt.

With the commencement of World War II, in President Roose-

[10] Quoted in an address to the Advertising Clubs of the World, Houston, Tex., May 12, 1925, by Jesse H. Neal, executive secretary, Associated Business Papers.

velt's administration, the business press began to occupy an important place in the planning and thinking of official Washington. Long before Pearl Harbor and the official entrance of our country into the conflict, editors of leading businesspapers in industries which were to become extremely vital to the war effort were in consultation with officials in preparation for what was then called M Day, a plan for the quick mobilization of industry.

It can now be said that, without the organized business press, the impact of the Japanese attack on Pearl Harbor could have been a much more devastating blow instead of, as it turned out, an added incentive to speed up the conversion of industry to war production. The schedules of industry were already blueprinted, and businesspaper editors were hard at work collecting know-how from the wealth of accumulated technical knowledge in their files, and from years of personal experience, when our country officially entered World War II.

One of the first officials to seek the co-operation of the business press in World War II was J. Edgar Hoover, chief of the Federal Bureau of Investigation. With his help, editors quickly told industrial management how to guard against sabotage and espionage.

In rapid succession these men called businesspaper editors into their councils: William S. Knudsen of General Motors, who became chief of OPM (Office of Production Management) and later lieutenant general, U.S. Army; Donald Nelson, vice-president of Sears, Roebuck, who became chairman of the War Production Board; Philip Reed, chairman of the board, General Electric Company, who became chief of the Bureau of Industry Branches; Floyd Odlum, financier, who became chief in the Contracts Division WPB; W. L. Batt, head of the S.K.F. industries, who became chief of the materials division of WPB, later a member of the United Nations War Materials Board; Edward Stettinius of United States Steel, who became one of the chiefs of WPB and later became Secretary of State; Charles E. Wilson, president of General Electric, second in command in WPB, and Theodore Quinn, then president of Maxon Advertising Agency, who held important WPB posts; Sidney J. Weinberg, senior partner of Goldman, Sachs, vice-chairman of WPB; Leon Henderson, director of the

Office of Price Administration; Chester Bowles, Mr. Henderson's successor, an advertising agency executive; Lessing Rosenwald of Sears, Roebuck, head of the Salvage Division, WPB; Secretary of the Treasury Henry Morgenthau, Jr.; James S. Knowlson, chief of the Division of Industry Operations.

In addition, army, navy, air, and maritime chiefs of staff and General Somervell of the Service of Supply sought the business press for aid in the task of converting a peaceful country into an arsenal for the United Nations.

"Help us find ways to increase managerial efficiency," pleaded Donald Nelson at an all-day session with 125 businesspaper editors in Washington soon after he took over as WPB chief.[11]

"The Government will lean heavily on the business press in its More Production Program," read the *Fortnightly Letter to Business Paper Editors* from the Office of War Information, July 30, 1943, as preparations for the Allied invasion of Europe were getting under way. "Materials will soon be available which will enable trade publications in almost every field *to carry the story to management*" (author's italics), declared Phil H. Stitt, chief, Business Press Section, OWI.

Problems of getting industrial scrap to the smelters, of conserving vital metals (and knowing what metals were vital), and vital paper, of mining more copper ore, of conserving high-speed cutting tools, of eliminating transportation bottlenecks, of explaining price ceilings, priorities, ration directives, of selling industry the 10 per cent payroll allotment plan for war bonds, of fighting for industrial unity; these were but a few of the problems laid at the door of the business press for expeditious and intelligent solution.

For a hundred thousand new executives in industry to train ten million green, unskilled workers in new tasks requiring skill and precision, in record time, was the herculean wartime task undertaken by industry in 1941 and 1942.

An Advisory Council of Businesspaper Editors was formed by Donald Nelson to consult with various members of the War Production Board. Publishers of businesspapers formed an Industry Advisory Committee to work with official Washington.

[11] War Production Board release No. 24249, Feb. 13, 1942.

Many businesspapers began specialized studies and analyses to aid the war effort. Businesspaper editors and their technical staffs prepared books and handbooks, manuals, booklets, and folders to instruct new men in high-precision work in arsenals and converted war plants, to help personnel trainers and others.

"Pearl Harbor caused no violent change in businesspapers," declared Stanley A. Knisely, executive vice-president of Associated Business Papers, Inc. *"All that changed was the problems of their readers* . . . for example, a mere handful of men understood the design and manufacture of high explosive shells. It was essential that this vital 'know-how' be passed along speedily and accurately to thousands in industry if we were to overtake the seven-year lead of the Axis. The same was true of tanks, cannon, powder, planes, ships and a thousand other wartime items. This became at once the primary job of the businesspaper editors."[12]

Some of the typical operations carried on by the business press in World War II were: taught new skills and duties; assisted in employee training; promoted more efficient use of manpower; helped in the production of fighting weapons; surveyed availability of strategic natural resources; promoted the salvage of scarce materials and equipment; advanced technical research and development of war goods; informed key personnel on newly developed materials and methods; helped to make teachers out of new foremen and department heads; kept various trades and industries currently informed on Government regulations and rulings; conveyed latest information on design, production, materials handling, power transmission and conservation; furnished by the request of the army and navy for distribution to military schools as guides and instructional helps, hundreds of thousands of reprints of businesspaper articles; advanced food preservation technics in canning, freezing, dehydration, and packaging—all necessary to feeding the soldiers and civilians—our own and our allies'.[13]

[12] *The Business Press at War*, by Stanley A. Knisely; a presentation made to various key government officials in Washington, in 1943, published by the Associated Business Papers, Inc.

[13] From a presentation prepared for the Reconstruction Finance Corporation and the U.S. Treasury Department by the Associated Business Papers, Inc., in August, 1944.

INTERPRETIVE JOURNALISM

The key concept of a businesspaper editor is that he is an interpreter. In describing the functions of the contemporary businesspaper editor, in this chapter, notice must be taken of two definite trends: One is the trend toward interpretive journalism, which is increasing. The other is the trend toward totality in the editorial pages rather than specialization. Coverage of the over-all picture is a natural corollary of interpretation. Together these may be called a trend toward *social reality*.

The businesspaper's editorial page today tries to do for the readers what each reader tries to do for himself: get a clear picture of his world as mirrored in the news pages, reach an understanding of what is back of the news events, and decide what is to be done about it. In short, the editor tries to give understanding to events and then helps the reader decide on a course of action.

The businesspaper editor, therefore, studies the news more analytically than any reader, in a search for news significance. He picks out news items that are seemingly unrelated. A news sense, which only experience can develop, tells him that a link exists between these items. He may recognize a link to news in some other field. Putting two and two together, he discovers a trend which he reports to the reader.

Knowledge of the whole is necessary for expert interpretation of any of the parts. The contemporary businesspaper editor must step down from his ivory tower and utilize as many personal contacts as he possibly can to get the over-all picture. By talking to informed people, attending meetings, reading books, traveling the markets and production centers, he equips himself with knowledge in many spheres that may *seem* far afield from his own specialized sphere, but in reality are one picture. For example, businesspaper editors write authoritatively on problems of federal taxation, labor legislation, and foreign policy. What reader, asks the editor, is immune to these three broad subjects?

The news editor on a businesspaper reports his impression of events as a news story. He must keep to a strict record or recital of the facts. The editor assesses this news in relation to other news events and in terms of the future. That is his function.

Where reporting stops and interpreting begins, there should be a clear line of demarcation. Reporting is for the news columns. Interpretation is for the editorial pages, although it is difficult for a good news reporter to eliminate himself completely. His very choice and placement of facts in his story and emphasis in terms of number of words given to any particular angle becomes to some degree interpretive. The reader, however, should know when he is reading news and when he is reading editorial comment. News and editorial should be plainly labeled or apparent to the reader.[14]

We have all heard it said many times that the function of a journalist is "to seek the truth in contemporary life and print it without fear and favor." What is truth? What kind of truth? "No one" wrote *PM*'s editor, "can inventory all the kinds of truth which the people of a great industrial democracy like ours should know in order to govern themselves better and to get more out of the lives they lead. It is only possible to talk in terms of *direction*."[15]

There is no short cut to being a businesspaper editor or to writing editorials on a businesspaper. Years of maturing, wide and deep knowledge of his field and related fields, and of the background of the news, these things fortify the businesspaper editor. He is the mouthpiece. On his editorial page he lays bare the soul, one might say, of the businesspaper. Here on the editorial page, and here alone, the businesspaper makes chief claim to a rightful place in the communication system. On his editorial page the businesspaper editor integrates news and trends, discusses, analyzes, interprets. Here issues are joined, defined, clarified, illuminated, so that readers may reach convictions, make *decisions*. Here, too, the editor not only guides and advises; he also persuades, urges action.

To be effective, editorial expression must come from a publica-

[14] See Chart 32, third standard of practice.
[15] Ralph Ingersoll, editor of *PM*, from a confidential office memorandum to his staff, May 14, 1940, a month before publication started.

tion that is *independent*, solvent, beyond the reach of pressure groups, a businesspaper which has already won the confidence of its field. Such confidence is not won easily or quickly.

Reader confidence is won over a long term of years, first by furnishing readers with unbiased news information and intelligent, unselfish service. Plainly this is the most powerful argument the salesmen of space on a paid circulation paper can use. For example, there is a vast difference between the practice a physician builds up and a practice he buys.

EDITORIAL CONTENT AND DISCONTENT

In a talk before the New York Business Paper Editors some years ago,[16] the author suggested that it would be better to speak of editorial content as editorial *discontent*. The editor should preach dissatisfaction with things as they are. Business journalism is in opposition to the *status quo*, for the prime objective of business journalism is to raise the status of industry, advance the status of the individual in industry, *improve* the standards of practice. It is the business of businesspaper editors, as Howard Ehrlich once put it in a talk on another occasion before the same group of editors, to *"blast the readers out of their indifference."* Mr. Ehrlich criticized business publications for being "too monotonous" in editorial content. "Don't follow a regular monthly pattern," he said, suggesting faster tempo, more brevity, showmanship. "And," he added, *"don't let your editorial scope narrow down to your field as isolated from the rest of the world of business. All men in business are vitally interested in general business progress. Don't make the reader buy general business magazines to learn about other industries."*[17] (Italics are the author's.)

Professor Roscoe Ellard, in an appraisal of editorials, made these criticisms: lack of vigor, lack of analytical quality, lack of free-

[16] "Planning Editorial Content," a talk by Julien Elfenbein before the New York Business Paper Editors, Town Hall Club, 1941.

[17] *The Future of Business Paper Publishing*, by Howard Ehrlich, executive vice-president, McGraw-Hill Publishing Co., before the New York Business Paper Editors, Town Hall, New York, Nov. 7, 1940.

dom, lack of accuracy, sloppy English, verbosity, business office timidity, failure to investigate fundamental facts.[18] Professor Ellard was chiefly criticizing newspaper editorials, and he went on to criticize them for political bias and a tendency to toady to corporate wealth. Some of this criticism can also be applied to some businesspaper editorials, but one specific criticism of newspaper editorials, which Professor Ellard made, does not apply: "Edited by morons for morons." The average normal American who reads a newspaper or listens to a radio has the literate capacity of a 14-year-old child, according to one of the classic textbooks on advertising.[19]

One of the reasons for the miscarriages seen too frequently in businesspaper advertising copy is the complex many advertising copywriters still possess that all audiences are on the same intellectual level. Industrial buyers and managing executives to whom the businesspaper editor addresses himself are usually on his intellectual level. The editor, like the copywriter, must not underestimate the intelligence of his readers.[20]

Editorial discontent is imagination-in-action. The operation of the universe is not a smooth, sustained, uninterrupted process; it is erratic, the result of jerks and jumps, like the behavior of electrons. A generation ago, Professors Max Planck and Albert Einstein and Prince Louis de Broglie gave traditional scientific thought a shake-up by their amendments to the so-called "laws of nature."[21] Just as nature abhors a vacuum and perfect symmetry, so balanced or frozen editorial content can become boresome or even distasteful. "The fellow who doesn't go on some kind of a binge once in a while—alcoholic, gastronomic or emotional—isn't comfortable to live with," R. O. Eastman told a group of businesspaper editors in a lecture on editorial balance. "It's the same with businesspapers," he added. "Editing is an art rather than a craft. It can't be done with a slide rule, planboard and T square. It is inter-

---

[18] "What Is the Matter with Today's Editorials?" *Editor & Publisher*, Jan. 6, 1934. Prof. Ellard is on the staff of Columbia School of Journalism.

[19] *Advertising*, by Kenneth M. Goode. Greenberg, New York, 1941.

[20] "Industrial Copy," by S. C. Eastman of Dozier-Graham-Eastman, Los Angeles advertising agency, in *Western Advertising*, July, 1944.

[21] The quantum and radiation theories.

pretive art as well as creative. And one of the most important things in any interpretive art is correct accentuation.

"So when we talk about good editorial balance, it is not with the slightest idea that such a thing can be accomplished through blind adherence to a set of rules. However, there *is* such a thing as good and bad balance."[22]

For analyzing the editorial content of businesspapers, members of the National Industrial Advertisers Association have proposed a formula evolved by the American Management Association, which departmentizes business as follows: management, production, finance, and selling.

An "M" formula is outlined by Douglas Woolf: (1) management, (2) merchandising, (3) methods, (4) men, (5) materials, and (6) mill engineering. Mr. Woolf has thus grouped his editorial contents in terms of the functions of the readers of *Textile World* of which he was for many years chief editor.[23] "Management," of course, is concerned with planning and supervision of men. They have many titles: administrators, sales managers and salesmen, superintendents, overseers, personnel directors, purchasing agents, engineers, mechanics, and various operating executives. "Materials" or "goods" in the view of businesspaper editors is the market. "Methods" are peculiar to different kinds of business operations; they are often best described in the form of a single case history. "Merchandising" involves the functions of buying and selling, advertising, promotion. These are elaborated upon in other chapters.

Most business publications range in content from the general to the specific; from national or international subjects to purely local coverage. Up front are the editorials, Washington news, feature articles of a general nature; then some bread-and-butter or know-how articles; a "case history," perhaps; then specialized interest departments; sales training; merchandising ideas; buyer news; manufacturer news; and routine business, such as calendars of coming events, personnel changes, clubs or association news, and

[22] R. O. Eastman, Eastman Research Organization, before New York Business Paper Editors, May 11, 1939, Town Hall Club.
[23] *The Business Paper Editor at Work*, by Douglas G. Woolf. McGraw-Hill, New York, 1936.

so on. One businesspaper has a department at the back called "Necrology." Specializing in death, bankruptcy, and litigation and then departmentizing these subjects is something most editors believe is better avoided. Deaths, bankruptcies, and lawsuits may or may not be important news. Sometimes they become news because they are published and given wide circulation. Only when the editor is certain such events are of sufficient interest to the majority of the readers should they be reported at all, and then treated like all other news and given a position on the news pages of the businesspaper according to their importance, not in a department.

Who Knows Real News?

In his once famous column "Today," the late Arthur Brisbane devoted himself one day to a contemplation of real news:

> When you read about news, as you do here, you can never be sure that the really important news is even mentioned. An ant, climbing a mountain, does not see the mountain.
> While Napoleon was waiting to cross the channel to attack England, contrary winds holding him back, he said to an attendant:
> *"Tell that American I can give him three minutes."*
> The American "talked three minutes"; Napoleon dismissed him, too busy to listen. The American was Fulton, trying to tell about his steamboat that could travel regardless of wind.
> Leonardo wrote constantly, devoted scores of pages to the art of mixing paints, but said nothing of Columbus' voyage, although it happened in his day.
> Faraday, son of an English blacksmith, announced his discovery of magneto electricity, basis of all electrical development, foundation of the world's electric companies, that employ billions of dollars and millions of men. Eminent British scientists agreed that Faraday's discovery was interesting, "but it would never be anything more than an amusing toy."[24]

Collier's Weekly once conducted a symposium on "What Is News?" Dr. MacDougall gives a cross section of the definitions obtained:

[24] "Today," by Arthur Brisbane, New York *American*, May 25, 1936.

WHAT IS NEWS?

News is whatever your readers want to know about.

Anything that enough people want to read is news provided it does not violate the canons of good taste and the laws of libel.

News is anything that happens in which people are interested.

News is anything that people will talk about. The more it will excite comment, the greater its value.

News is accurate and timely intelligence of happenings, discoveries, opinions, and matters of any sort which affect or interest the readers.

Whatever concerns public welfare, whatever interests or instructs the individual in any of his relations, activities, opinions, properties or personal conduct is news.

News is everything that happens, the inspiration of happenings and the result of such happenings.

News is the essential facts concerning any happening, event or idea that possesses human interest; that affects or has an influence on human life or happiness.

News is based on people, and is to be gauged entirely on how it interests other people.

News comprises all current activities which are of general human interest, and the best news is that which interests the most readers.

News is anything that interests a number of people; and the best news is that which has the greatest interest for the greatest number.[25]

The difference between the event and the news is clearly indicated in the definition of news by Webster's Comprehensive Encyclopedic Dictionary:

News: *recent intelligence regarding any event; fresh information of something that has lately taken place, or of something before unknown.*

The event itself is potential news; the reporter gives it significance. The event becomes real news when it is recorded, published, communicated to others who did not see the event. The interpretive comment of an editor lifts the event to a yet higher plane.

Malcolm Muir, former businesspaper publisher, described a "new editorial dimension" when he took over and reorganized *Newsweek*:

With this issue *Newsweek* continues its evolutionary achievements in the new editorial dimension—interpretation of expertly marshaled facts. Further broadening its scope beyond a digest of weekly events,

[25] *Newsroom Problems and Policies,* by Curtis D. MacDougall, Ph.D., professorial lecturer in journalism, Northwestern University. Macmillan, New York, 1941.

it becomes The Magazine of News Significance. Important happenings, in all fields of human endeavor not only will be mirrored with strict impartiality from yesterday's origins into today's actualities *but the possible effects on tomorrow will be interpreted.*[26]

Ferdinand Lundberg expressed the same idea thus:

Significant news is not what is happening all over the world but what is happening within a few square city blocks of the world's surface. *Vital news is not what has happened; such news is water off the dam, beyond control. Vital news is what is going to happen.*[27]

A sharp distinction between newspaper and technical paper must be carried in mind on the subject of news and reader interest. The technical reader is in a different frame of mind from the daily newspaper reader, as we pointed out earlier in this chapter. Gallup polls[28] show that comics are the most popular feature in a newspaper, read largely by adults. Other polls (wartime) put subject matter in this order for men newspaper readers: (1) war; (2) weather, labor, sports; (3) science, human interest, deaths, politics, crime; (4) accidents; (5) amusements, radio log, business. For women newspaper readers: (1) weather; (2) human interest, deaths; (3) accidents; (4) amusements; (5) crime, fashion, society, war.[29]

"Human interest," says Helen MacGill Hughes, "is the interest in the common fortunes, fears and fates of mankind, appearing in a new expression." In the introduction to her book, Robert E. Park, sociologist, defines human interest as "the universal element in news." He adds: "It is the ability to discover and interpret the human interest in the news that gives the reporter the character of a literary artist and the news story the character of literature."[30]

Events are not made by journalists; journalists simply reject,

[26] *Newsweek*, Oct. 4, 1937.
[27] *News-Letters, A Revolution in Journalism*, by Ferdinand Lundberg. Harper & Brothers, New York, 1940.
[28] American Institute of Public Opinion, Dr. George Horace Gallup.
[29] *The Press, Reader Habits, and Reader Interest*, by Chilton R. Bush, Ph.D., executive head, Division of Journalism, Stanford University (Calif.); chairman, National Council on Research, American Association for Schools and Departments of Journalism, and Darwin L. Teilhet, research associate, Stanford University, former account executive N. W. Ayer & Son.
[30] *News and the Human Interest Story*, by Helen MacGill Hughes. University of Chicago Press, 1940.

select, and project them. If an editor's staff is alive it usually finds more news between publication dates than the space budget will ever allow.[31] There is no limit to what may happen. There is always a limit to what can be published. In the rejection and selection of news, the physical limitation requires quick discrimination by newspaper editors and slow, careful weighing and judging of news values by businesspaper editors.

News editors on monthly or semimonthly businesspapers write up and follow up events as they happen during the month. As deadlines approach, some news items coalesce, others expand into bigger stories, some grow stale, some which originally were considered important assume insignificance. News editors, sometimes in consultation with the chief editor, find it necessary to kill some news items, condense or enlarge others, or combine related ones. Last-minute demands for extra advertising space often require quick reappraisal of all galleys of news and further killing, cutting or boiling down, to fit a reduced budget of editorial space.

Most folios are printed in 8-page or 16-page forms. A publication may have 64 pages (two 32's) or 72 pages (two 32's and an 8-page form). A four-page form can also be used. Unless a page is pasted in, a last-minute advertisement means cutting an editorial page or adding three.

Producing the editorial contents of a businesspaper month after month is like no other business. The editor faces unknown quantities with each new issue. His schedules are both fixed and flexible. His space budget is known and unknown. (Only his expense budget is fixed, rigid and precise.) How many new products will be revealed this month? How many personnel changes will take place? How many important events will break? What leader will die or resign? What firms will merge, or close down, or expand? How much advertising will the business office secure? If businessmen had to plan production of any other commodity with so many unknown quantities, such indefinite knowledge of volume or materials, as an editor must use in planning a businesspaper they would be more in sympathy with the problems of businesspaper editors. To most businesspaper editors, like all other kinds of

[31] Many businesspaper editors mail "Between Issues" news bulletins to their readers.

editors, news is paramount. Feature articles are often killed or held over rather than sacrifice news to keep within space limitations. The article may keep; news will not.

Editors withhold news sometimes in the public interest and sometimes because it has been given to them in confidence. As a result of the off-the-record conferences with Washington official-dom, businesspaper editors often become the repositories of vital news information weeks and even months before it is released for public consumption as "news." Sometimes the information is never released, in the public interest. Editors are told to forget it.

During World War II, Byron Price, director of the Office of Censorship, furnished every businesspaper editor with a guide-book for voluntary censorship of his own operations.

In the second edition of this Censorship Guide Book (Feb. 1, 1943), Mr. Price said to editors:

The basic facts of voluntary press censorship remain unchanged. The first of these facts is that the outcome of the war is a matter of vital personal concern to the future of every American citizen. The second is that the security of our armed forces and even of our homes and our liberties will be weakened in greater or less degree by every disclosure of information which helps the enemy. In other words, a maximum of accomplishment will be attained if editors will ask themselves with respect to any given detail, *"Is this information I would like to have if I were the enemy?"* and then act accordingly.[32]

Graduate of the editorial staffs of *Time*, *Life*, and *Fortune*, Ralph Ingersoll[33] in a confidential memorandum to his own staff a month before his unorthodox newspaper, *PM*, started publication, recorded his "respect" for these six elements in journalistic writing:

1. A due respect for the fact that a story can properly be begun at the beginning, the middle or the end—but that each story shall have all three components.
2. A definite interest in the personalities and characters of the people who make the news, as well as in the news itself.

[32] Code of Wartime Practices, U.S. Office of Censorship.
[33] Editor-publisher of *PM*, adless New York City tabloid, which is owned by Marshall Field III. Mr. Ingersoll served as a captain in World War II, wrote a book about the African Campaign.

3. An interest in the stage on which news is played.
4. A definite interest in the background and continuity of news—and a similar interest in appraising the future.
5. A definite interest in the significance and meaning of news.
6. A consuming interest in the story value of the news—if it gets much space it must be a *good* story.

INTERVIEWS AND CREATIVE WRITING

Seven rules for interviewing were discussed with businesspaper editors of New York by a business writer, John Allen Murphy.[34] The rules he follows are: (1) Prepare for the interview. (2) Use waiting time to get more information. (3) Ask for only a few minutes but take all the time you can. (4) Be casual and informal. (5) Take no notes. (6) Do not ask leading questions too early and spread out important questions. (7) Make the interview a discussion, not a quiz program.

There is little need to elaborate on the first and second rules. Basic strategy of all interviews is thoughtful preparation. The more familiar the interviewer is with his man, his habits and hobbies, his likes and dislikes, and his business interests, the easier the interview will be. "To learn his personality," a famous interviewer says, "study his photograph."[35] The interviewer had better know a lot about his own business: his businesspaper, its policy, its field, its publishers. On occasion, the interviewer himself may be subjected to a barrage of questions by the interviewee. The interview requires the utmost skill and the editor should not send an interviewer unless he has some polish and experience.

Many editors will protest Mr. Murphy's third rule. Most interviews are (and should be) by appointment. The approximate time limit of the interview should be known to both parties and respected by both. If the person interviewed wants to terminate it, little is to be gained by hanging on. If he deliberately prolongs the interview, cut it short when you have what you came for, and no

[34] "The Technique of Interviewing," by John Allen Murphy, from an address before New York Business Paper Editors, January, 1942.
[35] "The Art of the Interview," by Emil Ludwig, *Editor & Publisher*, July 18, 1936.

further advantage is to be gained by protracting it. Why should the person interviewed think a reporter's or an editor's time is completely at his disposal, or of no value? And vice versa.

On rule 4, being "casual and informal" depends on who is interviewed, the setting, and other circumstances. The writer has never found it possible to be as casual in interviewing the Chief Executive of the United States as he has in talking with the president of a factory making tinware. That does not mean that Paul Wooton[36] could not be just as casual with the President of the United States. The President calls him Paul and calls him often.

Rule 5 is debatable. Again the interviewer must be guided by the circumstances. Some interviews are given with an understanding that there will be no use of the interviewer's name. The author, at such interviews, nevertheless has often taken copious notes. The story needed facts, not authority. At any interview it should be clearly understood by both parties what the interviewer proposes to do with the information, when, and where, and why. Some interviewers ask for advance galleys of the story for okay before it goes to press. Businesspaper journalists often suggest this themselves to ensure accuracy as to both facts quoted and opinion interpreted. Formal authentication by the interviewee ensures the interviewer against charges of misquotation or inaccuracy after publication. An interviewer does not, however, have to submit his finished story unless that is the policy.

Some people form an unfavorable opinion of an interviewer if he does not take notes. They stop talking. True, some stop talking when you pull out a notebook. Why? The interviewer must find that out. The notebook may act like a camera on the person interviewed, make him self-conscious or freeze him up. Perhaps he does not want to be quoted. Or perhaps what he says will not stand up between quotation marks and he knows it. Business journalists never quote, as a general rule, without permission. Instinct, therefore, is an important sense to develop in interviewing. If you took no notes, be sure to write down what you heard as soon as possible after you depart. Do not trust your memory too long.

[36] Washington correspondent of McGraw-Hill businesspapers; president, National Conference of Business Paper Editors.

Rule 6 is based on experience. Although methods, as Mr. Murphy says himself, must vary with every newsman, the indirect approach is a favorite of both interviewers and good salesmen. In a way, the interviewer can profit by studying the technics of good salesmanship. He is also a salesman. He is selling his competence to project a man's views; selling the value of his publication as a carrier; selling his own intelligence to comprehend what the man has on his mind; selling his ability to judge or interpret its value to his paper's readership. The indirect approach, however, is knocked in the head when a pair of cold, steel-blue (or brown) eyes say as plainly as words "Come to the point," or when nervous fingers drum on the desk while you are wasting precious minutes praising an etching on the wall. An interviewer must keep all his nerves exposed, like the sandpapered finger tips of a cracksman. He must be all antennae during an important interview. He must be "a man without a skin . . . all eyes, all ears, all nerves of sense."

Rule 7 is important. The interviewer should never step into his prospect's presence without a carefully formulated plan for his story, unless it is an emergency interview, in which case he probably has the story outlined in his mind anyway. The plan of the interview must be flexible just as the interviewer's attitude must be adjustable to the situation he encounters when he begins his interview.

Defects in businesspaper writing, as outlined by Burton Bigelow, are: (1) slow start, bad lead, lack of "sex appeal" in the headline; (2) lack of pattern or order; (3) too much repetition: in-again-out-again-on-again-off-again technic; (4) imperfect and divided reference; (5) excessive use of personal pronoun; (6) verbosity; (7) cracks in writer's joints: paragraphs do not hang together; (8) lack of suspense: there must be momentum and sustained suspense; (9) use of dead verbs; (10) talking down: teacher to student, look you here, I'm telling you; (11) excessive inclusion or exclusion; (12) overuse of past tenses; (13) lack of summaries, intermediary and at the end; (14) lack of examples and illustrations; (15) lack of personalizing.[37]

[37] "Writing for Business Papers," from an address by Burton Bigelow, management consultant, before the New York Business Paper Editors, April 13, 1943.

Amplifying his criticism, Mr. Bigelow declares businesspaper writing must be objective: "start at a particular starting place and go to a definite destination." He believes the businesspaper article must "steal the reader's attention from something perhaps more interesting . . . then get action . . . achieve a purpose." He says: "stick to facts . . . you are dealing with a skeptical audience."

Both Mr. Murphy and Mr. Bigelow prefer what they term the "sharp-angle" type of article to the "encyclopedic check-list" or "bird's-eye-view" type.

The "sharp-angle" story is thus defined by John Allen Murphy:

My writing specialty is the sharp-angle story of hot news value, backed up with a lot of examples or case histories. I condense many interviews into one article. An hour's interview may be summed up in one sentence. Even an important interview may be covered in two or three paragraphs. Very few interviews today are worth a whole story by themselves. Any one executive or engineer or whoever he is, is only a tiny particle of the vast economic picture. What he has to say is not of world-rocking significance. What he has to say may become of far greater significance if it is combined with what a lot of other important men have to say. Under present world conditions the average one-interview story is pretty thin. The great value of the many-interview article is that it makes tabulation of points or trends possible. Tabulation is rapidly coming into journalism, just as it has long been a vital part of research.

During an average trip of a couple of weeks I will get the story on eight or ten businesses. I contend that only through the many-interview article can the story of most of these businesses be told. For the most part they are old, well-established, medium-sized concerns. I have found that seldom will business men of this character give out a formal interview. They don't want their business written up. They want to be left alone. Hundreds of business men in New England take this attitude. Yet these men are courteous. They will talk freely about their businesses and do not object to a writer using this information if it is not spotlighted too much in a "splash" story. They don't mind if incidents from these interviews are used in general stories. They often thank me for including them in such stories. If I asked them for an exclusive story about them, which I have often done, they would have given me an emphatic "No."[38]

[38] "Technique of Interviewing," a paper by John Allen Murphy, read before New York Business Paper Editors, January, 1942.

The thesis of the late Dr. Stephen Leacock's last book, *How to Write*,[39] is that writing originates in the brain, not in the elbow. Leacock quoted the famous humorist, Bill Nye, who once said in his column of "Answers to Correspondents":

"You write a splendid hand, you ought to write for the papers."

As we stated in the Preface, the work of the business journalist is a labor of definition, clarification, and illumination. In his *Tyranny of Words*, Stuart Chase says:

A good semantic discipline gives the power to separate mental machinery from tangible events; makes us conscious of abstracting; prevents us from peopling the universe with non-existent things . . . It checks us from acting *as if* fantasies were real events worth fighting and dying for. Look over the edges of abstractions and ask:
"What is really happening out there?"
"How do the facts really hang together out there?"
"What are people really doing out there?"[40]

REWRITE, COPYREADING, STYLE GUIDES

Businesspaper editorial staff workers, like newspaper workers, generally employ a style sheet. Sometimes they use the style book of a well-established publication. Usually prepared by the chief editor, the style sheet lists common errors for writers and copyreaders to avoid. Example: spelling Celanese[41] with a lower *c*; or St. Marys' blanket with the apostrophe misplaced; or using the trite word "pep." The style guide provides uniformity, accuracy, and easy reference but when the style guide becomes too obese and ponderous it will slow up copyreaders and writers. Style sheets should be short and general. The carefully edited back issues of a businesspaper are good style guides. New staff members should study the editor's blue-penciled corrections on their copy and find out *why* the changes were made.

One of the important posts on a businesspaper editorial staff is the rewrite man or woman. His job is twofold: (1) He revamps

[39] *How to Write*, Stephen Leacock, professor of political science, McGill University, Dodd, Mead, New York, 1943.
[40] *The Tyranny of Words*, by Stuart Chase, Harcourt, Brace, New York, 1938.
[41] Trade-mark of a private corporation.

The Symbol or Term	How Used	Its Meaning
⌐ ⌐	")Deadlines("	Note the quotation marks
═	John Doe	Set in small capitals
∿	publisher	Set boldface
───	editor	Set in italics
˒	John, Jane	Note comma
⊙ ✕	the end⊙the end✕	Note period
		Story is not completed
more or ↓		Story is completed
③⓪ or #⃝		
no ¶	ᴺᵒ¶The print shop	Do not paragraph
¶ ⌐ ⌐	¶ The ⌐The ⌐The	Paragraph
	The shop⌐print	Transpose words
	pⱥiⱥnt	Transpose characters
∼ stet	The ~~print~~ shop	Restore the text
	Main⌐ street	Join separated matter
═	Exclude me ~~out~~	Delete matter crossed out
≡	r̲	Make it a capital letter
⁄	E̸	Make it a small letter
⌒	Ed itor	Close up
⌣	consumer⁄goods	Separate
⁄	next The ˄ day	Insert letter or word
⌢	pres.	Spell out
⌒	president	Abbreviate
○	six	Make it a digit
○	6	Spell it out
		Indent on both margins
⌐ ⌐	⌐The diamond market is in Maiden Lane⌐	

CHART 33. COPYREADING SYMBOLS

CR	Take out letter, letters, or words indicated.
#	Insert space where indicated.
⊙	Turn inverted letter indicated.
lc	Set in lower-case type.
wf	Wrong font.
×	Broken letter Must be replaced.
ital	Reset in italic type the matter indicated.
rom	Reset in roman (regular) type the matter indicated.
bf.	Reset in boldface type word, or words, indicated.
⊙	Insert period where indicated.
tr	Transpose letters or words as indicated.
stet	Let it stand as it is. Disregard all marks above dots.
/ = /	Insert hyphen where indicated.
eq #	Equalize spacing.
[or]	Move over to the point indicated.
	[if to the left; if to the right]
⌐⌐	Lower to the point indicated.
⌐⌐	Raise to the point indicated.
⟨⟩	Insert comma where indicated.
⟨⟩	Insert apostrophe where indicated.
⟨⟩ ⟨⟩	Enclose in quotation marks.
H	Replace with a capital the letter or letters indicated.
⊥	Push down space which is showing up.
C	Draw the word together.
Out, see copy	Used when words left out are to be set from copy and inserted as indicated.
spell out ○	Spell out all words marked with a circle.
¶	Start a new paragraph as indicated.
No ¶	Should not be a separate paragraph. Run in.
?	Query to author. Encircled in red.
=	Out of alignment. Straighten.
em	1-em dash.
⊠	Indent 1 em.

Prepared by *Sales Management*

CHART 34. PROOFREADER'S SYMBOLS

original copy which the paper receives in the form of articles, shorts or news items, and publicity releases. (2) He rewrites articles and news items relating to his paper's fields which appear in daily newspapers, general magazines, or competitive business-papers. All clippings sent in generally find their way to his desk. Often he is a graduate reporter—or he may combine outside re-porting with rewrite. He also takes stories over the telephone. He may improve or boil down copy written by other staff members, or field editors and correspondents. He also acts as fact-confirmer. He also interviews office visitors (with stories) who are not impor-tant enough for the editor's time. Since news is dynamic and al-ways changing, the rewrite man must also bring news stories up to date. All outside publications are routed to his desk for survey and study. Once a news story is published it is legitimate news for any other competing publication to lift. Since it is a paper's duty to give its readers as much news as it can, the rewrite man combs the competitive papers for news which may have escaped his own paper's reporters. Most printshops employ expert proofreaders in their composing rooms, but the rewrite man often acts as proof-reader to double-check against errors.

The copyreader's, or proofreader's basic tools are style sheet, dictionary, Thesaurus, almanacs, directories, Who's Who, ency-clopedia, Adverb Finder, Bartlett's Quotations, clipping files, or "morgue," the house library, correspondence files, back copies of his businesspaper, or the publication's card file index, a guide of symbols or copyreading and proofreading marks and terms (Charts 33 and 35), a type chart, his telephone, typewriter, and sharp pencils.

Sales Management, a businesspaper giving horizontal coverage to all management problems of industry, gives the following sug-gestions to its own copyreaders and rewrite people:

SUGGESTIONS FOR COPY READING AND REWRITING[42]

1. Have your style sheet beside you.
2. Give the article a preliminary reading.
3. After your preliminary reading, decide if anything is *organically*

[42] From *Sales Management* manual for editorial workers.

wrong with the article. (Example: bad lead that needs re-writing.) (Example: portion needs change of form: quotes that need to be thrown into straight exposition or vice versa; sequences that would gain in clarity and speed by ABC tabulation.) If so, do the re-writing first. If the article has to be entirely re-typed, copyread the entire manuscript so that in the re-copying you will come out with clean copy that needs little additional editing.

4. Before you start to work on any article look at the signature. We have five standard forms:

   a. The article which is unsigned—the straight report.
   b. The article which is signed by a name, without further identification. ("By Lester B. Colby")
   c. The article set up as an interview ("Based on an interview by Lester B. Colby with Joseph W. Zilch, President, Zilch Manufacturing Co., Chicago").
   d. The article signed by a company executive ("By Joseph W. Zilch, President, Zilch Manufacturing Co., Chicago").
   e. The article which is written in first person but is signed "As told to Lester B. Colby by Joseph W. Zilch, President, Zilch Manufacturing Co., Chicago."

   The signature sets the point of view for the article. Naturally, material signed as in d and e above must be first person throughout. In the case of c, both the reporter and the man interviewed can and do speak.

5. Check to see that the company name and line of business is clearly defined not later than the second paragraph of the article. Preferably, it should show in the head or blurb.

6. If there are included in the article extensive facts about the company history, background, and personnel which seem to slow up the story, ask yourself if these should be taken out of the article entirely and presented in a separate box.

7. After your first reading, analyze carefully the *flavor* of the story: Does the presentation seem too flippant? Sound "feminine" in the write-up? Lack sophistication because of failure to use good business language? Have a publicity flavor? If anything seems to be wrong with the flavor of the story, this, of course, will have to be corrected in the editing.

8. Reading for the printer: Use a sharp, black pencil. If there is too much interlining in a paragraph or paragraphs, re-type and paste over the original. Break up excessively long paragraphs and combine groups

of paragraphs in manuscripts which have too much paragraph break-up without good reason.

Watch editorialization, adjectives, adverbs, words with queer connotation. See that opinions are quoted. Watch for redundancy. See if you can substitute active, strong, colorful verbs for "flat" inactive verbs.

9. Is there in the article any material you could take out and use in a picture caption, thus cutting over-all length?

10. If, after reading a manuscript, you think it has not achieved the utmost in clarity, ask yourself if we could improve the presentation by some special art work—special map, pictograph, etc.?

11. Particularly where there are sequences of big company names in an article, do not trust your memory on spelling and the expression of corporate names. Check with the Red Book. Watch media names particularly. (Example: A recent article mentioned five or six advertisers on the "Red Network"—there is no longer any Red Network— it is The National Broadcasting Co.)

12. Beware of the article that trails off into anti-climax at the end. Many writers seem to feel that they have to fashion some sort of a trailer after the story has really ended. You can often cut such material.

13. Try as you handle *Sales Management* material to develop your editorial judgment. Who will read the article? Is it, for example, primarily for presidents and general managers or is it an article about a bread-and-butter problem of sales management which is likely to be of greater interest to the sales manager? If the article is expected to be of primary interest to research men, you may want to lean in the direction of leaving in the article more facts about the research techniques involved than would otherwise be true. Is the article of special interest to any classification of our advertisers and prospects? (If so, the salesmen may want copies of it before the publishing date.)

Headline Writing

The headlines of a story or article in a businesspaper do three basic things: (1) *sell* the story; (2) *tell* the story; (3) *dress* the story. The format of a businesspaper will determine headline style, type size, type family and other factors, but the three basic points are universal. In the headline you sell or fail to sell the reader. To

The "Happy Family" Sales Force: What Keeps It Buoyant and Productive?

Answer: The sales manager who looks upon every man on the force primarily as a human being with family responsibilities, financial problems, "relative" troubles, emotional up's and down's—and who treats every one considerately as an individual rather than as a cog in a business machine.

Based on an interview with

1 MILTON A. KOTTINGER
Assistant General Sales Manager,
California Conserving Co.,
San Francisco

Distributors on the Way Out? I Don't Believe It!

A Zenith executive appraises the probable situation in post-war distribution. He finds: No evidence that changes will be radical, no discernible tendency to eliminate distributors. He believes many new methods will develop, but they will be evolutionary.

2 BY J. J. NANCE
Vice-President and Director of Sales
Zenith Radio Corporation
Chicago

Branded & Advertised Wallpapers Pull United Out of Red Ink

Over a year ago United Wallpaper Factories, Inc., decided to invest $800,000 in a complete new marketing plan. It called for promotion of wallpapers by brand, national advertising, a research program to insure quality. The result of the first year's operation: A $216,000 net loss turned into a $320,000 net profit.

Speakers' Club Gives Executives Polish & Poise on the Platform

A group of business men in Bridgeport felt themselves hampered by inability to express themselves clearly and forcefully before others. So they formed a study forum, practiced, analyzed, and practiced some more. Their new skills have proved to be assets.

3 BY M. S. SULLIVAN

4

Shipshape Tools Make Sure-Footed Salesmen

Do buyers who demand facts find too many of your salesmen mentally undressed? Do your men refer too many questions to the home office? If so, they need better sales equipment. Raybestos-Manhattan's fine selling tools may give you some ideas.

5 BY J. J. DE MARIO
Advertising Manager, The Manhattan Rubber Mfg. Division
Raybestos-Manhattan, Inc.
Passaic, N. J.

One Product, One Price, One Market: The Policy That Built Schaefer

Built soundly on low-pressure selling and persistent advertising, Schaefer's 1,300,000 barrels for 1940 represent an all-time 99-year high. Volume has expanded every year since Repeal.

6

Corning Glass has price maintenance contracts in force in every state that has passed an enabling law. Wholesalers and retailers, thus lifted out of cut-rate dog-fights, are cheering . . . and the substantially increasing volume on Pyrex has enabled the company to pass on to consumers fat savings in the form of lower prices.

7 **We'll Fight to Keep Fair Trade— Because We Know It Works**

BY

W. A. KATES
General Sales Manager,
Corning Glass Works,
Corning, N. Y.

So You Think Radio Is Only for "Big Money" Advertisers?

This analysis of talent-cost-per-listener shows that certain types of programs within financial reach of many a modest advertiser are producing results far out of proportion to their cost.

8 BY LOUIS HONIG
Director of Research, Erwin, Wasey & Co.,
San Francisco

Curve Control Crisis: Frenzied Femmes Want Guns and Girdles

Some intimate news from SM's Chicago reporter on the state of things in the buttock-and-bust-control business.

9 BY LESTER B. COLBY

Swift Employes Turn in 17,588 Ideas in '42; 3,044 Are Accepted

A suggestion plan for workers has paid handsome dividends for this big Chicago meat packing house. Last year the management paid out more than $62,000 for ideas submitted from the ranks.

10

That "Happier Tomorrow": If We Want It, We Must Plan Today

Business can cushion the shocks of re-conversion if it will. But if we are to avoid wholesale unemployment and a more intensive form of government-managed economy, every company will have to share the load. Are you planning now to do your part to win the peace—with the same sense of responsibility that you feel about helping to win the war?

11

12

No Spine, No Spirit, No Sparkle: Is Your House Organ Like That?

If it is, it's a weak sister, and probably isn't earning its keep. You can resuscitate it by the application of good business paper technique to its editorial content. The "how" type of story is still unbeatable. Not enough house organs use it.

Thirteen Mistakes To Avoid in Your Post-War Planning

Business as a whole is untrained in the skills required for intelligent long-range planning. As in every other operation, however, there is a technique for doing it, and it's fully as important to understand the pitfalls as it is to analyze the positive objectives

13 BY BURTON BIGELOW
Burton Bigelow Organization
New York City

What Happened When War Wiped Out $17,000,000 of Our Annual Volume

Not until trucks were frozen and the company faced the possibility of having to disband their entire sales force did White Motors discover the real possibilities for volume and profit inherent in service, theretofore the firm's "Also Ran" department.

14 BY HAROLD D. LAIDLEY
Manager, Sales Development
The White Motor Company
Cleveland

I Make a Wager: After V-Day Thousands of Salesmen Will Fly

There are many logical reasons for believing that tomorrow's salesmen will operate their own planes. Mr. Watkins states the case.

16 BY ROY A. WATKINS
Executive Vice-President and General Manager
Howard Aircraft Corp.
Chicago

TWA Training Capsules Pack Laughs with Lessons

Would you know a "Longslugg" if you met one? Or a "Jerp," or a "Bidgit" or a "Tellagotn?" See how TWA has invented and used these entertaining characters to help management do a routine job of administering painless basic training to all employes.

15

Two Helicopters in Every Garage

Before we grow delirious over 200-seater ocean clippers, a televised World Series, and prefabricated houses we can assemble, in six hours, maybe we'd better look for ways to improve the little homely gadgets we use every day. Personally, we want a pineapple corer long enough to go through a pineapple!

17 BY T. HARRY THOMPSON

New York a Ghost Town? Phooey!

So you think it's true that Manhattan (with four other counties thrown in) has been sold back to the Indians for a second-hand set of s'dora and ten dollars in Confederate currency? Maybe it's just a rumor. Let's take a careful look at the record.

18

CHART 35.   SAMPLE HEADLINES

get his attention to the story you must arouse his interest. That is the purpose of the headline. The headline must also tell the story, summarize it or at least bring out the most important point in the story. The third factor is related to the first two. If the page is attractive the reader's eye will linger. On a page without illustration the headline must arrest attention and focus interest. The value of a good article can be lost on a page that lacks balance, good arrangement and headlines that sell and tell the story.

PRINCIPLES GOVERNING THE WRITING OF GOOD HEADS[43]

REMEMBER WHEN YOU WRITE HEADLINES FOR SALES MANAGEMENT THAT OUR READERS ARE BOTH SOPHISTICATED AND HARD HEADED.

DO NOT WRITE THE HEADLINE FOR A STORY YOU HAVEN'T READ.

1. A good headline is truthful. It neither undersells, nor oversells the story. (See headline seven)
> (Overbroad statements made in top head sometimes need to be qualified in the blurb in order to achieve truthfulness.)

2. A good headline is in tune with the article—light if the article is light, etc.

3. A good headline has horizontal appeal—sells the story.
   Some basic elements that have good head appeal:

   a. Fights (Headline two)
   b. Changes
   c. News of timeliness
   d. Checklists
   e. Spectacular figures
   f. Solution to some common problem
   g. Competition
   h. Big jobs done quickly
   i. Promise of specific information
   j. Threats, dangers
   k. Errors or mistakes
   l. Forecast or prognostication

4. A good headline has unity—does not try to do too many things at once.

5. A good headline is specific.

6. A good headline avoids mechanical elements which confuse the reader or slow up reading
> (Examples: Two hyphens in the same head; two apostrophes; unfortunate juxtaposition of figures.)

[43] *Ibid.*

7. A good headline contrasts well with other heads in the same issue to make a palatable editorial menu.

(Think of the reader "shopping" through the book to see what he wants to read. Watch for too many question heads or "how" heads in the same book.)

8. A good headline has color, liveliness, movement, rhythm, feeling of spontaneity.

How to achieve:

a. Use of colorful words and expressions as opposed to millrun phrases and clauses, trite expressions.
b. Use of analogy, other figures of speech
c. Use of active voice
d. Use of alliteration
e. Wise use of slang and colloquialisms
f. Use of balanced or contrasting pairs of words
g. Use of strong, active verbs
h. Use of informality
i. Use of curiosity.

9. A good headline is properly tuned to its position in the book. Note especially in connection with lead articles.

10. A good headline, other things being equal, is short and speedy. Use and hold to short words as much as possible.

11. A good headline exploits *justifiable* opportunities for good propaganda.

12. A good headline does not in any way embarrass good friends or customers.

MOST COMMON FAULTS IN HEADS

1. Mixed figures of speech.
2. Too long, with too many multi-syllable words.
3. Failure to tell enough to sell—failure to be specific.
4. Bad echoes.

Analysis of Sample Headlines From Sales Management Magazine
[See Chart 34]

1. sells story . . . common problem . . . colorful words 2. fights . . . challenge 3. rhythm . . . alliteration 4. crisis . . . justifiable propaganda 5. short . . . alliterative 6. sequence of balanced phrases 7. strong . . . does not oversell or undersell 8. change of pace . . . interrogatory 9. timed to pitch of the article 10. bad head . . . elements

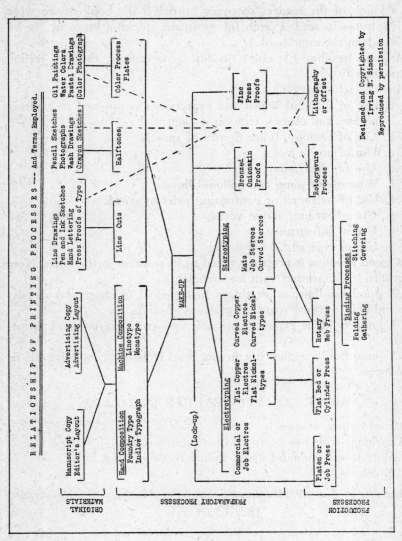

CHART 36. RELATIONSHIP OF PRINTING PROCESSES

confusing 11. wish fulfillment 12. balanced phrases 13. promises specific information . . . checklists are always good 14. big figures 15. bright and light in keeping with article 16. forecast always good 17. good hyperbole 18. wise use of slang or colloquialism.

TYPE CASTING AND PRINTING

Anyone connected with journalism or ambitious to make journalism a career must have a love for and some experience and knowledge of printing. The life of Benjamin Franklin or Johannes Gutenberg or a general history of printing is a good start. Scores of books on printing may be found today in any library. In New York City educational courses in the elements of printing and printing processes are available under the auspices of the New York Employing Printers Association. Many schools and colleges also give courses in printing and engraving.

Get into a fair-sized print shop and see what goes on. Younger members of businesspaper editorial staffs find plenty of opportunities to get into the print shop, or the engraver's, or the bindery. What happens to copy or proofs after they leave the editorial rooms is something a staff worker must understand by having seen the transformation with his own eyes before he can appreciate why copy is written and edited a certain way, or why proofs are marked a certain way.

In the interest of efficiency in sending copy to the printer, most businesspaper editors "cast" their copy so that they know how many words a story runs to, without counting each word, as soon as it is typed. A sample type-casting chart which acts as a guide to the stenographers in the editorial workroom is shown on page 248.

This is not complete but will give the general idea. In the first column, "1″, 6 pc," means one inch width or six picas, which is a standard width this particular editor uses for captions alongside of illustrations. The regular column width on his magazine is 13½ ems or picas. The type page is 7 by 10 inches. A page 7 inches wide is therefore 42½ picas wide and if divided into two columns, the width of one column will be 20½ picas. A pica of space will divide the two columns without use of a rule. The typist knows

CHART FOR CASTING TYPE

Type Face	Number of Typewriter Characters					
	1″ 6 pc	1 col 13½ pc	2 col to pg 20½ pc	2 col 28 pc	3 col 42½ pc	Lines per Inch
Body type 8 Pt Old Style Solid UL	18	38	60	79	122	9
Editorials—1st para- graph only 10 Pt Old Style UL	16	37	57	75	117	7
Captions 8/10 Bodoni Bold UL	15	38	57	78	117	7
Boxes 10 Pt Metro Med UL	18	40	60	82	123	7 (less 10 characters for box use)
8/9 Old Style UL	18	38	60	79	122	8

that, if her instructions are to type for a one-column box in 10-point Metro Medium, she can get only 18 typewriter characters to a line to match 18 characters of Metro Medium type in size 10 point in a one-column box.

PROPAGANDA AND IMPROPERGANDA

As a technic for influencing human action, inaction or reaction, propaganda is as old as human communication. It is done by *manipulating* spoken, written, pictorial, or musical representations. Political assassination, for example, is propaganda by deed.[44] But mass subjugation and mass annihilation may be accomplished by the propaganda of ideas followed up by military power. Ivy Lee,[45] famous publicist, called propaganda a "bad word," and said its evil lay in "failure to disclose the source of information." That is but one of its evils. Much propaganda today discloses its source

[44] *Propaganda*, by H. D. Lasswell, *Encyclopedia of the Social Sciences*, Vol. 12, pp. 521-522. Macmillan, New York, 1934.
[45] *Publicity*, by Ivy Lee. Industries Publishing Co., 1925.

without hesitation. The source may have a fancy name incorporating the card-stacking term "institute," "foundation," or "national" as dressing. The word "propaganda" is slippery; thus it has been given many slippery concepts.

Walter Lippmann[46] calls propaganda "the manufacture of consent . . . now based on analysis rather than rule-of-thumb."

Combination of modern communication and psychological research have made propaganda a formidable weapon whose uses every journalist should understand. As journalists, we must be constant students of propaganda, and with eyes open we can each be our own judges of whether on recognition it is good or bad, right or wrong, useful or dangerous. The successful journalist must, as Marquis Childs says, "be able to smell lying propaganda."[47] To identify propaganda is to avoid the pitfalls which are encountered, as Doob points out, when thinkers try to distinguish between education and propaganda.[48]

Propaganda is now universally recognized as a weapon[49] of military as well as economic warfare. It would be naïve to assume that propaganda stops when military war stops. *The battle for the kingdom of the mind never stops.* Its most powerful weapon is the IDEA. Technics vary as ideas change. The battle goes on. During World War II, the United States spent somewhere around $50 million a year for counter-foreign propaganda and "political warfare," whereas Germany, according to Reston of the *Times*, spent $234 million a year for foreign propaganda.[50]

Leonard Doob defines propaganda as "*a systematic attempt by an interested individual, or group of individuals, to control the attitudes of groups of individuals through the use of suggestion, and consequently to control their actions.*"

Huxley says, "history pursues an undulatory course because self-conscious men and women grow tired of a mode of thought and feeling which has lasted for more than a certain time. Propa-

---

[46] *Public Opinion*, by Walter Lippmann. Macmillan, 1929.

[47] "Propaganda in War," Forum of the Air, July 13, 1943, Marquis Childs, Washington correspondent, St. Louis *Post-Dispatch*.

[48] *Propaganda—Its Psychology and Technique*, by Leonard W. Doob. Henry Holt, New York, 1935.

[49] *Propaganda Is a Weapon*—radio broadcast series, by Bryce Oliver.

[50] *Prelude to Victory*, by James B. Reston, Knopf, New York, 1942.

ganda gives force and direction to the successive movements of feeling and desire, but it does not do much to create those movements . . . the propagandist is a man who canalizes an existing stream. In a land where there is no water he digs in vain."[51]

"The power of suggestion," which is Dean Ackerman's definition of journalism, is a force which, unfortunately, is often more greatly appreciated by the publicist than it is by the journalist. Dean Ackerman observes:

Publicists have long known both of the existence and the usefulness of this power. It has been used to elect and defeat candidates for public office, to initiate and destroy public confidence in administrative and legislative proposals, to stampede a nation into a prohibition hysteria, and to reverse the majorities fourteen years later. The use as well as the misuse of information has made the power of suggestion the decisive force in world affairs. It can cause or prevent war. It can strengthen or destroy a democracy. It can build or wreck a nation.[52]

SEVEN PROPAGANDA DEVICES

Formulated by the Institute for Propaganda Analysis[53]

1. NAME CALLING: use of terms of hate and fear such as atheist, radical, red, fascist, dictator, communist, agitator, alien, utopian, idealist, tory, economic royalist, propagandist, troublemaker, racketeer and isolationist. A proud word in 1939 isolationist was a swear word in 1941.

2. GLITTERING GENERALITIES: use of virtue words such as honor, liberty, freedom, social justice, loyalty, American Way, constitution-defender, idealism, public service.

3. TRANSFER: use of emotion-rousing symbols such as *Cross* for Christian Church, *Flag* for Nation, *Uncle Sam* for public opinion. Transferring authority, sanction or prestige from things respected to things the press agent is paid to promote.

4. TESTIMONIAL: use of "big names" not only to plug patent medicines,

[51] "Notes on Propaganda," by Aldous Huxley, *Harper's Magazine*, Vol. 174, December, 1936.
[52] Carl W. Ackerman, dean, Columbia University School of Journalism.
[53] *The Fine Art of Propaganda*, edited by Alfred McClung Lee and Elizabeth Bryant Lee, Harcourt, Brace, New York, 1939; see also
How to Detect Propaganda, Propaganda Analysis, Vol. I, pp. 1-4, November, 1937, Institute for Propaganda Analysis, Inc., Columbia University, New York.

chewing gum or tobacco but also social, political or economic issues. One insidious device under this heading is grants and fellowships for purely propaganda purposes bestowed on colleges and universities by business concerns; another is the retainer to college professors for "consultation."[54]

5. PLAIN FOLKS: use of the age-old confidence winner. Businessmen use it on factory workers, politicians use it on voters; "I'm-just-plain-folks-like-you-all"; "I'm your neighbor—you can trust me."

6. BAND WAGON: use of "follow the crowd" technics: "My father was a Republican"; "Everybody's doing it"; "You're out of step"; "Be Regular"; "He's one of us"; "Don't Throw Your Vote Away."

7. CARD STACKING: use of the crooked approach, the fake build-up, smoke screen, red herring across the trail, lies, distortions, censorship, omission of facts, false testimony, half truths, confusion. This is the most difficult form to detect of all. Here must be included use of manipulated "public opinion polls" and needled "surveys," misuse of labels such as "national," "international," "institute," "foundation," "council," or "congress" in private undertakings to mislead people into thinking a quasi-public or public institution is soliciting funds or engaging in propaganda. Under such high sounding names as "Mothers of America, Inc.," "Protection of American Homes," "Liberty League," and "America First," many noxious organizations serve as "fronts"[55] for reactionary and revolutionary pressure groups who often use the names of well-known persons on their letterhead without permission, or by some subterfuge. Another card-stacking device is the use of facts to give a wholly erroneous impression. A fact may seem complete and yet upon examination by an expert, a certified public accountant, for example, be incomplete. Some writers pick isolated phrases which, apart from their original context, tell a different story. A familiar "card-stacking" device is the use of the "average" denominator, for example: A makes $20,000 a year; B, C and D each make $1,000 a year. Therefore, all four enjoy an "average" income of nearly $6,000 a year. This is the "high standard of living" technic popular with middle classes who own a car and an "electric kitchen." Then there is the "stockholder" technic: "More than 82,000 men and 64,000 women hold shares of U.S. Steel Common" is a statement one is likely to hear or read. No clue given to the size of their *individual* holdings

[54] *Partners in Plunder*, by J. B. Matthews and R. E. Shallcross, Covici-Friede, New York, 1935.
[55] *Under Cover*, by John Roy Carlson. Dutton, New York, 1943.

or indication of how much voice these 64,000 people had in the management of the U.S. Steel Corporation. The truth is most of them had no voice. The great year for distribution of stock ownership was 1929. In that year, three-tenths of one per cent of the population received 78 per cent of the dividends reported by individuals.[56] This is the same as saying, out of every 300 persons, one got 78 cents of every dollar of corporate dividends and the other 299 divided 22 cents between them! These are facts the propagandist shuffles to the center of the deck. The card stacking statistician lets you draw this card: "The total number of holders of corporate securities in our country is estimated at ten million," or this one: "The *public* owns the great corporations of our country."[57]

Knowledge of these or other propaganda devices does not make one an expert propaganda detective. Eternal vigilance is necessary. The propagandists think up new ones. Their technics improve as quickly as they are exposed. Besides, there are always large areas of gullibility, as Sinclair Lewis shows in his book.[58]

There is yet another device known as the *Emotional Stereotype*, a familiar tool of the biased reporter. Here is how Professor S. S. Sargent[59] contrasted two terms used to express similar ideas in two leading daily newspapers:

CHICAGO TRIBUNE	NEW YORK TIMES
radical	progressive
government witch hunt	Senate investigation
regimentation	regulation
communist CIO leader	maritime leader
labor agitator	labor organizer
dole	home relief
farm dictatorship	crop control
loyal workers	non-strikers
inquisitor	investigator
alien	foreign

[56] Report of the Temporary National Economic Committee, March 1941.

[57] "Of all corporations reporting, one-tenth of one per cent owned 52 per cent of the assets of all of them. Less than 5 per cent of them owned 87 per cent of the assets of all of them." Bureau of Internal Revenue, 1935, from the Report of the Temporary National Economic Committee, p. 11.

[58] *Gideon Planish*, by Sinclair Lewis. Random House, New York.

[59] *Sociometry*, Vol. II, 1939.

The word "idealism" which appears in the context of the Nobel Peace award prompted Allen Upward[60] to canvass a group of intellectuals for their definition of that term. He got these sundry answers for idealism: fanatical, altruistic, not practical, exact, poetical, intangible, sentimental, true, what cannot be proved, opposite of materialism, something to do with imaginative powers.

"Find the *referent*" is a good rule to follow. "When people can agree on the thing to which their words refer, minds meet . . . the communication line is cleared," Stuart Chase says.[61]

Another propaganda device is "illicit silence" about an event or person which permits an erroneous impression to prevail.[62]

More regularly than the regular paid contributor and quite as faithfully as the most loyal salaried member, the self-appointed staff members bring their gratis contributions to the editorial desk. (Sometimes they prefer to ignore the subtleties and send their releases to the advertising manager's desk.)

SELF-APPOINTED STAFF MEMBER: THE PUBLICIST

The publicist (or press agent) is often better educated, better trained, and better paid than a given publication's own staff writers or the editor. Call him what you will: press agent, ballyhoo artist, publicity hound, shirt-stuffer, space grabber, ghost writer, propagandist, publicity man, publicist, or public relations counsel— from his own point of view he performs an important function. He plays a spotlight on items of news interest which reporter and editor might have unwittingly passed by. He focuses attention. He is middleman between the interests he serves (corporation, pressure group, bureau, underground, or circus) and the press. In other words, he, too, is a communication medium.

Let us be perfectly candid about the press agent. Editors often call on him for help in getting material and preparing articles. It is to be expected that his help will generally be of a biased nature; he is hired to write the kind of story or present the facts his

[60] *The New Word*, Allen Upward. Mitchell Kennerley, New York, 1910.
[61] *The Tyranny of Words*, by Stuart Chase. Harcourt, Brace, New York, 1938.
[62] *Propaganda Is a Weapon*, by Bryce Oliver, radio news commentator.

employer wants presented. By the same token he may suppress or soft-pedal unpleasant facts.[63] The term "press agent" is an obvious misnomer. He is the agent not of the press but of the publicity seeker.

Free publicity has been a great success: banks, railroads, charities, social institutions, trade associations, public utilities, political parties, the army and the navy, state and federal governments, the church, schools, even the press, the great, the near-great, and the would-be-great employ publicity men.

Two of the best-known publicists of modern times are the late Ivy Lee, described by Flynn[64] as "the man who merchandised John D. Rockefeller to the American people,"[65] and the nephew of Dr. Sigmund Freud, Edward L. Bernays, "U. S. Publicist No. 1," according to *Time*.

Underlying reason for the existence of the press agent, according to Walter Lippmann,[66] is the reluctance of groups of people or business concerns, who crave or need publicity, to trust the legitimate press reporter's sense of discretion on certain matters. Another reason may be that many concerns do not trust the sense of discretion of their own board chairmen or corporation presidents or other officials when these individuals are exposed to an interview by the press. Much better to seek shelter behind the trained and shrewd public relations counselor who understands company policy and company objectives and also public capacity for understanding these things. There is an efficiency reason, too. Some companies are sources of "news"—day-to-day news from many departments. By channeling this information from one source, efficiency is attained—also accuracy. Also, there is no chance for conflicting stories.

Often the publicity man succeeds in getting a larger budget for

[63] "I know a few who will tell you the whole truth about their client," declares one businesspaper editor. "These men always get a favorable hearing . . . They perform a much more valuable service for their client than those who seek to cover up anything."

[64] "The Science of Ballyhoo," by John T. Flynn, *Atlantic Monthly*, Vol. 149, May, 1932.

[65] Ivy Lee "sold" Mr. Rockefeller, Sr., the public relations value of philanthropy and the gifts exceeded half a billion dollars.

[66] *Public Opinion*, Walter Lippmann. Macmillan, New York, 1927.

his activities than the same corporation's advertising manager. If you believe clippings are "results," he can often show more *tangible results* from free publicity than the advertising man can show from paid advertising. Look at his bulging scrapbooks of newspaper and magazine "editorial" clippings. He will painstakingly estimate for his employers the value of all those clippings in terms of their cost had it been "advertising linage." It may run into hundreds of thousands of dollars, on that basis. He will also quote the circulation figures of papers that have published his stuff, the aggregate often running into millions of readers. "And," he will point out to his employer, "this appeared in the *editorial columns*, which no amount of money can buy."

By the simple device of providing a press clipping bureau[67] with samples of his publicity releases and a list of the publications they were released to, the press agent causes an unending stream of clippings to pour into his office past an unending stream of publicity releases flowing out of his office.

The legitimacy of "public relations" cannot be successfully challenged. Many publications hire publicity men themselves for exactly the same purpose: to furnish the "legitimate editorial columns" of other media with handouts about themselves or their advertisers, or both. Publication editors send releases to radio editors and radio editors send releases to publication editors.

The publicity man often uses a stage setting for his releases or handouts: a cocktail party, a luncheon, dinner (or even breakfast), a theater party, a sports event, a fashion show, a cooking school, a forum or clinic—to mention a few devices. Well-known speakers or celebrities are sometimes employed as drawing cards; also bathing beauties or Powers models.

A modern technic of press-agentry is the so-called "news bureau," the "fashion bureau," and the alleged "press association," distributing miles of news "galleys," tons of glossy photographs and cartoons, "big-name" feature articles, and even tailor-made "editorials" to the legitimate press without charge. Smaller newspapers eat it up. It costs nothing and is usually better than their local staff could turn out. The business press is more selective.

---

[67] Dozens of these bureaus function in the country.

The pride which the publicist takes in his "profession" is a growing pride. Attempts to organize professional groups of certified public relations counselors have been partially successful.[68] Many publicity men now disclose the source of the handout. Much as he likes to publicize his own name, the publicity agent can be modesty itself, for a valuable consideration. He never signs his name to the many speeches delivered at banquets and great conventions by business tycoons or in legislatures, parliaments, and other forums. His name does not appear in the many economic books he prepares for big-name authors who advance the interests or the ideologies of certain groups.

One of the most prolific contributors of "letters to the editor" is the publicity man who signs himself "A Reader." He knows the value of that letter column in the daily newspaper right on the editor's page. *Vox populi, vox Dei.* Or, perhaps, Disraeli is correct: "The public mind is the creation of the Master Writers."[69]

At the top of many publicity releases sent out by advertisers and by advertising agencies you will find a printed legend to the effect that the "editor is at liberty to reject the release in whole or in part" and no hard feelings!

Some publicists for powerful pressure groups often hold what seem to be "independent" positions on leading independent publications and their names are as well-known as those of presidents and kings. The LaFollette Committee submitted evidence to Congress that one well-known New York newspaper columnist and radio commentator had received fat checks from a certain association of manufacturers for his "services" and from a utility-controlled propaganda bureau for radio records of his famous voice in action. These records (transcriptions) were put on at smaller stations at times more convenient to the listener than to this particular New York columnist. It worked fine.

Dr. Ralph D. Casey, who was a member of the committee on pressure groups of the Social Science Research Council, points out that "what one group of intelligent citizens may believe is

---

[68] There is an Association of Publicity Men in New York City which sets up standards of practice as a qualification for membership.

[69] "*Avec plaisir; chi tace accousente.*"

propaganda will be described by another as news."[70] The thing to be avoided is unjustified distrust either by the editor or by the reader of all information emanating from a publicity man. Speaking before the American Society of Newspaper Editors some years ago, Herbert Bayard Swope, then editor of the old New York *World* said:

We each of us have some standard of judgment whereby we can separate proper from improperganda. At least I have been able to discover a certain method whereby we can resolve all our doubts. Every utterance that is devoted at all to special pleading is propaganda.

Standing between the press agent or publicist or propagandist and his readership there is always the businesspaper editor. Permitted to exercise his own judgment and discriminatory sense of news values, he can examine a publicity release as he would any other piece of news. Is it real news? No news should be acceptable without some examination or test of its validity. Sometimes by probing deeper into a publicity release a better story may be turned up. The editor's nose for news must develop a keen sense of smell for propaganda.

A valuable institution would be a national clearinghouse collating, tabulating, and publishing the sums of money spent and amount (linage) of free space obtained for publicity and public relations in newspapers, magazines, businesspapers and radio. In connection with such a clearinghouse on free publicity there should be a public museum of simple exhibits, graphic pictures and charts, actual releases and campaign plans, explaining the economics of advertising, publicity, and propaganda, the technics, the devices, and their reaction on human relationships. Portable or mobile museums like these should be shown in schools and colleges. Such an institution, impartially conducted, could make a valuable contribution to journalism.

[70] "The Press, Propaganda and Pressure Groups," by Ralph D. Casey, *Annals of the American Academy of Political and Social Science*, January, 1942. Director of the School of Journalism, University of Minnesota, and editor of the *Journalism Quarterly*, former president of the American Association of Schools and Departments of Journalism.

QUALIFICATIONS OF A BUSINESS JOURNALIST

No one should be employed on the staff of the editor of a businesspaper who does not possess the qualities for being an editor:

1. Nose for news, instinctive curiosity, natural inquisitiveness.

2. Native ability to organize, integrate, and analyze facts as well as collect and report them.

3. Accuracy, integrity, speed. Only in the realm of pure science, as Frank Kent[71] points out, is there as high a premium on accuracy, or so prompt a penalty, as on the press. Nowhere in any business is so great a proportion of accuracy demanded or expected. Error is not only conspicuous, it is remembered. Even a truthful report of a false utterance is blamed on the editor, says Lee White. One error in a thousand statements of fact brings adverse criticism for the entire issue of a publication, and no word of praise for all the effort expended to produce that issue.[72] "Accuracy," Mr. White says, "involves more than a simple statement of fact. In reporting the news it involves choice, appraisal, proportion and display."

4. Personality, nerve, tactfulness, aliveness, initiative.

5. Interest in human values, in the meaning of news, in the stage on which events become drama, the background and continuity of news, in the people who make news, in the totality of human performance.

6. Liberal education.

7. Semantic discipline: knowledge of use and *misuse* of words and propaganda devices. Power to distinguish between real events and fantasy.

8. Acquired technical skill: most editors prefer and many insist that applicants for staff positions already have training or experience with technics of the field in which his businesspaper specializes. Others require training in journalism and newspaper or magazine experience (editorial department) as qualifications.

9. Desire to make journalism a career, not a steppingstone to some other occupation.

[71] Frank Kent, editor of the Baltimore *Sun*, from *Newsroom Problems and Policies*. Macmillan, New York, 1941.

[72] "The Press and the Public," by Lee A. White, Washington correspondent, *Journalism Quarterly*, Vol. 17, September, 1940.

10. Character. This, of course, is the most important qualification of all, for this or any other job on earth.

DUTY SPECIFICATIONS OF THE EDITOR'S STAFF

Secretary: Unequivocally a most important editorial staff member. Usually a woman, her first qualification must be a negative one: the absolute and utter absence of any desire whatever to be a writer or an editor and wear her hat or smoke cigarettes while at work. She is an expert in stenography and in decoding scribbled notes and corrections; she clips, pastes, files. Her work is diplomatic, confidential, sympathetic, and philosophical. She must *know how* the entire organization functions, eventually she will know how the editor's particular industry functions, know how the printer functions, know how the editor's mind functions, and know how the staff should function to get the paper out on time.

Managing Editor: He is responsible to the editor for staff production and performance. Theoretically, he gets out the magazine. As a matter of fact, working editors personally pitch in and help. But the managing editor knows the mechanical problems involved, keeps a record of the releases of copy to printer and engraver, builds the magazine day by day as this material comes back, and makes up for the folio. Often he is entirely an inside man who occasionally, but rarely, gets an outside assignment. "The chief editor," writes Douglas Woolf, "who has the proper type of managing editor is successful in his own profession. The one who has not such an assistant is only half there."[73]

Editorial Consultants: These are technical advisers and writers who perform special tasks for the editor, sometimes residing in Washington or other key cities, sometimes (incognito) in the heart of the industry in which they may be leaders. Sometimes they are full-time members of headquarters staffs.

Technical Assistants: As pointed out in Chapter 1 on Definitions, every businesspaper is a trade paper, an industrial paper, a tech-

[73] *The Business Paper Editor at Work*, by Douglas G. Woolf, editor of *Textile World*. McGraw-Hill, New York, 1936.

nical paper. Every field of human activity has certain *technics* which require constant explanation, reiteration, and elaboration. For this task, there is the *technical* editorial assistant.

Also, in every field the product or service must be sold, and the *technics* of selling, known as merchandising, call for the service of the merchandising editorial assistant.

Associate Editors: Understudies to the managing editor are the associate editors who assume responsibility for the economics of the industry covered, the study of articles and news in competitive businesspapers and papers in related fields, development of regional and foreign correspondence, contact in related fields, and special tasks. They release the senior editor for more creative work and long-range economic study.

Market and News Editors: The market editor is interested primarily in new commodities: goods or services; uses, design, prices, packaging, transportation facilities, devices for selling, promotion, advertising, displaying. The news editor is interested in people and events. There is no strong line of demarcation between the duties of these two editors—both men pick up valuable leads for each other's departments. The news editor holds a key position on the staff. The piece of news he passes on to the editor's desk may start a series of ripples in many departments of the publication, especially the business office. It may be news of a merger of two companies, a new discovery in production or fabrication, the entry into the field of a new type of producer or distributor, the collapse of an important house, a startling announcement of change of policy. The news editor maintains close liaison with all staff members, regional representatives, and correspondents.

Assistant Editors: These men study manuscripts, cover conventions and meetings, share some of the responsibilities of news and market coverage, rewrite, and make themselves generally available and useful.

The actual specifications of the different jobs in the editorial organization of one of the country's leading businesspapers, covering the huge chemical field, were drawn up by the chief editor, so that each man would know his specific responsibilities, the area of his activity, and the responsibilities of his coworkers. Copies also were furnished to the publisher and other publishing executives so that they would understand clearly the lines of demarcation in editorial functions. The duty-specification outline will be found in Appendix V.

EDITOR'S FIELD ORGANIZATION

Every businesspaper has a staff of field editors and writers of its own or else employs a group of free-lance correspondents, strategically located, who follow certain specified routines in gathering news information for the editors. These fieldmen also do special articles or interviews, usually on assignment. Some articles carry no signature or by-line. Sometimes their interviews are published with by-lines. In some cases the field editor or correspondent simply acts as agent of the editor in securing signed articles from authorities in the field. In other cases the fieldman ghost-writes the article.

Free-lance correspondents for businesspapers often take permanent positions or move away or end their association for other reasons. Considerable turnover takes place among such correspondents. One publishing house in the merchandising field issues an "Instruction Sheet" to new correspondents, which follows:

INSTRUCTIONS TO CORRESPONDENTS

Issues are planned 60 days in advance and assembled material should be in our hands at least 90 days in advance. Many good articles are rejected because they arrive too late.

In an article we are interested not only in what was done, but why it was done, a detailed how it was done, and the results obtained. Material must embrace the departments in a retail store or shop over which our readers act as buyers or managers.

Articles should not run over 500 words and should have some illustrative material such as window displays, interior displays, photo of buyer, manager or salespeople; ads, mailing pieces, etc.

We do not use fiction or poetry or information designed for the ultimate consumer.

We cannot exploit any brand in an article, but it is permissible to mention a number of brands carried in a retailer's stock.

Photographs must be on glossy paper, size not smaller than 3" x 5"—sharp contrast with clear detail; identified on back with name of contributor, store and complete description. If cards or signs appear in photo, text should be reproduced on reverse side of the photo.

We welcome "*shorts*"—interesting events briefly reported.

We welcome "merchandising ideas"—brief descriptions of retail promotions which contain the seed of an idea some other buyer in a store somewhere else can apply in his department.

MSS. should be typewritten, double spaced, read and corrected before mailing. Contributor's name and address should appear in upper left hand corner; name of magazine it is intended for and number of words should appear in the upper right hand corner. *PROPER NAMES* must be double checked for spelling. MSS. will not be returned unless accompanied by self-addressed stamped envelope.

We do not use articles or interviews unless name and address of the store and name of buyer is included. Articles about anonymous places, persons or stores not acceptable. Interviews with buyers should be submitted to the buyer for his O.K. and initials.

In describing promotions be careful they are not built around the sale of seconds, irregulars or close-outs, as we do not encourage this type of promotion.

RATES OF PAYMENT: $1.00 for items up to 65 words. $1.00 for a newspaper ad. $2.00 for photographs. All other material 1¢ a word. Payment is made about the 15th of the month following month of issue.

Payments to Contributors

The correspondent is usually paid for the articles, if the person whose signature appears on it is not the type who would accept a fee for an article or did not actually write the article. If the correspondent is not the actual author of the article, and the author is paid, the correspondent gets paid for his time, if he secured the article.

Field editors and staff writers in the field are generally on salary and devote all their time to one publisher. Free-lance correspondents are paid by the article, or by the number of words, although sometimes correspondents are paid by the month for their work.

DETAILED ANALYSIS OF EDITORIAL DEPARTMENT EXPENSES FOR	MONTHS ENDED	194				
	Current Month	Budget	___Months to ___194	Budget		
EDITORIAL OFFICE COSTS						
Business News						
Exchanges and Clippings						
Reprints						
Miscellaneous						
Office Postage						
Stationery and Supplies						
Telephone and Telegraph						
TOTAL:-						
EDITORIAL SERVICE						
Photos						
Engravings						
Illustration Dept.-Drafting						
" " Laboratory						
TOTAL:-						

CHART 37. ANALYSIS OF EDITORIAL EXPENSE

They have the privilege of writing for other businesspapers although usually not for direct competitors.

Some publishers have established prices per word for contributions. Other publishers permit the chief editor to be the judge of the value of each contribution. He accepts or rejects the contributed article, he determines how much of it will be used, when it will be used, and what it is worth. This includes text, and accompanying material such as illustrations, charts, maps, and statistical tables. Payments run from one cent per word to hundreds of dollars for articles which may run to only 1,000 or 2,000 words. Photographs vary usually from $2 to $10, unless specially ordered, and depending on the nature and value of the subject. Business News Service pays $1,000 for articles by big-name writers which it secures for member businesspapers every month.

Mss. Inventory Control

On large businesspapers, averaging from 100 to 150 pages of editorial content a month, plenty of editorial material must be secured well in advance. It is equally important to be able to plan a balanced editorial diet for each succeeding issue. *Factory Management & Maintenance*, serving all kinds of manufacturing industries, meets this problem with a well-organized system for collecting, filing, scheduling, and paying for contributions. *Factory* numbers among its more than 22,000 readers such executives as managers, plant superintendents, maintenance engineers, mechanics, electricians, cost control heads, time and motion engineers, production designers, and a miscellany of other specialists. The chief editor has a staff of associate editors, consulting editors, and assistant editors. To these editors all contributed and solicited manuscripts are distributed for analysis, editing, and preparation for publication. Each editor gets the articles relating to his particular department.

Three form letters facilitate the disposal of mss.: (1) acknowledgment, which goes out on receipt of the ms.; (2) rejection, after careful consideration without delay; (3) acceptance, after due consideration. Special mss., particularly where they have been solicited by the publication, are naturally given special handling in correspondence with the author. The following three form letters, however, enable the chief editor's secretary, in the majority of cases, to relieve him of a large amount of correspondence:

1: Acknowledgment

Dear Mr. _____

We acknowledge receipt of your contribution, "_____
_____," dated _____. It will be given prompt consideration and you will be advised as to its acceptance or rejection.

Your consideration of FACTORY MANAGEMENT AND MAINTENANCE as indicated by your sending the article to us is appreciated and we hope that the subject matter and our requirements will be such that the contribution can be accepted.

Very truly yours,

_____

Editor

2: Rejection

Dear Mr. _____

I regret the necessity of informing you that the contribution, "_____
_____," submitted recently, cannot be accepted because it does not fill any of the present editorial requirements of FACTORY MANAGEMENT AND MAINTENANCE.

I appreciate your consideration of FACTORY, and am sorry that we must return the manuscript, which is attached.

Very truly yours,

_____

Editor

3: Acceptance

Dear Mr. _____

I am glad to tell you that we have accepted your contribution, "_____
_____." It will be published as soon as possible. You will understand, however, that in selecting contributions for specific issues we must give consideration to priority as well as to immediate requirements.

As soon as the article has been edited your name will be placed on our contributors' pay sheet, after which about two weeks will be required for the order for payment to pass through our Accounting Department and the check to be mailed. Please do not think that the matter of payment has been overlooked if you do not receive your check for several weeks.

Very truly yours,

_____

Editor

Contributions that are accepted are immediately entered in a "Contribution Book" and assigned a number. Columns on ruled sheets in this book list the number, title, type of article, author, date received, editor to whom assigned, reference to pay sheet, amount paid, and date published.

SAMPLE SHEET FROM CONTRIBUTION BOOK FOR RECORDING ARTICLES

No.	Title	Kind of Article	Author	Recd.	Ed.	Pay Sheet	Amt.	Pub.

A ms. card is also made out for accepted articles:

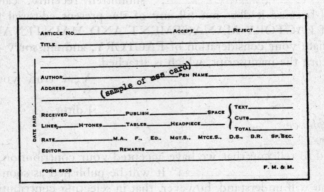

M.A.—Management Article   Mgt.S.—Management Short
Mtce.S.—Maintenance Sheet   D.S.—Data Sheet
B.R.—Book Review   Sp.Sec.—Special Section
F.—Filler   Ed.—Editorial

The ms. card is placed in the "to be paid" section of a ms. file box. Later it is filed numerically, according to the article classification. After publication this ms. card is removed from the "current issue" drawer and placed in the "morgue" drawer for six months.

A copy of the original ms. is then made with this form printed at the top of the first page to act as record and guide:

COPY FOR	Name of publication	8 9 on 9½ 10 11__ 13½ 20 20½ 42__		WANTED	
				Date	Hour
	Set the name of publication and the following information as catchline			Sent to Composing Room	
_____FORM	Art No.	H. T.	Tables	Date	Hour
	Editor	L. C.	Captions	Received from Comp. Room	
	Dept.	Class	Panels	Date	Hour

Form 5003

The accepted ms. also gets a folder bearing number, title, author's name, and classification. Illustrations, correspondence, and all other material relating to this ms. are kept within this folder until it is assigned by the chief editor to a special editor to prepare for publication. Meanwhile the original ms. is placed in a special envelope with identifying information on its face. This envelope is placed in a "current issue" drawer for six months.

FACE OF THE MS. FOLDER

Corrected Title _____	Article No. _____
	Date Recd. _____
Original Title _____	Date Edited _____
	Scheduled For _____
Author _____	Date Published _____
Address _____	Disposition of Photo-
Editor _____	graphs _____
Paid $_____ Date _____	
	Disposition of Drawings
Accepted Rejected	Reprints:
To Mgr. Ed.	Number
Compensation	Style
Return:	Size
Manuscript	Cover
Drawings	Quotations
Blueprints	Charge to
Photographs	Special Instructions
Cuts	

Before this folder is disposed of, at the end of six months, important correspondence is transferred to the correspondence files.

A smaller "Manuscript Envelope" contains galleys and proofs of halftones and line cuts relative to the particular ms. and bears this information on the face:

MANUSCRIPT ENVELOPE

Article No. _____   Dept. _____
Title _____
Edited By _____   Text _____
Author _____   Half Tones _____
Date to Printer _____   Line cuts _____
Proofs to Editor _____   Tables _____
Corrections Recd. _____   Panels _____
                              Total _____

THE SCHEDULE BOARD FOR PLANNING ISSUES

The chief editor of *Factory Management & Maintenance* uses an Acme Visible Record book as his schedule board, to keep track of ms. inventory and to plan issues with a balanced editorial diet. Only major articles are listed. Tabs on the visible index, bearing number, title of ms. and author's name, are either white, red, blue, or yellow. Red tabs mean that the article is not yet in the house although already scheduled. Blue tabs indicate articles on "Management" and yellow tabs refer to articles on "Maintenance." The chief editor easily shifts the movable tabs as he plans a current or future issue. Editorial meetings are held for this purpose and the visible record of mss., as shown in the Schedule Board, makes it easy to hold such meetings down to a minimum of time.

Because of the necessity of long-range planning, *Factory* pays for a ms. upon acceptance, although the article may not be used immediately. As soon as the article is edited, the author's name is entered on a "pay sheet" and the order for payment is passed on to the accounting department. The chief editor keeps a duplicate of each pay sheet, which carries spaces for the titles of 24 mss., and lists the number, author, address, title of article, amount paid, bank cancellation and check number, for convenience in corresponding with contributors:

No.   Editorial Manuscript   Issue of Month of_____Date Paid_____

No.	Name	Full Address	Title of Article	Amt.	Bank Canc.	Check No.

Vol. No.   Date Mailed   Approved by

Editorial Budget Control

Budgets of space and money to be spent for salaries, traveling, entertainment, contributions (mss.), editorial services (photography, art, engravings, telephone and telegraph, exchanges, clipping bureaus, etc.), office administration (reprints, postage, stationery), are given to chief editors by the publisher or general manager. The budgets will vary according to the requirements of different kinds of businesspapers.

Some publishers object to "averaging" the budget at the end of the year and insist that, for example, if the budget for engraving is $200 a month, an editor may not spend $100 one month and $300 the next. Other publishers do not object to what an editor spends if, at the end of the year, a monthly "average" is well within the budget limits. A detailed analysis of editorial department expenses is provided to many editors by the accounting department (see Chart 37).

STATEMENT OF INCOME AND EXPENSES	(MONTH) MONTHLY FIGURES				(YEAR) YEAR TO DATE		
	Current Month	Budget	Last Month	Same Mo. Last Yr.	This Year	Budget	Last Year
INCOME - ADVERTISING							
Display Advertising							
Searchlight Advertising							
Service Sales							
TOTAL							
Less Agency Commissions							
ADVERTISING INCOME							
EXPENSES							
2% Cash Discount - Advertising Collections							
Advertising							
Display Office - Salaries							
" " - Traveling							
" " - Costs							
" " - Direct Promotion							
Territorial - Salaries & Commissions							
" - Traveling							
Bad Debts							
Searchlight Dept. - Promoted Costs							
Copy Service Dept. " "							
Sales Admin. & Prom. " "							
TOTAL							
Editorial							
Salaries							
Traveling							
Contributions (Manuscripts)							
Editorial Service							
Office Costs							
Editorial Administration							
TOTAL							
Mechanical and Mailing							
Printing							
Paper and Supplies							
Postage - Second Class							
TOTAL							
Conventions and Associations							
General and Administrative - Direct							
General and Administrative - Promoted							
Special Capital Costs							
TOTAL COSTS (Excluding Circulation)							
NET INCOME (Excluding Circulation)							
CIRCULATION INCOME							
CIRCULATION EXPENSES							
CIRCULATION NET INCOME							
Direct Mail - Net Income							
TOTAL GROSS INCOME							
TOTAL EXPENSES							
TOTAL NET INCOME							
PROVISION FOR ACCRUED TAXES							

CHART 38. STATEMENT OF INCOME AND EXPENSES

Some chief editors, in large publishing organizations, who have profit-sharing arrangements, are furnished with complete break-down statements of income and expenses on their own publications each month (see Chart 38). This knowledge serves as an incentive to correct uneconomic methods and improve the paper's profit position. Many editors keep records themselves where it is not the practice of the accounting department to furnish such records. An editor should know as much as possible about publishing costs on his own paper.

LAWS GOVERNING BUSINESS JOURNALISTS

The Unique Characteristics of Libel

Every businesspaper editor must be able to answer this question: *How far can I go in publishing an article, a story, an editorial, or a letter, without becoming involved in a libel suit or threat of a libel suit?*

To clear up confusion over the terms "defamation," "libel," and "slander," remember this: A false statement about a person to his discredit is defamation. If it is by word of mouth, it is slander. If it is done in print, writing, or by cartoon, picture, diagram, sign, or in some other permanent form, it is libel.

A libel may be defined as a malicious publication tending to blacken the reputation of a living person so as to expose him to public hatred, contempt, or ridicule.[74]

This kind of libel is known as a civil libel.

A criminal libel is a publication which tends to incite a riot or some other form of violence against the government or publication of an obscenity or blasphemy.

Freedom of the press, as we all know, is a guaranty by the Constitution of the United States, in the First Amendment adopted in 1791. It is also a guaranty in several state constitutions. Under this guaranty a publisher may publish what he wishes, true or false. Moreover, in New York State, a publisher cannot be enjoined *in advance* from publishing an article on the ground that it is false

[74] 17 Ruling Case Law, Section I, Paragraph 2, Eighteen American Decisions, 105.

or libelous (Article I, Section VIII of the New York State Constitution).

The brakes on the constitutional guaranty of freedom of press and speech are the laws of defamation, libel, slander, breach of peace, and treason.

A businesspaper editor, in other words, may publish what he pleases without legal interference, but once published, if it is a civil libel, the injured party or parties may sue to recover damages. If it appears that the publication was also malicious, the injured party can recover additional or punitive damages.

If a criminal libel has been published, the state sues in its own name.

In a discussion of libel before the New York Business Paper Editors,[75] Harry H. Van Aken, of DeWitt, Van Aken & Nast, specialists in libel law, pointed out certain *unique* characteristics of libel actions in our law. To recover damages in an ordinary lawsuit, the plaintiff must produce evidence to prove he was damaged, and in many cases must prove the amount of damage suffered. In a libel suit, however, the plaintiff need only prove that the libel was published. If the publication appears libelous *on its face*, the law *presumes* that it is a false statement, *presumes* that it was published maliciously, and *presumes* that it has damaged the plaintiff. The jury is the sole judge of the amount of damages.

In other words, a plaintiff in a libel suit, where an article is libelous on its face, may simply offer the libelous article in evidence and rest his case without proving any damages or even taking the witness stand, and he has a good chance to win the case and collect the damages the jury decides upon.

The Word "Alleged" Is No Protection

It is no defense to write "it is rumored" or "it is alleged" that someone has done something, or to quote someone else as saying that someone has done something. Nor is the use of inference or innuendo or any subtlety a defense to libel if the average reader can spell out the commission of a disgraceful or criminal charge against a person by reading between the lines of your publication.

[75] Town Hall Club. Feb. 9, 1939.

The publisher's liability arises when he publishes a libelous statement, and all persons who take part in the *procurement, composition, and publication* of libel are responsible. That includes the reporter or author who wrote it, the editor who approved it, the publisher (whether individual proprietor or corporation) of the businesspaper which published it; even the printer who prints a libel at the request of another is responsible for its publication. The original publisher of a libel, however, is not responsible for its *independent* subsequent publication by others.

Moreover, Section 1352 of our penal law provides that any person who willfully states, delivers, or transmits to any manager, editor, publisher, or reporter, or any employee of a publisher, any statement which if published would be a libel is guilty of a misdemeanor.

Section 1353 goes a step further and says such a person will be guilty of a misdemeanor if the statement is made or transmitted with *intent* that same shall be published.

Four Defenses to Libel

1. *Truth:* This is the best defense to a civil suit to recover money damages for libel, but proof of the truth must be as broad as the charge. The motives must be good and the ends justifiable. A true story with a misleading headline may be interpreted as a half-truth.

Exception to this defense, which business journalists should remember, is that under the penal law of the State of New York and other states, it is a crime to libel the memory of the dead.

A well-trained businesspaper reporter or editor must seek to secure the entire truth from his source of information, and if he is close to his deadline and the truth is in doubt, it would be the wiser policy to leave out the story until it can be investigated further.

2. *Privilege:* The defense of privilege is the second complete defense. It is provided by statute (Civil Practice Act, Section 337) in New York, that a fair and true report of public, official, and judicial proceedings is privileged. This does not mean that you have to publish everything that takes place in a court or legislative

proceeding, in order for it to be fair or true. It may be an abridged report. This includes the proceedings of Congress.

3. *Fair Comment:* For the defense of fair comment to succeed against an action for libel, the facts on which the comment is based must be true and the comment fair. A businesspaper, like any other publication, is free to make a fair comment on all matters of public concern. This extends to criticism of government, utilities, books, magazine articles, plays, movies, etc. The court decides whether the field is within the range of public interest. The jury decides whether the comment is fair. A published retraction or apology may lessen or eliminate the amount of damages; it does not eliminate the libel, if one exists, but it tends to prove a lack of intent or malice. This third defense is important to the editorial writer who must comment on events of public interest affecting his industry.

4. *Statute of Limitations:* This is a technical defense. In New York State, the Statute of Limitations against the bringing of action for libel or slander is one year from date of publication of the article. The fact that the magazine containing the so-called libelous article is in the publisher's library or in some other library open to the public and may not be seen for several months after the publication date, does not extend the Statute of Limitations. The Court of Appeals has held that the cause of action arose and the Statute of Limitations began to run from the time the first publication was made.

Civil Rights Law, or "Right of Privacy"

More subtle than libel for a business journalist is the danger which in New York is called civil rights law, and in most other states protects one under the common law "right of privacy." There are provisions in this law which prohibit the use of a picture or portrait, or letter or the name of a living person, for advertising or trade purposes without written consent. If you use a picture from one of the picture agencies, of a living person, the agency usually furnishes copy of a "release" from such person. Be sure it is a reputable agency and that they have a bona fide release if you are in doubt. Never publish a private letter without consent of the signer.

Contempt

There are also provisions of our law which make the comment of an editor or reporter concerning a case *pending* before a court of law for decision punishable as contempt of court. Such remarks may be construed as attempts to intimidate the judge.

Letters and Telegrams

Letters and telegrams which a business journalist sends out may be dynamite, not only as a base for libel suits, but because they may be the base of legal commitment which should never be made without the advice of competent counsel.

Copyright

The law of copyright protects the literary form of an article or the identical manner or sequence of statement. Copyright does not protect the news element of a story once it is published. News appearing in daily papers, for example, is often rewritten by other dailies, magazines, or businesspapers.

Copyright is provided by Article I, Section VIII, Paragraph 8 of the Constitution of the United States. Application for copyright is filed with the Register of Copyrights, Library of Congress, Washington, D.C. Two copies of the work must be deposited. The fee for unpublished works or photographs is $1 and for published works or photographs, $2. Notice of copyright must appear on the published article. An article or articles and pictures in a businesspaper may be copyrighted by filing one complete issue with the $2 fee. The copyright extends for 28 years with the right of renewal for another 28 years. However, if one had no right to claim ownership to a work or illustration in the first place, the mere securing of a copyright is no protection against the rightful owner.

Trade-Marks

Trade-marks also have statutory protection. They may be registered in the U.S. Patent Office after a search for similarity with existing trade-marks. But the privilege of placing under a trade-mark the phrase "Reg. U.S. Pat. Off." is denied until one year from the date of the first public use of the trade-mark. A lawyer is employed in the registration of a trade-mark and the registration fee is higher ($25). Like the copyright, the registration of a trade-mark does not protect a person from suit by one claiming prior ownership for use of a similar or the same trade-mark. Unfair use by another of copyrighted material or a registered trade-mark may lead to a damage suit for infringement and an action in equity to enjoin against further infringement.

Legal Concept of a Businesspaper Publishing Business

While its functions are obviously quasi-public, the law regards a businesspaper publisher's business as a private enterprise and the publisher need not accept advertising or advertising contracts. The courts have ruled that, if a publication could be held liable for refusal to accept advertising, it could also be held liable for refusal to print a news item.

Post-Office Regulations

To have second-class mailing privileges, a businesspaper must conform to certain strict postal laws and regulations. For example, the publication must issue from a known office. It must be published with regularity and maintain a legitimate list of subscribers. It must be published for the dissemination of information of a public character, devoted to the arts and sciences, literature, or some special industry. Matter that tends to incite to riot, murder, arson, or assassination, contains obscene literature or pictures, or information on a lottery is nonmailable.

Censorship

In time of great national emergency, such as war, censorship may be imposed on journalists prior to publication. In ordinary times, freedom of the press means publication without censorship.

On the Record

Public records may be inspected and reported by the press, but this does not include diplomatic documents, the files of the President of the United States, or the files of law-enforcing agencies such as the Federal Bureau of Investigation or the Police Department, where it would not be in the public interest to make such records available.

Off the Record

At meetings between reporters and government agencies, an official will sometimes state that what he has to say is "off the record." In such cases, businesspaper representatives respect the request, since they are interested in the background information which an official might otherwise hesitate to give them if he thought he was going to be quoted. If such a confidence is broken, the reporter or editor may suffer nothing more than the displeasure of the official, but he jeopardizes the future opportunities of his colleagues to enjoy the confidence of this official. Moreover, when he publishes off-the-record information, while it may not be libelous, it may be contrary to the public interest. The official is usually a better judge than the reporter. All this also applies to the request: "Don't quote me." Here a man usually means that he has no objection to the publication of the essence of his statement, but does object to his name being associated in any way with that publication.

Preventive Law

The old axiom that an ounce of prevention is worth a pound of cure is a good one for business journalists to follow. Ask yourself, *Is this true?* Be sure your information comes from reliable sources. Confirm important news or statements of fact by checking the source. Get important interviews O.K.'d by the person interviewed, or by his superior if necessary. Get important stories about firms approved by a responsible official of the firm.

When anything looks libelous on its face, rewrite it or consult your legal counsel.

Ask yourself, *Does this article or picture constitute an invasion of anyone's right of privacy?*

Check, and be sure there are written releases or written permissions to publish in connection with all pictures, cartoons, diagrams, and quoted articles.

Avoid litigation, because even the winner of a lawsuit may be the loser.

CHAPTER XII

THE FUTURE OF BUSINESS JOURNALISM

*"As with all instruments of multiplication the critical question
is as to the function and quality of the object one is multiplying."*
—LEWIS MUMFORD, *Technics and Civilization.*

INTEGRATED BUSINESS JOURNALISM

IN THE beginning of this book the nine functions performed by
the businesspaper were listed:

1. *Adult education function:* providing the technical "know-how"
information on operations, products and services to key managers and
supervisors responsible for production and distribution.

2. *News function:* gathering, organizing, and disseminating business
news intelligence.

3. *Editorial function:* criticizing, guiding, crusading, and pioneering.

4. *Integrating function:* revealing the relationship of the parts to the
whole. Interpreting the meaning of news events and forecasting trends.

5. *Forum function:* Town Hall in print. A meeting place for
self-expression by management, producer and distributor, and other
readers.

6. *Advertising function:* selling and merchandising in print by means
of advertising messages.

7. *Research function:* market analyses, surveys, and studies.

8. *Public relations function:* giving information to the public, to
the government, and to industry and labor about the particular segment of industry a businesspaper represents.

9. *Public utility function:* the responsibility to provide continuous
service at fair rates in return for the franchise from the public guaranteeing freedom to the press to print the truth without fear or
prejudice.

The future of business journalism depends upon the expansion
and greater exercise of the fourth function—*integration*. To give

understanding to the sequence and totality of events is one of the most urgent needs of business, and that is what we mean by integrated business journalism.

Business leaders constantly deplore the fact that the average businessman is too much of a specialist in his own particular field. They urge businessmen to give more attention and understanding to the problems of other businessmen in other segments of industry. Businesspapermen also have remained specialists, too much so, in the particular fields of enterprise covered by their publications. The future demands that businesspapermen become specialists in private enterprise, specialists in democracy, specialists in political man as well as economic man.

Development of the integrating function in business journalism does not mean that less consideration need be given to the other basic functions. The other functions, too, require broadening in order to meet the challenge of the future.

Adult Education Becoming More Important

The huge training programs inaugurated in American war plants and in our armed services have whetted the desire of millions of men and women for the kind of technical knowledge found in the columns of the businesspaper. Hundreds of thousands have acquired the habit of reading and study. New textbooks, manuals, charts, educational films, and reprints from businesspapers have stimulated their interest in production and distribution technics. They want factual information about new products, new equipment, new processes. They want the latest know-how so that they can keep up with the times in their chosen occupations or professions. One businesspaper publishing house in 1944 had a waiting list of 40,000 new subscribers, held up by the paper shortage. This is not an isolated example. Waiting lists of new kinds of subscribers for virtually all leading businesspapers indicates a definite trend which may change the entire concept of businesspaper circulation. Businesspapers may have to ease up their circulation controls so as to include not only those who are top management and those who are actual buyers or purchasing agents of goods and services, but in order also to include thousands upon thousands of new readers who now demand the type of adult education and editorial guidance which the businesspaper is so well-designed to give them.

These additional thousands of new readers, while neither buyers nor sellers, will wield an ever-increasing influence in business decisions made by top management in the emergent economy. The new circulation concept points a trend to sell businesspaper space on the basis of *power* rather than numbers of readers and this in turn should revolutionize the advertising rate structure of the business press, which is arbitrarily based on numbers of readers.

This disinclination of businesspaper publishers to charge adequately for the tremendous amount of *power* they furnish has held back the businesspaper editor in his desire to improve his product. It has held back the business office in its desire to make more scientific market studies. The future will see a greater appreciation of the business press by the business press itself.

Spot News Becoming Less Important

Spot business news may diminish in importance as a part of the regular editions of businesspapers, as the news functions of other media expand. Today business news is everyone's news. Not only do the radio, newspapers, and general magazines now give coverage to business news, but there has sprung up a group of weekly business news magazines and business newsletter services. Television, the electric teletype, phototransmission, and facsimile will pass out of the experimental stages to become competitors in the transmission of spot news. The reader of a businesspaper that is published monthly does not want to read stale news. The mere repetition of a news event has little interest. When the businesspaper tells the reader what the news event means to his job, to his industry, and to the economy as a whole, that is a different matter. The businesspaper reader's news needs are interpretation, analysis, integration.

Publication of product or equipment news, however, will always remain the province of the businesspaper. In the highly competitive postwar era, this kind of news will be in great demand.

Many businesspapers publish between-issues news bulletins or newsletters in order to transmit news intelligence quickly to their readers and advertisers. This service accomplishes a fourfold purpose: (1) it reports the news while it is still news; (2) it meets the competition of other news agencies; (3) it provides accurate information to offset inaccurate, false, or rumored information often published by less careful agencies; (4) it leaves more pages in the editorial space budget of the businesspaper for constructive articles of education, interpretation, and criticism.

MECHANICAL IMPROVEMENTS

In the graphic arts we will see the employment of heat-set, quick-drying inks, lighter weight paper, more color, use of plastic plates, greater speed in letterpress and automatic folding, new binding glues which will permit magazines to lie flat when open. Great improvements are being made in offset printing. Greater use will be made of the small Webb perfecting presses to handle economically 32-page forms printing in two to four colors on small runs. There will be greater use of the stereotype and of photo-imposing and typesetting machines working on strip or page film.

During the war businesspapers used lighter weight paper and sacrificed the quality of printing and engraving because of the emergency. Research in the chemical relationship between papers and inks will result in the economical use of much lighter papers, but with finishes that will permit better printing than was accomplished even on the heavy coated stocks before the war. Most businesspapers also trimmed their page size to save paper, thereby sacrificing margins and attractive layout. The future will see greater consideration given to the design of a page and the presentation of a story in typography and illustration. *Fortune* magazine has set a high standard of excellence in this respect.

There will be faster transmission of copy and layout from editor to printer by wire through the development of the teletypesetter.

The editor's secretary will put his copy directly on the teletype ribbon for automatic transmission to the printer's linotype machine. "In fact," as one businesspaper editor put it, "the editor's secretary will set the type." Another development, still in the experimental stage, is impressionless printing. The ink is lifted from the printing plate to the paper by electrostatic action.

DEFINITION OF COMMUNICATION

All these technological and mechanical improvements underwrite the future of the businesspaper as a more efficient "instrument of multiplication." But the critical question, as Mumford says, in the quotation at the head of this chapter, is as to the *function* and *quality* of the object one is multiplying.

There is a world of difference between an instrument of communication and communication itself. Communication is the end result whether one uses radio, television, or the smoke signals of the ancients to convey a message from sender to receiver. Thomas Carlyle used the wrong term when he said civilization was transportation. Carlyle really meant that civilization was communication. Transportation can never be anything but a *medium* of communication. The highway, the seaway, the airway, radio waves, cables, and wires are communication lines. The telephone, telegraph, and radio are simply instruments which have supplanted the ram's-horn and the tom-tom. Planes, ships, trucks and automobiles, magazines, newspapers, and businesspapers are carriers. Printed, written, and spoken words are merely symbols of communication. Supreme Court Justice Robert Jackson describes the human mind as a "besieged stronghold . . . constantly bombarded with symbols: words, pictures, charts, slogans, sounds, signs, colors, gestures. We react to these symbols to the degree that we understand their meaning." Communication lines extend the range of human knowledge, but they also extend the range of human error. It is the quality of what goes over these communication lines, what understandings, sharings, agreements and like meanings, what integration of objectives is achieved, that makes real communication. The future of the businesspaper as an instrument of communication obviously depends on how well we train men and women to perform the various functions of business journalism.

TOMORROW'S SCHOOL OF JOURNALISM

President Robert Hutchins of the University of Chicago told a luncheon meeting of the Inland Daily Press Association in Chicago:

What education cannot do is prepare men and women for specific jobs All it can hope to do is to train their minds so that they can adjust themselves to any job. *So the shadiest educational ventures under respectable auspices are the schools of journalism.* They exist in defiance of the obvious fact that the best preparation for journalism is a good education. *Journalism itself can be learned only by being a journalist.*[1] (Italics are the author's.)

Dr. J. L. Morrill, vice-president of Ohio State University, labeled Dr. Hutchins's contention as "adult argument" and declared that "it has little appeal for the eager youngster anxious to get at the work of his choice, and almost no validity in the psychology of learning." Dr. Morrill went on to assert that in his opinion instruction in journalism was "a priceless instrument of educational motivation."[2] We agree with Dr. Morrill.

New situations created daily by a world in revolution underline the *need* for the ablest type of men and women in business journalism of the future. In order adequately to equip a new generation of business journalists, it will be necessary to broaden the base of journalism schools. The students of journalism must be provided with a broad background of knowledge of all the arts and sciences that govern human society. They should have a clearer conception of the role and duty of communications in human society. The school of journalism should be a miniature world community where student journalists can "practice" business journalism in collaboration with student enterprisers in the school of business administration or the school of marketing. The

[1] "Is There a Legitimate Place for Journalistic Instruction?" *Quill*, March, 1938.
[2] *Ibid.*

business journalism students should cover the trials of the school of law and the clinics of the school of medicine and the sessions of the schools of diplomacy, comparative government, and foreign trade. There should be more effective synthesis between all advanced college courses and the school of journalism.

The late Willard Bleyer said, " . . . a well organized course in reporting involves *a survey of the whole community and all its important activities*, as a means of showing students how to discover and evaluate the news that they may furnish. Thus, it serves to correlate the work of news gathering and news writing with what students have learned in psychology, economics and similar subjects."[3] (Italics are the author's.)

Many competent observers believe that greater status and recognition should be given to the vital work of teachers of journalism and teachers of business administration, not only by paying them higher salaries but by more frequent employment of their talents in public enterprises and business projects.

In journalism, Mencken says, "Most of the hard work must be done by men who depend less upon inspiration than upon *sound professional competence*. The greater the competence of such men, the more accurate, intelligent and useful are our papers. And the greater their sense of professional dignity, the more honorable and conscientious is the craft they practice. I believe schools of journalism tend to improve them in both directions."[4]

BUSINESS JOURNALISM—BUSINESS OR PROFESSION?

Journalism has become both a big business and an important profession. The distinction, as Dean Ackerman of the Pulitzer School of Journalism, Columbia University, has drawn it, is between the *business* of the publisher and the *profession* of the editor.

In reply to a statement by the New York *Herald Tribune* that

[3] "What Schools of Journalism Are Trying to Do," by Dr. Willard G. Bleyer, *Journalism Quarterly*, March, 1931. See also *Main Currents in the History of American Journalism* (Houghton, Mifflin, Boston, 1927) and *The Profession of Journalism* (Atlantic Monthly Press, Boston, 1918). Dr. Bleyer was director of the School of Journalism, University of Wisconsin.

[4] *Reflections on Journalism*, by H L. Mencken. Knopf, New York, 1930.

the press was a quasi-public utility, the eminent businesspaper, *Wall Street Journal*, declared on Jan. 20, 1935:

It is flatly untrue, but there is much ignorance and hypocrisy about the matter calling for plain speaking. A newspaper is a private enterprise owing nothing whatever to the public, which grants it no franchise. It is therefore "affected" with no public interest. It is emphatically the property of its owner, who is selling a manufactured product at his own risk . . . there are many newspaper owners willing enough to encourage the public in the delusion that it is the editor of a newspaper who dictates the selection of news and the expression of opinion. He only does so subject to correction and suggestions of the proprietor of the paper who, most properly, considers his newspaper a plain business proposition. It is just that, no more and certainly no less.

The editor of the *Wall Street Journal* in 1935 was William Peter Hamilton. The present editor, W. H. Grimes, in a letter to the author on Sept. 2, 1943, clarified his position on the quasi-public character of the press:

Whatever may have been Mr. Hamilton's thoughts on the matter, the fact is that he was editor of *The Wall Street Journal* in fact as well as in name, and that the owners of the paper did not attempt to correct or suggest what opinions he should express. During my term as editor of *The Wall Street Journal* I have never received a single suggestion from the owners of the paper as to editorial policy. Obviously a newspaper does have duties and obligations to the people it serves and to its community.

Social Responsibility of the Business Journalist

"Those who undertake to interpret and clarify the facts of human life and human relations . . ." wrote Frank Parker Stockbridge,[5] "have a responsibility which is as highly charged with social import as the physician for the relief of the ills of the human body, the clergyman for the moral and spiritual welfare of his parishioners' souls; a responsibility of far greater social consequences than that of the lawyer and the engineer and immeasur-

[5] "The Problem of the Press," *Nineteenth Century*, February, 1939.

ably greater than that of the farmer, the businessman or the banker."

Sir Norman Angell recognized the quasi-public utility nature of the press when he wrote:

"... *unless certain decisions can be made with some degree of wisdom by multitudes of men, on the basis of the kind of knowledge transmitted by the press, our civilization must break down.*"[6]

The business press has a dual personality. It is a private enterprise, a business operated for profit by businessmen, as was shown in the chapters on the functions of advertising, circulation, and promotion managers, and in the chapter on the functions of the publisher. That it is also a quasi-public institution, essential to the preservation of all other private enterprise in a free democratic society, and to the preservation of society itself, was shown in the chapter on the function of the editor.

Unlike other institutions, however, the business press is not tax-free; it is not supported by voluntary contributions, nor is it endowed. The press does, as we have already pointed out, enjoy a special privilege in the use of the mails, a subsidy granted in the public interest.[7] To survive, however, an independent business-paper must make money. But even in that respect as a private business it differs from other private producers of commodities.

As we pointed out in the chapter on the advertising manager, the chief source of revenue of a businesspaper is not the sale of the product to its logical consumer, the reader. The subscription price the reader pays does not even cover the mechanical cost of producing one copy of the publication. The profits of the business press come from the advertisers who regard the businesspaper as a logical, effective carrier of their own business messages to the same readers, who are or may become the customers for their products.

But that is not the sole reason for the advertiser's use of the

[6] "A Plea for Professional Standards," *Quill*, December, 1934.
[7] Subsidy of $90 million a year in less-than-cost postage rates. See *Function of the Advertising Manager*, Chap. VIII.

businesspaper. The advertiser looks upon the businesspaper as a spokesman for his industry, an independent spokesman, a champion of his rights as a private enterpriser, and of the rights of all private enterprise, a crusader against those forces which would destroy or injure the industry, a pioneer for the improvement of industry standards; and finally, he looks upon his businesspaper as a line of communication, to bring back to him the news it gathers and the interpretation of news and events which affect or may affect his private business enterprise, his particular field, and all industry. He, too, is a reader. Were the business press but a *carrier* of advertising messages, in the way that a truck transports bundles of papers, advertisers could as easily go to any job printer and have the printer run off and staple together their several advertising messages. These printed and bound messages the advertisers could then furnish to any mailing concern together with their customer lists, with instructions to send them out periodically to their customers. The businesspaper is not a catalogue.

By merely making money, by merely being a successful business enterprise, the business press does not fulfill its obligation to industry or its assignment for the future. Business journalism cannot afford, any more than can medicine or law, to look upon its enterprise as a "plain business proposition" or as "a calling owing nothing whatever to the public."

Contrary to the cynical view of the former editor of the *Wall Street Journal*, the press does enjoy a franchise from the public, a franchise denied to other private enterprises. It enjoys a constitutional guaranty of freedom to speak out and at the same time to protect its sources of information. The press cannot be enjoined or censored in advance of publication. "When this one form of private business was singled out and hedged around with a special protection," wrote the celebrated columnist and author, Herbert Agar, "the American people said: 'we believe the press can make a great contribution to the life of a free people. To make this contribution the press must be free from outside control of its policies. Therefore, we forbid our government to interfere with the printing of decent news or decent opinions.' "[8]

[8] *Quill*, October, 1938.

But the freedom of the press, like every other so-called right in the Constitution, is indeed a *privilege*, not a right. It is, as Mr. Agar said in the same article, "a burden laid on the press, not a promise that the press can do what it likes." He pointed out, as others have done, that the Bill of Rights itself is not a statement of what man naturally inherits; it is a statement of what our fathers tried to win for themselves.

THE BUSINESSPAPER'S COMPETITION

The businesspaper competes for part of the producer's advertising dollar. It also competes for people's reading time. But, while the specialized business press believes it is entitled to a larger share of both dollars and readers, competition looms ahead to give it less of each. Competent observers see competition for the businesspaper's advertising dollar becoming more severe from these media: (1) general magazines; (2) news magazines; (3) newspapers; (4) radio.[9] Each of these general media stresses industrial news today. During the war these media carried industrial advertising of corporations in war work who felt a need to keep in close contact with the public as well as the trade. The general media regard this as a trend and have no intention of giving up industrial advertising, which before the war appeared solely in businesspapers.

Another competitor of the specialized business press is the so-called horizontal businesspaper, of which *Fortune* and *Modern Industry* are excellent examples. Some publishers of specialized, or vertical, papers also publish horizontal types.

The answer to this competition for dollars and readers is more aggressive exercise of the nine functions of business journalism, especially the functions of integrated journalism and public relations. As Mr. Howard Ehrlich says, "no one has a God-given franchise to be the exclusive purveyor of business news to men in business."[10]

[9] See Paul F. Lazarsfeld, Ph.D., *Radio and the Printed Page. Journalism Quarterly*, Vol. 18, March, 1941.
[10] Before the Associated Business Paper publishers, Westchester Country Club, Rye, N. Y., May, 1944.

Public Relations and the Business Press

The device of public relations and the device of self-government (called the trade association) have developed along parallel lines with technological improvements in industry. The trade association, as discussed at length in Chapter VI, is the alternative to bureaucratic control of industry by government. As a framework for self-discipline and self-regulation in business journalism itself, the trade associations in the field of businesspaper publishing must become more aggressive, encourage more publishers to join their ranks, and endorse their codes of fair practice, and thus strengthen the position of the business press in organized society.

There is also need for a public relations program to strengthen the position of the business press in the economic competition between all media which will highlight the future. The businesspaper, which lays claim to being the spokesman for industry, up to now has been pouring the voice of industry into the ear of industry alone, with an occasional aside to government. In the future it will be necessary for the business press to explain, defend, and also courageously criticize industry before all those who live by industry, which is the public at large as well as government, labor, and capital. By making its own functions and services more intelligible to the public, the business press at the same time will be staking out its own future security.

A broad study of the businesspaper as a force in production and distribution, through its adult education function, and a deeper inquiry into the needs of businesspaper readers should head the agenda for the future. A comparative study of expenditures for public relations in all fields should be undertaken. A study of trade associations is a must for the future. Other needed inquiries are patent law reform, the bottlenecks in scientific and technical research, the strengthening and enforcement of laws against monopolies and international cartels.

The Needs of the Reader

The businesspaper must become much more conscious of the needs of its readers. These needs will differ from the needs of

CHART 39

CHARACTERISTICS OF A PROFESSION*

By Louis Dembitz Brandeis
Late Justice of the Supreme Court of the U. S.

EACH commencement season we are told by the college reports the number of graduates who have selected the professions as their occupations and the number of those who will enter business. The time has come for abandoning such a classification. Business should be, and to some extent already is, one of the professions. The once meagre list of the learned professions is being constantly enlarged. Engineering in its many branches already takes rank beside law, medicine and theology. Forestry and scientific agriculture are securing places of honor. The new professions of manufacturing, of merchandising, of transportation and of finance must soon gain recognition. The establishment of business schools in our universities is a manifestation of the modern conception of business.

The peculiar characteristics of a profession as distinguished from other occupations, I take to be these:

First: A profession is an occupation for which the necessary preliminary training is intellectual in character, involving knowledge and to some extent learning, as distinguished from mere skill.

Second: It is an occupation which is pursued largely for others and not merely for one's self.

Third: It is an occupation in which the amount of financial return is not the accepted measure of success.

Is not each of these characteristics found today in business worthily pursued?

The recognized professions, however, definitely reject the size of the financial return as the measure of success. They select as their test, excellence of performance in the broadest sense—and include, among other things, advance in the particular occupation and service to the community. These are the basis of all worthy reputations in the recognized professions. In them a large income is the ordinary incident of success; but he who exaggerates the value of the incident is apt to fail of real success.

* From an address delivered at Brown University Commencement Day, 1912. Published in *System*, October, 1912. *Business—A Profession* by Louis D. Brandeis; Small, Maynard & Company, Boston, 1914.

yesterday, as businesspapers add new types of readers. It will become the duty of the American businesspaper editor to observe the workings of industry all over the globe. No country anywhere in the world is content to remain entirely agrarian. Every nation will want to industrialize, to mass-produce as a means for national or social security. The businesspaper editor will be the world reporter of better methods of low-cost production and distribution. It will no longer be satisfactory for his reporters in France to be Frenchmen, in Germany to be Germans, or in Russia, Russians. His observers, analysts, and interpreters in every part of the globe will be Americans, members of his own staff; and neither the editor nor his staff members anywhere in the world will be farther away from editorial headquarters than 60 hours' flying time.

In the Preface to this book appears a statement by Archibald Mac-Leish that "the war for men's minds can only be won by a labor of clarification and definition and illumination." Such labors, as we have tried to show, are the daily functions of business journalism. In the last book of his great trilogy, *The Condition of Man*, Lewis Mumford declares: "The function of work is to provide man with a living: not for the purpose of enlarging his capacities to consume, but of liberating his capacities to create." The more man creates, whether of goods or services, artifacts or symbols, the greater will be his need for the know-how of the specialized businesspaper.

We have seen the way the business press in the first half of this century provided the know-how for more efficient mass production, culminating in the greatest production achievement of all times during World War II. To maintain these high production levels and provide work for all who want to work in the second half of our century, the know-how of more efficient mass distribution becomes the paramount peacetime assignment of business journalism.

[11] *Technics and Civilization* (1934); *The Culture of Cities* (1938); *The Condition of Man* (1944); Harcourt, Brace & Co., New York.

AMERICAN BUSINESSPAPERS BEFORE 1900[1]

1795: *New York Prices Current-Rater*
    New York Commercial
1808: *Butchers' and Packers Gazette*
1815: *General Shipping and Commercial List*
1825: *American Journal of Pharmacy*
1826: *Journal of the Franklin Institute*
1827: *Journal of Commerce*
1832: *American Railroad Journal*
    (now *Railway Mechanical Engineer*). A half dozen other railroad journals in Boston, Philadelphia, Cincinnati, Chicago, and New York all argued for a railroad to the Pacific Coast. (Henry V. Poor, editor in 1848.)
1836: *Thompson's Bank Note and Commercial Reporter*
    (Then *Thompson's American Bank Report* and, in 1877, *American Banker*.) Started as daily bulletin on rates of currency exchange. John Thompson, founder and editor, laid foundation for *American Banker*. He retired in 1865. (In 1836 he was first to organize a national bank in New York—the First National Bank.) In 1877 he founded Chase National Bank, named after his close friend and coworker, Salmon P. Chase.
1838: *Blast Furnace & Steel Plant*
    Started as *Pittsburgh American Manufacturer*
1839: *Merchants' Magazine and Commercial Review*
    (no advertising)

[1] The long gap between the dates of inventions that sowed the seeds of new industries and the actual founding dates of nineteenth century businesspapers devoted to such industries, when compared to the shortened gap between discoveries and new business papers in this century, clearly indicates the fast tempo of the twentieth century. This list, incidentally, is incomplete. See Vols. I, II, III, *A History of American Magazines*, by Frank Luther Mott. Harvard University Press, 1938.

1839-1909: *American Journal of Dental Science*

1844: *Price Current-Grain Reporter*

1845: *Scientific American*

> Rufus Porter, the founder, was a shoemaker's apprentice and house painter, invented a camera obscura in 1820; became peddler of a "revolving almanac" he had invented. Many other inventions—signal telegraph, fire alarm, fog whistle, washing machine, rotary plow, portable house, corn sheller, flying ship are his.

1846: *United States Economist and Dry Goods Reporter*

> First—*Dry Goods Reporter and Commercial Glance*
> Second—*United States Economist and Dry Goods Reporter*
> Third—*Dry Goods Economist*
> Fourth—*Department Store Economist*
> Founded 1846 by W. B. Burroughs

1845-78: *Mining Journal*

> (Marquette, Mich.)

1846: *Bankers Magazine*

> Founded by I. Smith Homans

1850: *American Journal of the Medical Science* (Phila.) and *Boston Medical & Surgical Journal*

> were two oldest. Dr. Isaac Hays, editor and founder of *American Journal*, scores of others—some specialized.

1851: *Shoe & Leather Reporter*

1852: *Wall Street Journal* (not related to paper of same name started in 1889)

1852-1867: *American Journal of Photography*

1852-1856: *Ink Fountain*

> For printers

1852-1853: *American Telegraph Magazine*

1853-current: *American Insurance Digest & Insurance Monitor*

> Absorbed the old *Insurance Monitor* (1853)—oldest insurance businesspaper

1853-61: *Mining Magazine*

1855: *Iron Age*

> Started as *Hardware Man's Newspaper and American Manufacturers' Circular*. In 1911, Conde Nast set up fabulous United Publishers Corp. which acquired papers ranging from *Les Jardin des Modes* to *Iron Age*, *Motor Age*, *Automobile*, *Vanity Fair*, and *Vogue*. Nast died in September, 1942. Iva

Patcévitch, successor. Nast company's majority stockholder in 1942 was prominent English publishing peer, Lord Camrose.

1855-92 *Typographic Advertiser* (Phila.)
  For printers; several others.

1855: *Hardware Age*
  (Established 1855, succeeding and embodying *Hardware*, New York; *Stoves and Hardware Reporter*, St. Louis; *Western Hardware Journal*, Omaha; *Iron Age Hardware*, New York; *Hardware Reporter*, St. Louis; *Hardware Salesman*, Chicago; *Hardware Dealers Magazine*, New York; and *Good Hardware*, New York.

1856: *Railway Gazette*

1857: *Shoe & Leather Reporter* (N.Y.)
  Later moved to Boston

1857-current: *The American Druggists' Circular and Chemical Gazette*
  Founded by Henry Bridgman, apothecary and druggist. Fought nostrums and adulteration and published annual trade directories for 40 years. John H. Snively enjoyed longest term as editor (1886-1904).

1857-83: *Harness and Carriage Journal*

1859-current: *Weekly Underwriter* (insurance)

1859-1936: *Dental Cosmos* (Philadelphia)
  Published by S. S. White Dental Supply Co.

1859-current: *American Gas Journal*
  Started as *American Gas-Light Journal and Mining Reporter*

1858-71: *Coach-Makers Magazine*

1859: *Hub*
  Later *Automotive Manufacturer*

1862-current: *Trade of the West*
  Later *American Manufacture and Iron World*
  Later *Steel and Iron* (Pittsburgh)

1862-86: *American Spirit and Wine Trade Review*

1862: *American Druggist*

1863-current: *Army & Navy Journal*
  The U.S. Army and Navy Journal and Gazette of the Regular and Volunteer Forces changed in 1926 to *Gazette of the Land, Sea, Air*. Captain William C. Church, editor; young soldier who fought with General W. T. Sherman and Silas Casey. Started it in 1863 in New York. Also his brother

Francis P. Church (both sons of the Rev. Pharcellus Church,
founder of Baptist newspaper, New York *Chronicle*).

1863-current: *International Iron Molders Journal* (Cincinnati)

1864-67: *Pacific Index*
> Became *American Mining Index* (N.Y.)

1864: *National Builder*

1864: *Photographic Journal of America*

1865: *Tobacco Leaf*
> C. Pfirshing, founder.

1865-66: *Petroleum Gazette and Scientific Journal*

1865: *Commercial & Financial Chronicle*

1865: *Vehicle Monthly*
> (now *Motor Vehicle Monthly*)

1866: *American Law Review* (Boston)
> Edited by Oliver Wendell Holmes (legal journal); by 1885,
> 43 law journals listed in *Jones' Index*.

1866: *Engineering & Mining Journal*
> Started as the *American Journal of Mining* in 1866—8
> mergers.

1866-75: *Journal of Applied Chemistry*

1866: *American Journal of Mining*
> Became *Engineering & Mining Journal*, 1869, in fourth year.
> G. F. Dawson, first editor; oldest of McGraw-Hill papers.
> Weekly, 1866-1929. Published in 1906 by Hill Publishing Co.;
> McGraw-Hill since 1917. Absorbed *Coal & Iron Record*,
> *Mining Review*, *Polytechnic Review*, *Mining & Metallurgy*,
> *Mining Magazine*, *Mining & Engineering World*, *Mining &
> Scientific Press*.

1866-86: *Inventor's and Manufacturers' Gazette*

1866-90: *Printers Circular* (Philadelphia)

1866-75: *Printing Gazette* (Cleveland)

1867: *Advertisers' Gazette*

1867-current: *Insurance News Graphic*
> Now *Southwestern Insurance News Graphic*, Dallas, Tex.

1867: *Iron Trade Review*
> Became *Steel* in 1930

1865-current: *U.S. Review* (insurance)

1868-current: *N. Y. Spectator: An American Review of Life Insurance*

1868-current: *American Brewer*
> 5 or 6 others.

1868-96: *Manufacturers' Review and Industrial Record* (New York)

1868-95: *American Journal of Art*
Chas. D. Lakey. In 1872 became *American Builder* and, later, *Builder and Woodworker*

1868: *Real Estate Record*

1868: *Textile World*
Started in 1868 as *Manufacturers Review and Industrial Record*; *Textile World*, 1888.

1869-87: *Van Nostrand's Electric Engineering Magazine*
"Electric" was dropped from title in 1879. David Van Nostrand, editor and publisher until death in 1866. Merger with *American Railroad Journal* in 1887.

1869-current: *American Grocer* (New York)

1869-current: *Coal Trade Journal*

1869: *Jewelers' Circular-Keystone*
Started in 1869 as *American Horological Journal*

1869: Forty medical journals started; 300 to 400 published by 1885

1870-current: *Insurance Index*

1870: *American Cabinet Maker and Upholsterer*
In 1919 became *Furniture Buyer and Decorator*; and *Carpet Trade Review*, now *Carpet and Upholstery Trade Review*. Subsidiary (1880-1932) was *Furniture Trade Review*.

1870-77: *American Chemist*

1870-72: *Petroleum Monthly*
Succeeded by *Monthly Petroleum Trade Report* (1873-1882) and by *Oil City Derrick* (1871-current).

1871: *Casket and Sunnyside*

1871-1929: *Dry Goods Reporter* (Chicago)

1871-88: *American Journal of Fabrics & Dry Goods Bulletin*
Later *Merchant World* in 1886.

1871: *New Remedies*
Changed in 1892 to *American Druggist*. Bought in 1892 by Ashbel R. Elliott. Caswell O. Mayo, editor. Merged *Pharmaceutical Record* and *Market Review* (1881-1893) and called it *American Druggist and Pharm. Record*. Bought, 1927, by Hearst.

1872-current: *Standard* (insurance)

1872-79: *Clothier and Hatter*

     Split into   { *Clothier & Furnisher*   { *American Hatter*
                 { *Hatter and Furrier*—then   { *Furrier*
                           (now *Fur Trade Review*)

     Clothier & Furnisher merged in 1927 into
     Haberdasher and called *Haberdasher and the Clothier and Furnisher*.

1872: *Pepper Trade Journal*

1873-current. *Insurance Age-Journal*

1873: *Western Hotel Reporter* (San Francisco)
     Numerous others in hotel field.

1873: *American Miller*
     Oldest milling journal. Amalgamation of eight other milling journals.

1873-93: *Sewing Machine Journal* (New York)

1873-1928: *American Stationer* (Brooklyn)

1873: *American Lumberman*

1874-1917: *Engineering News*
     Founded by George H. Frost. Began as *Engineer and Surveyor*. In April, 1917, consolidated with McGraw-Hill's *Engineering Record*, which had been founded in New York by Henry C. Meyer in 1877 as *Plumber & Sanitary Engineer*. Changed in 1880 to *Sanitary Engineer*. Combined journal became *Engineering News-Record*. Absorbed the *Contractor* (1892) in 1918.

1874-77: *American Laboratory* (Boston)

1874-1931: *Metal Worker, Plumber & Steam Fitter*
     In 1921, became *Sanitary & Heating Engineering*; in 1929, became *Sanitary and Heating Age*.

1874: *Western Tobacco Journal*

1874: *Confectioners Journal*

1874: *American Fashion Review*
     Called *Sartorial Art Journal* since 1887.
     Others: *Furnishing Gazette, Tailors' Review, American Tailor & Cutter*.

1874-1926: *New York Insurance Critic*
     20 journals founded in post bellum period (1865) continued 50 years; 9 are still published.

1874: *Electrical World*
     Started as a local telegraphers' journal in New York. in 1874; four mergers.
     1874—the *Operator*; then the *Operator and Electrical World*.

1874: *Engineering News-Record*

1874: *Crockery & Glass Journal*
>Merged with *China & Glass Guide* and *Pottery* half of *House Furnishing Goods Journal*

1875-1920: *Fabrics, Fancy Goods & Notions*

1875-87: *Grain and Provision Review*

1876-current: *Millinery Trade Review*

1876: *Casket* (Rochester)
>Undertakers' journal. Founded by Albert H. Nirdlinger. Merged with *Sunnyside* (1871) Casket Manufacturers house organ in 1925 (*Casket and Sunnyside*).

1876: *American Architect and Building News* (Boston)
>Jas. R. Osgood & Co. Editor, Wm. P. Longfellow. Changed in 1890 to *Architecture & Building*. In 1921 absorbed *Architectural Review*. Acquired by Hearst in 1929. In 1890 absorbed *Builders Magazine*.

1876-current: *Railway Age*
>E. H. Talbott. Merged with *Railway Gazette*, 1908, as *Railway Age-Gazette*, 1909.
>
>W. H. Boardman, E. A. Simmons, and others formed publishing company. Boardman long editor and publisher of the *Gazette*, edited new paper three or four years and then in 1912 Samuel O. Dunn took over. Changed to *Railway Age* in 1918.

1876: *Brewers Journal*
>Started as *Western Brewer*.

1877-current: *Geyer's Stationer*

1877-1904: *Ice Trade Journal*

1877: *Water Works Engineering*

1877-current: *American Machinist*

1877: *American Hairdresser*
>First in beauty industry as *American Hairdresser & Perfumer*.

1877: *Fire Engineering*
>Started *National Firemen's Journal*

1877-current: *Geyer's Stationer & Business Equipment Topics*

1877-1934: *Retail Grocers' Advocate*

1877-1902: *Shoe & Leather Review* (Chicago)

1877-1893: *Sewing Machine News* (New York)

1877: *American Machinist*
>Jackson Bailey, editor until 1888. Horace B. Miller, first publisher. McGraw-Hill in 1917.

1877-1892: *New York Mining Record*

1878: *Marine Engineering & Shipping Review*

1878-current: *Rough Notes*
> Third oldest insurance journal.

1878-1913: *Stoves and Hardware Reporter* (St. Louis)

1878-current: *Canning Trade*

1878-current: *Spice Mill*

1878-1901: *Mining and Metallurgical Journal*

1878: *Modern Miller* (Moline)
> as *Grain Gleaner*.

1878-current: *National Laundry Journal* (Chicago)

1878: *Paper Mill & Wood Pulp News* (Philadelphia)
> Founded by Lyman D. Post. Moved to New York in 1885.

1879: *Tradesman* (Atlanta)
> Became *Southern Hardware and Implement Journal*, 1919.

1879-current: *Butchers' Advocate and Market Journal*

1879: *Furniture Manufacturer*

1879-current: *Textile Colorist* (Philadelphia)

1879-1893: *Pottery and Glassware Reporter*

1879-1923: *Sewing Machine Advocate*

1879: *American Contractor* (Chicago)
> Now *General Building Contractor*.

1879: *Southwestern Miller* (Kansas City)

1879-1930: *Carpentry and Building*
> F. David Williams.
>
> In 1910 called *Building Age*.

1879-1913: *American Chemical Journal*
> Edited at Johns Hopkins by Ira Remsen. Absorbed by the American Chemical Society (1879).

1879-1886: *Barbers National Journal* (Philadelphia)

1879-current: *American Hairdresser and Perfumer* (New York)

1879-current: *Army & Navy Register*

1879: *Western Undertaker* (Grand Rapids)
> Called American Funeral Director in 1930.

1880-current: *American Artisan* (Chicago)
> Hardware and hot-air heat.

1880-1892: *American Engineer*
> Started by John W. Weston.

1880-1898: *Paper World*

1880: *Steam*

1881-1909: *Glovers' Journal* (Gloversville, N.Y.)

1881-1888: *Petroleum Age*

1881: *The American Press*

1881: *American Funeral Director*

1882: *Factory*

> Started 1882 as *Review of the Telegraph & Telephone*; *Electrical Review*, 1883-18921; *Industrial Engineering*, 1922-1931; *Maintenance Engineering* (New York) 1931-1932; *Factory Management and Maintenance*, 1932-current; absorbed several other papers. Charles W. Peters, great editor, 1891-1921.

1882: *American Silk Journal*

1882-1930: *American Elevator and Grain Trade*

1882-1929: *American Jeweler*

1882: *Wood Worker*

1882: *Steel*

> Started 1882 as the *Trade Review*; then *Iron Trade Review* (1888); *Steel* in 1930.

1882-1901: *Boots and Shoes*

> Called *Boots and Shoes Weekly* after 1899, New York.

1882: *Leather Manufacturer*

1882-1899: *Mechanics*

> Became *Engineering-Mechanics* in 1892.

1882-1887: *American Chemical Review* (Chicago)

1882-current: *Boot and Shoe Recorder*

> Known first as the *Great National Shoe Weekly*.

1882-1889: *American Electrician*

> F. L. Pope, editor. Changed to *Electrician & Electrical Engineer* in 1884 and *Electrical Engineer* in 1888. Finally merged with *Electrical World*.

1882: *Miller's Review* (Philadelphia)

> Moved to Atlanta, Ga., 1924. Absorbed *Dixie Miller* (1892-1924) and called *Miller's Review* and *Dixie Miller*.

1882: *Building*

> Wm. T. Comstock's weekly.

1882-1902: *American Laundry Journal* (Troy)

1882-1915: *Printing Trade News* (New York)

1883: *Gas Age-Record & Natural Gas*

1883: *Western Architect & Builder*

> *Building Witness* in 1913.

1883: *Electrical World* (*Operator*, 1874)
> Founded by W. J. Johnston. Separated the same year *World* absorbed *Operator* in 1885 and half dozen other papers.

1883: *Boston Journal of Chemistry*
> *Popular Science* in 1883.

1883-1934: *Keystone*

1883: *Inland Printer* (Chicago)
> H. H. Hill, editor.

1884: *Telegraph Operator*
> Became *Electrical World.*

1884: *Transit Journal*

1884: *Street Railway Journal*
> Now *Electric Railway Journal.*

1884: *Power*
> Swetland took over *Power* in 1884, called it *Power-Steam.* In 1892 name reverted to *Power.*
>
> In 1908 absorbed *Chicago Engineer*, called *Power and the Engineer.*
>
> In 1904 bought by Hill Publishing Co., which became Mc-Graw-Hill in merger of 1917.
>
> Also absorbed: *Science & Industry, Mechanics Magazine, Steam Electric Magazine, Engineers Review, Safety Valve, The Stationary Engineer, Steam Engineering, The Mechanical Engineer.*

1884: *Editor & Publisher*
> Started as the *Journalist*, 1884. Merged *Newspaperdom*, 1892; *Fourth Estate*, 1894.

1884: *Midas Criterion*
> Oldest liquor publication. Started in Chicago by William Mida.

1884-current: *Manufacturing Jeweler*

1884-1930 *Milk Reporter*

1884: *Fishing Gazette*

1884-current: *National Glass Budget*

1884-1913: *Leather Gazette*
> (In 1888 called *Shoe & Leather Gazette*, St. Louis)

1885: *American Printer*
> Five mergers.

1885: *Hardware Age*
> Seven mergers.

1885: *Railway Engineering*

1887: *Bakers Helper*

1887: *Electrical West*
> Started, 1887, as *Pacific Lumberman, Contractor & Electrician.*

1888: *Hardware & Metal*

1888: *Printers' Ink.* In 1867 Geo. P. Rowell founded *Advertisers' Gazette*, its predecessor. Name changed in 1871 to *American Newspaper Reporter*

1888:-1925 *Newspaperdom*
> H. Craig Dare, publisher. Purchased in 1925 by *Editor & Publisher.*

1889-current: *Wall Street Journal*

1889: *National Provisioner*
> Meat-packing industry

1890: *Hide & Leather*
> With *Shoe Factory.*

1891: *Factory*
> Started as *Factory and Industrial Management.*

1892: *Embalmer's Monthly and National Funeral Director*

1892: *Shears*

1892: *Foundry*

1892: *Brick & Clay Record*
> First, *Clay*, 1892; *Brick*, 1894; merger, 1912.

1892: *Men's Wear*; started as *Chicago Herald Gazette*; then *Chicago Apparel Gazette.*

1892: *Hotel Monthly*

1892: *House Furnishing Review*
> Oldest housewares and appliance magazine incorporating four other papers: *Home Equipment, House Furnishing Journal, Housewares Merchandising*, and *Creative Design.*

1893: *Starchroom Laundry Journal*
> Oldest in power laundry industry.

1893: *Daily News Record*

1895: *Automotive Industries*
> *Horseless Age*—first auto businesspaper printed in English (1899, *Automobile & Motor Review*). Now *Automotive Industries. Horseless Age* merged in 1918.

1896: *Power Plant Engineering*; Started as *Practical Engineer*

1896: *Automobile Trade Journal*
    First "cycle trade journal." "Cycle" was not dropped until
    1912. In 1899, *Cycle and Automobile Trade Journal.*
1897: *National Underwriter*
1898: *Cotton*
1898: *Luggage & Leather Goods*
1899: *Timberman*
1899: *Sporting Goods Dealer*

1. EXTRAORDINARY WARTIME CONFERENCE WITH LEADERS OF INDUSTRY

Dec. 10-11, 1942
Program

Thursday, December 10, 1942:

9:30 A.M.—General Motors Board Room,
General Motors Building, 57th St. & Broadway

Mr. Alfred P. Sloan, Chairman of the Board
Mr. Charles E. Wilson, President
and other G. M. officials

Subject—Transportation and Manpower

11:00 A.M.—New York Central Board Room
New York Central Building

Mr. F. E. Williamson, President New York Central Railroad and other available railroad officials to be invited for us by Mr. Williamson

Subject—Transportation and Manpower

12:15 Noon—Return to Waldof-Astoria, Le Perroquet Suite for brief interview with Clyde Vandeburg, Assistant Director, OWI, who is making special trip from Washington, D. C. to meet our group.

12:30 Noon—LUNCH at Waldorf-Astoria Hotel
Le Perroquet Suite
Speaker—Col. W. Gibson Carey, Jr. (Chief, Army Specialist Corps—President, Yale & Towne Mfg. Co.)

Subject—"Some Thoughts on the Post-War Situation"

3:00 P.M.—Luncheon room of American Cyanamid Company
30 Rockefeller Plaza (Radio City—Room 6433)

Mr. William B. Bell, President
American Cyanamid Company
Mr. M. C. Whittaker, Vice-President
Dr. Walter S. Landis, Vice-President

Subject—Patents and proposed changes in patent laws.

4:00 P.M.—Board room of Standard Oil Company of New Jersey
Officials of Standard Oil Company of New Jersey

Subject—Synthetic Rubber Progress and Manpower

5:30 P.M.—Back at Waldorf-Astoria, Le Perroquet Suite
Speaker—Lewis H. Brown, President
Johns-Manville Company

Subject—Manpower, Management's Attitude

6:30 P.M.—Or sooner following interview with Mr. Brown—
COCKTAILS

7:30 P.M.—DINNER—Le Perroquet Suite, Waldorf-Astoria Hotel
Speaker—Frederick · C. Crawford, President,
National Association of Manufacturers

Friday, December 11, 1942
9:15 A.M.—Offices of Associated Merchandising Corp., and the
Retailers' Research Association at 1440 Broadway.
corner West 40th Street.
Conference Room A—on the 8th Floor
General Subject—Wartime Trends in Distribution
Speakers—Introductory remarks by Phillip J. Reilly,
Director of both Associated Merchandising Corpora-
tion AMC and Retail Research Association RRA
R. O. Bergdahl, General Merchandise Manager, AMC

Subject—Market Problems
A. C. Thompson, Assistant to Director in charge of
RRA
Subject—Store Operation under Wartime Restrictions.

10:45 A.M.—General Foods Company, Offices 250 Park Avenue
Mr. Colby Chester, Chairman, and
Mr. C. M. Francis, President

Subject—Food Supply and Rationing

2. WARTIME WASHINGTON CONFERENCE OF BUSINESSPAPER EDITORS WITH GOVERNMENT

Washington meeting—June 11-12, 1943
(To indicate the type of pictures that can be secured from OWI, an exhibit of pictures will be shown throughout the day at the Hotel Statler, which is headquarters)

Friday, June 11
8:30 A.M.—Breakfast—South American Room, Hotel Statler
Speaker: Leon Henderson, former Price Administrator, will discuss the price situation from the outside looking in.
Annual business meeting—election of officers for the ensuing fiscal year.

11:00 A.M.—Executive Offices, the White House
Conference with President Roosevelt
Presentation by the President of a watch to Paul Wooton, president of the National Conference of Business Paper Editors.

12 Noon —Room 1202 Federal Reserve Building, 20th & Constitution Avenue, N. W. Conference with Judge Fred M. Vinson, new director, Economic Stabilization Board.

1:00 P.M.—Luncheon—South American Room, Hotel Statler
Speaker: Dr. Louis Stark, labor correspondent of the New York *Times*

3:30 P.M.—Room 5109 Social Security Building
Conference with Donald Nelson, chairman of the WPB, and top officials of the Office of War Information.

5:00 P.M.—Reception—Federal Room, Hotel Statler
Chester Davis, Chief, War Food Administration,
guest of honor.

7:00 P.M.—Dinner—South American Room, Hotel Statler
Admiral Sir Percy Noble, Royal British Navy,
Lt. Cmdr. Grace Lally, U.S. Navy Nurse Corps.

Saturday, June 12—Group Sessions
10:00 A.M.—Room 5109 Social Security Building
Discussion of the future of the machine tool industry
with Charles E. Wilson,
Executive Vice-Chairman, WPB
Discussion with Elmer Davis, Director,
Office of War Information

11:00 A.M.—Room 5414 Social Security Building
Discussion of the situation surrounding consumer sup-
ply with Arthur D. Whiteside, Vice Chairman for
Civilian Supply, WPB

11:30 A.M.—Room 5109 Social Security Building
Conference with Hiland G. Batcheller,
Director, Steel Division, WPB

2:00 P.M.—Room 5133 Interstate Commerce Building
Transportation Conference with Henry McCarthy,
Director of the Division of Traffic, Office of Defense
Transportation and John L. Rogers, Director, Division
of Motor Transport, ODT

3. NATIONAL CONFERENCE ON BUSINESS PAPER EDITORS

Washington Meeting—June 9, 1944

8:30 A.M.   Breakfast—South American Room, Hotel Statler
Speakers:
W. L. Clayton, Surplus War Property Administrator
9:45 A.M.   Lt. Gen. Brehon Somervell, Commanding General,
Army Service Forces
First showing War Department motion picture "Earth
Movers"

11:00 A.M.   State Department Gate, West Executive Avenue,
                                          The White House
             Conference with President Roosevelt

12:30 P.M.   South American Room, Hotel Statler
             Speakers:
                 Lawrence Appley, Deputy Chairman, War Manpower
                     Commission, who will discuss the new manpower
                     order.
                 Dr. Emerson Schmidt, Chief Economist, Chamber of
                     Commerce of the United States (on leave from the
                     University of Minnesota).

3:30 P.M.   Room 5440 Social Security Building
             Speakers:
                 Charles E. Wilson,[1] Executive Vice Chairman, War
                     Production Board.
                 Elmer Davis, Director, Office of War Information
                 Edward Falck, Director, Office of War Utilities
                 Herbert M. Faust, Director, Salvage Division
                 F. J. Solon,[2] Forest Products Bureau

6:30 P.M.   Cocktails—Foyer, South American Room, Hotel Statler

7:30 P.M.   Dinner—South American Room, Hotel Statler
                 Dr. W. Y. Elliott, Director, Office of Civilian Re-
                     quirements

[1] President, The General Electric Company.
[2] Vice-President and Sales Director, Owens-Illinois Glass Co.

FUNCTIONS OF BUSINESSPAPER ADVERTISING
1. IN THE DISTRIBUTIVE FIELD[1]

1. To announce new products, new styles.
2. To feature store displays.
3. To offer deals.
4. To talk about profits and turnover.
5. To seek new outlets.
6. To sell with reason-why appeal.
7. To merchandise national advertising.
8. To proclaim product's leadership.
9. To discuss price.
10. To show market opportunities.
11. To point out the advantages of quality.
12. To suggest merchandising methods.
13. To urge use of dealer manuals.
14. To suggest what to say to consumer.
15. To offer consumer literature.
16. To combat false impressions.
17. To play up manufacturer's trade-mark.
18. To glorify manufacturers' salesmen.
19. To show how product should be sold or serviced.
20. To announce contests for dealers.
21. To get retailers to concentrate on full line.
22. To advertise in-stock service, or consignment plans.
23. To combat substitution.
24. To feature dealer testimonials.
25. To announce consumer contests.
26. To suggest seasonal or timely tie-ups.
27. To warn against patent and trade-mark infringements.
28. To carry institutional messages.
29. To announce manufacturer's sales policy.
30. To sell by premium offers.
31. To suggest related selling ideas.
32. To tie in with news events.
33. To discuss product design.

[1] "Sales to Dealers Through Trade Papers," an article in *Printers' Ink Monthly*, September, 1935.

34. To gain acceptance for products that are a part of finished articles.

35. To show quality by means of tests.

2. IN THE TRANSFORMATIVE FIELD[2]

1. To assist Salesmen in Their Selling Job
2. To Reach Executives that Salesmen Cannot Reach
3. To Strengthen Salesmen's Morale
4. Institutional Advertising
5. To Fill in Between Salesmen's Calls
6. To Gain Acceptance for Materials and Parts
7. To Establish Quality
8. To Tell of New Developments
9. To Secure Use of Company's Trade Name by Fabricators
10. To Introduce New Products
11. To Create a Favorable Disposition toward the Product
12. To Establish the Speed and Scope of Company's Service Facilities
13. To Keep Name and Product Before Buying Audience
14. To Broaden the Market
15. To Hold the Market
16. To Dramatize or Emphasize Trade-Mark
17. To Give Information about Product Advantages
18. To Get a Trial Order
19. To Get Inquiries and Leads
20. To Promote Better Product Design
21. To Offer Literature
22. To Provide Customers and Prospects with Helpful Information
23. To Sell the Idea of Adopting a Process
24. To Tie in Product with Names of Satisfied Users
25. To Advertise Installations
26. To Replace Obsolescent Equipment
27. To Offset Seasonal Decline in Sales
28. To Cite Performance Tests
29. To Advertise Repair Parts Service
30. To Feature Tests
31. To Tie in with Exhibits and Trade Shows
32. To Quicken Interest of Distributors
33. To Show Uses of the Product; to Create New Uses

[2] *Printers' Ink Monthly*, December, 1935.

34. To Establish Jobber as Source of Supply
35. To Feature a Maintenance Service
36. To Gain Good-Will of Machine Operators
37. To Get Architects and Engineers to Specify a Product
38. To Stress Efficiency and Economy of a Maintenance Product
39. To Show How to Make or Save Money
40. To Forestall Patent Expirations
41. To Show How to Make Better Products
42. To Cultivate Future Buyers

EDITORIAL STYLE MANUAL FOR BUSINESSPAPER

This guide is based on a model compiled by George Fox Mott, from the style guide of The New York Times, *Chicago* Tribune, *Baltimore* Sun, *and leading schools of journalism.*

GENERAL INSTRUCTIONS

Use a typewriter in preparing all copy.

Write on copy paper size 8x11.

Begin every story in the middle of the sheet, number each page at the top.

Write on one side of a sheet only.

Keep a one-inch margin on each side of the page and at the bottom.

Double-space all copy to provide room for guide lines, corrections, and other markings by the editor.

Write the name of the author in the upper left-hand corner of the first page and a word, or phrase, symbolic of the story in the upper left-hand corner of each page.

Place the word "more" at the end of each page if there is more than one page.

Use symbol "#" or word "end" to signify the conclusion of story.

Avoid long paragraphs, unnecessary words, and choppy sentences. Four typewritten lines generally make a satisfactory length for a paragraph.

Do not begin succeeding paragraphs with the same word.

Avoid the use of the same sentence structure continually—vary it.

Do not overwork any writing device; such as, the practice of beginning a paragraph with a direct quotation.

Hackneyed words and expressions, "fine" writing, and sensational phrases are to be avoided as much as possible.

Do not begin a new paragraph on the last line of a page.

Always read a story over before turning it in to the editor—unless time prohibits.

Read the story in the paper and note the changes.

Never write more than one story on a sheet.

Make copy conform to the authorized style sheet.

Use the most reliable sources of information, such as: city directory, almanac, dictionary, telephone directories, the Bible, a concordance. and an encyclopedia.

Abbreviations

(*When in Doubt Spell It Out*)

Abbreviate:

Names of states only when they follow names of cities: *Rockford, Ill.*

Names of months that contain more than five letters, but only in dates: *Dec. 20.*

The phrases *master of arts, doctor of philosophy*, etc.: *M.A.*

Hours of the day: *7 p. m.*

Railway and railroad, when initials are used for the name of the railroad: *C. M. St. P & P. Ry.*

The titles *Dr., Mr., Mrs., the Rev., M., Mme.*, and *Mlle.*

All other titles only when the first name or initials are used: *Gov. E. B. Jones.*

Nouns expressed in figures: *No. 3,469.*

Saint, Mount, and *Fort* before names: *Ft. Wayne.*

The word *and* to *&* only in business titles: *John Jones & Co.*

Common designations of weights and measures when occurring several times in a story: *1 yd. by 15 yds.*

Books of the Bible when the name of the book contains more than one syllable.

Names of political parties when used in statistics or parenthetically.

Senior and *junior* when used after names.

Do not abbreviate:

Auxiliary nouns when used as parts of names: Harvard *college*, Central *street.*

The word *Christmas.*

The word *per cent*, except in tabulations.

The word *cents*, except in tabulations.

Christian names.

Names of centuries.

Points of the compass except with figures.

Years, except in referring to college classes.

Names of cities.

Days of the week.

Professor to *prof.* and other colloquialisms except before a full name.

Et cetera to &c. Use etc.

ADDRESSES

Spell out numbered streets up to Tenth, inclusive.

Write it John D. Jones, 932 Pilmant Street.

If there is no street address, make it John D. Jones, Marshall (name of town).

CAPITALIZATION
(*When in Doubt Do Not Capitalize*)

Capitalize:

Names of political parties, religious denominations, and religious orders.

Names of races and nationalities, athletic teams and clubs.

Horses' and dogs' names, but do not use quotation marks also.

Seasons of the year, months, days.

Directions when used to denote national subdivisions.

Political and geographical divisions and regions when used as nouns.

Titles when they precede proper nouns.

First and principal words when in titles of plays, books, etc.

Abbreviations of college degrees.

Names of varieties of flowers, fruits, etc. when derived from names of persons or places: *Herefords, American Beauty roses*.

Names of companies, except words denoting form: First National *bank*.

Names of legislative acts: *Volstead act*.

All cabinet officers: *Secretary of Labor*.

All proper nouns.

Nicknames of cities, states, nations: *Wolverine, Windy City*.

Words signifying divisions of real estate or documents: *Room 43*.

Names of places or official residences: *Vatican*.

Do not capitalize:

Points of the compass: *northeast*.

College degrees when spelled out.

Auxiliary nouns.

The word *former* when it precedes a title.

Names of national, state, and city bodies.

Names of the mythical Greek and Roman or heathen deities.

The abbreviations a.m. and p.m.

Common religious terms, scripture, gospels.

Names of studies except languages.

Scientific names of plants and animals.

Titles when they follow a name: *John Jones, chief botanist.*

Names of college classes.

Titles in lists of officers.

Common nouns that originally were proper nouns.

Debate questions, except first word.

Adjectives derived from proper nouns which have lost their original associations.

Such words as gulf, island, lake, county, district, and ward when used singly.

FIGURES

Numbers from one to ten, inclusive, should be spelled out; eleven and higher should be written as digits.

Use *10 p.m.*

Write it *March 15, 1936* and *Sept. 15, 1939.* Omit st., rd., th., after dates.

Use figures for all sums of money, scores, telephone numbers, street numbers, degrees of temperature, times in races, automobile numbers, latitudes and longitudes, distances, votes, betting odds, ages, percentages, and dimensions. Certain phrases involving the use of figures should be spelled out: *one case in a hundred.*

If a sentence begins with a number, spell it out.

In sentences requiring more than one numeral, one below and the other above ten, spell out both except in tabulations of such material.

Write it *50th.*

All numbers in statistical material should be written in figures.

Avoid unnecessary ciphers: *9 a.m.,* not *9:00 a.m.; $10,000* not *$10,000.00; $5 billion,* not *$5,000,000,000.*

Spell out fractions, except after figures.

Spell out ordinal names of streets.

PUNCTUATION
Apostrophe

Use an apostrophe to make clear the omission of a letter: *can't, it's.*

Use it to indicate possession except in pronouns: *John's,* but not *their's.*

Use it in making plurals of letters, but not of figures: early *'90s,* four *A's.*

Use but one to indicate common possesssion: *John and Mary's car.*

Omit before common contractions like varsity, bus, phone, plane, possum.

Use it in unusual plurals: *Co.'s, D.A.R.'s.*

Omit in *Lawyers association, Fencers club.*

Use with year of college classes: *'40.*

Colon and Semi-Colon

Use a colon after a statement introducing a direct quotation of one or more sentences.

Use the colon to introduce a series: *Those elected are: president,* etc.

Use the colon to introduce a resolution: *Resolved:*

Use the colon between chapter and verse in scripture references: *John 3:16-18.*

Use it in giving the time of day: *7:35 a.m.*

Use the semi-colon to separate coordinate clauses of the same sentence when they are not separated by a coordinate conjunction: *There are the Indians; we should have taken the other trail.*

A semi-colon should be used to separate a series of names and addresses.

It should be used in giving election results: *Johnson, 4,657; Jamestown, 2,390.*

Comma

Use a comma whenever the meaning is doubtful, and a comma will make it clear.

Use the comma to set off appositives.

When an adverbial clause begins a sentence, separate it from what follows by a comma.

When a clause ending in a verb is immediately followed by another verb, a comma should separate the verbs: *Whatever is, is right.*

A non-restrictive adjective clause should be set off by commas.

A comma should be used to separate the parts of a compound sentence.

Separate the parts of a date by commas: *Thursday, Feb. 2, 1938.*

Use commas to set off parenthetical matter.

Set off by commas a noun used in direct address: *John, when did you arrive?*

Adjectives modifying the same noun should be separated by commas.

Omit the comma before *of* in such a construction as *Mary Brown of Chicago.*

Use the comma in scores: *Juniors, 2; Freshmen, 2.*

Dash

Use a dash after a man's name placed at the beginning of a series of interviews: *Henry Keith—I have nothing to say.* (Quotation marks are omitted with this form.)

Use dashes to indicate broken speech.

Use a dash to indicate a sudden breaking off in a direct quotation.

Use a dash to set off a parenthetical expression.

Use it to indicate omission of letters.

Hyphen

Use the hyphen with prefixes joined to proper names: *un-American.*

Use it in measures only if employed as an adjective: *3-in. valve.*

Use it in titles that begin with the word *vice.*

Compound numbers and fractions take it: *two-thirds.*

In compound adjectives use the hyphen.

Between a prefix and a proper noun it is to be used.

Omit the hyphen in words whose first syllable ends with the same letter as begins the second syllable: *cooperate, reelect.*

In combinations of nouns omit the hyphen: *today, tonight.*

Leave it out of civil and military titles: *attorney general.*

Omit it from Latin forms: *ex officio member.*

Omit it from such phrases as *newly married couple, well known person.*

Write the following as shown: anybody, everybody, nobody, somebody, anyone, everyone, no one, some one.

When two words are united to express a new meaning they should be either printed as one word or hyphenated.

When each of the words of which a compound is formed retains its original accent, they should be united by a hyphen.

Parenthesis and Bracket

Avoid parentheses as much as possible. When parentheses are used, punctuate the remainder of the sentence as if the parentheses and the inclosed words were not there.

When the name of the state, though not a part of the title of a newspaper, is given with the title, use this form: *Mankato (Minn.) Free Press.*

Brackets should be used to inclose a phrase already marked by parentheses.

Use parentheses to inclose figures that indicate subject divisions: *Five points were raised: (1) cost of construction, etc.*

When a legislator's political party and state are to be indicated in short: *Sen. John Jones (Dem., N. Y.)* use parentheses.

Use brackets to inclose matter inserted by someone other than the author: *They [the Jesuits] are expected to take action.*

Period

Omit the period after headings, captions, subheads, figures, paragraph numbers, single-line heads, Roman numerals, letters used in formulas, the words *per cent* and *pro tem.*

Use a period with all abbreviations except government agencies like AAA, CCC.

Use a series of three or six periods to indicate omission of quoted matter: . . .

Use a period with the abbreviation of a college degree: *A.B.*

Use before the last parenthesis mark when an entire sentence is enclosed: (See other story on Page o.)

Use after the last mark if final words of a sentence are parenthetical: *Once the book was stolen (at least so they said).*

Omit the period after nicknames.

Never use it after *Miss* but always after *Mr.* and *Mrs.*

Quotation Mark

Use quotation marks when naming books, paintings, operas, magazine articles, songs, dramas, subjects of lectures, and topics of sermons.

Use them at the beginning of each paragraph of a continuous quotation of several paragraphs, but only at the end of the last paragraph.

Outside periods and commas use quotation marks, but put them inside question marks, exclamation points, colons, and semi-colons, except in cases where the punctuation is part of the quotation.

When quoting a quotation: A quotation within a quotation requires single quotation marks, but a third quotation reverts to double quotation marks. Use them to set off a word of unusual meaning or an unfamiliar, excessively slangy, or coined word the first time it is used. Quotes are unnecessary thereafter.

Use them when quoting all direct testimony, conversation, and interviews given in direct form, except when the name of the speaker of the Q. and A. (question and answer form) with a dash precedes.

Use quotation marks for all quotations when they are to be set in the same type and measure as the context, but not when they are in a narrower measure of smaller type.

Avoid quotation marks when naming characters in plays or novels, with names of newspapers or other periodicals, with common nicknames except when used with the full name, and with names of vessels, animals, and sleeping cars.

Titles

Always give initials or first names of persons the first time they appear: use either initials or first names; never say *Mr. William H. Conley*, or *Mr. Wm. Conley*; make it *William H. Conley* and, for second reference, *Mr. Conley*.

Give first names of unmarried women, not initials only: *Miss Mary Carney*.

Put *the Rev.* before a minister's full or last name: *The Rev. John Jones* and *The Rev. Mr. Jones*. Priests, on second reference, are called *Father*.

A Catholic sister's rank is given but not her last name, unless in exceptional cases or in case of death.

Never write it *Mrs. Doctor* or *Mrs. Professor*.

Avoid long and awkward titles before a proper name: *Joseph V. Jones, superintendent of public works*.

Write it *Mr. and Mrs. John Jones*, not *John Jones and wife*.

Use Miss before an unmarried woman's name.

Avoid *Mesdames* and *Messrs.* before groups of names.

OUTLINE OF EXACT DUTY SPECIFICATIONS ON A LARGE BUSINESSPAPER EDITORIAL STAFF

Editor

Major responsibility: editorial policy and performance, budget, etc. Representative on Editorial Board and Intracompany Committees.

Departmental responsibility: Editorial pages.

Contacts and Coverages:
American Institute of Chemical Engineers
(immediate past president, 1943)
American Chemical Society
Society of Chemical Industry of Great Britain (director, 1943)
Manufacturing Chemists Association
War Production Board
War Manpower Commission
National Research Council
Engineers Council for Professional Development
Society for the Promotion of Engineering Education
National Conference of Business Paper Editors.

Managing Editor

Major responsibilities: materials of construction, metals and alloys, plastics, electrochemicals, pulp and paper, rubber—natural and synthetic, paint and varnish, etc.

Departmental responsibilities: Pictured Flowsheets, Front Cover, News of Products and Materials, Personals and Obituaries.

Contacts and Coverage:
Electrochemical Society, Inc. (vice-president, 1943, member of Executive Committee)

Technical Association of Pulp and Paper Industry (chairman,
Materials of Const. Committee, 1943)
Society of Plastics Industry
American Society for Testing Materials
American Chemical Society
American Institute of Chemical Engineers (chairman, Committee
on Public Relations, 1943).

Associate Editor

Major responsibilities: Chemical engineering equipment (design,
application and performance), theory and practice of chemical
engineering unit operations, heavy chemicals, rayon and textiles,
glass and ceramics.

Departmental responsibilities: Equipment News, Plant Notebook,
Manufacturers' Publications.

Contacts and Coverage:
American Society of Mechanical Engineers
(Secretary, Process Industries Division)
American Ceramic Society
National Exposition of Chemical Industries
Power Show.

Market Editor

Major responsibilities: economics of chemical industries, coverage of
markets for chemicals and allied materials, coverage of chemical
engineering news.

Departmental responsibilities: Chemical Engineering News, Chemical
Economics and Markets, Current Prices, News from Abroad, Industrial Notes.

Contacts with:
Chemical Market Research Group.

Assistant Editor

Major responsibilities: coverage of organic chemical and petroleum
industries, meetings and conventions, papers and abstracts, professional development, particularly of younger engineers.

Departmental responsibilities: meetings and conventions, calendar, manufacturers' publications (with T.R.O.), Equipment News (Assists T.R.O.).[1]

Contacts and Coverage:
   Junior Chemical Engineers of New York (president, 1943)
   American Institute of Chemical Engineers (coeditor, Student Chapter Bulletin, 1943)
   American Chemical Society
   American Institute of Chemists
   American Petroleum Institute.

Assistant Editor:

Major responsibilities: applications of chemical engineering equipment in process industries (sharing part time as research director for Business Department). Maintenance and repair, Washington rulings and directives.

Departmental responsibilities: Interpreting Official Washington, Log of Engineering Experience.

Contacts and Coverage:
   Oils and Fats
   Soap and Glycerine
   Dyes and Intermediates (with J.R.C.).

Assistant Editor:

Major responsibilities: production schedules, relations with printer, mechanics of layout and make-up of magazine, books, and current literature.

Departmental responsibilities: Chemical Engineers Book Shelf, Governmental Publications (with R.S.M.), Readers' Views and Comments, Foreign Literature, Abstracts.

Contacts:
   Transportation
   Packaging and Shipping.

Editorial Consultant

Major responsibility: editorial adviser and writer on Washington topics of technical interest, chemical engineering education, relations

[1] Initials indicate names of other staff members.

with governmental and technical departments, coverage of various process industries (see below).

Departmental responsibility: Washington highlights, government publications.
Industry Coverage:
Gas & Fuel (Coal Products)
Fertilizer
Foods, especially Oils and Fats (with N.G.F.).

Contacts and Coverage:
American Gas Association
National Fertilizer Association
A.I.C.H.E., A.C.S., S.P.E.E., etc.

Other Regional Representatives and Consultants
Contact work only.

A streamlined businesspaper editorial staff is that of *Modern Industry*, which has eleven editors with these specialized titles: chief editor, associate editor, contributing editor, managing editor, consulting (news interpretation) editor, industrial relations editor, technical editor, economics editor, Washington editor, postwar plans editor, materials editor, European editor. Three assistant editors help the chief editor.

TERMINOLOGY: TECHNICAL TERMS, ABBREVIATIONS, AND JOURNALESE

A.A.—Author's Alterations, corrections made in proofs by an author in contrast to those made by printer's proofreader.

A.B.P.—Associated Business Papers.

AD.—Advertisement.

ADD.—Additional news material to be appended to a story.

AGATE—Type measuring 5½ points in depth. Newspaper columns and advertisements are measured in agate lines.

ALLEY.—Print shop aisle.

A.N.A.—Association of National Advertisers.

ART.—Illustrations.

ASSIGNMENT.—A reporter's designated task.

BAD COPY.—Illegible, indistinct or improperly edited manuscript.

BANK.—Lower section of a headline: a table on which set type is placed.

BANNER or BANNER LINE.—A page-wide head in large type.

BEAT.—A reporter's regular territory for news coverage; a story published solely by one newspaper.

BEN DAY.—Term referring to mechanical process for shading line engravings.

B.F.—Bold or black face type.

BIO.—Biographical sketch.

BIG BERTHA.—Large sports camera.

BLEED PAGE.—Type or illustration which runs off the edge of page.

BLIND INTERVIEW.—An interview which does not reveal name of interviewed person.

BLURB.—Summary or description of an article.

BODY TYPE.—Type in which the major part of the businesspaper is set.

BOILERPLATE.—Syndicate or publicity material in metal-plate form.

BOLDFACE.—Darker or heavier type impression as contrasted to light face.

BORDER.—Type-metal strips used to box a story or head.

BOX.—Type bordered by rules.

BOX HEAD.—A headline enclosed by a border.

BOX STORY.—A story enclosed in a box.

BREAK.—The point at which a story continues from one page or one column to another; a story "breaks" when it is available for publication.

BULL.—Fillers, material to fill space.

BY-LINE.—Signature above a story.

BY-LINE STORY.—A signed story.

C.G.O.—Can go over, meaning some of the copy can be set for the back of the publication.

C. and L.C.—Capital and lower-case letters.

CANNED COPY.—Material received from publicity offices or press agents.

CAPS.—Contraction for capitals.

CAPTION.—Explanation of a photograph, illustration, or diagram.

CASE.—Cabinet or type where printer works.

CAST.—To mold for electrotyping or stereotyping; to calculate from copy amount of space it will take in type.

CATCH LINE.—Same as slug.

C.C.A.—Controlled Circulation Audit.

CHASE.—Metal frame used for holding, in page form, type and cuts ready for printing.

CHECK UP.—To verify information.

CHINA WHITE.—Paint used to retouch photos.

CLIPS.—Clippings from newspapers or morgue files.

CLIP SHEET.—Publicity prepared in sheet form for easy use.

COL.—Column.

COLUMN.—A department regularly published; a row of type.

COMPOSING ROOM.—Department where type is set.

COMPOSITOR.—Person who sets type.

CONDENSED TYPE.—Type which is narrower than standard width; other widths include: standard, extended, and extra-condensed.

COPY.—Manuscript or typewritten pages to be set by printer.

CORRESPONDENT.—Out-of-town reporter.

COVER.—To get the facts or be responsible for a story.

CREDIT LINE.—Line acknowledging source of a story or cut.

CROP.—Trim or cut down a picture or engraving.

CRUSADE.—A campaign for reform or improvement.

CUT.—An engraving; to shorten a story.

CUTLINE.—Caption for a cut.

DASHES.—Short lines which separate parts of a headline, headlines and stories, and stories from each other. Normally, dashes separating parts of a headline are short and those separating stories somewhat longer.

DATE LINE.—Place of origin and date put at the beginning of non-local news.

DEAD.—News material, especially type that is no longer usable.

DEADLINE.—The time when a story must be completed or an edition goes to press.

DIRTY COPY.—Copy containing many corrections.

DISPLAY TYPE.—Large, prominent, or ornamental type used to make headlines or advertisements conspicuous.

DOPE.—Advance news information, frequently rumor.

DRESS.—Makeup of paper involving styles and size of type and headlines.

DUMMY.—Diagram showing the layout of a page.

EDITORIALIZE.—Inclusion of opinion in a news story or headline.

ELECTRO.—An electrotype of a metal cut.

EM.—A measure of type width.

EN.—One-half em.

EXCHANGE.—Copies of other papers received on an exchange basis.

EXTRACT.—An excerpt or quotation from a periodical or book.

FAKE.—A fraudulent, invented story.

FEATURE.—A story which, though timely and interesting, is not exactly news; to feature a story is to give prominence to it; the significant fact of a story.

FILLER.—Material which can be used at any time or to fill space.

FINGERNAILS.—Slang for parentheses.

FIVE W's.—Who? What? When? Where? Why?

FLASH.—A message giving first brief news of an event.

FLIMSY.—Thin carbon copy of a manuscript or wired story.

FLUSH AND HANG.—First line set even with left margin and subsequent lines indented one em or more.

FOLIO.—A page; a page number.

FOOTLINE.—Line at bottom of page containing name of publication and folio number.

FOOTNOTE.—A note of explanation to clarify text to which it refers.

FORM.—A page of type locked in a chase and ready for press.

FOTOG.—Photographer.

FOUR "A's".—American Association of Advertising Agencies.

FURNITURE.—Wood or metal pieces, less high than type, used for packing type in order that a form may be locked.

F.Y.I.—For your information.

GALLEY.—An oblong metal tray for holding type.

GALLEY PROOF.—An imprint of type on a strip of paper made while the type is being held in the galley for corrections.

GHOST WRITER.—An unknown writer who produces copy to be signed by persons of prominence.

GREEN COPY.—Bound copy of first run of a magazine off the press, lacking final check on make ready and color register.

GREEN PROOF.—Uncorrected proof.

GUIDE LINE.—A word or words placed at the top of copy to identify it; slug line.

GUTTER.—A piece of vertical furniture used to separate columns, or space between columns.

HAIRLINE BOXES.—Thin-line boxes.

HALF STICK.—Type set in half-column width.

HALF-TONE.—A picture that is photographed on metal through a screen and chemically or electrolytically etched.

HANDOUT.—Statement prepared for publication.

HED TO CUM.—Instruction to printer on copy that headline will follow later.

HEAD.—Short for headline; headings of news stories.

HEAD SCHEDULE.—Listing of type faces, sizes, left with printer by editor to follow according to numerical designation.

HICKEY.—A defect in typography. A large bundle of papers or magazines which a handler tosses on a truck.

HOLE.—Vacancy on a page.

HOUSE ORGAN.—A publication issued at regular intervals by a business house to employees, salesmen and customers.

HOT NEWS.—Up-to-the-minute and important news.

HTC, HTK.—"Head to come," used when a story is rushed to the composing room before the head is written.

HUMAN INTEREST.—A story or phase of the news appealing emotionally.

INDENT.—Instruction to the compositor to start a line a specified distance in from the margin; 2 or 4 page printed piece, usually advertising, bound into the book without a folio.

INITIAL LETTER.—Usually first letter of first word word of paragraph that is decorative in design.

I.N.S.—International News Service.

INSERT.—New copy to be incorporated in a story that has gone to the composing room. Also refers to an advertisement bound into the businesspaper but printed elsewhere.

INTERVIEW.—A conference for the purpose of obtaining news.

ITALS.—Italics.

JUSTIFYING, JUSTIFICATION.—Spacing out a line to fill a column or type to fill a form.

KILL.—To exclude from copy; to destroy a story in type.

LABEL.—A colorless headline.

LAYOUT.—A sheet ruled into columns representing a page on which the positions of stories or stories and advertising are indicated.

L.C.—Lower case.

LEAD.—(Pronounced leed). The introduction (sentence or paragraph) of a news story; the chief story of the day.

LEAD.—(Pronounced led). Thin metal pieces for spacing out lines of type.

LEG MAN or LEGGER.—One who gathers news but does not write it.

LIBEL.—A false or defamatory presentation.

LIBRARY.—Files of newspaper clippings and other reference matter.

LIGATURE.—Two or more letters of type cast on the same body.

LIGHT FACE.—Thinner or lighter characters as contrasted with bold face.

LINE CUT.—An illustration that is reproduced in metal without the use of a screen.

LINO.—Linotype, a machine for setting type.

LOCK-UP.—The locking of a type-form before it is moved to press or stereo room.

LOG.—A book of assignments.

LOGOTYPE.—A single type which contains two or more letters.

LUDLOW TYPOGRAPH.—Machine for casting display composition on slugs. Primarily for slugs.

MAKE OVER.—To rearrange a page of type or pages to accommodate new stories or to better the appearance.

MAKE READY.—The backing up of engravings with strips of paper so that metal surface is level with type surface.

MAKE-UP.—The placement of stories, pictures and advertisements on a page.

MANUSCRIPT or MS.—Anything written by hand or typewritten as distinguished from printed matter.

MASTHEAD.—The editorial page heading that supplies information about the publication.

MAT.—Matrix; the papier-mâché mold of a page of type used for making a stereotype plate; the linotype brass mold for casting type.

MILLINE.—An agate line of advertising appearing in one million copies of a publication.

MORGUE.—A reference file of clippings, photographs and other useful information.

MORTISE.—Space or notch cut into and through printing block or plate so that type matter or other material may be inserted.

MUST.—Instruction on copy meaning that it must be printed without fail.

NAME PLATE.—Businesspaper's name as carried on Page One.

N.B.P.—National Business Paper Publishers.

NOSE FOR NEWS.—Aptness in sensing news.

NOTCH.—See mortise.

OBIT.—Obituary; general biographical information, not necessarily that of a dead person.

ODD PAGE.—A page bearing an odd folio, such as 5, 7, 11; a right-hand page.

O.K.'D PROOF.—Page proof bearing the O.K. of the author or some other person having authority to pass on its correctness.

PAGE OPP.—Page opposite, meaning page opposite the editorial page.

PAGE PROOF.—Proof of the whole page.

PERSONAL.—A brief news items concerning one or more persons.

PHOTO-ENGRAVING.—See half-tone.

PICA.—Twelve-point type.

PICK-UP.—Standing type that is to be included with new copy; an instruction to the composing room to include such type with that which is being set.

PIED.—Type that is in disorder and unusable.

PIX.—Pictures.

PLATE.—A page of type which is cast in metal and is ready for locking on the press; an electrotype or half-tone.

PLAY UP.—To display a story prominently.

POINT.—Measurement for type sizes, a point being 1/72 of an inch.

POLICY.—A newspaper's stand on a public issue.

PREFERRED POSITION.—An ad sold to appear opposite outstanding text material in magazine.

PREPRINT.—Material printed in advance of its publication in a regular issue of the businesspaper.

PRESS AGENT.—Publicity person employed by private interest.

PRESS PROOF.—A proof taken on a job or cylinder press.

PRINTER.—Employees of the composing room who correct type or assemble it in chases as directed.

PROOF.—An imprint taken on paper so that errors may be corrected.

PROOFREADER.—One who corrects proof against the copy.

PUFF.—Publicity story that is personal.

PULLING A PROOF.—Obtaining an impression of type.

PUNCH.—Vigor and snap in words, stories, and headlines.

PUT TO BED.—Locking up the forms in preparation for printing an edition.

QUERY.—Correspondent's synopsis, indicating existence and nature of a story. On the basis of the summary the editor designates the number of words desired.

QUOIN.—Device used for locking type in a form.

QUOTE.—Quotation mark.

RAILROAD.—To rush copy in an emergency to the composing room without careful editing.

REGISTRATION.—Lining up color plates, so that the impressions hit perfectly.

RELEASE.—An instruction to print a story set earlier and held for late disposition.

REPRODUCTION or REPRO PROOF.—Exceptionally clear and sharp proofs from type which can be used for reproduction.

REVISE.—Proof taken after type has been corrected.

REWRITE.—To write a story again, to improve, lengthen, or shorten it.

REWRITE MAN.—One who rewrites stories appearing in newspapers or other magazines.

ROMAN.—A class of type taken originally from manuscript books of the Romans and which is distinct from italics.

ROTO.—Rotogravure.

RULE.—A metal strip which is the height of the type and prints as a line. Column rules make the printed lines which separate the columns of a paper.

RUN.—A reporter's regular territory. Press Run is number of copies printed.

RUN-AROUND.—Type to be set around a cut of odd measure.

RUSH.—Instruction on copy to insure rapid handling in the composing room.

S.S.—Same size (a mark on engraver's copy).

SACRED COW.—Slang for material of interest to the publisher or superior editors which must be printed.

SCHEDULE.—A list of assignments kept by the editor; a list of stories edited and headed by a copy editor; a dummy page.

SCOOP.—An exclusive story printed by only one paper.

SEE COPY.—Copydesk instruction to the composing room to refer to the copy for verification.

SET FLUSH.—Instruction to set without paragraph indentation or margin.

SHOULDER.—Top surface of type; also anchoring for a cut attached to a wood block.

SHOUTS.—Exclamation points.

SIGNATURE.—1) Letter or figure placed at bottom of each sheet of book or pamphlet as direction to binder in arranging or folding sheets 2) The printed sheet, so marked, on the form from which it is printed.

SKED.—Schedule.

SLANT.—Emphasis placed on a particular aspect of a policy story.

SLUG.—Notation placed on copy to identify it; a guide line in type.

SMALL CAPS.—Small capital letters.

SMASH.—A sensational story.

SOB STUFF.—Stories that are sentimental and designed to appeal to the sympathy of the reader.

SOLID.—Type set without leads separating the lines.

SPOT NEWS.—Unexpected, live, important news.

SQUIB.—A brief news item.

STEREO.—A stereotype metal cut made from a paper matrix.

STET.—Let it stand.

STALE.—Old news.

STICK.—A measuring unit for type equaling two inches: a type holder.

STONE.—A stone or metal-topped bench or table upon which a page is assembled.

STORY.—An article written by a reporter.

STRAIGHT NEWS.—An unembellished account of news facts.

STRING.—Clippings pasted together in a strip or scrap book.

STYLE BOOK or STYLE SHEET.—Rules of style governing a paper.

SUBHEAD.—A line of type differing from body type and used to break up a long story.

SUMMARY.—A brief statement of a news story.

TELEGRAPH NEWS.—Stories received by telegram.

TELEPHOTO.—Photograph received by wire.

TEXT.—Body of matter as distinct from heads or footnotes.

THUMBNAIL.—Small, referring to sketch or biography.

TIE UP.—Type form bound with cord.

TIGHT PAPER.—A paper so filled with advertisements that a reduction
of news space is necessary.

TIP.—Information suggesting a news story.

TITLE-LINE.—By-line.

TOE NAILS.—Parentheses.

TR.—Transpose.

TRIM.—To shorten a story.

TRIM SIZE.—Size of a page when trimmed by cutting in the magazine
bindery.

TWO-LINE INITIAL, TWO-LINE FIGURE.—Initial and figure two lines in
depth.

TYPO.—Typographical mistake.

U. and L.C.—Upper and lower case.

UNDERLINE.—Explanation under a cut.

UNQUOTE.—Indication of the end of a direct quotation.

WHEN ROOM.—Story may be used at any time.

WHIFF.—Publicity of small news value.

WIDOW.—A short line at the top of a column.

WOODEN HEAD.—Meaningless headline.

WRONG FACE, WRONG FONT.—Type differing in style or size from that
specified.

ZERO-HOUR.—Last minute for receiving news before the paper goes to
press.

THIRTY (The end)

INDEX

Abbreviations, 325-33
Ackerman, Carl W., 250, 284
Addison, Joseph, quotation, 54
Adult education function of businesspapers, 3, 279, 289
Advertising, 139-41
  budgets, 144, 147
  copy, 157-58, 161
  cost control, 134
  department, 160-61
  functions, 310-12
  publication orders, 142
  rates, 140, 151-59
  revenue, 141
  sales volume, 19, 148-53, 156
  subsidies, 142-43
Advertising agency commissions, 151-
  54, 157-60
Advertising associations, 91-101
Advertising Council, 99
Advertising Federation of America, 101
Advertising function of businesspapers,
  4, 122
Advertising press, 85, 88
Advertising sales manager, 139-61
  success factors, 146-49
Agar, Herbert, 287
Agnew, Hugh E., 9, 85, 124 n., 159, 169
Agricultural press, 66, 91
Aldrich, Paul I., 75
American Arbitration Association, 109,
  117
American Association of Advertising
  Agencies, 98-99
American Association of Manufac-
  turers, 86
American businesspapers, 65-86, 293-304
American press associations, 91-99
American Railway Magazine Editors'
  Association, 83
American revolution, 58
Anderson, Arthur D., 79
Angell, Sir Norman, 286
Anshen, Melvin, 22, 51, 55
Arbitration organizations, 109, 117

Army and Navy Journal, 75
Arnold, Thurman, 14-15
Artman, James, 71, 72
Associated Business Papers, 10, 97, 130-
  38
  sales volume, 152
Association of American Advertisers,
  177
Association of National Advertisers,
  100, 154, 177
Associations, advertising, 91, 97-101
  editors', 103-104
  press, 91-98
  professional, 106-10
  promotional, 102
  trade, 106-18
Audit Bureau of Circulations, 97, 101,
  177-82, 188, 191, 200 n.
  foreign, 179 n.
Automobile industry press, 71-72, 74-75
Avery, Frank L., 182-86, 195 n.
Awards, annual, 105, 206

"Baby Snooksers," 209
Barron, Clarence W., 89
Baruch, Bernard, 111
Beard, Miriam, 57
Benn Bros., Ltd., 61-62
Berle, A. A., Jr., 31 n.
Bernays, Edward L., 254
Bernheimer, Charles L., 117
Bigelow, Burton, 235
Bill, Ray, 105
Blackburn, James E., Jr., 191 n.
Bleyer, Willard G., 284
Boardman, W. H., 68, 74
Bourse, 56
Boyd, Robert, 77
Brad-Vern reports, 102
Brandeis, Louis D., 290
Bridgman, Henry, 75
Brisbane, Arthur, 228
Brisco, Norris A., 39 n.
British trade press, 60-64
Brown, James W., 87

335

Date Du